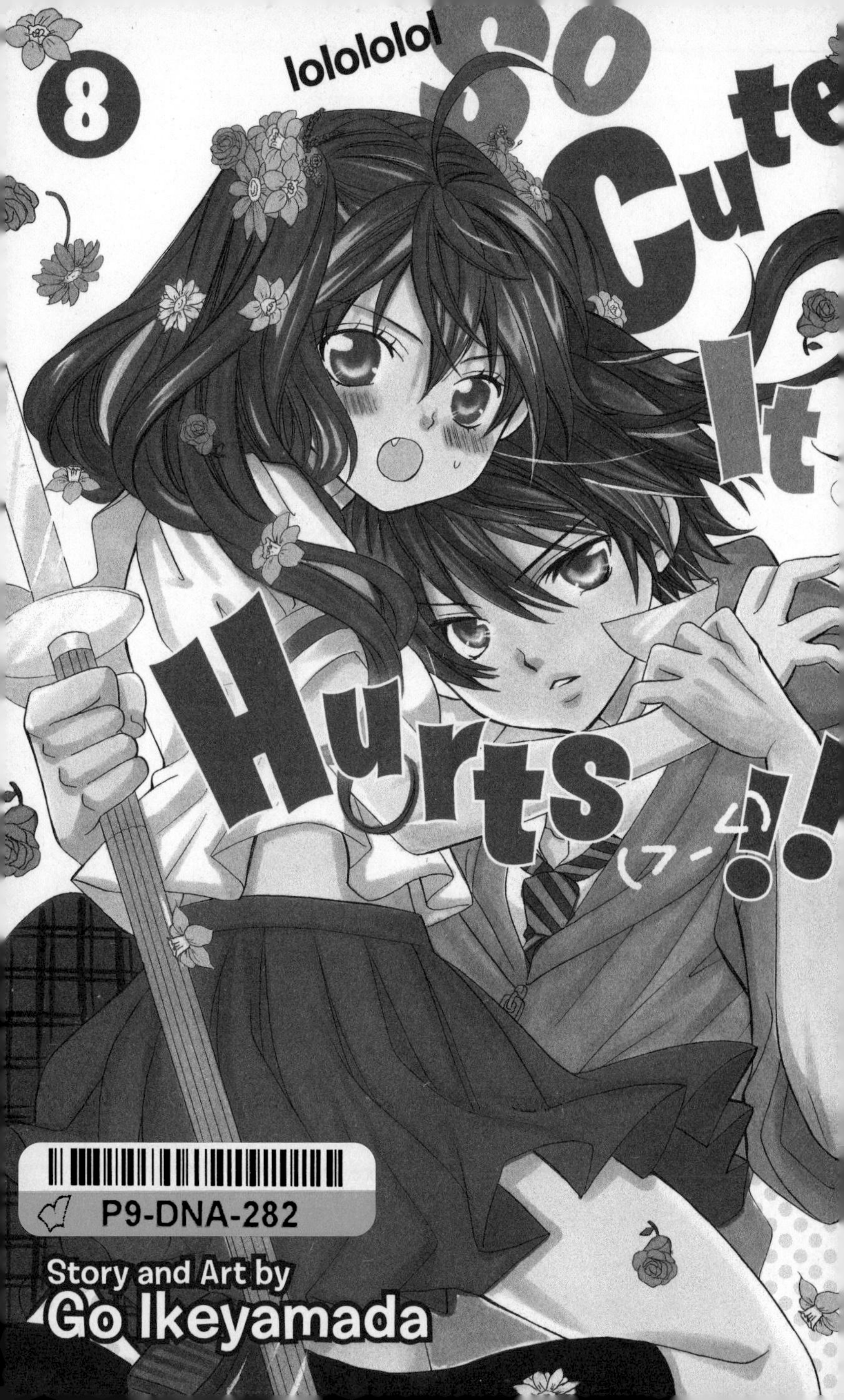
8
lolololol
So Cute It Hurts!!
Story and Art by
Go Ikeyamada

CHARACTERS

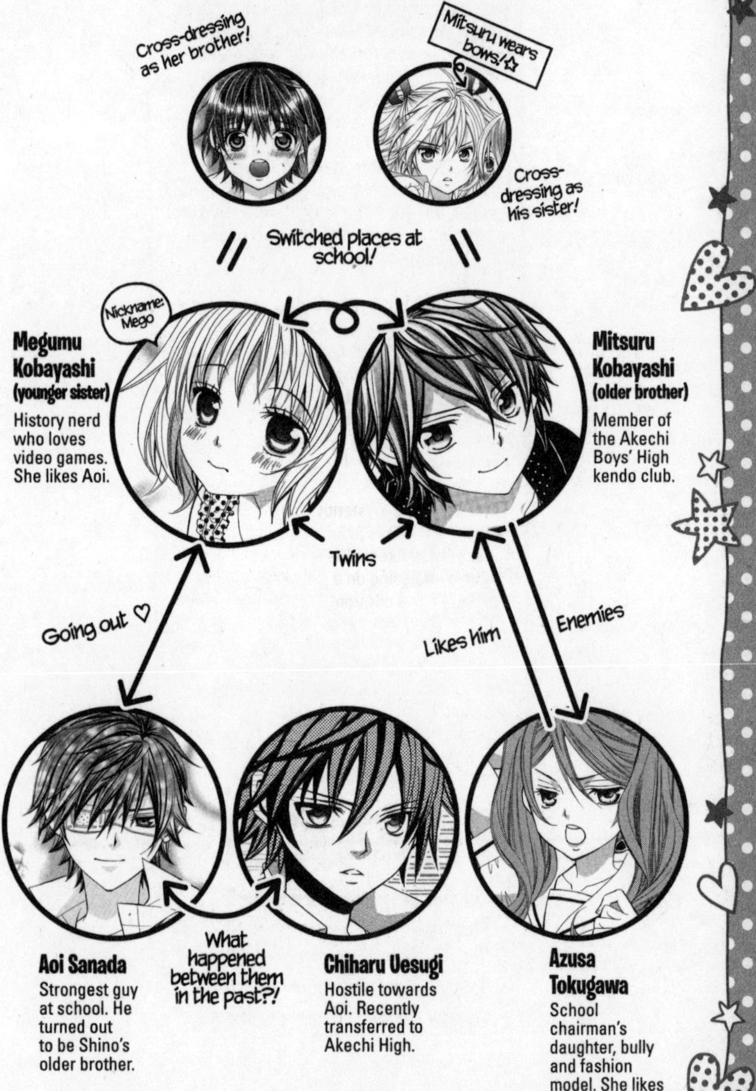

Cross-dressing as her brother!
Mitsuru wears bows!☆
Cross-dressing as his sister!
Switched places at school!
Nickname: Mego
Megumu Kobayashi (younger sister)
History nerd who loves video games. She likes Aoi.
Mitsuru Kobayashi (older brother)
Member of the Akechi Boys' High kendo club.
Twins
Going out ♡
Likes him
Enemies
Aoi Sanada
Strongest guy at school. He turned out to be Shino's older brother.
What happened between them in the past?!
Chiharu Uesugi
Hostile towards Aoi. Recently transferred to Akechi High.
Azusa Tokugawa
School chairman's daughter, bully and fashion model. She likes Mitsuru.

STORY

★ Mitsuru and Megumu are twins. One day they switch places and go to each other's school for a week! That's when Megumu falls in love with Aoi and Mitsuru falls in love with Shino. Azusa and Aoi both discover the twins' ruse but keep quiet for reasons of their own. When the week is over, Megumu declares her love for Aoi, and they start dating. They need to stay two feet apart because of Aoi's extreme discomfort around women, but they plan to work on it. Mitsuru is rejected by Shino, but Azusa starts to have feelings for him.

★ Later, Mitsuru rescues Azusa when someone tries to attack her. Worried, Mitsuru swaps places with Megumu again so he can be Azusa's bodyguard. During the course of his duties, he accidentally kisses her cheek, which makes her blush bright red. Suddenly, Mitsuru begins to see Azusa as more than just an adversary.

★ Meanwhile, a mysterious boy named Uesugi, who seems to hate Aoi, has transferred to Akechi High. He blackmails Megumu into going on a date with him by holding her first gift from Aoi hostage. When he pretends to toss the present into the river, Megumu jumps in after it and ends up almost drowning. Uesugi pulls her from the river, and although he's impressed by her devotion, he still takes advantage of her unconscious state to snap a compromising photo to send to Aoi…

CONTENTS

So Cute It Hurts!! (7-4)

I FELT LIKE I WAS FLOATING.

I WAS HAVING A HAPPY DREAM...

...WHERE AOI WAS CARRYING ME LIKE A PRINCESS.

Chapter 36

HELLO. I'M GO IKEYAMADA.
THANK YOU FOR PICKING UP MY 51ST BOOK!!
THIS IS VOLUME 8 OF *SO CUTE IT HURTS!!*
I DREW AZUSA AND MITSURU ON THE COVER. ♪♪
I'VE BEEN LOOKING FORWARD TO DRAWING THESE TWO ON A COVER, SO I REALLY PUT MY SOUL INTO WORKING ON THIS ILLUSTRATION. ♪ I LOVE THE FLOWERS IN AZUSA'S HAIR. ♪
I HOPE WHEN YOU READ THE STORY YOU'LL GET WHY I INCLUDED THE FLOWERS. (SMILE) ♪♪

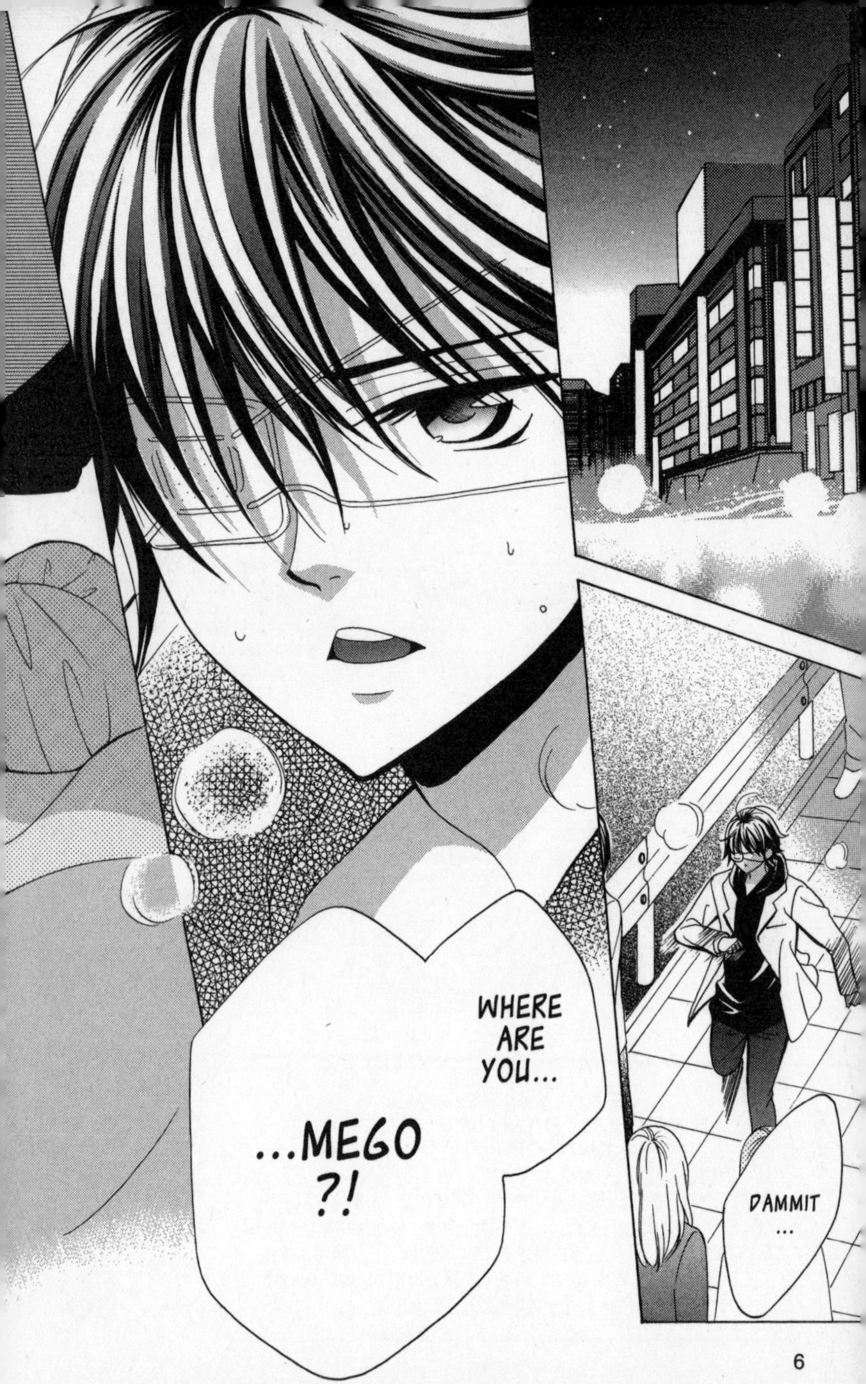
DAMMIT ...
WHERE ARE YOU...
...MEGO ?!

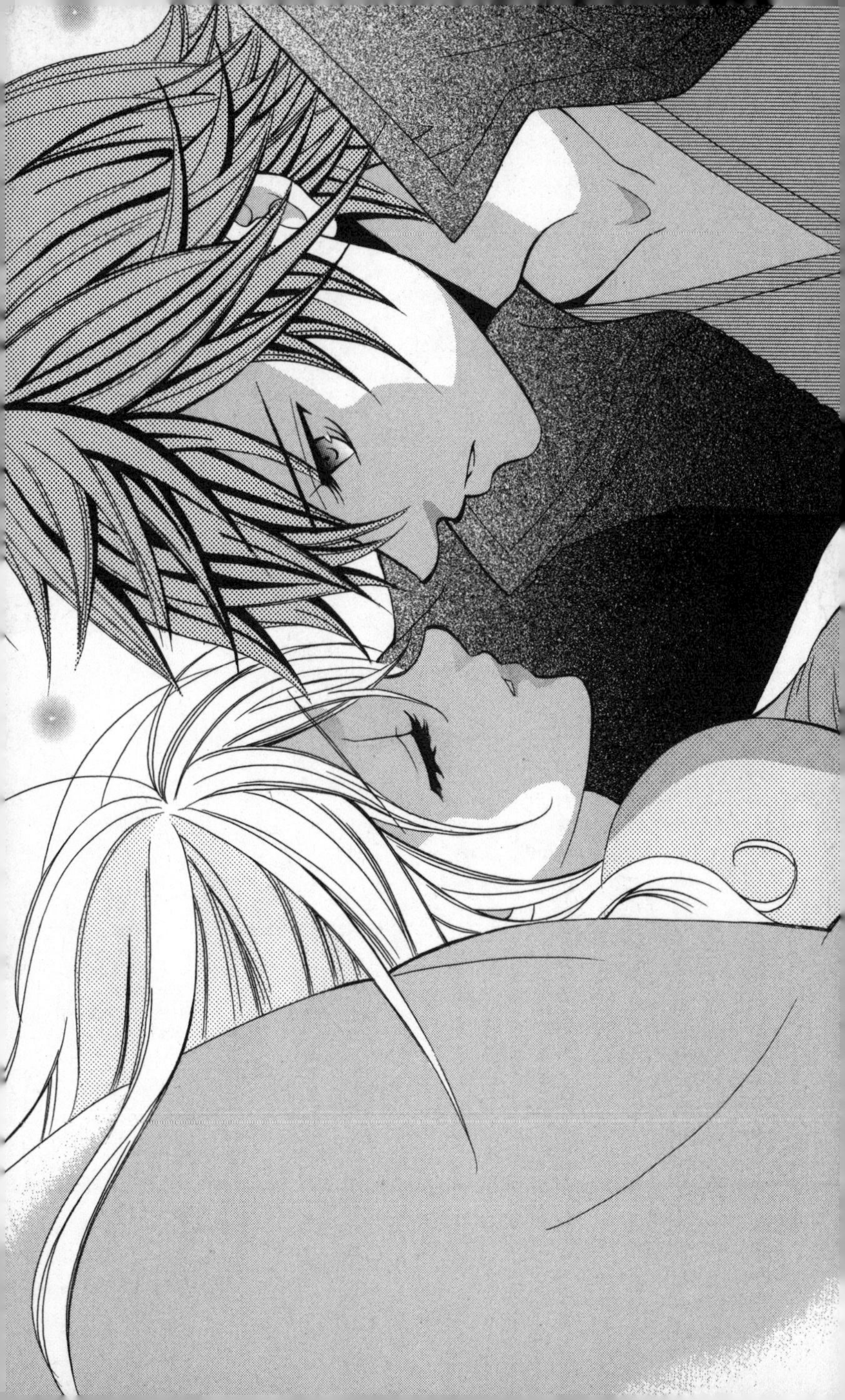

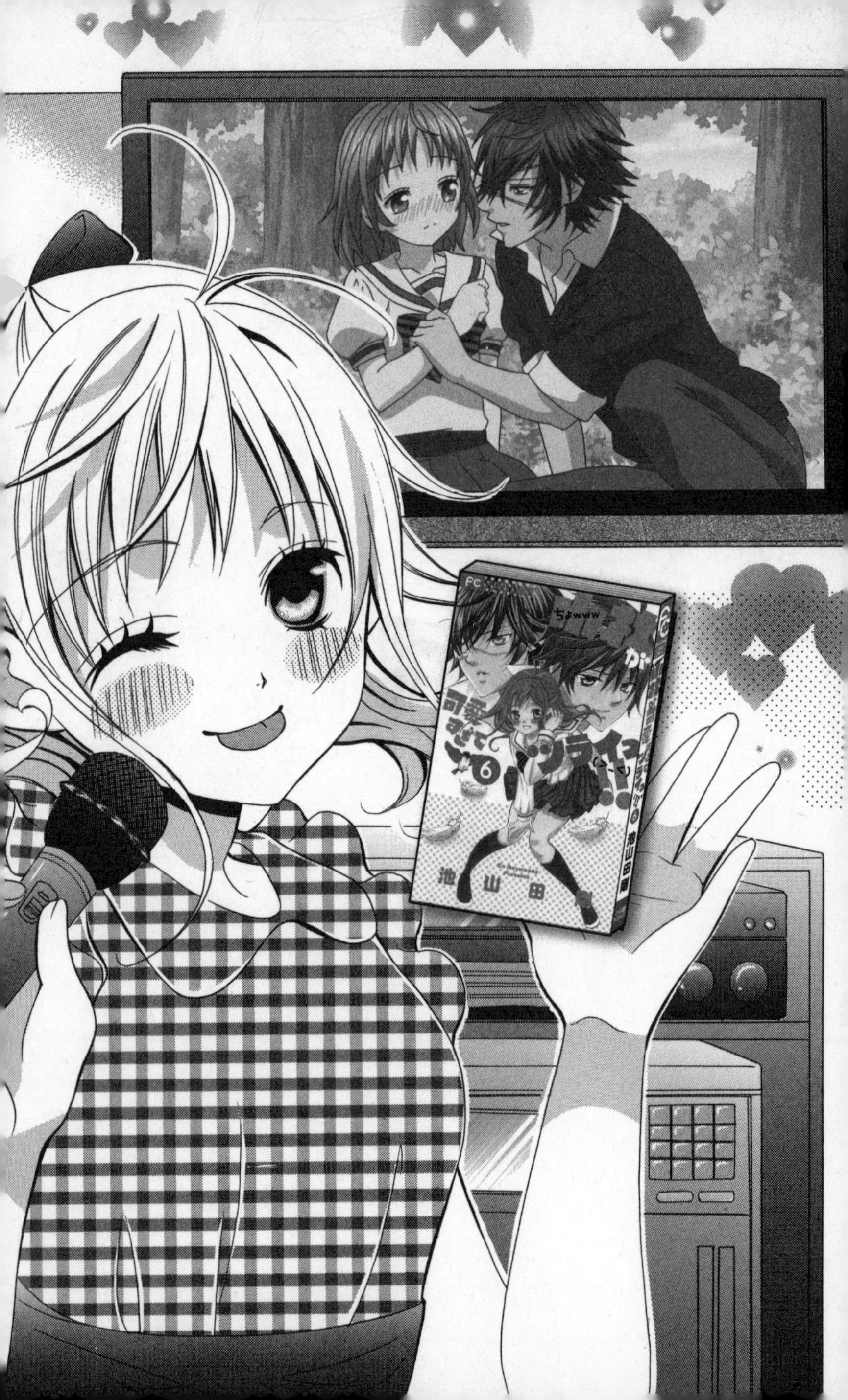
FC
ちょwww
6
池山田

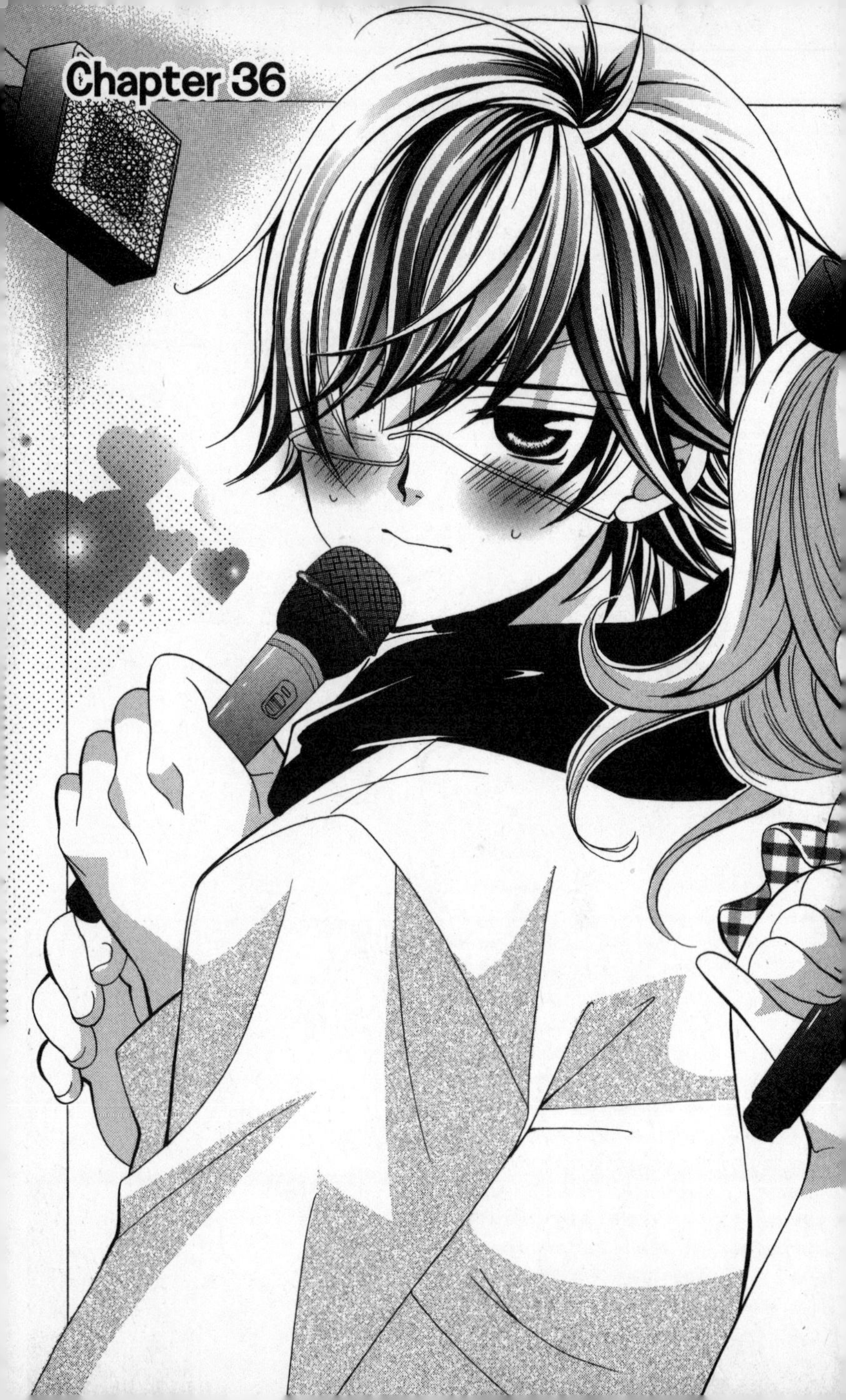
Chapter 36

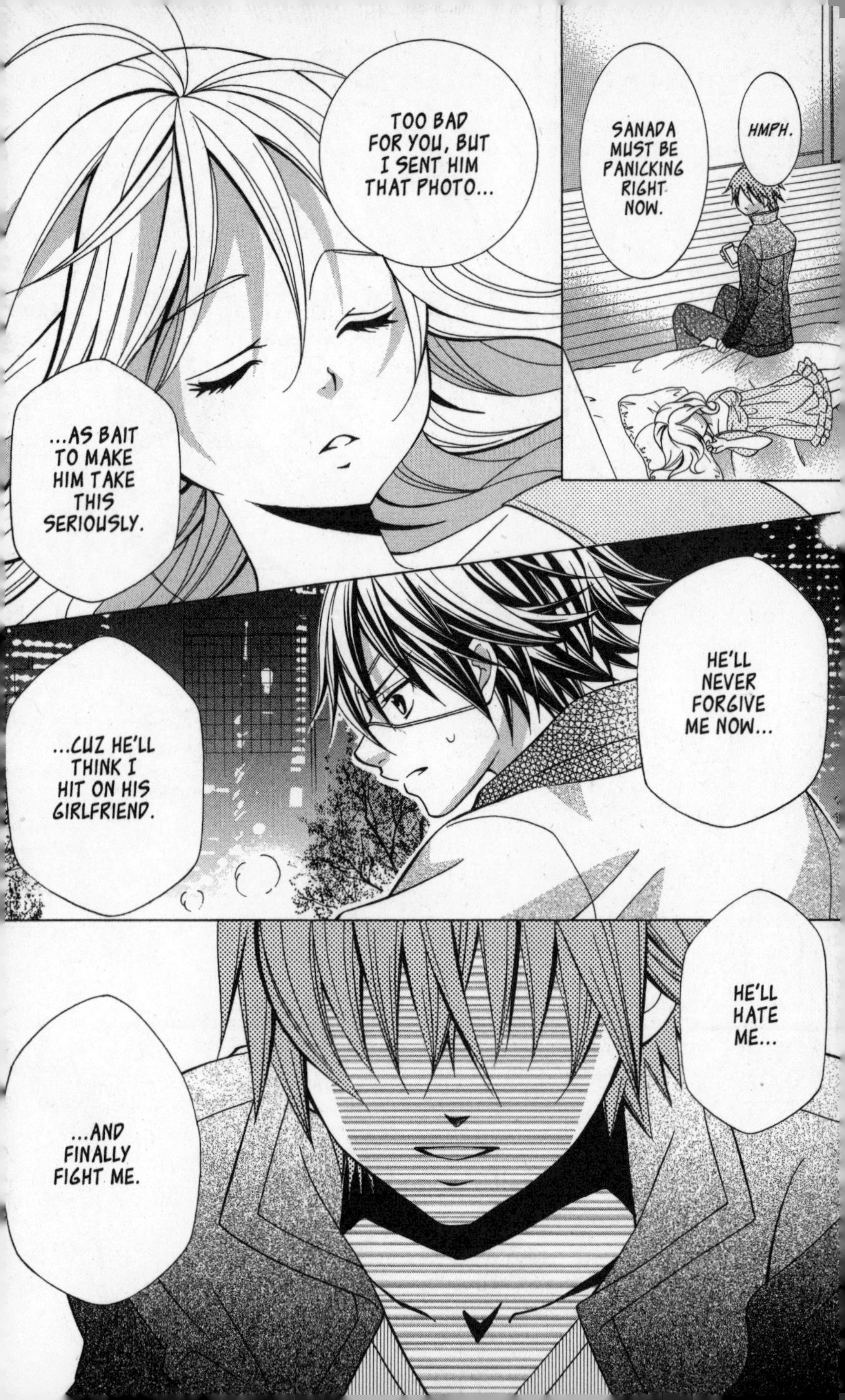
HMPH.
SANADA MUST BE PANICKING RIGHT NOW.
TOO BAD FOR YOU, BUT I SENT HIM THAT PHOTO...
...AS BAIT TO MAKE HIM TAKE THIS SERIOUSLY.
HE'LL NEVER FORGIVE ME NOW...
...CUZ HE'LL THINK I HIT ON HIS GIRLFRIEND.
HE'LL HATE ME...
...AND FINALLY FIGHT ME.

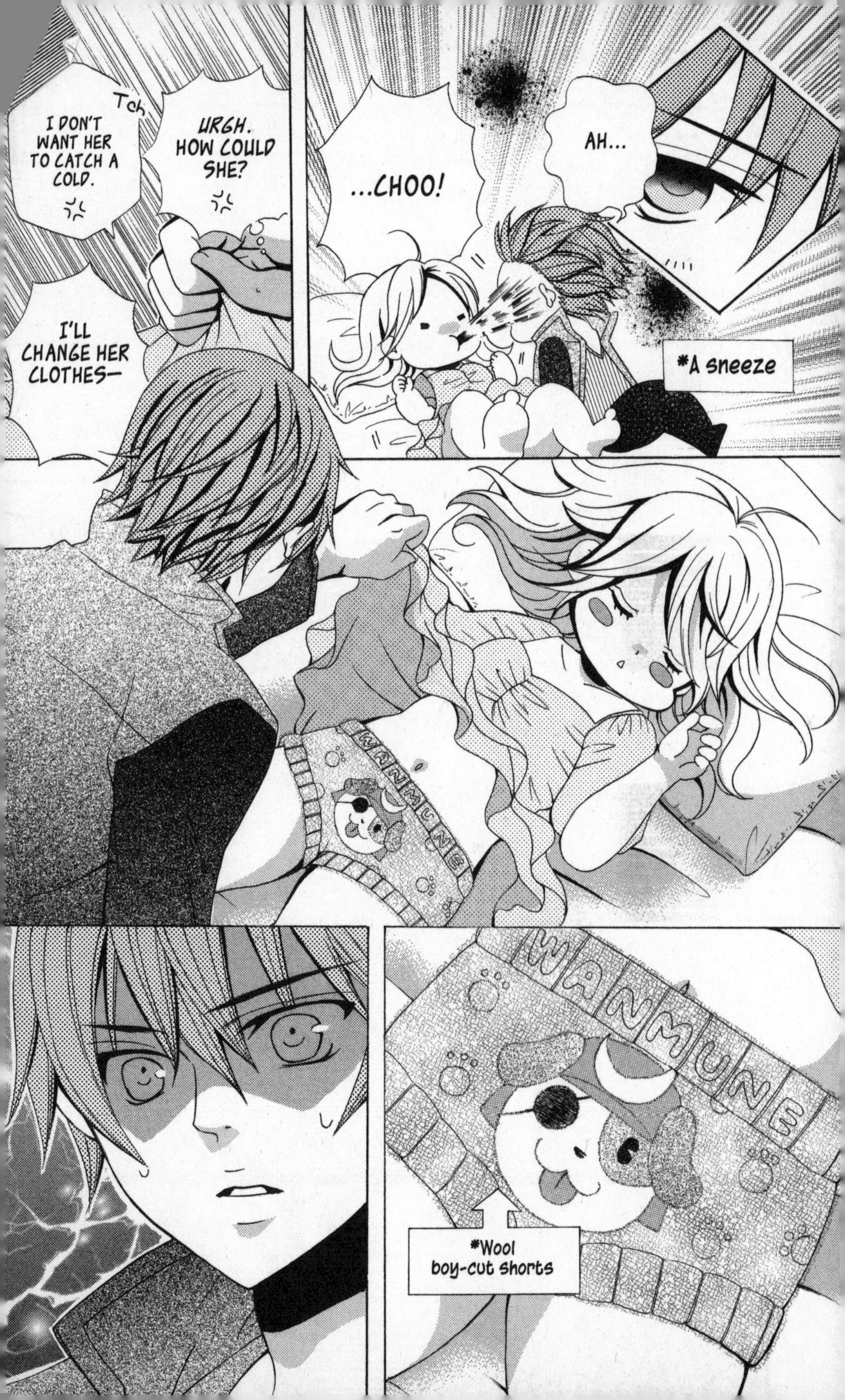
AH...
...CHOO!
*A sneeze
URGH. HOW COULD SHE?
Tch
I DON'T WANT HER TO CATCH A COLD.
I'LL CHANGE HER CLOTHES—
WANMUNE
WANMUNE
*Wool boy-cut shorts

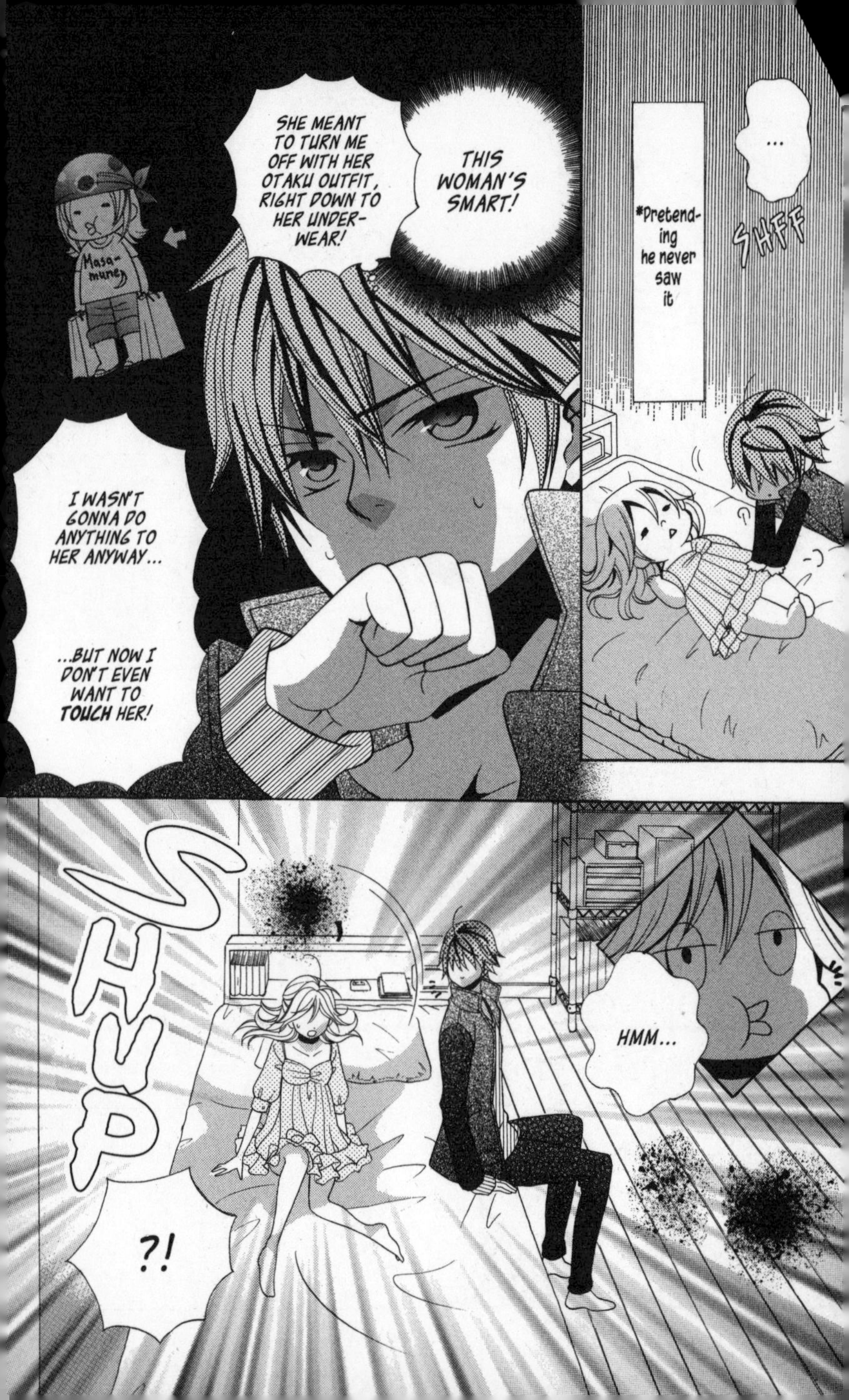
...
SHFF
*Pretending he never saw it
THIS WOMAN'S SMART!
SHE MEANT TO TURN ME OFF WITH HER OTAKU OUTFIT, RIGHT DOWN TO HER UNDERWEAR!
Masamune
I WASN'T GONNA DO ANYTHING TO HER ANYWAY...
...BUT NOW I DON'T EVEN WANT TO TOUCH HER!
HMM...
SHUP
?!

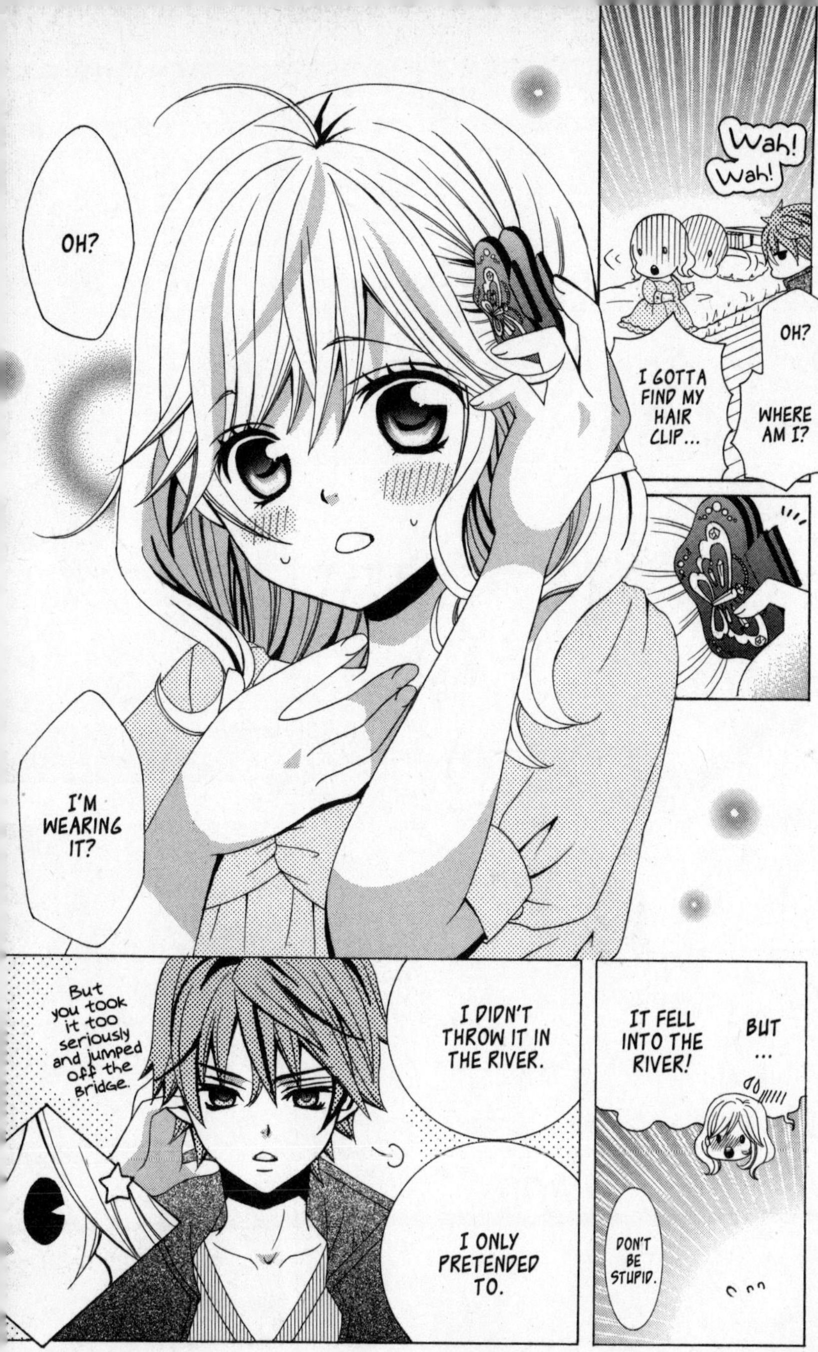
Wah! Wah!
OH? WHERE AM I?
I GOTTA FIND MY HAIR CLIP...
OH?
I'M WEARING IT?
BUT ...
IT FELL INTO THE RIVER!
DON'T BE STUPID.
I DIDN'T THROW IT IN THE RIVER.
I ONLY PRETENDED TO.
But you took it too seriously and jumped off the bridge.

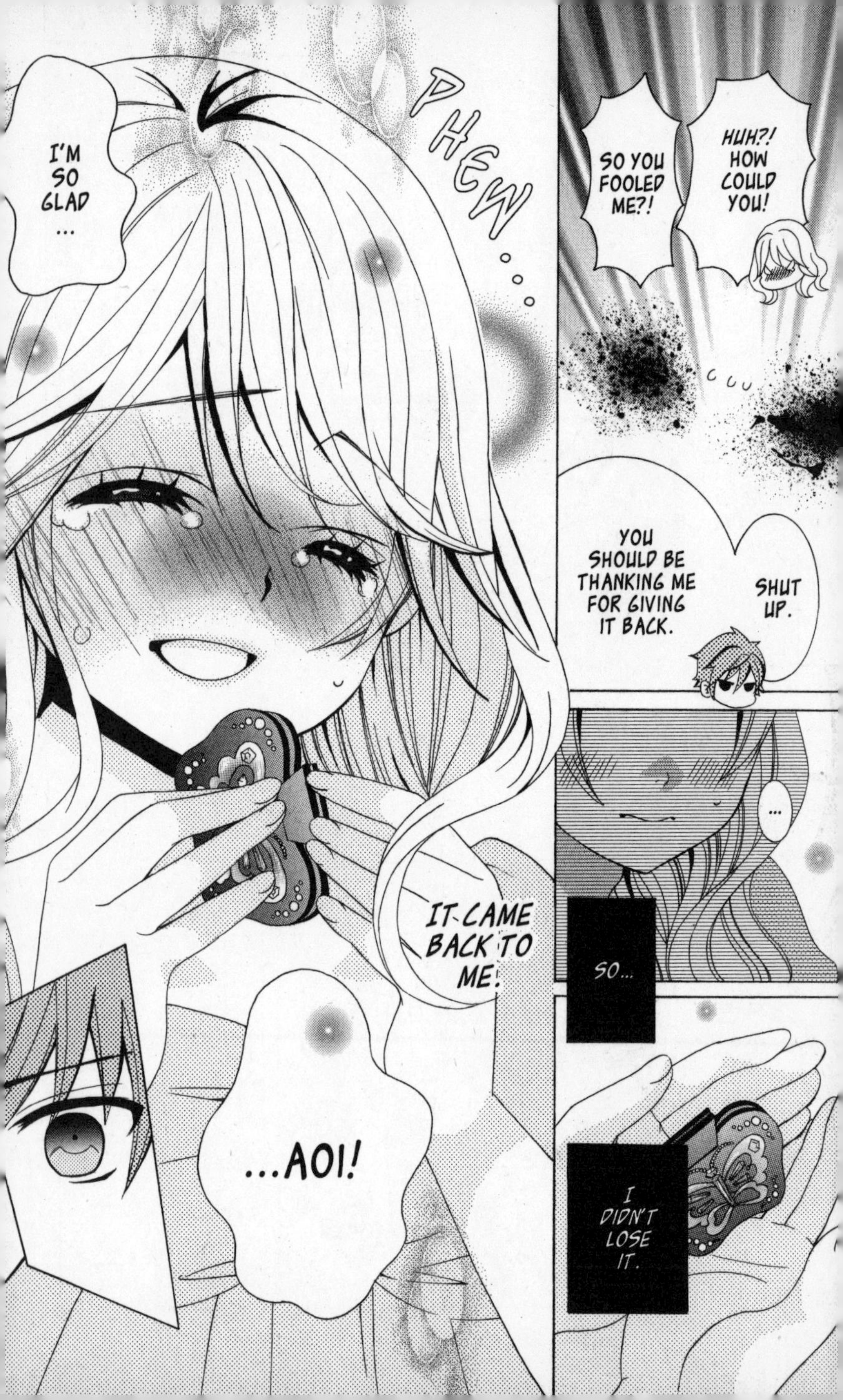
HUH?! HOW COULD YOU!
SO YOU FOOLED ME?!
SHUT UP.
YOU SHOULD BE THANKING ME FOR GIVING IT BACK.
...
SO...
I DIDN'T LOSE IT.
PHEW...
I'M SO GLAD...
IT CAME BACK TO ME!
...AOI!

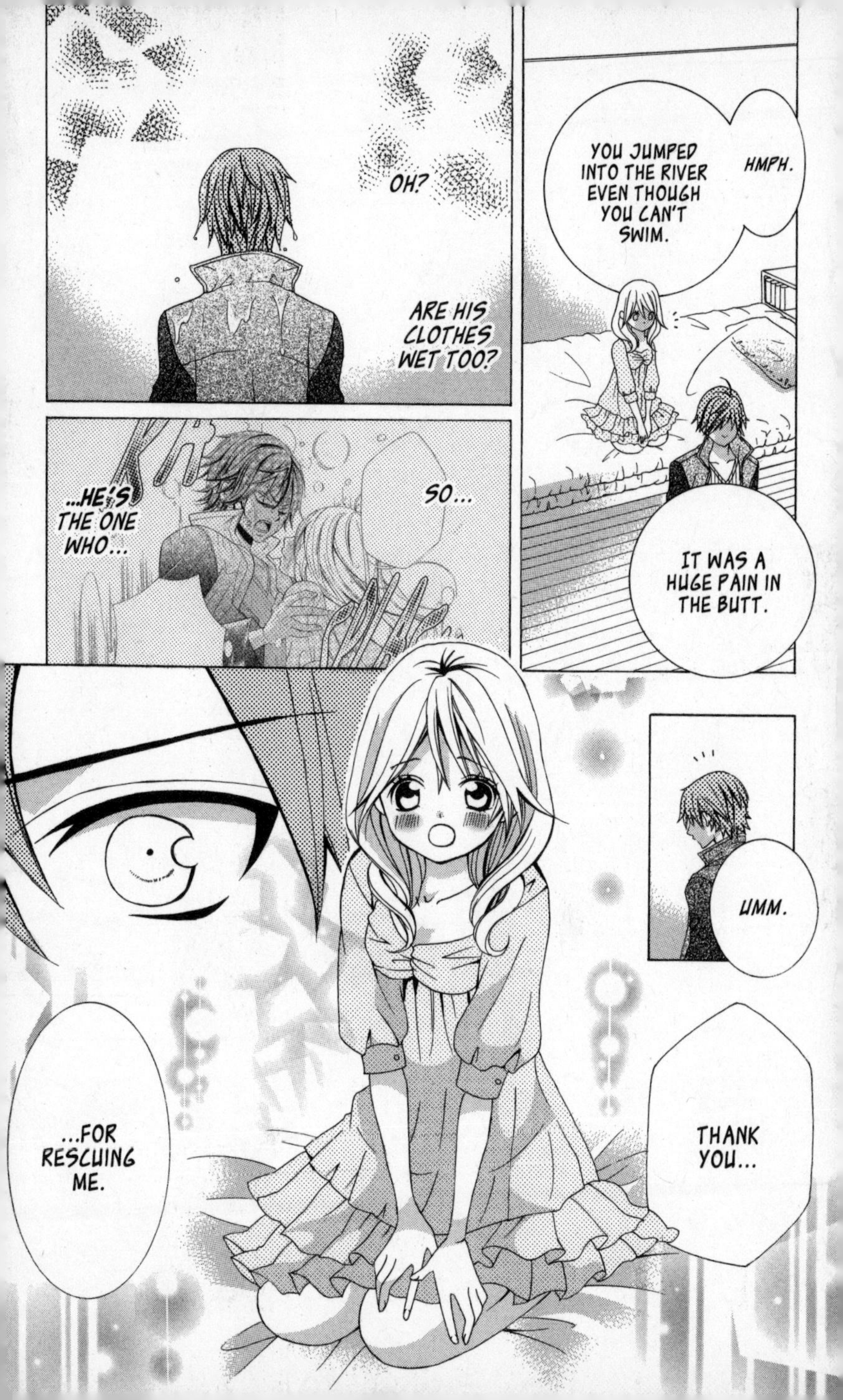
HMPH.
YOU JUMPED INTO THE RIVER EVEN THOUGH YOU CAN'T SWIM.
IT WAS A HUGE PAIN IN THE BUTT.
OH?
ARE HIS CLOTHES WET TOO?
SO...
...HE'S THE ONE WHO...
UMM.
THANK YOU...
...FOR RESCUING ME.

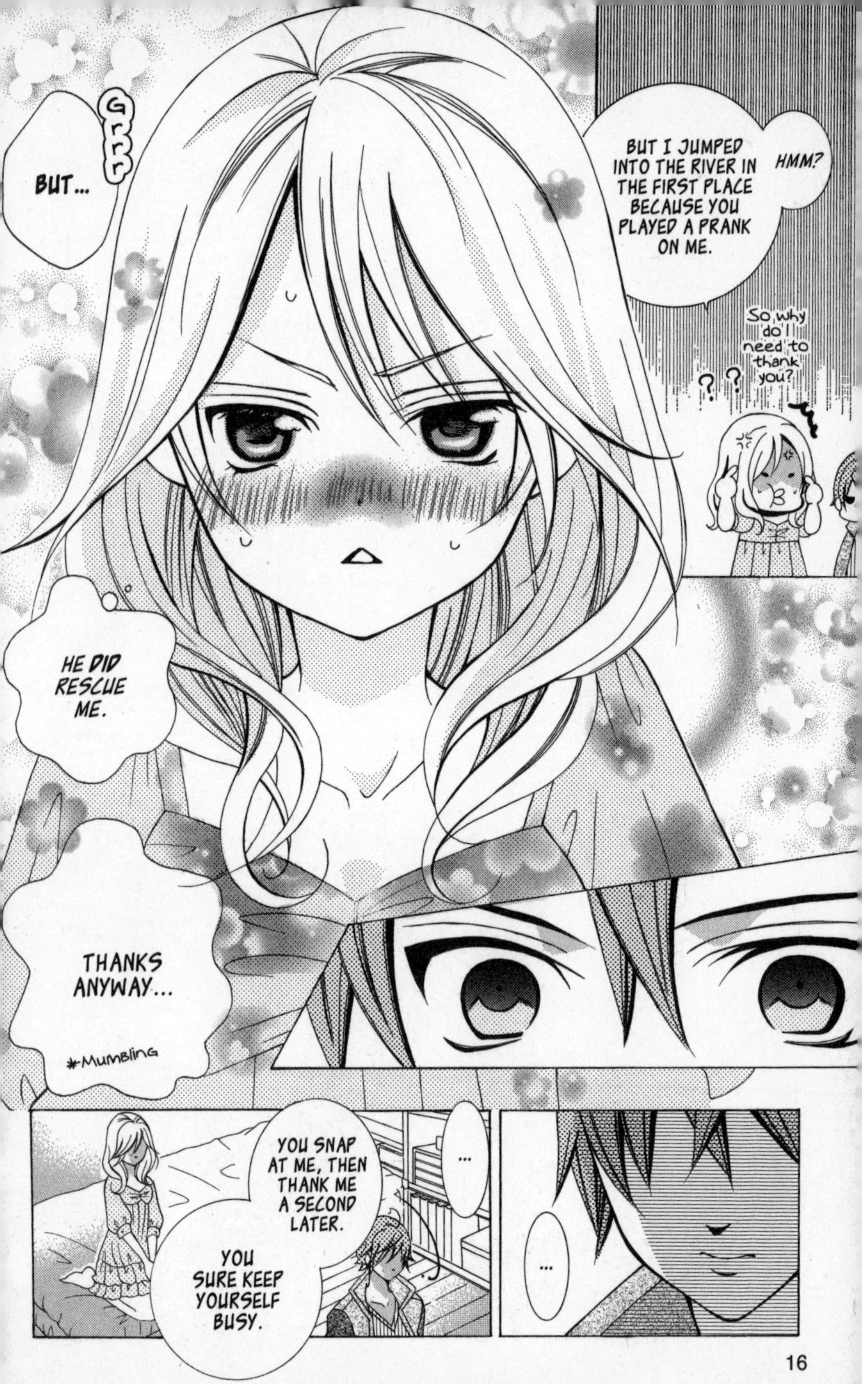
HMM?
BUT I JUMPED INTO THE RIVER IN THE FIRST PLACE BECAUSE YOU PLAYED A PRANK ON ME.
So why do I need to thank you?
Grrr
BUT...
HE DID RESCUE ME.
THANKS ANYWAY...
*Mumbling
...
...
YOU SNAP AT ME, THEN THANK ME A SECOND LATER.
YOU SURE KEEP YOURSELF BUSY.

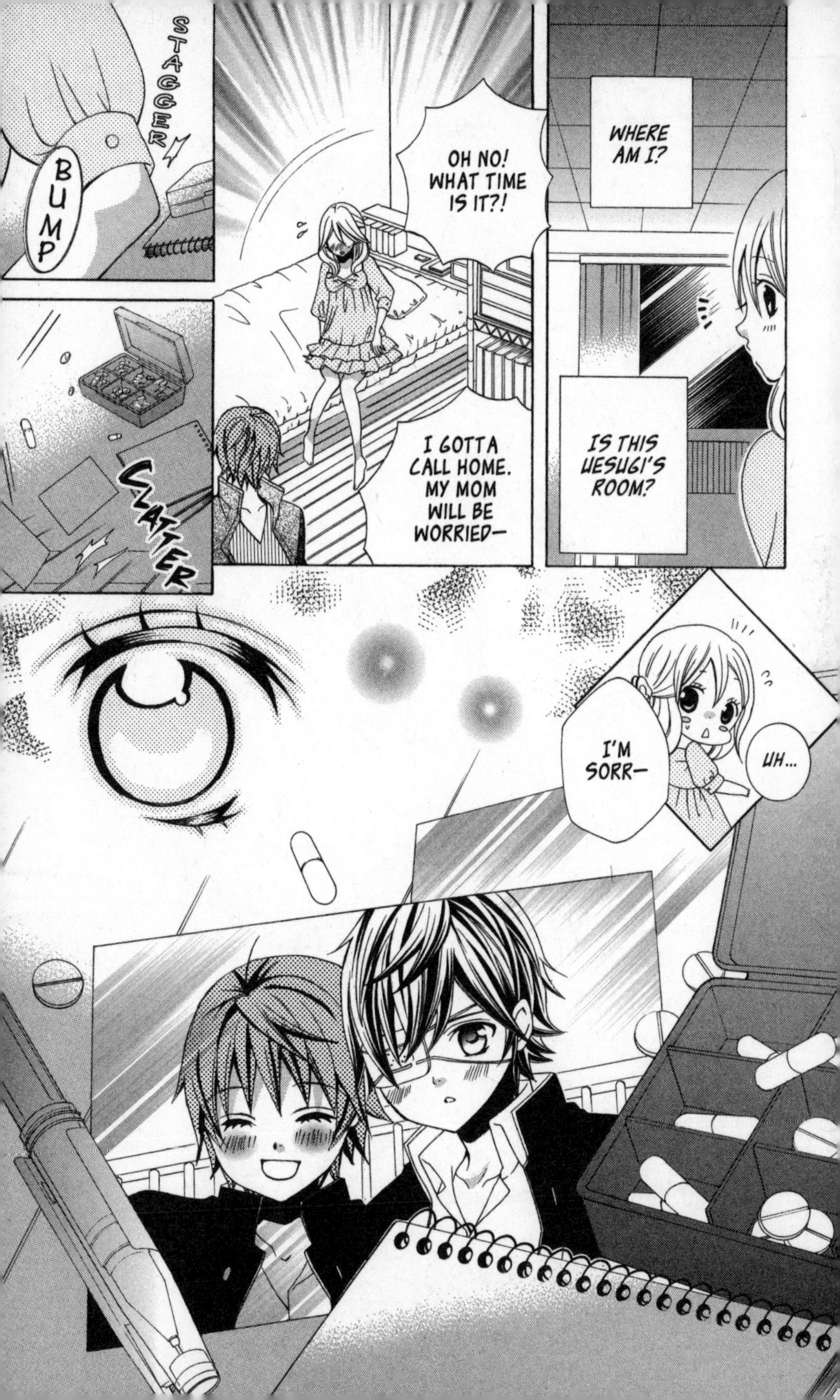
WHERE AM I?
IS THIS UESUGI'S ROOM?
OH NO! WHAT TIME IS IT?!
I GOTTA CALL HOME. MY MOM WILL BE WORRIED—
STAGGER
BUMP
CLATTER
UH...
I'M SORR—

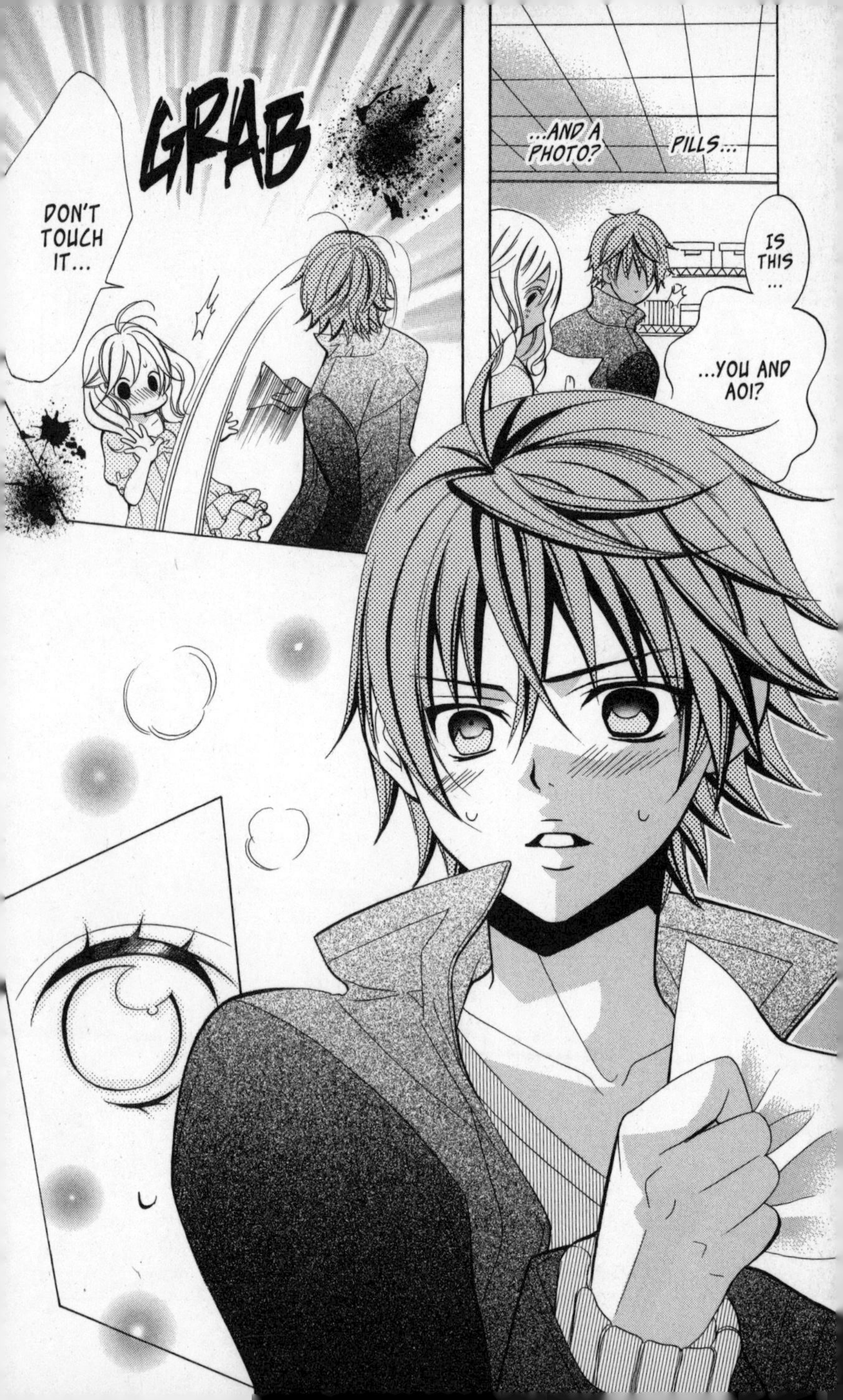
PILLS...
...AND A PHOTO?
IS THIS ...
...YOU AND AOI?
GRAB
DON'T TOUCH IT...

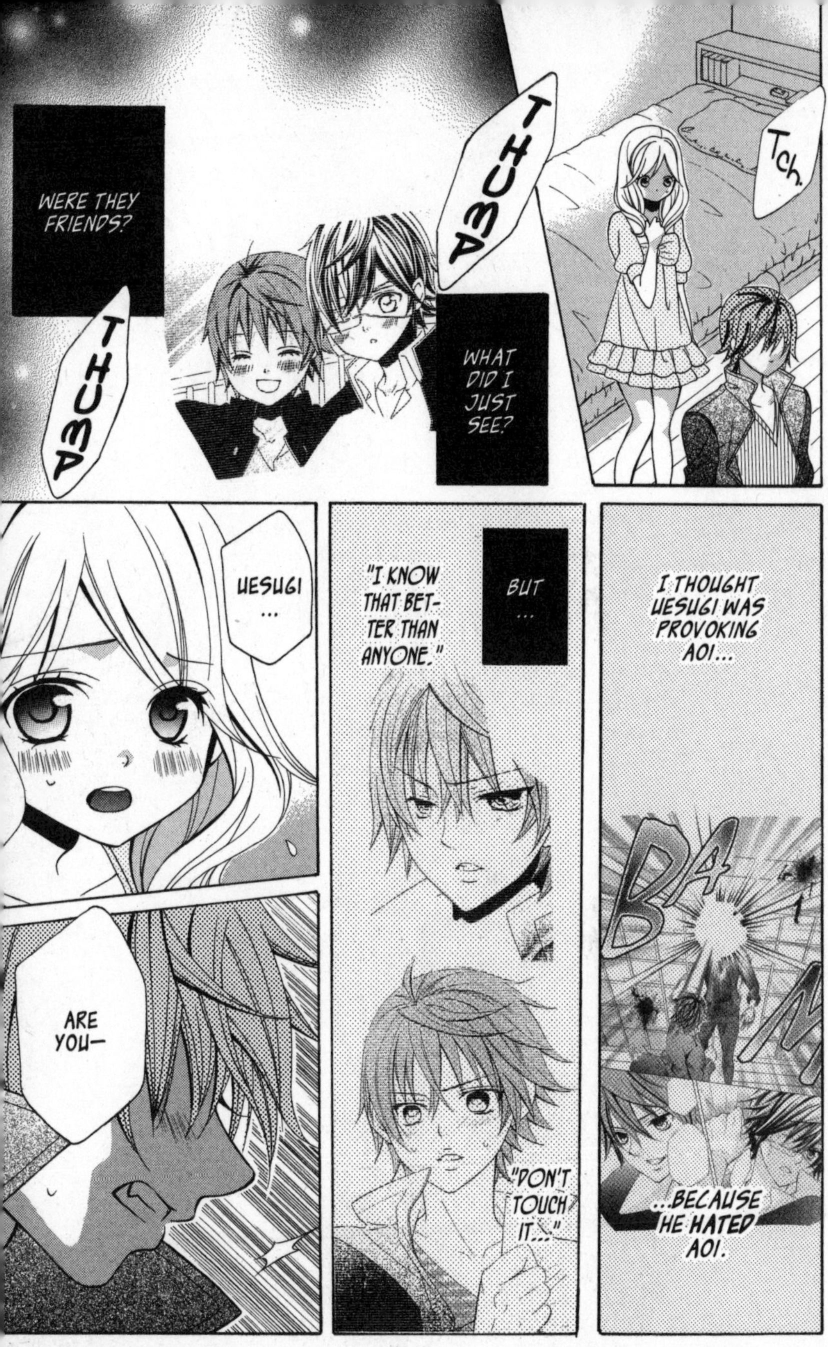
Tch.
THUMP
WHAT DID I JUST SEE?
WERE THEY FRIENDS?
THUMP
I THOUGHT UESUGI WAS PROVOKING AOI...
BAM
...BECAUSE HE HATED AOI.
BUT...
"I KNOW THAT BETTER THAN ANYONE."
"DON'T TOUCH IT..."
UESUGI...
ARE YOU—

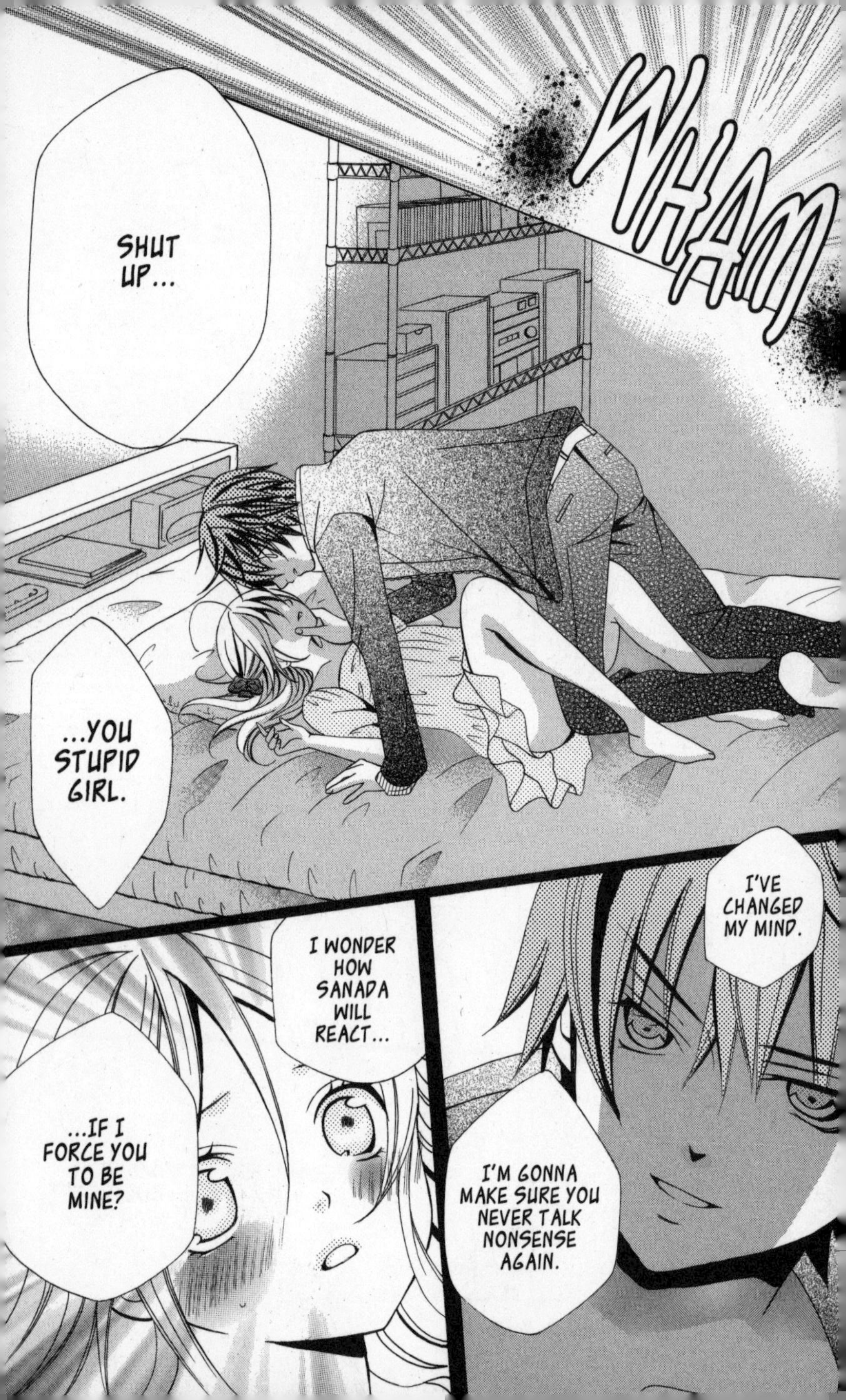
WHAM
SHUT UP...
...YOU STUPID GIRL.
I'VE CHANGED MY MIND.
I'M GONNA MAKE SURE YOU NEVER TALK NONSENSE AGAIN.
I WONDER HOW SANADA WILL REACT...
...IF I FORCE YOU TO BE MINE?

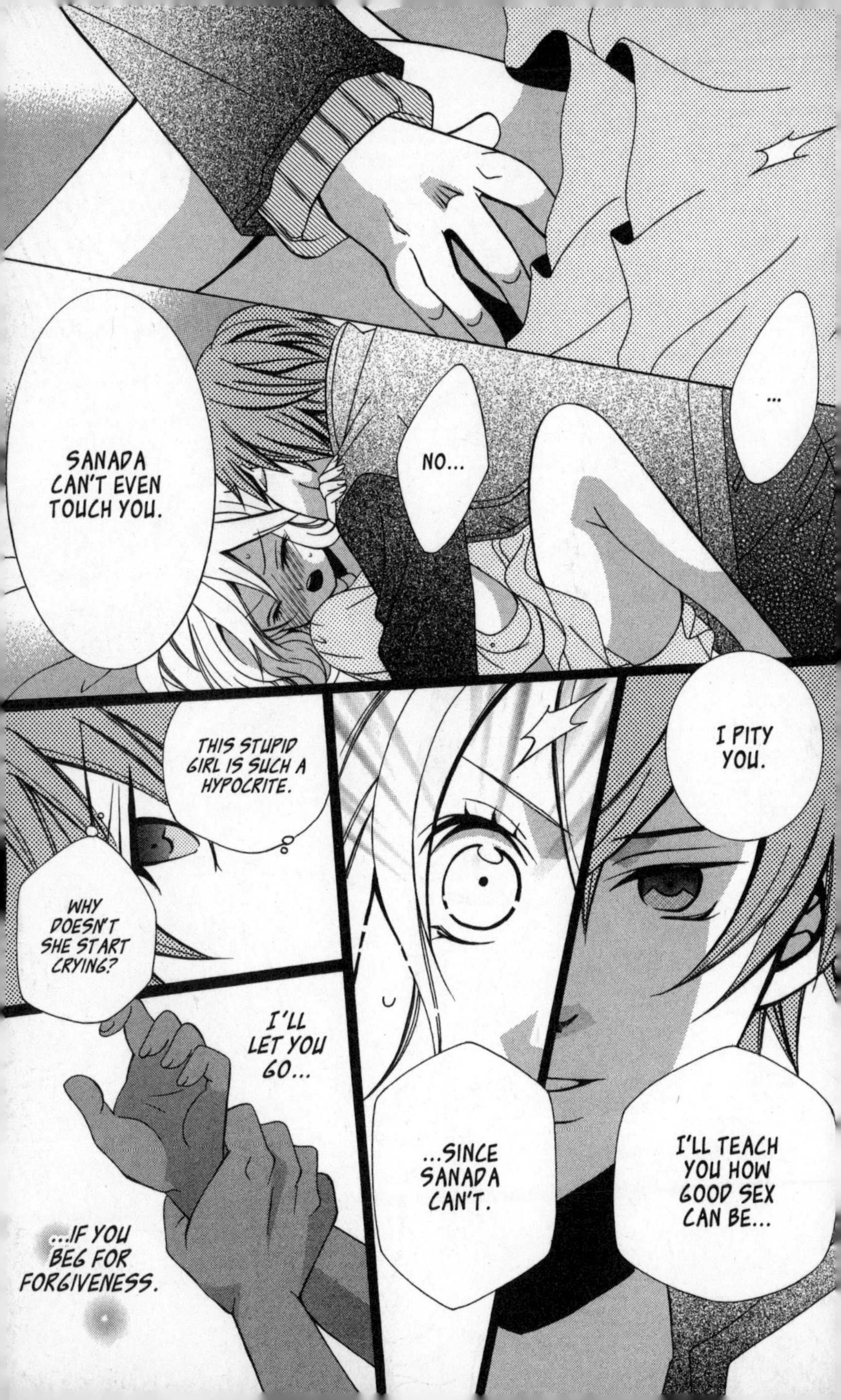
...
NO...
SANADA CAN'T EVEN TOUCH YOU.
I PITY YOU.
I'LL TEACH YOU HOW GOOD SEX CAN BE...
...SINCE SANADA CAN'T.
THIS STUPID GIRL IS SUCH A HYPOCRITE.
WHY DOESN'T SHE START CRYING?
I'LL LET YOU GO...
...IF YOU BEG FOR FORGIVENESS.

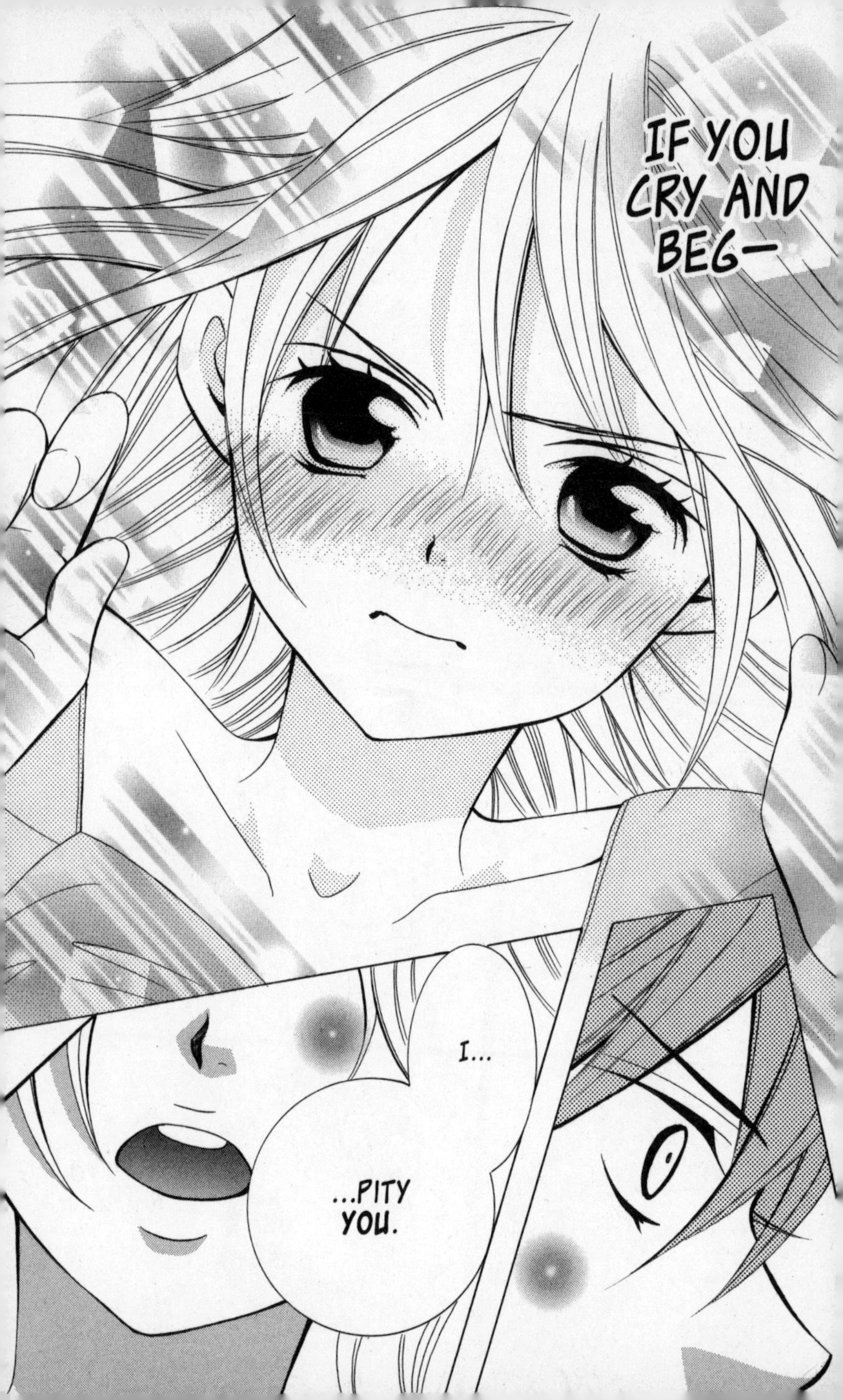
IF YOU CRY AND BEG—
I...
...PITY YOU.

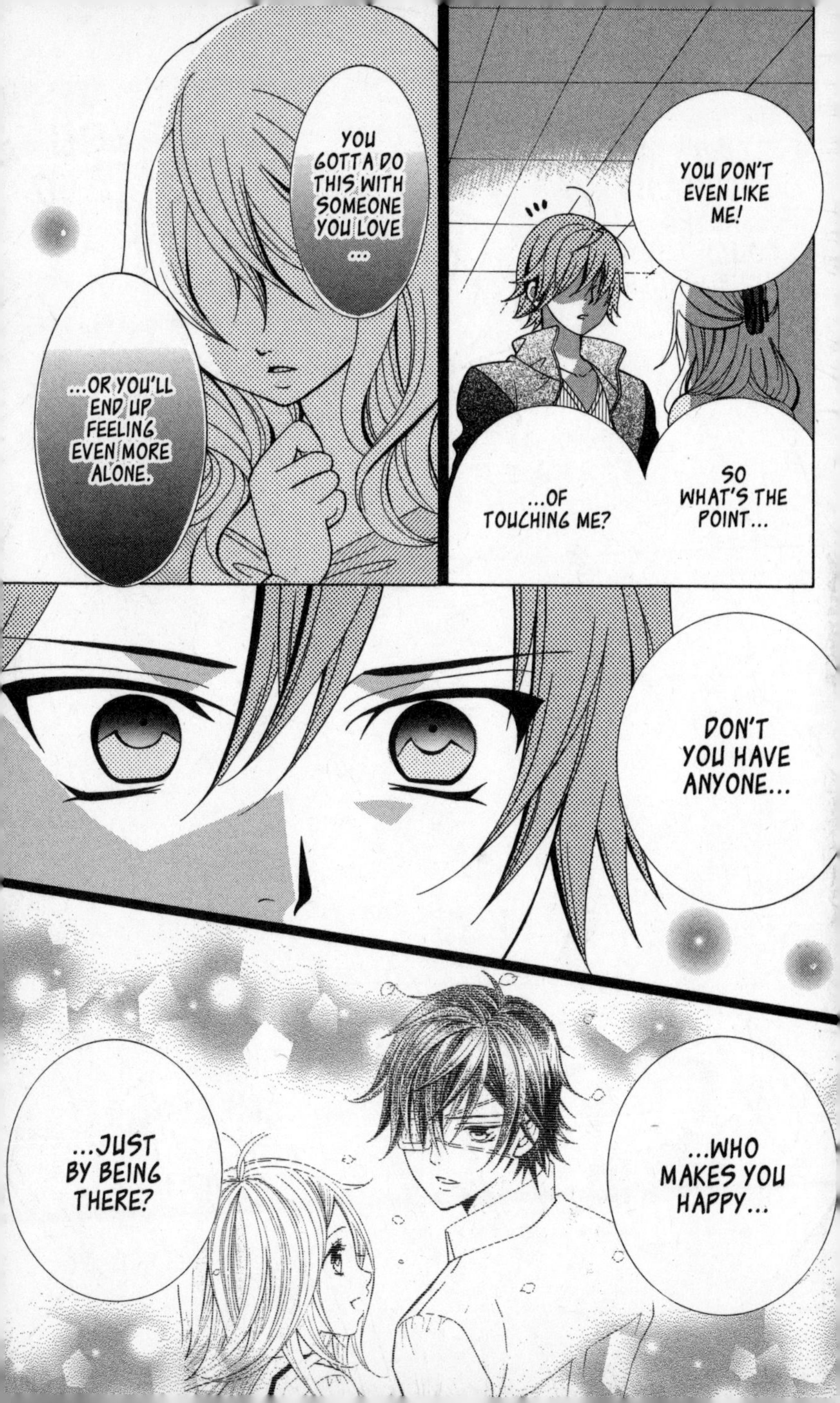
YOU DON'T EVEN LIKE ME!
SO WHAT'S THE POINT...
...OF TOUCHING ME?
YOU GOTTA DO THIS WITH SOMEONE YOU LOVE...
...OR YOU'LL END UP FEELING EVEN MORE ALONE.
DON'T YOU HAVE ANYONE...
...WHO MAKES YOU HAPPY...
...JUST BY BEING THERE?

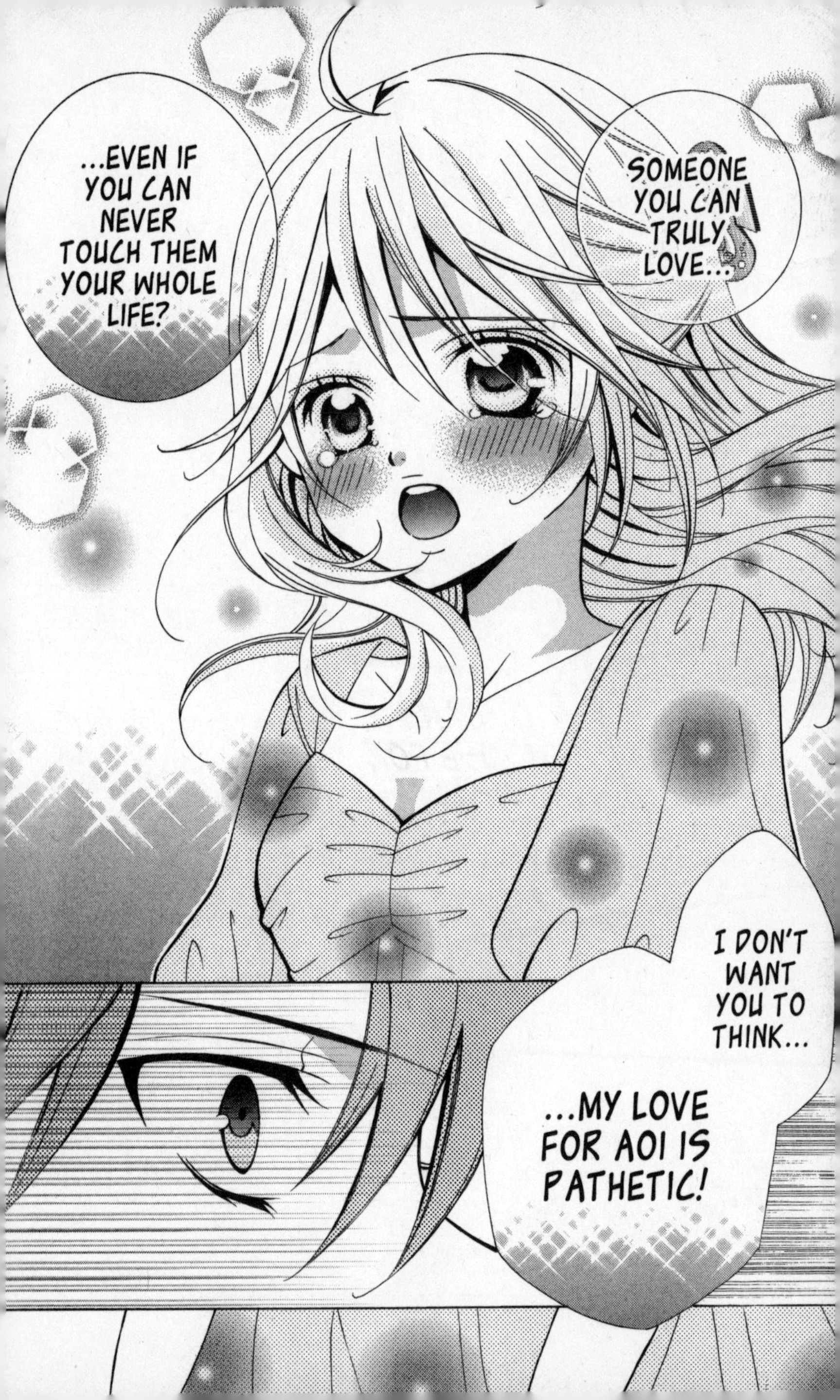
SOMEONE YOU CAN TRULY LOVE...
...EVEN IF YOU CAN NEVER TOUCH THEM YOUR WHOLE LIFE?
I DON'T WANT YOU TO THINK...
...MY LOVE FOR AOI IS PATHETIC!

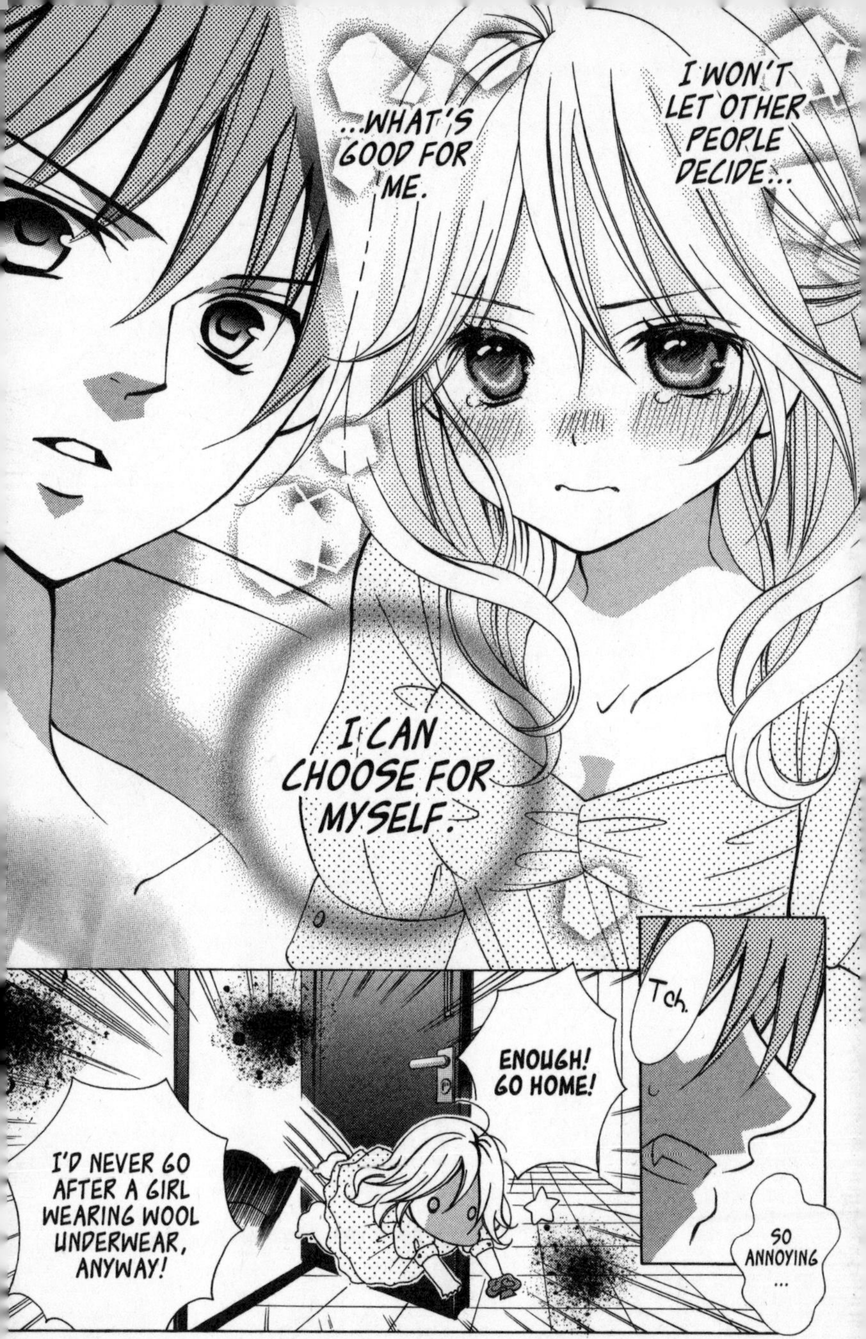
I WON'T LET OTHER PEOPLE DECIDE...
...WHAT'S GOOD FOR ME.
I CAN CHOOSE FOR MYSELF.
Tch.
SO ANNOYING ...
ENOUGH! GO HOME!
I'D NEVER GO AFTER A GIRL WEARING WOOL UNDERWEAR, ANYWAY!

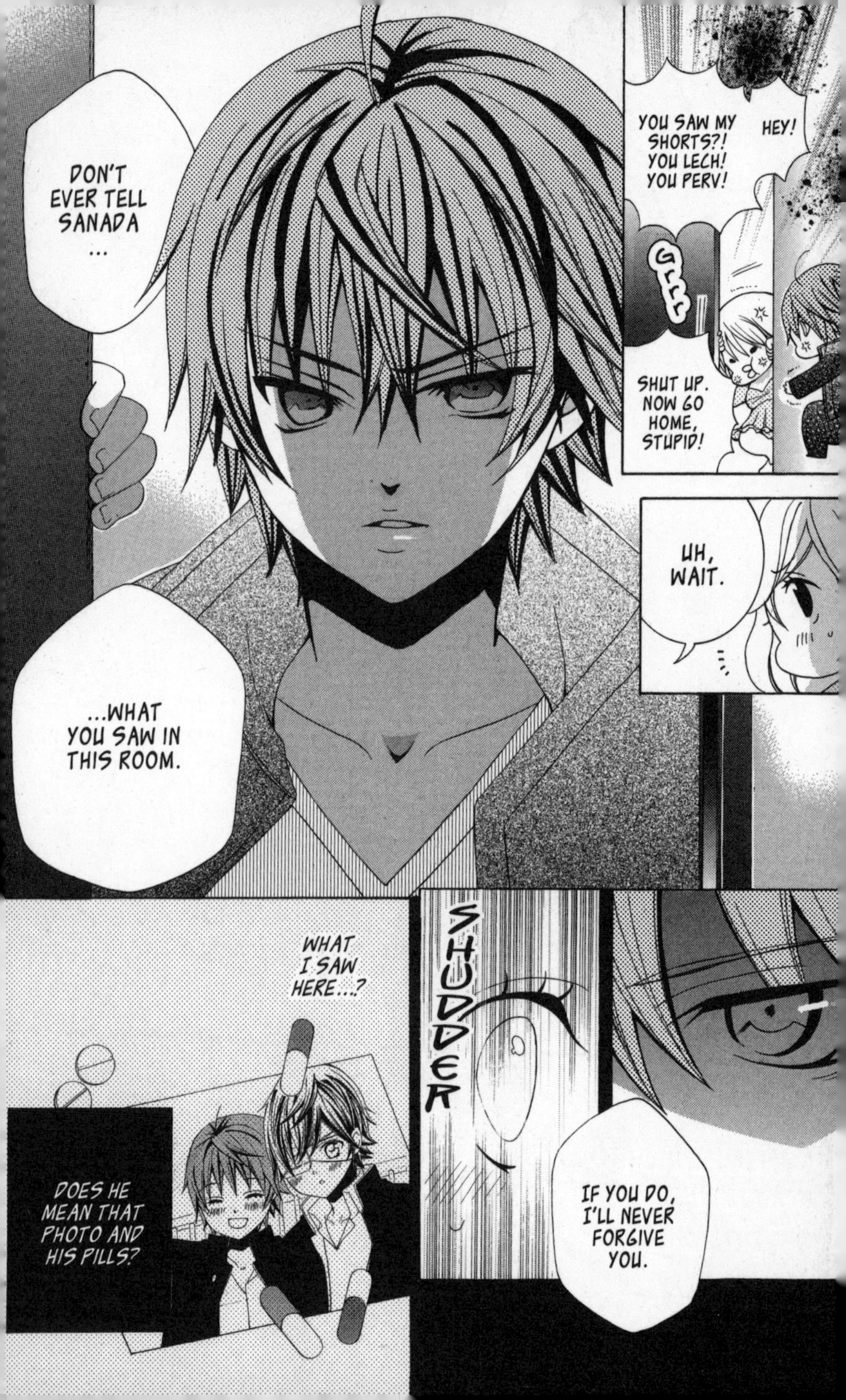
HEY!
YOU SAW MY SHORTS?! YOU LECH! YOU PERV!
Grrr
SHUT UP. NOW GO HOME, STUPID!
UH, WAIT.
DON'T EVER TELL SANADA ...
...WHAT YOU SAW IN THIS ROOM.
IF YOU DO, I'LL NEVER FORGIVE YOU.
SHUDDER
WHAT I SAW HERE...?
DOES HE MEAN THAT PHOTO AND HIS PILLS?

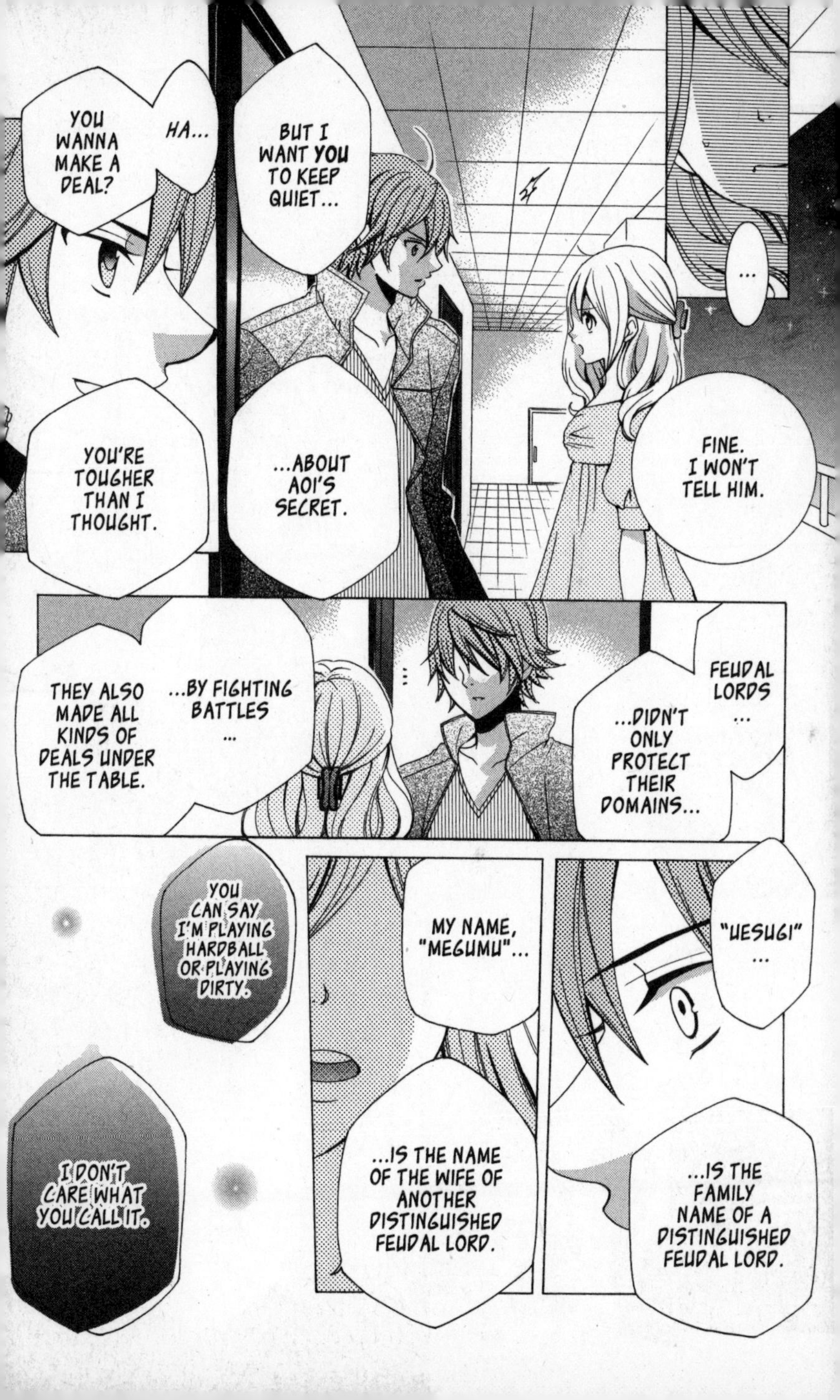
...
FINE. I WON'T TELL HIM.
BUT I WANT YOU TO KEEP QUIET...
...ABOUT AOI'S SECRET.
HA...
YOU WANNA MAKE A DEAL?
YOU'RE TOUGHER THAN I THOUGHT.
FEUDAL LORDS ...
...DIDN'T ONLY PROTECT THEIR DOMAINS...
...BY FIGHTING BATTLES ...
THEY ALSO MADE ALL KINDS OF DEALS UNDER THE TABLE.
"UESUGI" ...
...IS THE FAMILY NAME OF A DISTINGUISHED FEUDAL LORD.
MY NAME, "MEGUMU"...
...IS THE NAME OF THE WIFE OF ANOTHER DISTINGUISHED FEUDAL LORD.
YOU CAN SAY I'M PLAYING HARDBALL OR PLAYING DIRTY.
I DON'T CARE WHAT YOU CALL IT.

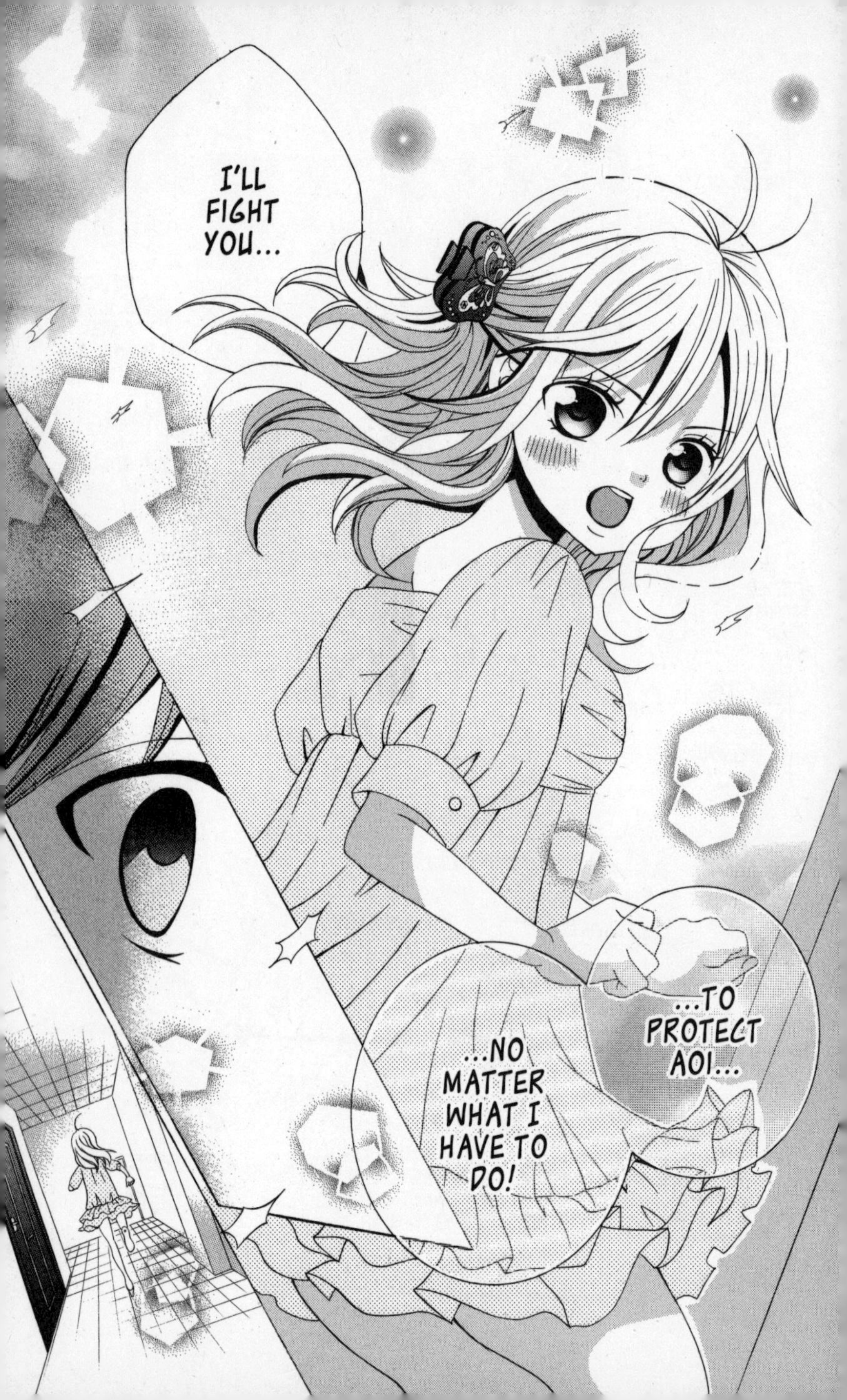
I'LL FIGHT YOU...
...TO PROTECT AOI...
...NO MATTER WHAT I HAVE TO DO!

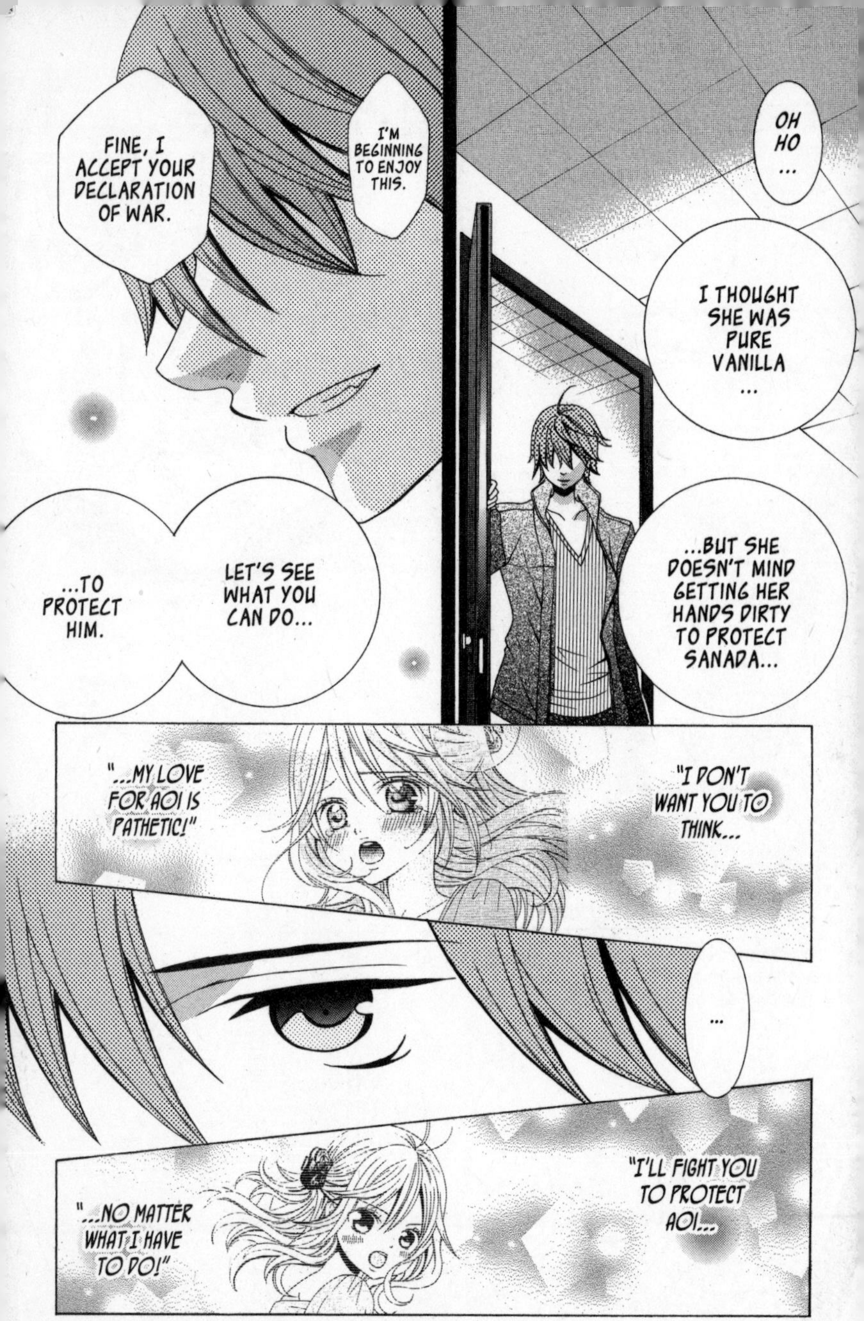
OH HO ...
I THOUGHT SHE WAS PURE VANILLA ...
...BUT SHE DOESN'T MIND GETTING HER HANDS DIRTY TO PROTECT SANADA...
I'M BEGINNING TO ENJOY THIS.
FINE, I ACCEPT YOUR DECLARATION OF WAR.
LET'S SEE WHAT YOU CAN DO...
...TO PROTECT HIM.
"I DON'T WANT YOU TO THINK...
"...MY LOVE FOR AOI IS PATHETIC!"
...
"I'LL FIGHT YOU TO PROTECT AOI...
"...NO MATTER WHAT I HAVE TO DO!"

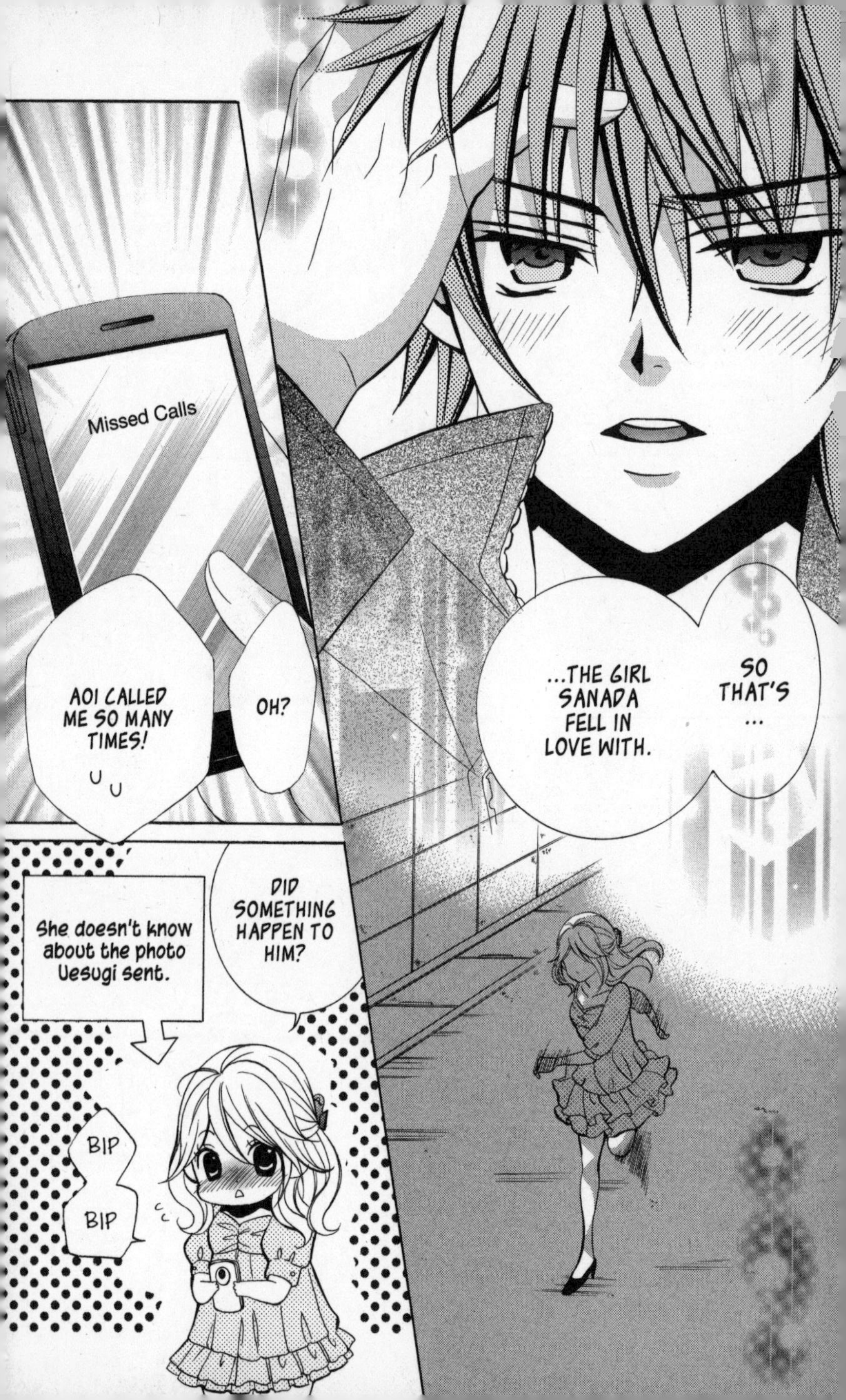
SO THAT'S...
...THE GIRL SANADA FELL IN LOVE WITH.
Missed Calls
OH?
AOI CALLED ME SO MANY TIMES!
DID SOMETHING HAPPEN TO HIM?
She doesn't know about the photo Uesugi sent.
BIP
BIP

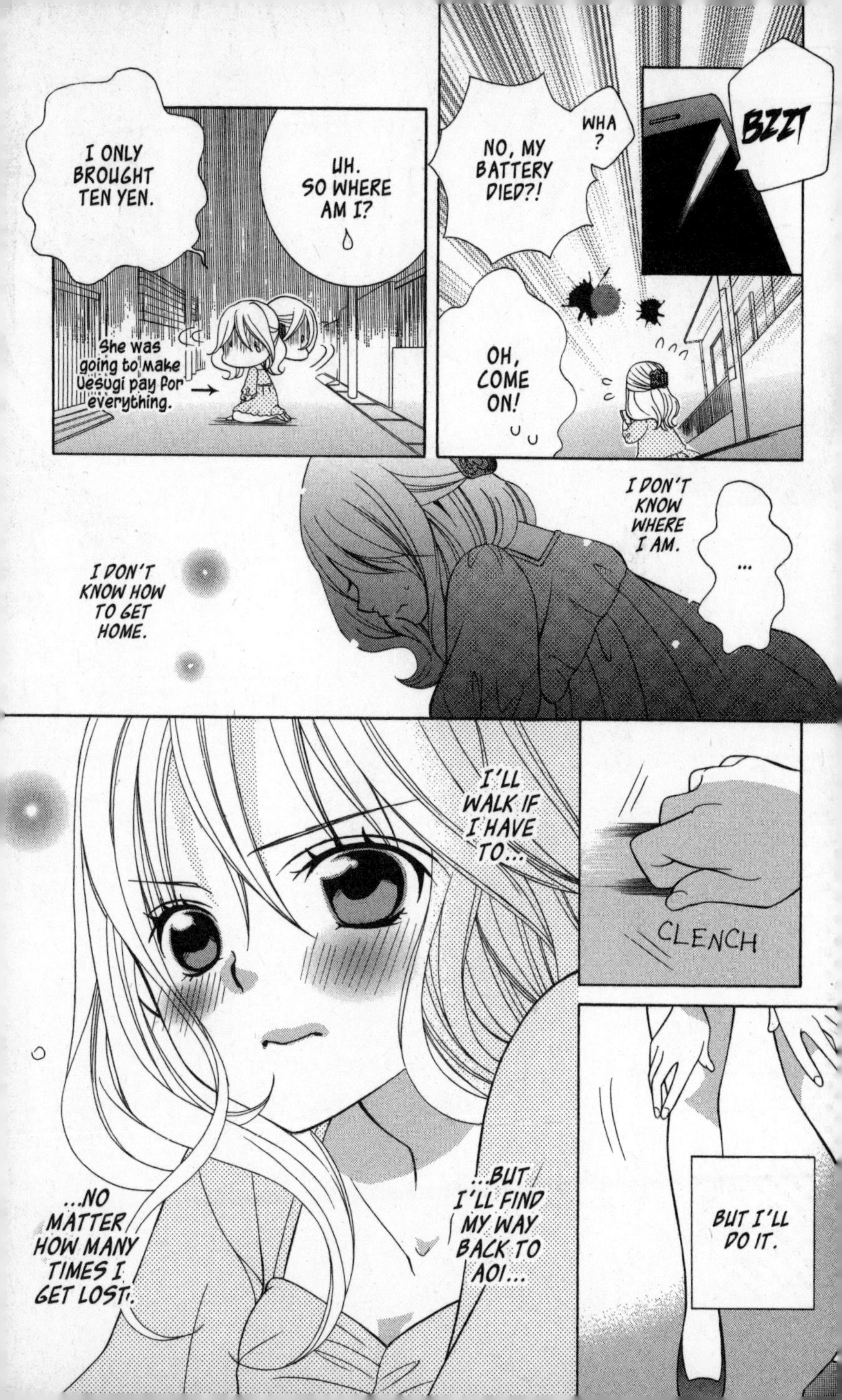
BZZT
WHA?
NO, MY BATTERY DIED?!
OH, COME ON!
UH. SO WHERE AM I?
I ONLY BROUGHT TEN YEN.
She was going to make Uesugi pay for everything.
I DON'T KNOW WHERE I AM.
...
I DON'T KNOW HOW TO GET HOME.
CLENCH
BUT I'LL DO IT.
I'LL WALK IF I HAVE TO...
...BUT I'LL FIND MY WAY BACK TO AOI...
...NO MATTER HOW MANY TIMES I GET LOST.

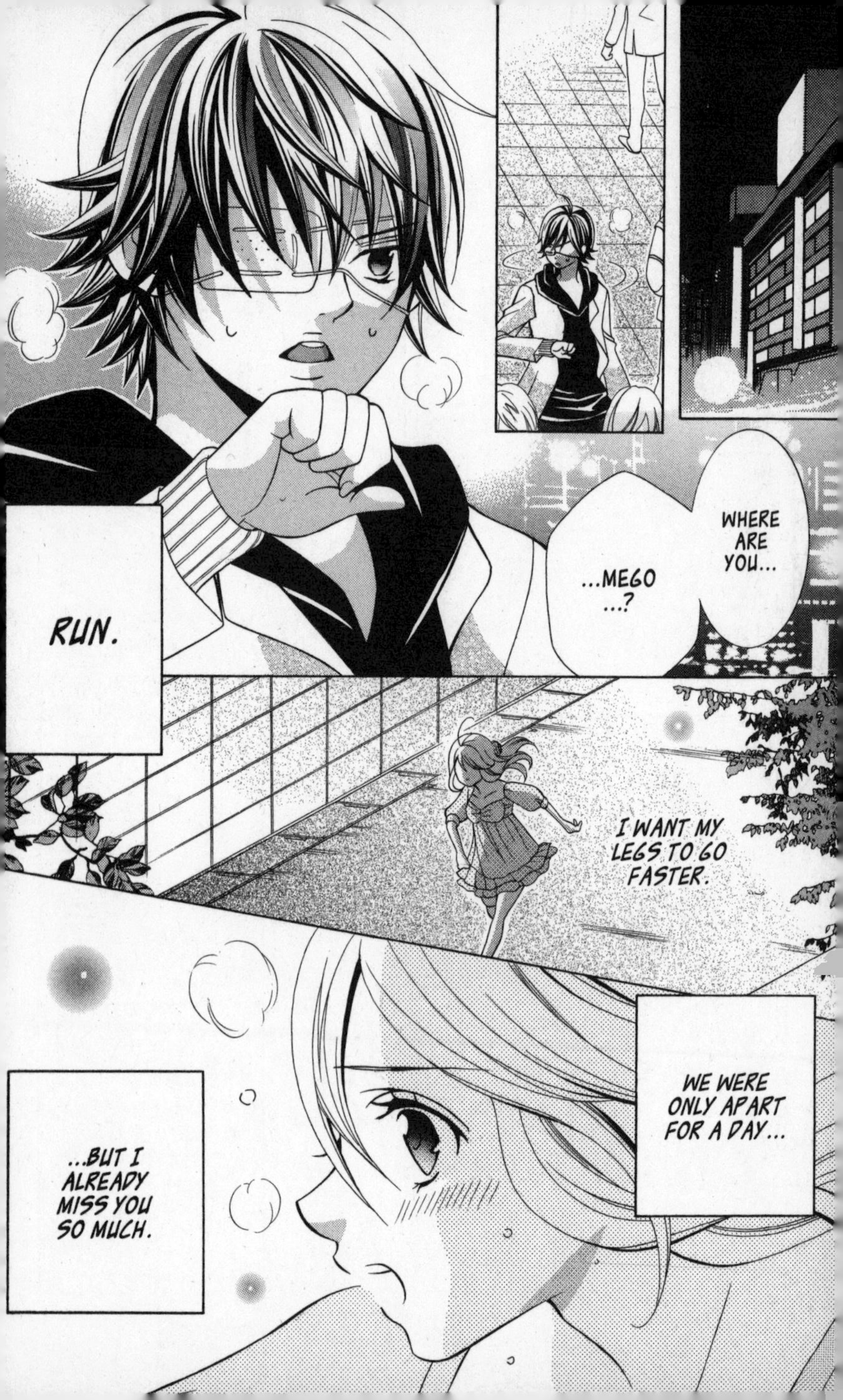
WHERE ARE YOU... ...MEGO ...?
RUN.
I WANT MY LEGS TO GO FASTER.
WE WERE ONLY APART FOR A DAY...
...BUT I ALREADY MISS YOU SO MUCH.

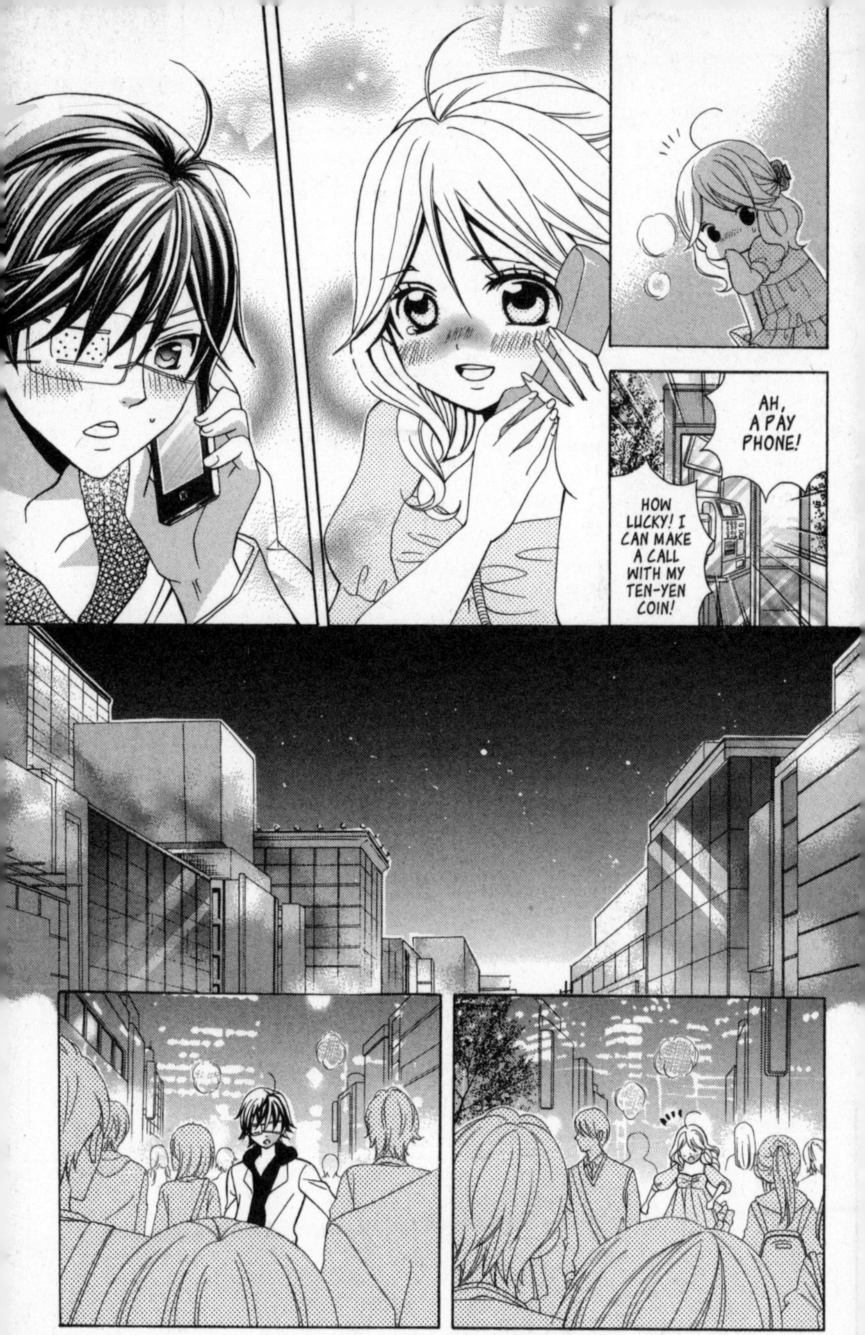
AH, A PAY PHONE!
HOW LUCKY! I CAN MAKE A CALL WITH MY TEN-YEN COIN!

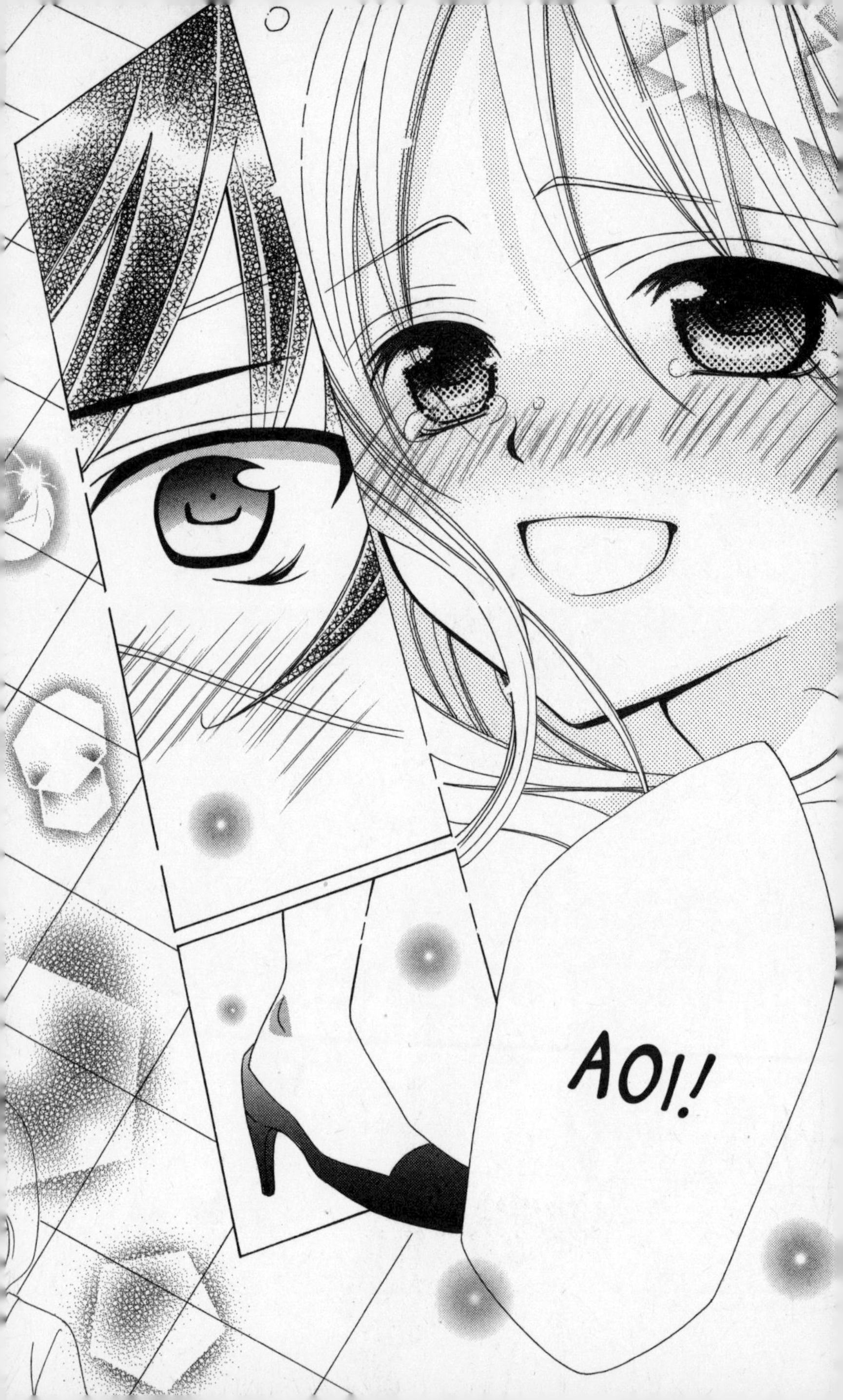
AOI!

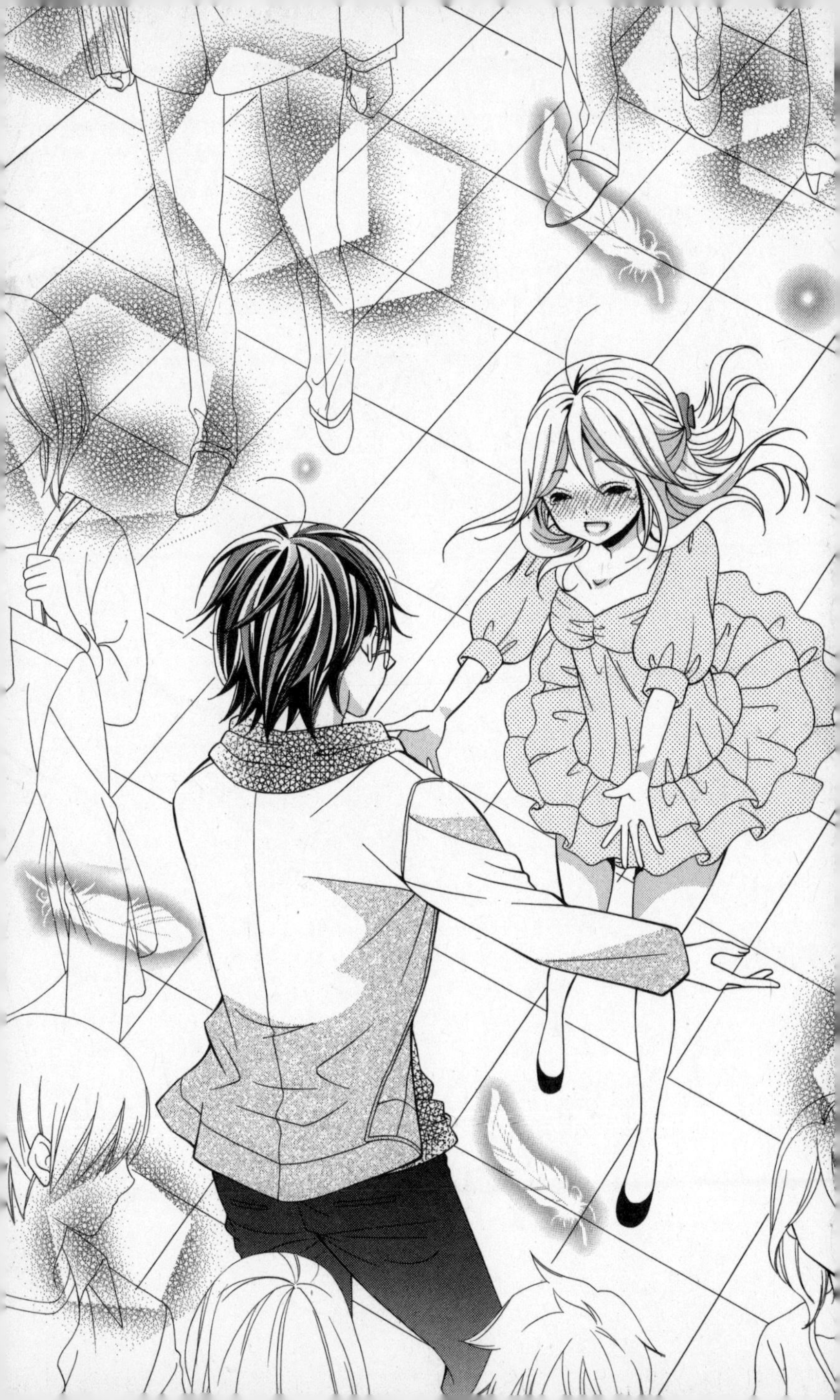

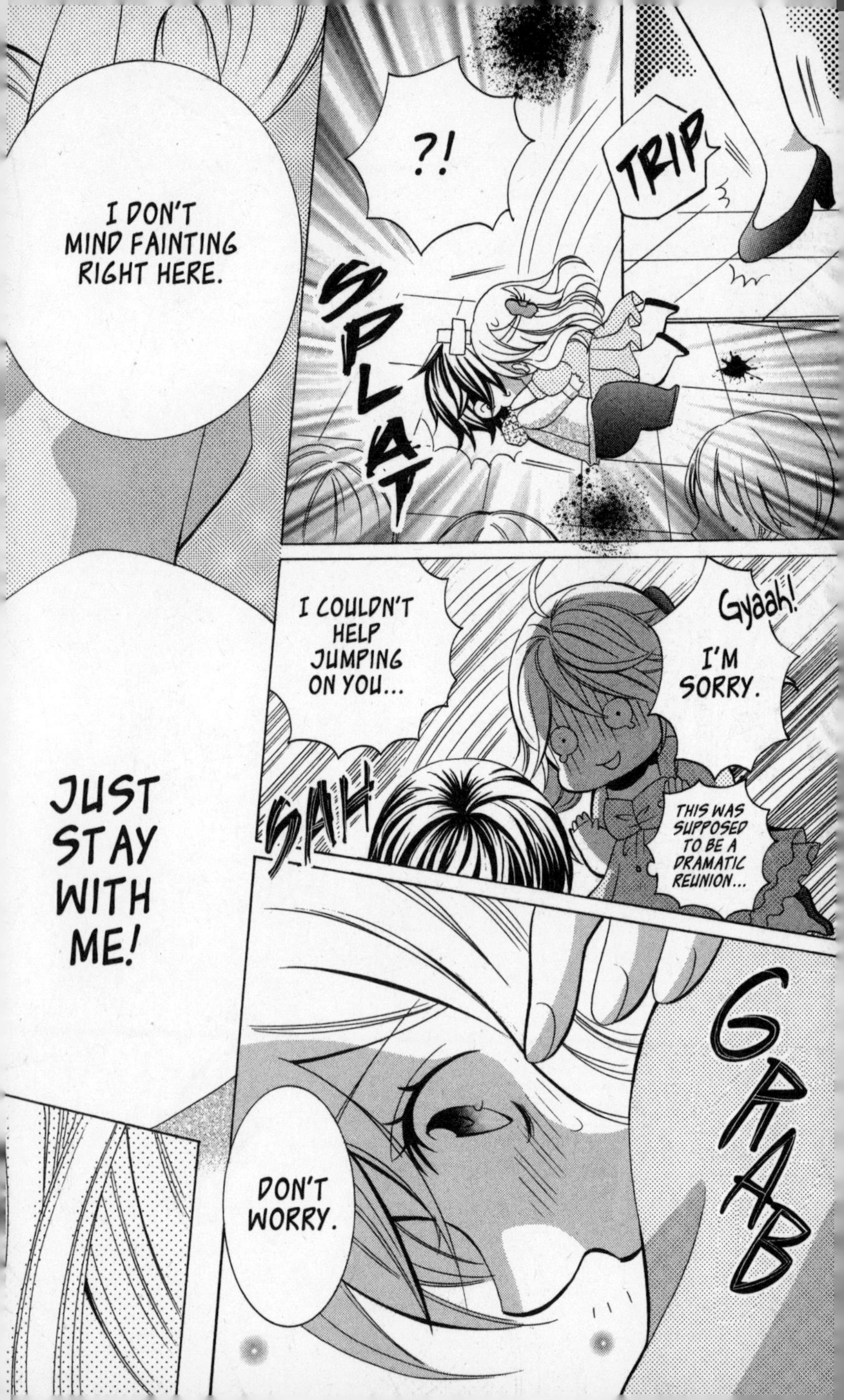
TRIP
?!
SPLAT
Gyaah!
I'M SORRY.
I COULDN'T HELP JUMPING ON YOU...
THIS WAS SUPPOSED TO BE A DRAMATIC REUNION...
SAH
GRAB
DON'T WORRY.
I DON'T MIND FAINTING RIGHT HERE.
JUST STAY WITH ME!

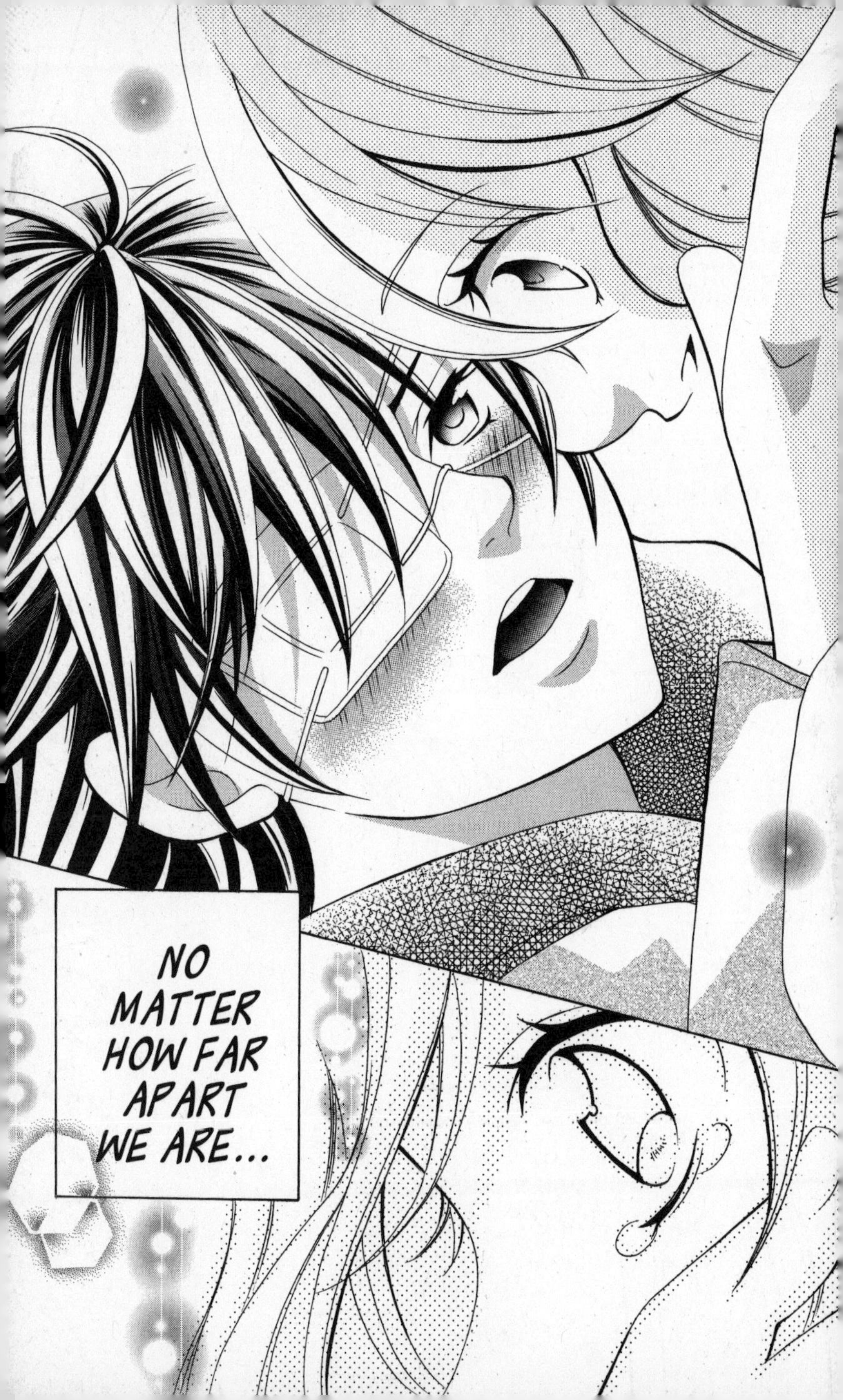
NO MATTER HOW FAR APART WE ARE...

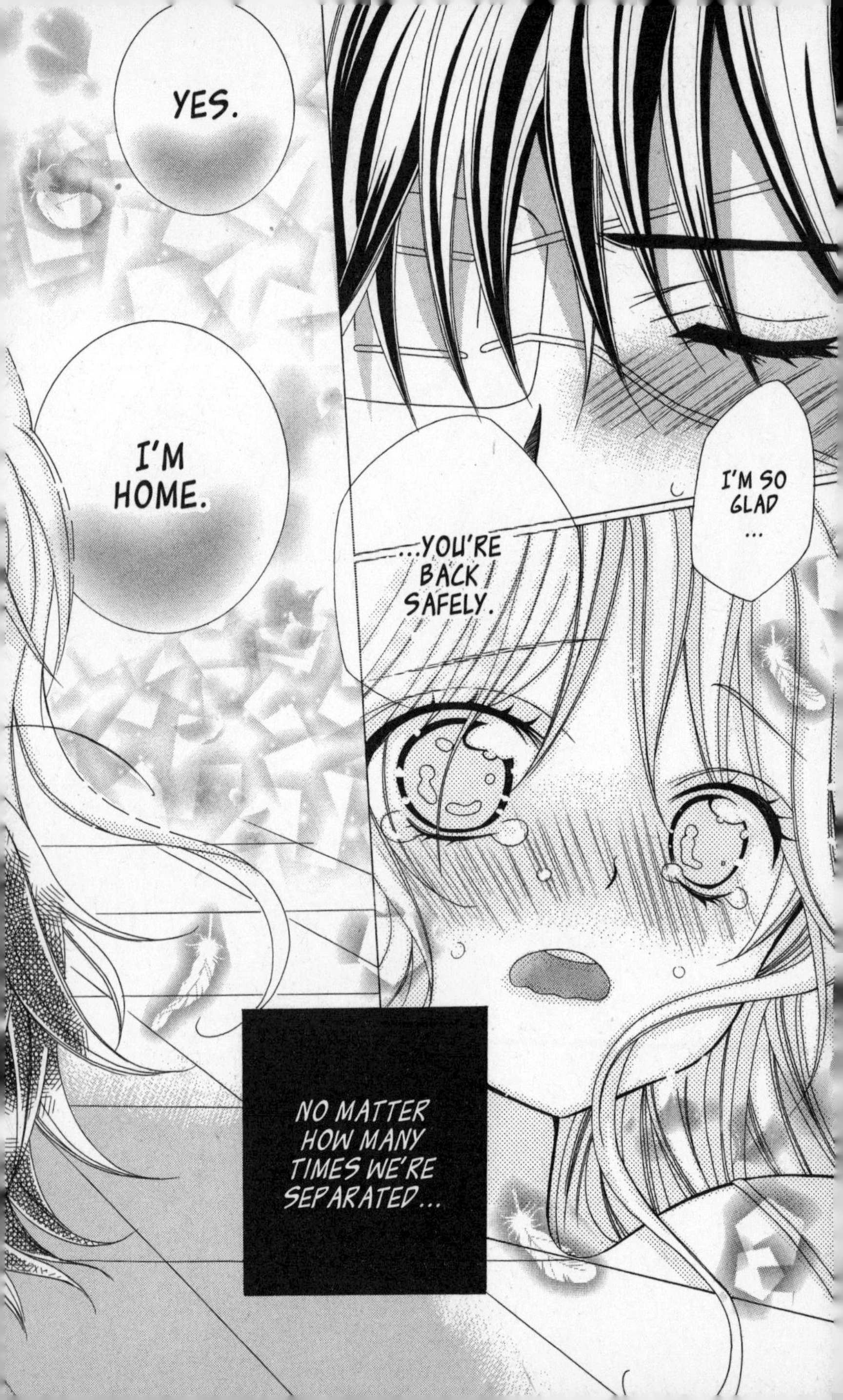
I'M SO GLAD ...
...YOU'RE BACK SAFELY.
YES.
I'M HOME.
NO MATTER HOW MANY TIMES WE'RE SEPARATED...

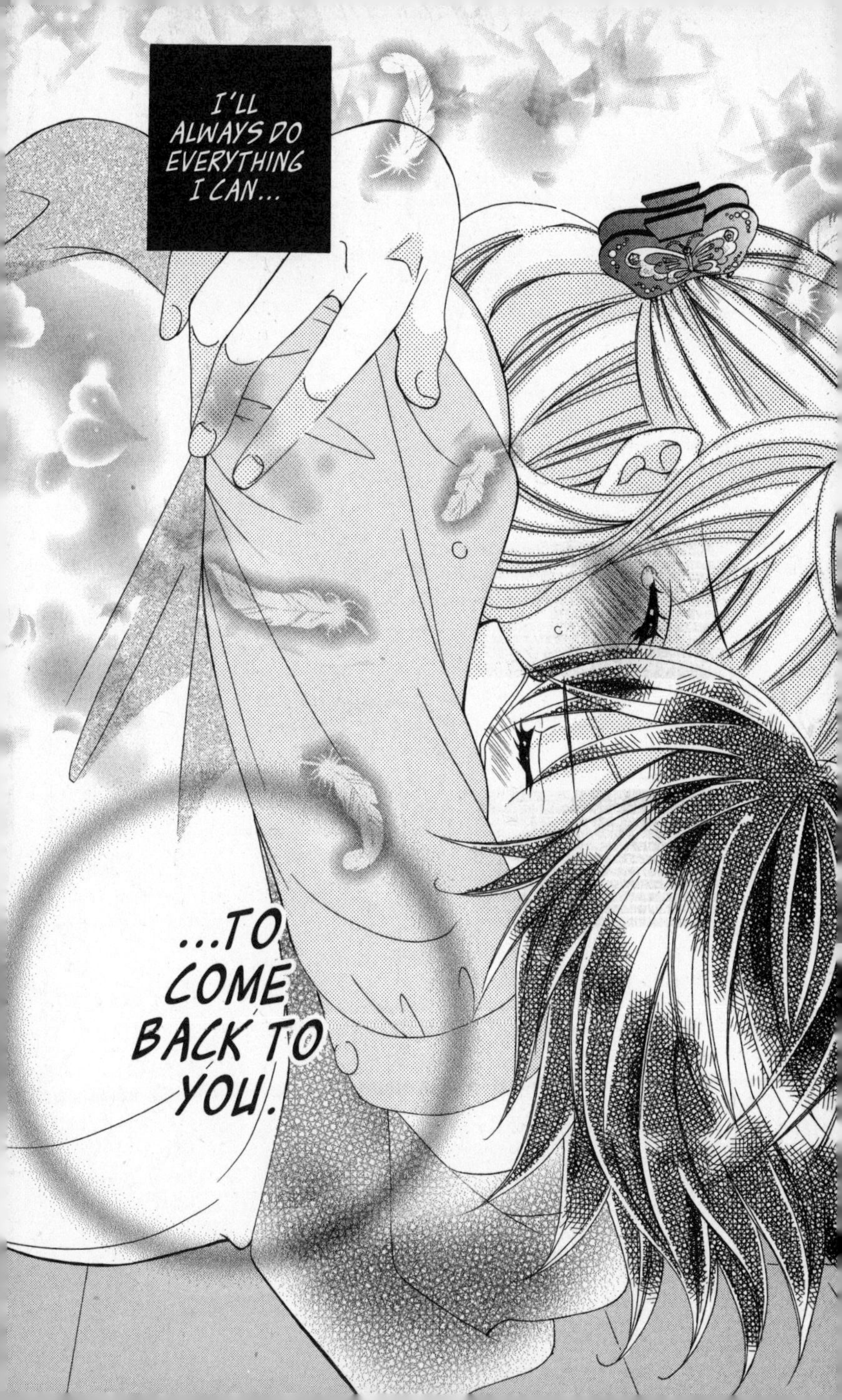
I'LL ALWAYS DO EVERYTHING I CAN...
...TO COME BACK TO YOU.

EVERYONE'S DRAWINGS ARE SO CUTE, THEY HURT!!

SO CUTE! FAN ART FEATURE ♥

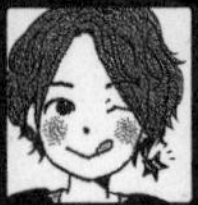

Shoji

Editor Shoji has commented on each one this time too!!

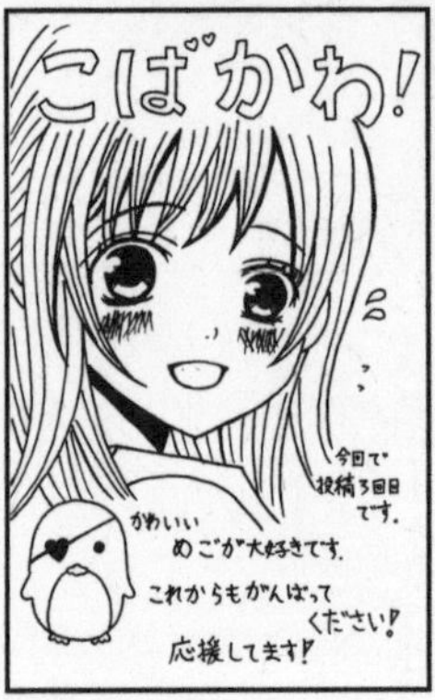

こばかわ!
今回で投稿3回目です。
かわいいめごが大好きです。
これからもがんばってください!
応援してます!

Pako☆ (Saitama)
Ed.: Both Mego and the eye-patch penguin are super cute. ♥ ←

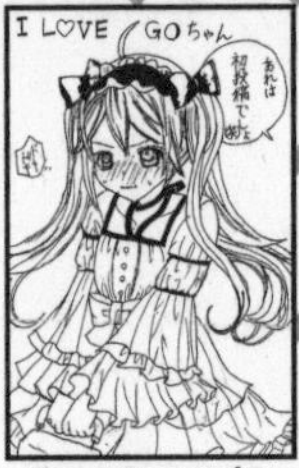

I LOVE GOちゃん

↑ Mana Iwata (Osaka)
Ed.: Azusa is actually girlish!

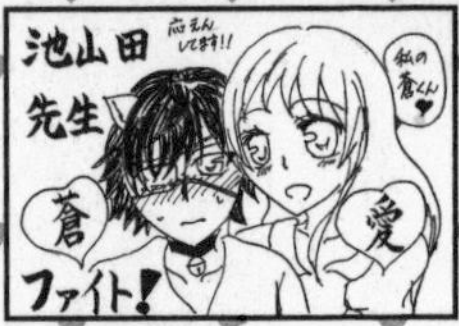

池山田先生
応えんしてます!!
私の蒼くん♥
蒼
愛
ファイト!

Mitchan (Saga) ↑
Ed.: I love the cat-eared Aoi!!

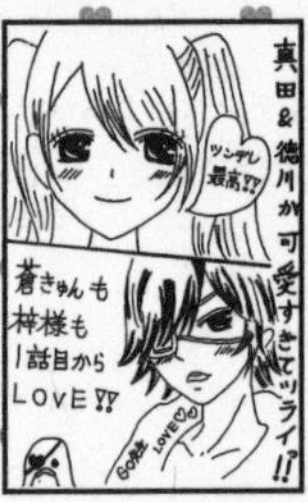

真田&徳川が可愛すぎてツライ!!
ツンデレ最高!?
蒼きゅんも梓様も1話目からLOVE!!

Sakura Shishido (Tokushima)
Ed.: Azusa and Aoi are rarely drawn together! ←

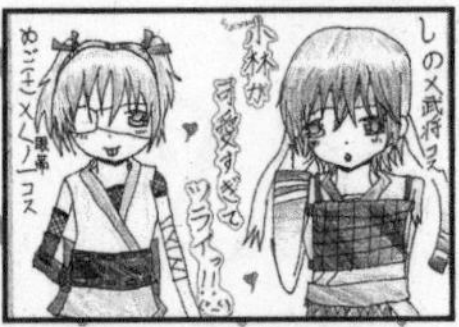

小林が可愛すぎてツライっ!!

Hyo Iyokono (Saitama) ↑
Ed.: Their cosplay is cool!!

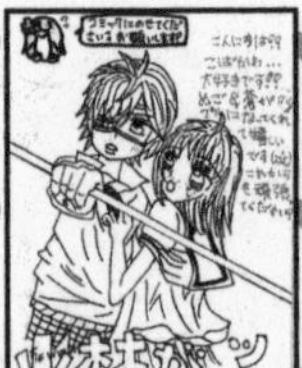

小林が可愛すぎてツライ!!

Koyuki Hirano (Toyama)
Ed.: Aoi looks cool protecting Mego!! ←

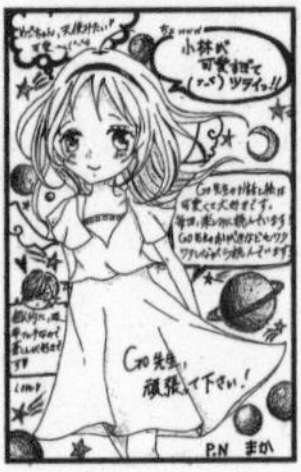

小林が可愛すぎて(アハ)ツライ!!
GO先生、頑張って下さい!
P.N まか

Maka (Tochigi)
Ed.: Mego looks like an angel. ♥ ←

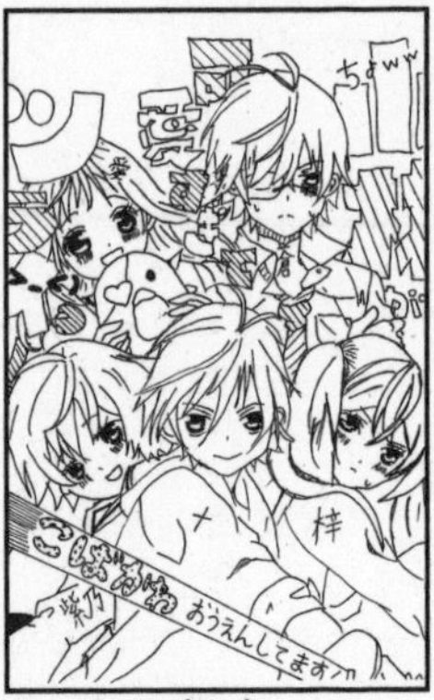

こばかわ おうえんしてます!

Yuna Kanbe (Mie) ↑
Ed.: Everyone's here! The drawing is super gorgeous!

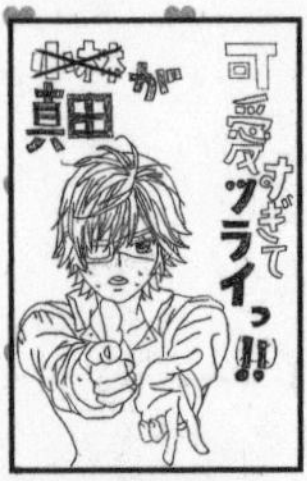

小林が
真田
可愛すぎてツライっ!!

Maaya Takashima (Ishikawa) ↑
Ed.: S-so the title's gonna change...

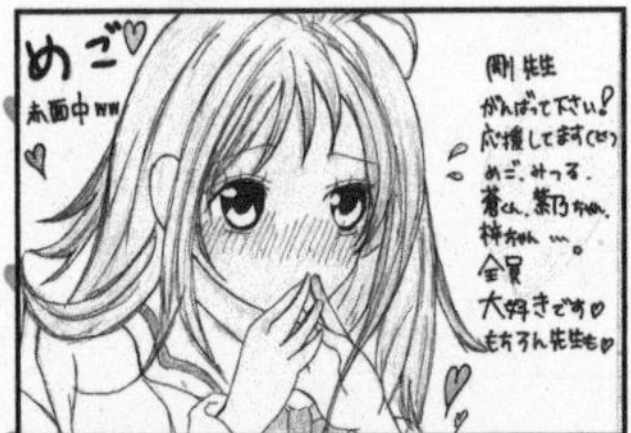

めご♥
剛先生
がんばって下さい!
全員
大好きです♥

Chiffon ♡ (Aomori) ↑
Ed.: The blushing Mego...is way too cute!!

Chapter 37

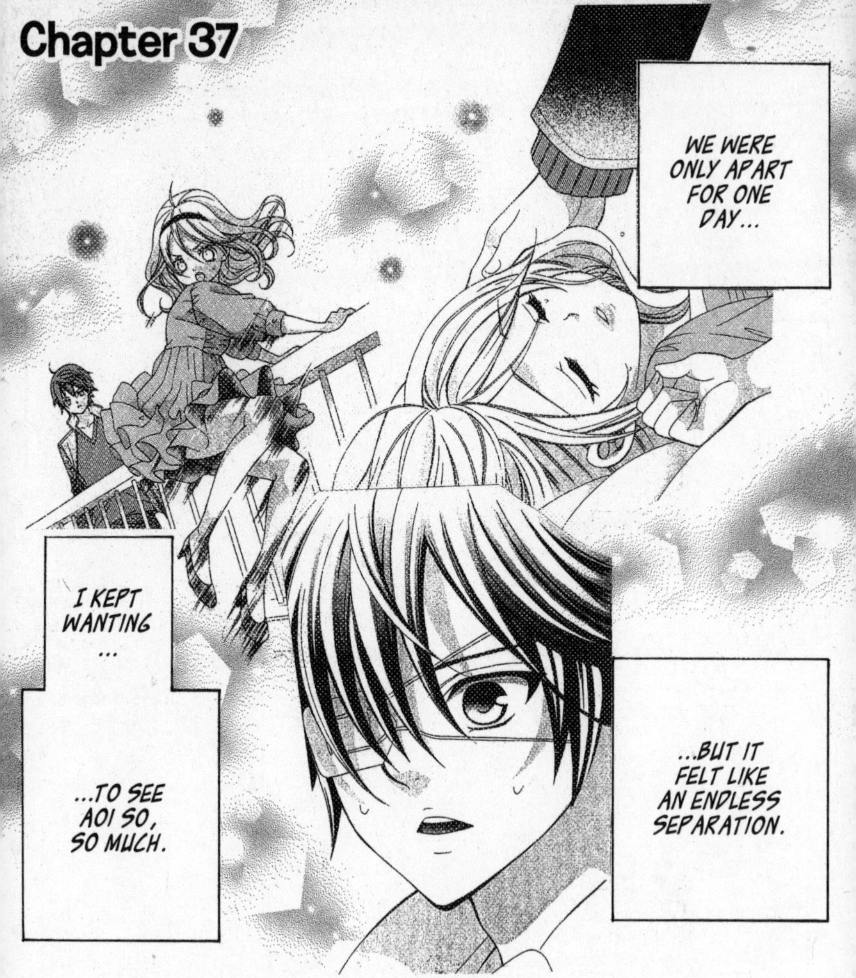
WE WERE ONLY APART FOR ONE DAY...
...BUT IT FELT LIKE AN ENDLESS SEPARATION.
I KEPT WANTING ...
...TO SEE AOI SO, SO MUCH.

THANK YOU FOR ALWAYS SENDING ME LOVELY LETTERS AND DRAWINGS. ♡♡ THEY MAKE ME SO, SO HAPPY. ♡♡ I HOPE YOU SEND YOUR THOUGHTS AND DRAWINGS AFTER READING VOLUME 8. ♡

GO IKEYAMADA
C/O SHOJO BEAT
VIZ MEDIA, LLC
P.O. BOX 77010
SAN FRANCISCO, CA
94107 (^o^)

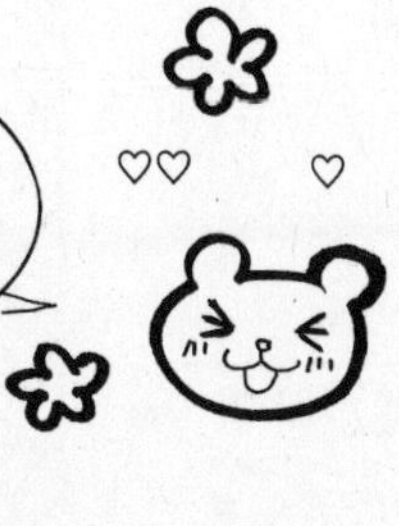

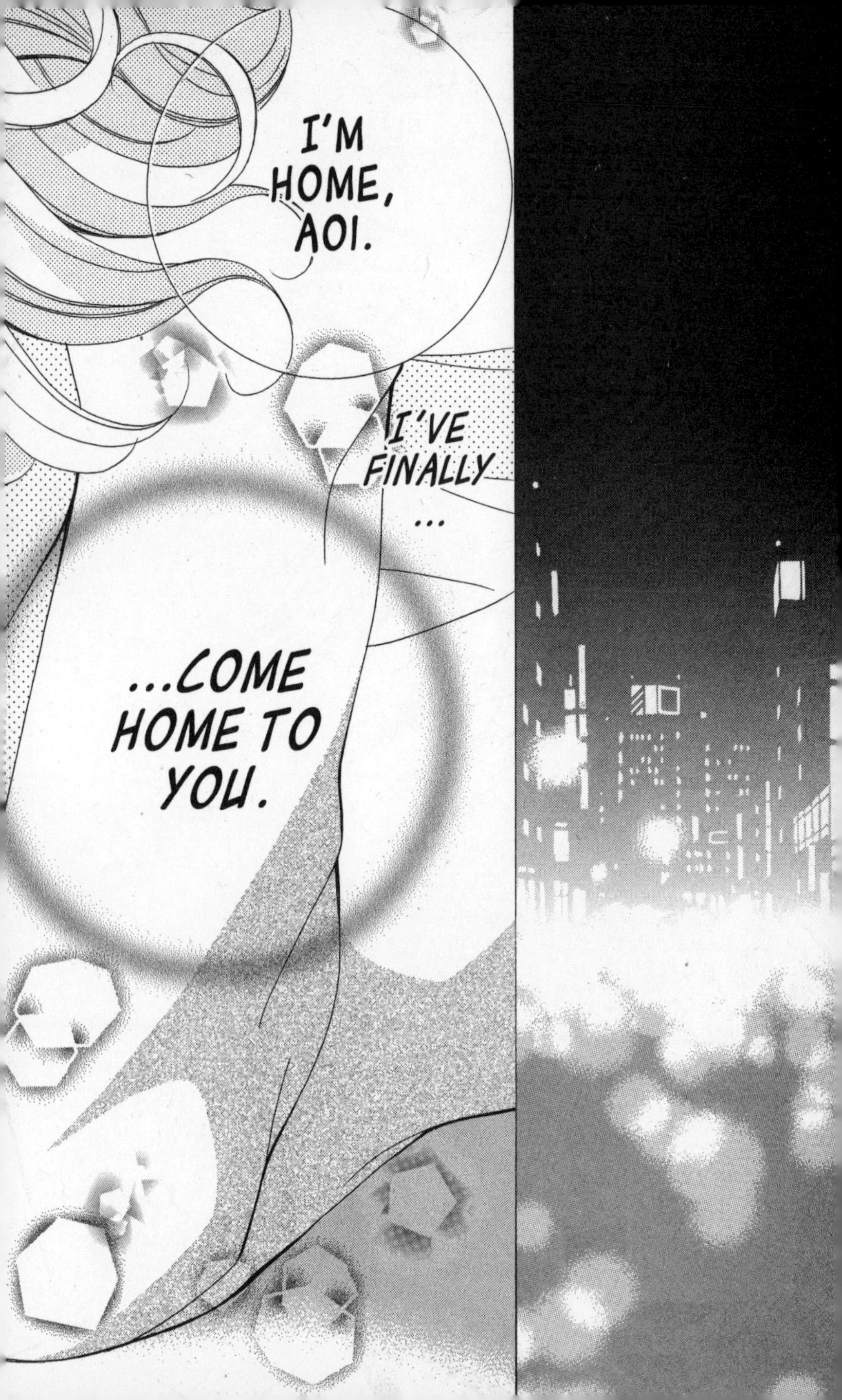
I'M HOME, AOI.
I'VE FINALLY...
...COME HOME TO YOU.

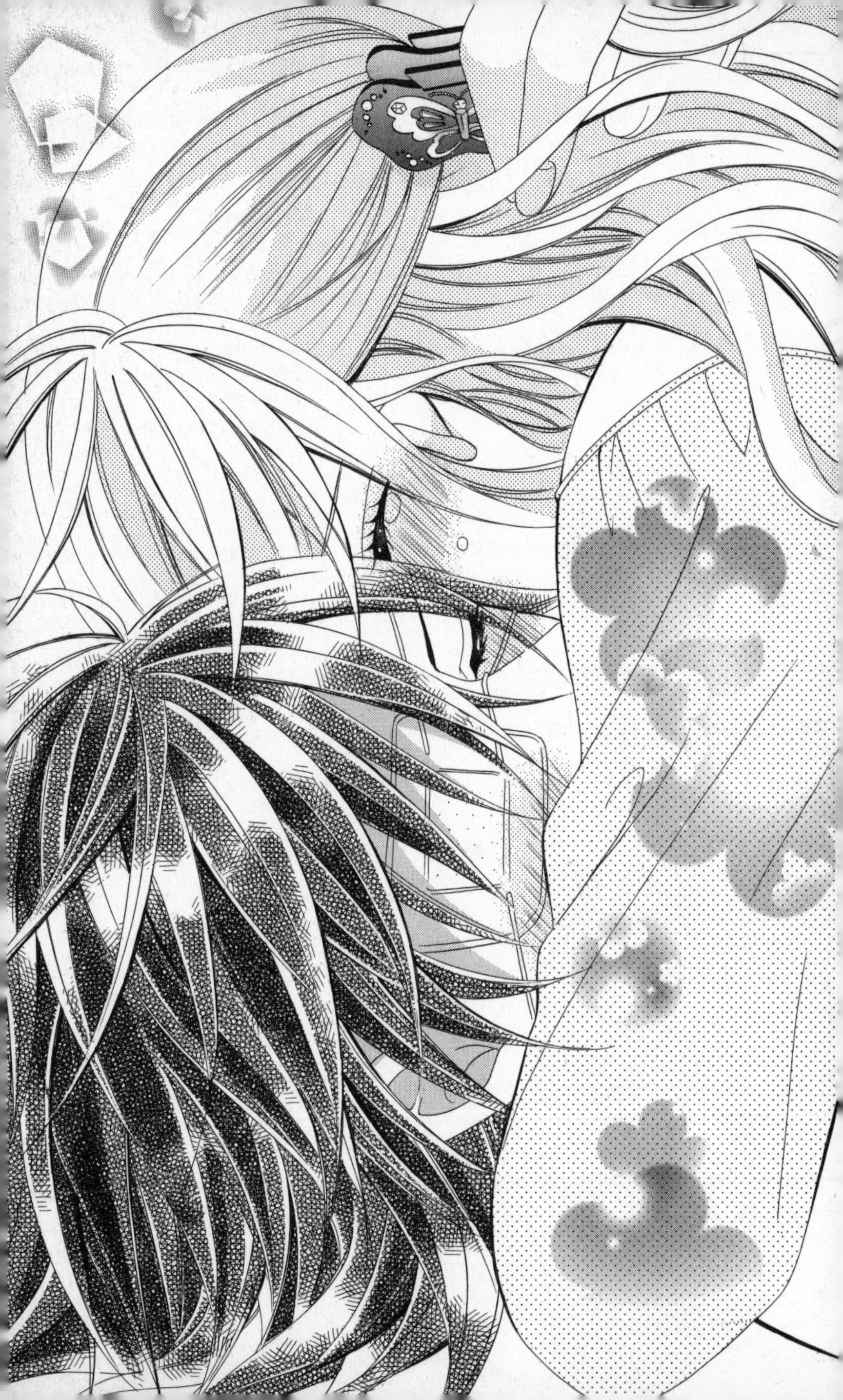

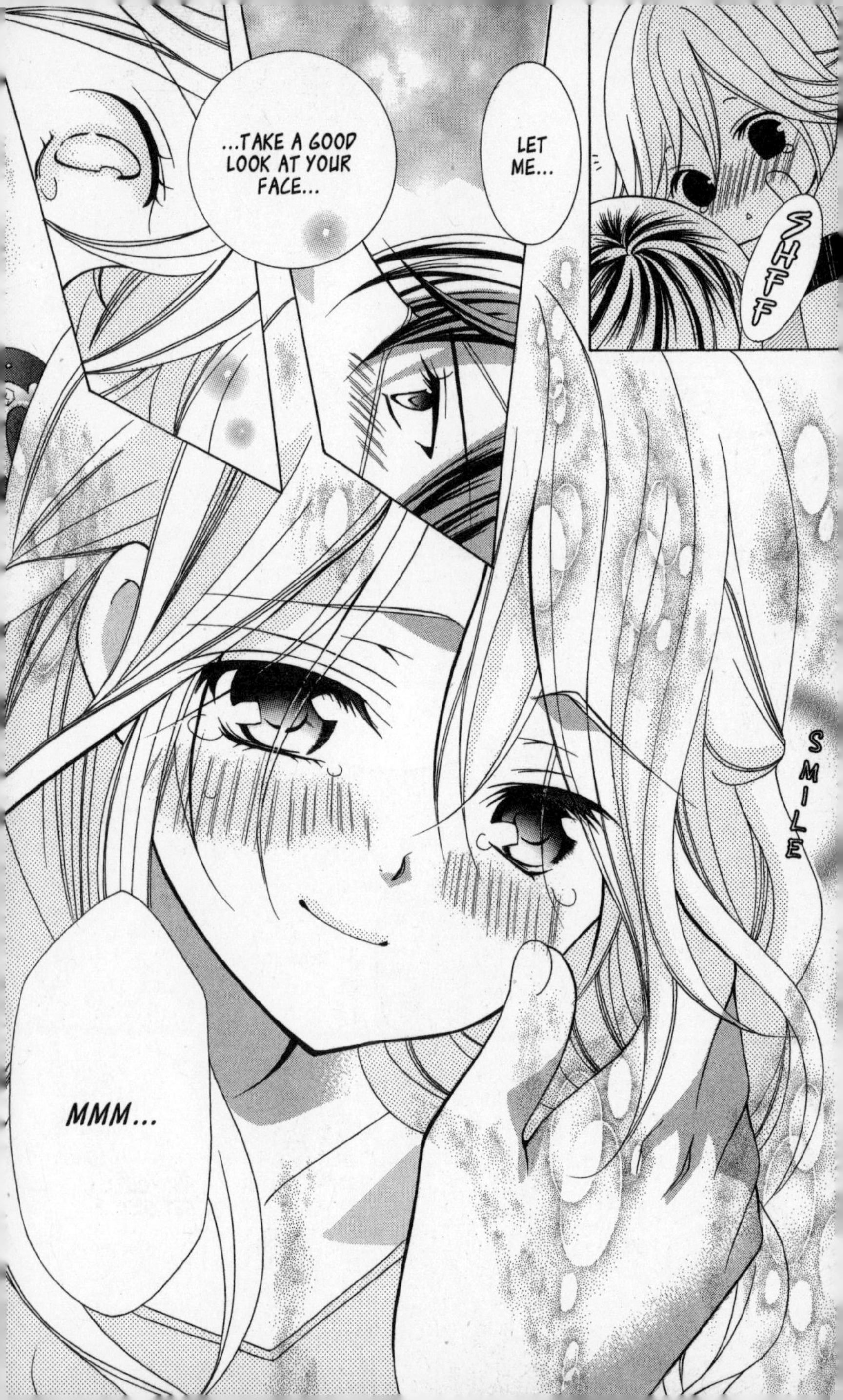
SHFF
LET ME...
...TAKE A GOOD LOOK AT YOUR FACE...
SMILE
MMM...

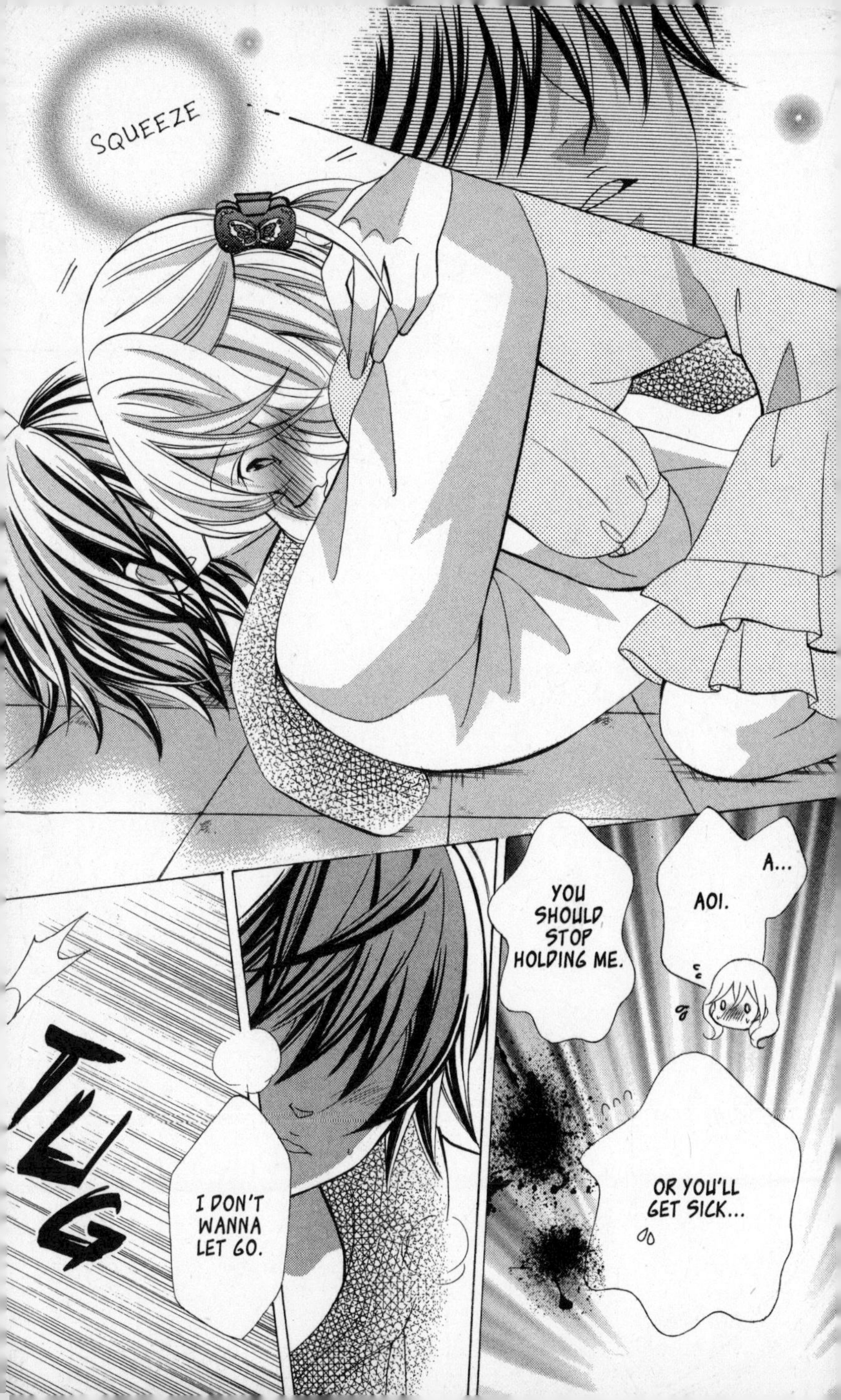
SQUEEZE
A... AOI.
YOU SHOULD STOP HOLDING ME.
OR YOU'LL GET SICK...
TUG
I DON'T WANNA LET GO.

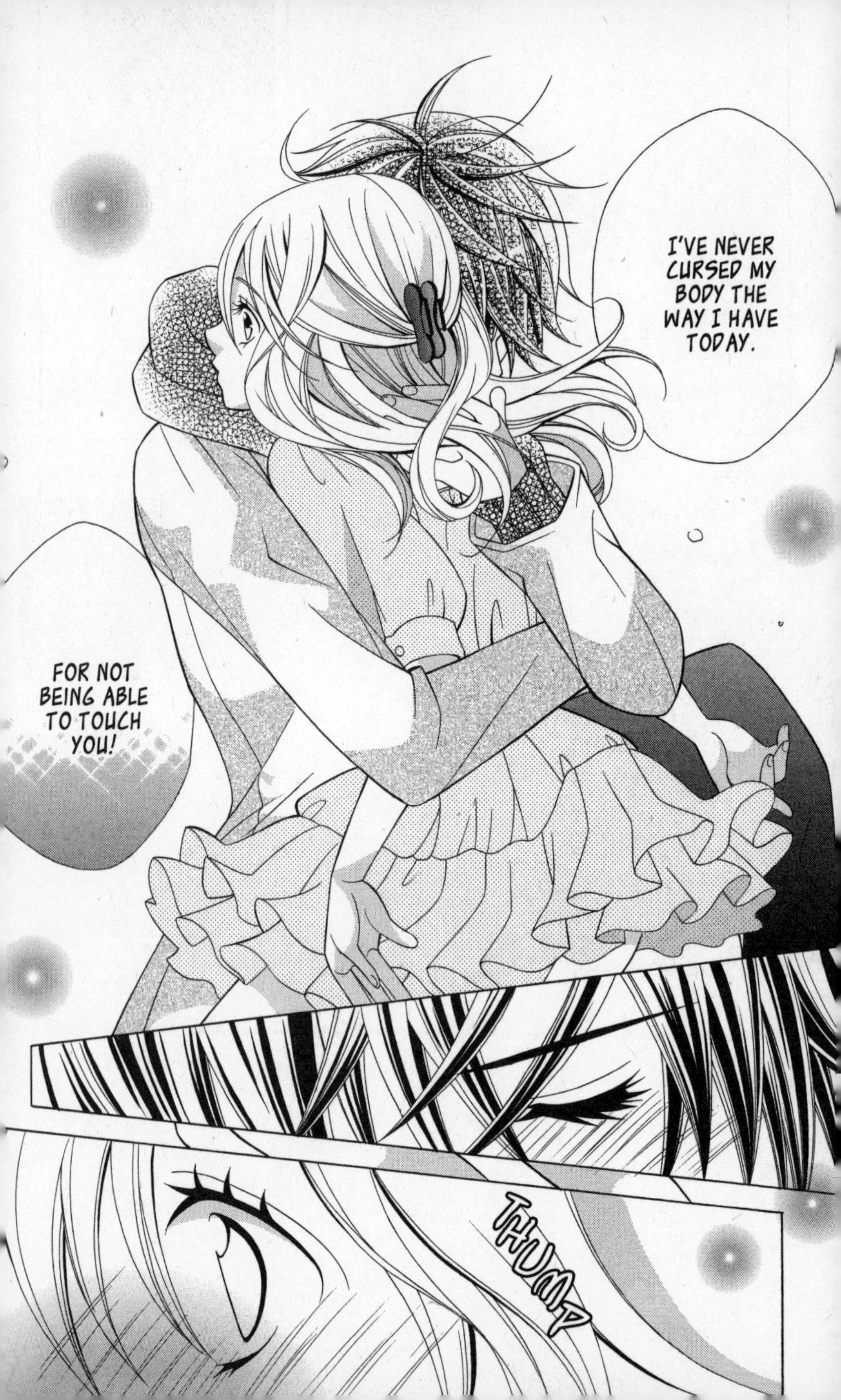
I'VE NEVER CURSED MY BODY THE WAY I HAVE TODAY.
FOR NOT BEING ABLE TO TOUCH YOU!
THUMP

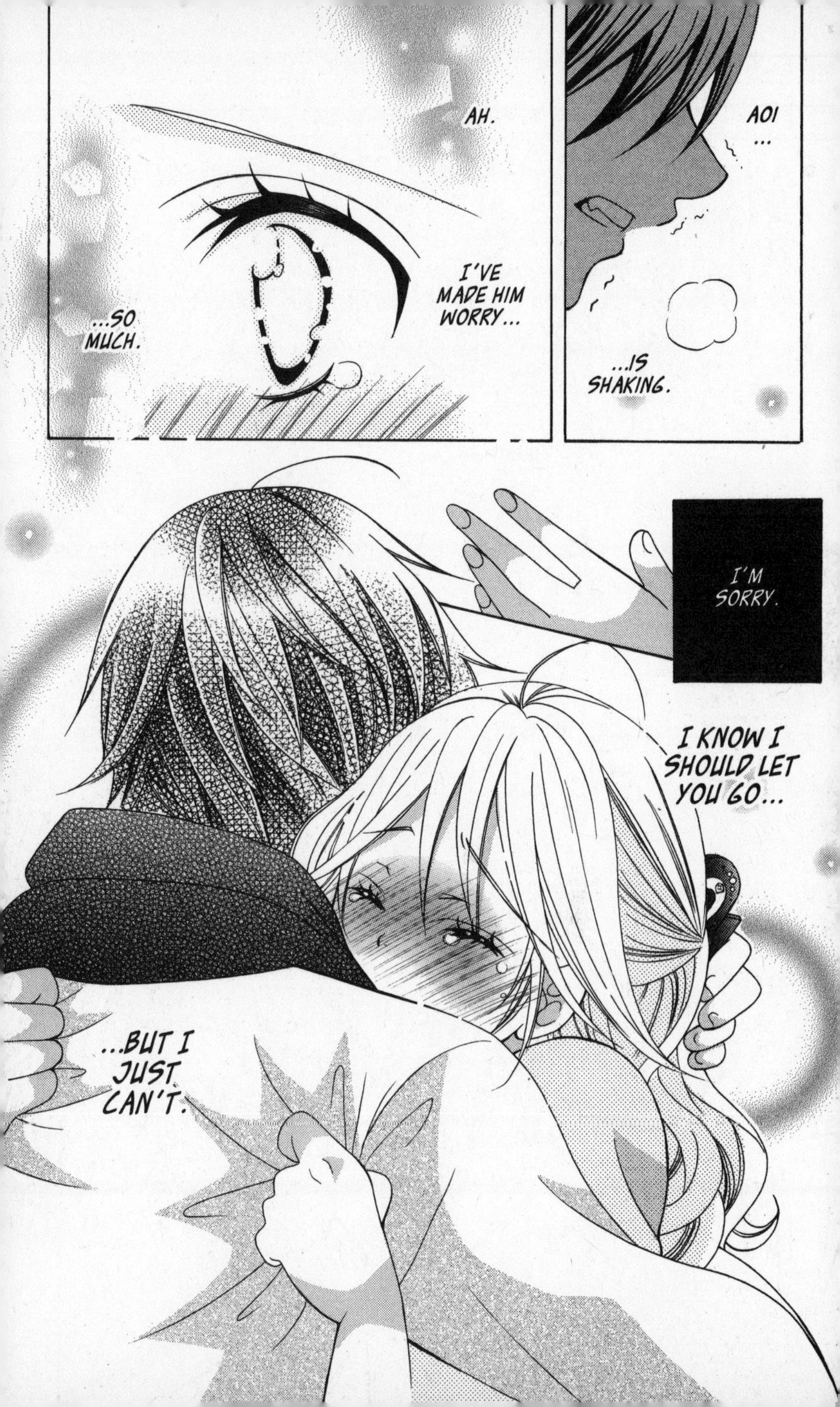
AOI ...
...IS SHAKING.
AH.
I'VE MADE HIM WORRY...
...SO MUCH.
I'M SORRY.
I KNOW I SHOULD LET YOU GO...
...BUT I JUST CAN'T.

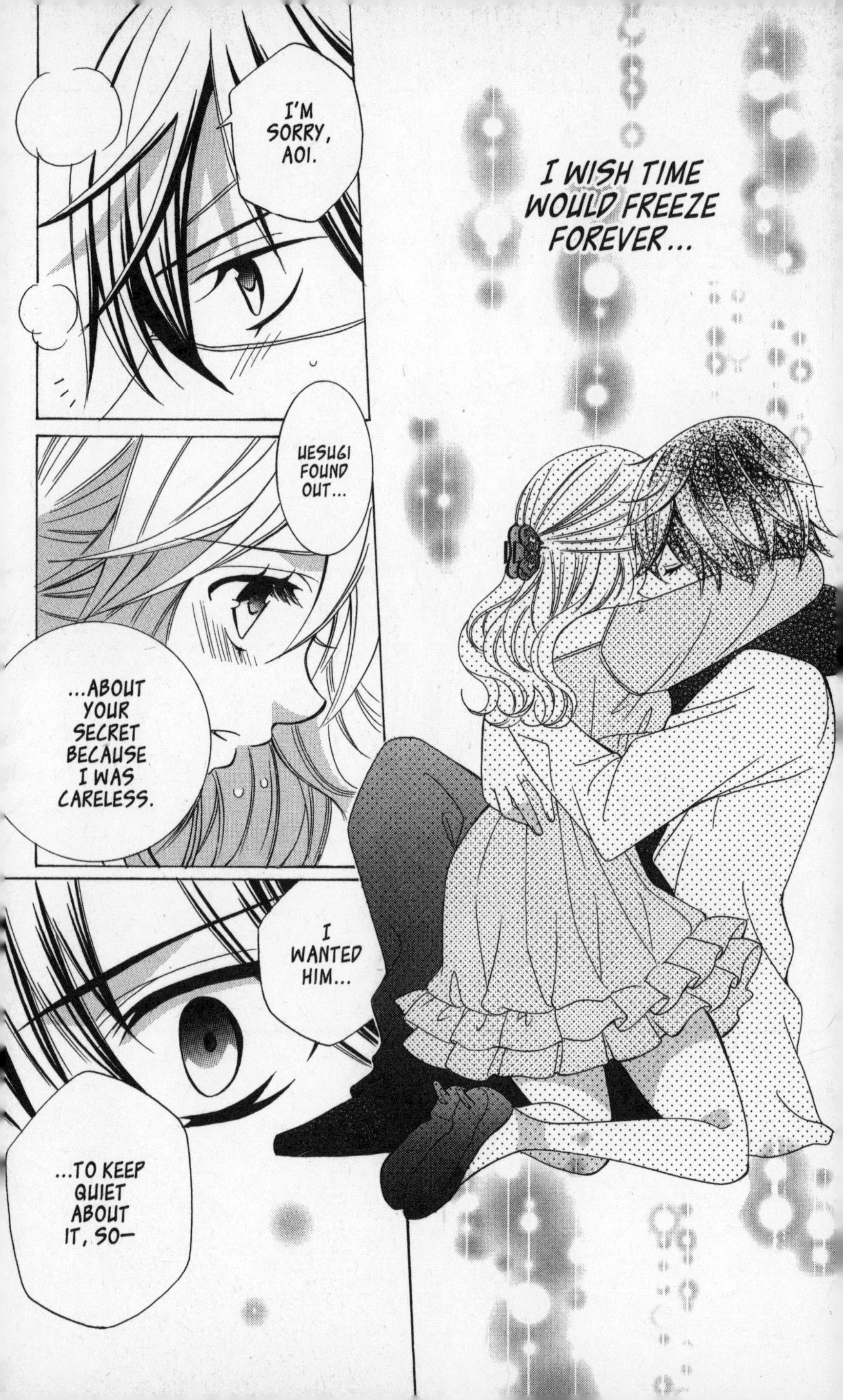
I WISH TIME WOULD FREEZE FOREVER...
I'M SORRY, AOI.
UESUGI FOUND OUT...
...ABOUT YOUR SECRET BECAUSE I WAS CARELESS.
I WANTED HIM...
...TO KEEP QUIET ABOUT IT, SO—

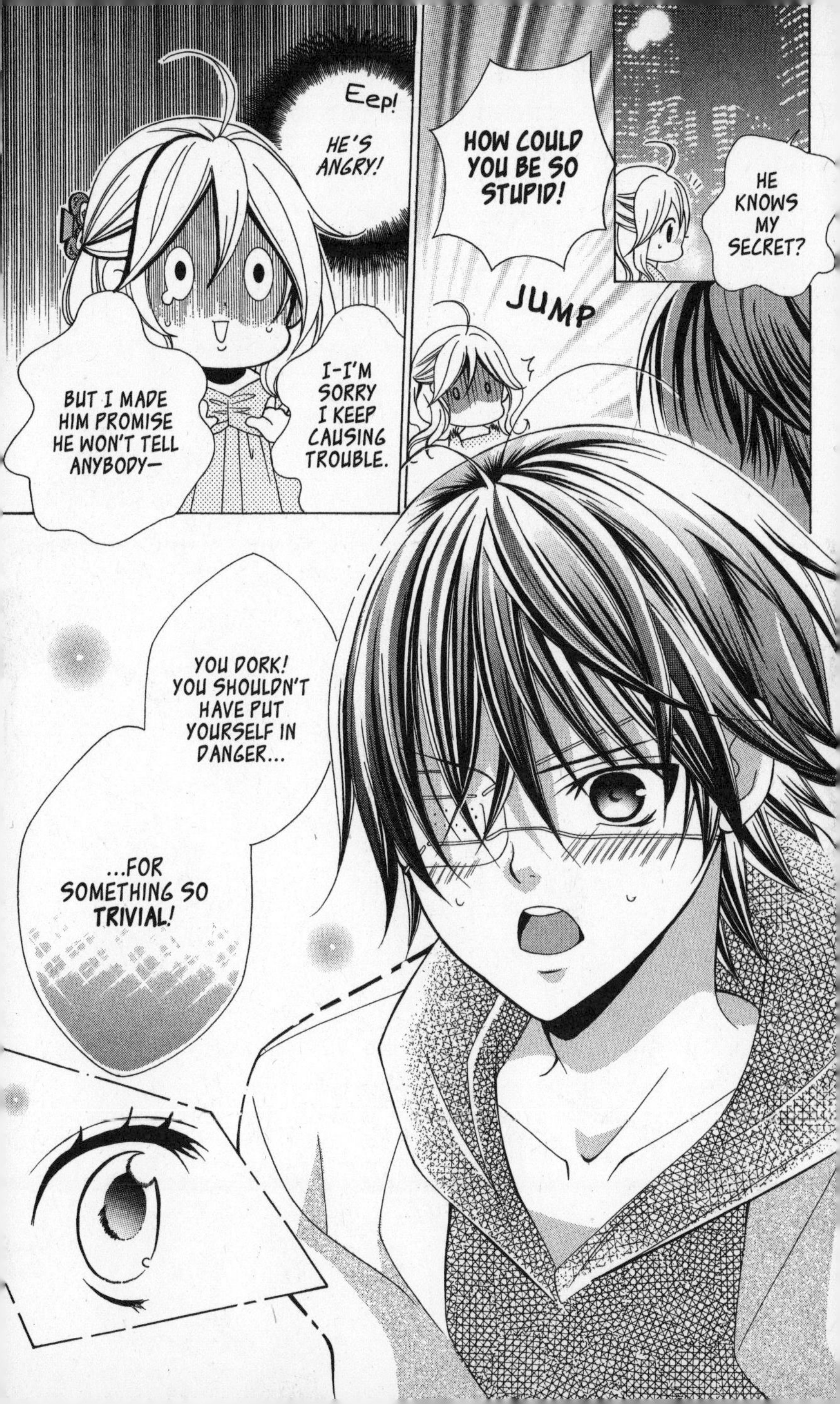
HE KNOWS MY SECRET?
HOW COULD YOU BE SO STUPID!
JUMP
Eep!
HE'S ANGRY!
I-I'M SORRY I KEEP CAUSING TROUBLE.
BUT I MADE HIM PROMISE HE WON'T TELL ANYBODY—
YOU DORK! YOU SHOULDN'T HAVE PUT YOURSELF IN DANGER...
...FOR SOMETHING SO TRIVIAL!

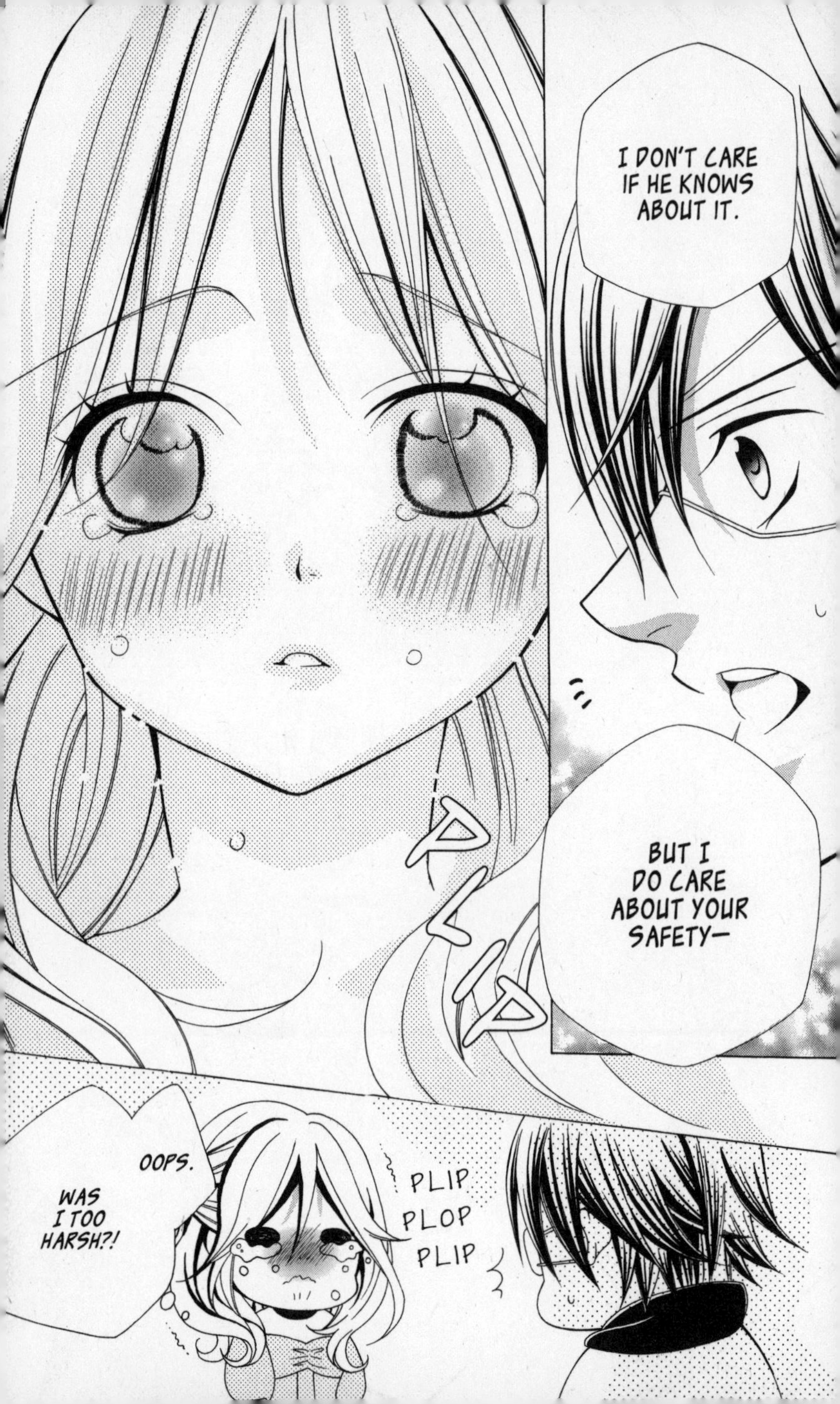
I DON'T CARE IF HE KNOWS ABOUT IT.
BUT I DO CARE ABOUT YOUR SAFETY—
PLIP
PLIP PLOP PLIP
OOPS.
WAS I TOO HARSH?!

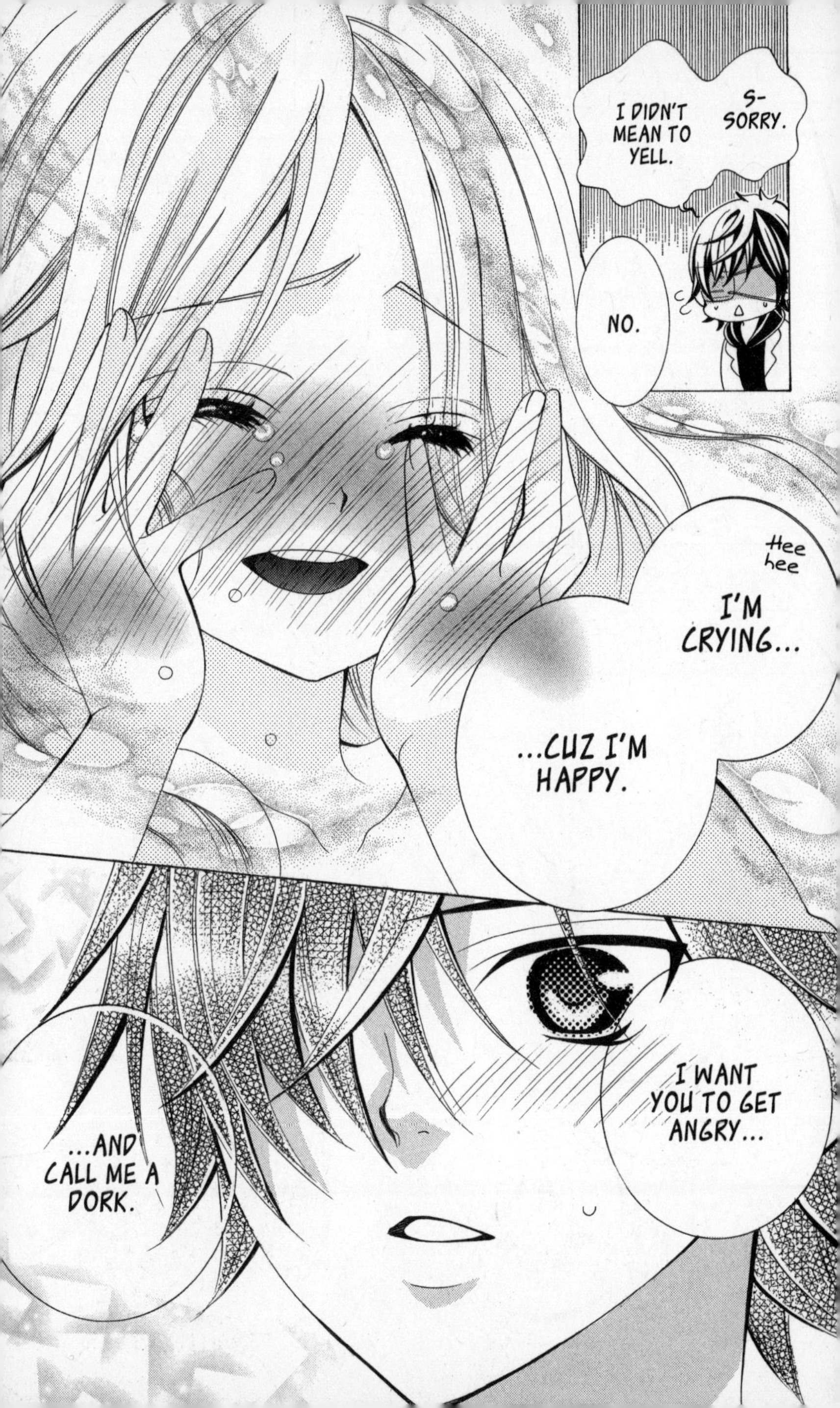
S-SORRY.
I DIDN'T MEAN TO YELL.
NO.
Hee hee
I'M CRYING...
...CUZ I'M HAPPY.
I WANT YOU TO GET ANGRY...
...AND CALL ME A DORK.

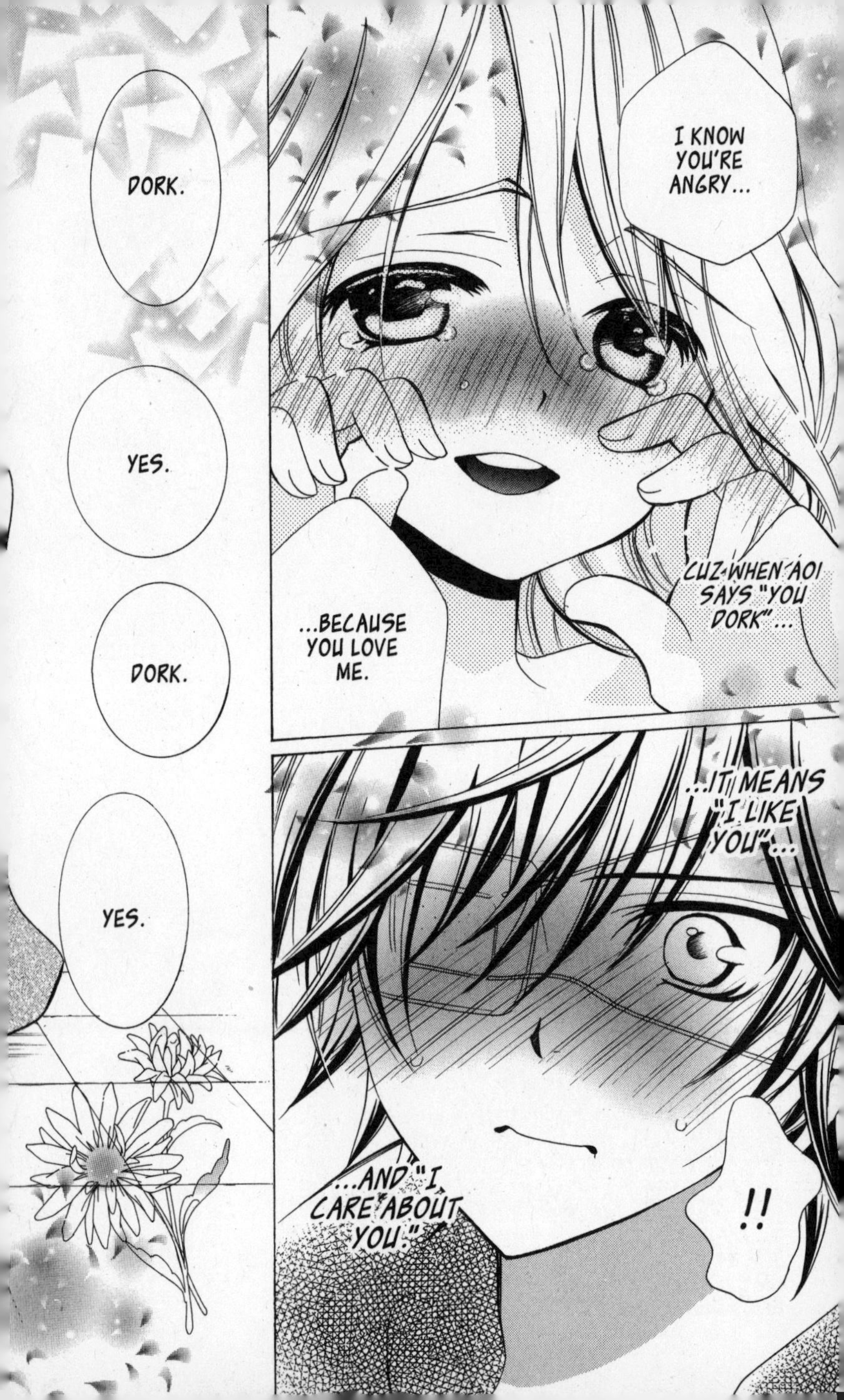
I KNOW YOU'RE ANGRY...
...BECAUSE YOU LOVE ME.
CUZ WHEN AOI SAYS "YOU DORK"...
...IT MEANS "I LIKE YOU"...
!!
...AND "I CARE ABOUT YOU."
DORK.
YES.
DORK.
YES.

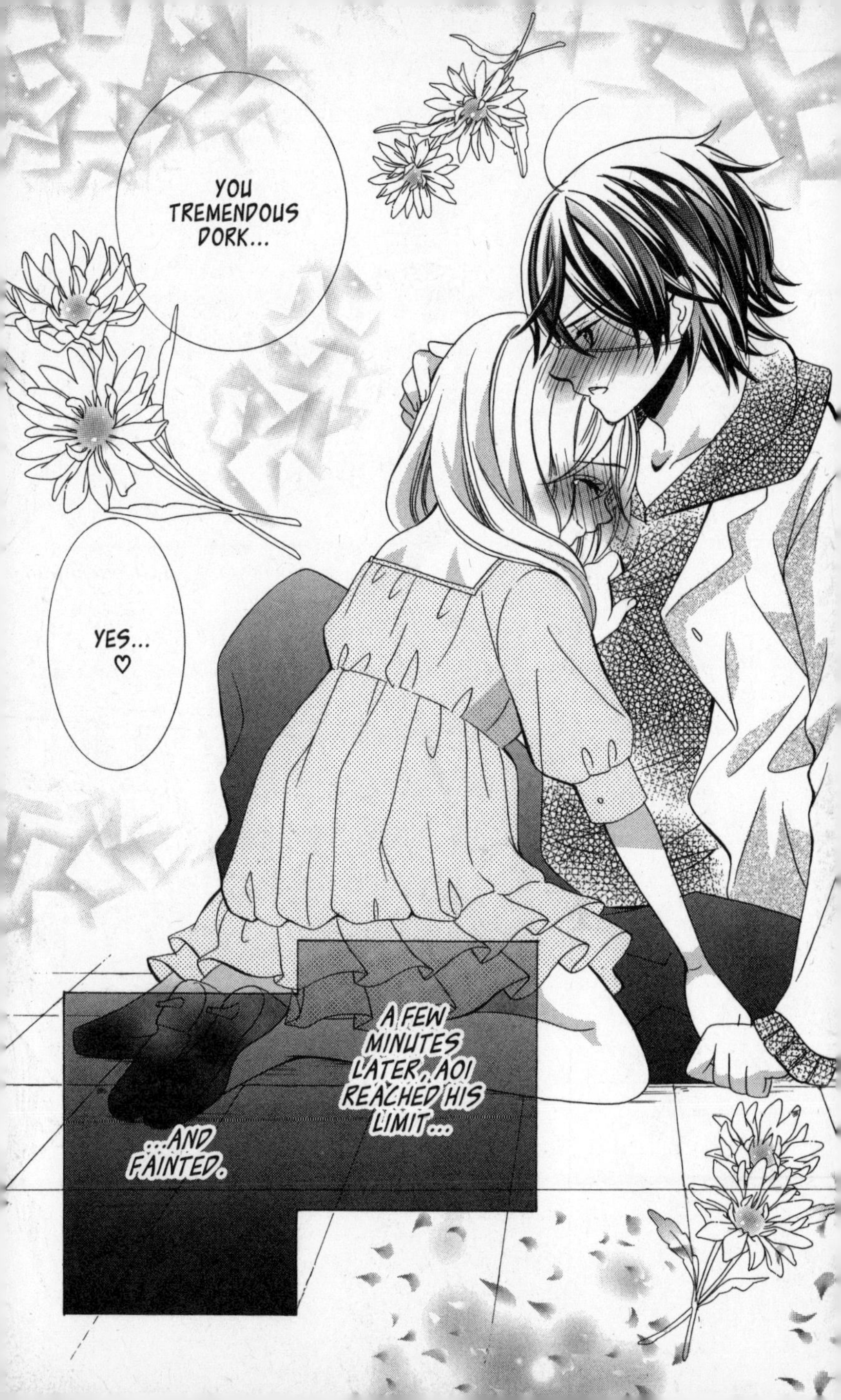
YOU TREMENDOUS DORK...
YES... ♡
A FEW MINUTES LATER, AOI REACHED HIS LIMIT...
...AND FAINTED.

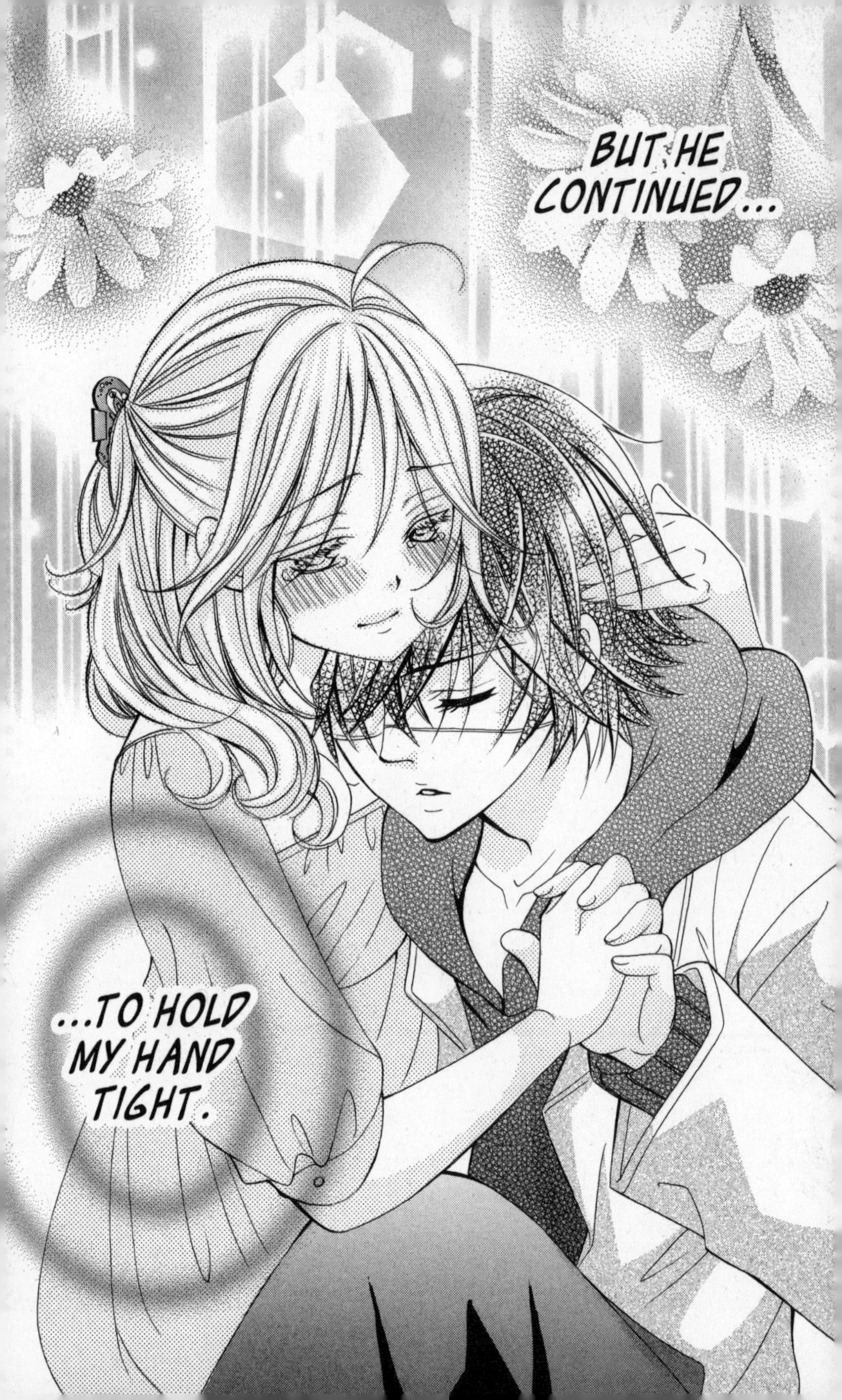
BUT HE CONTINUED...
...TO HOLD MY HAND TIGHT.

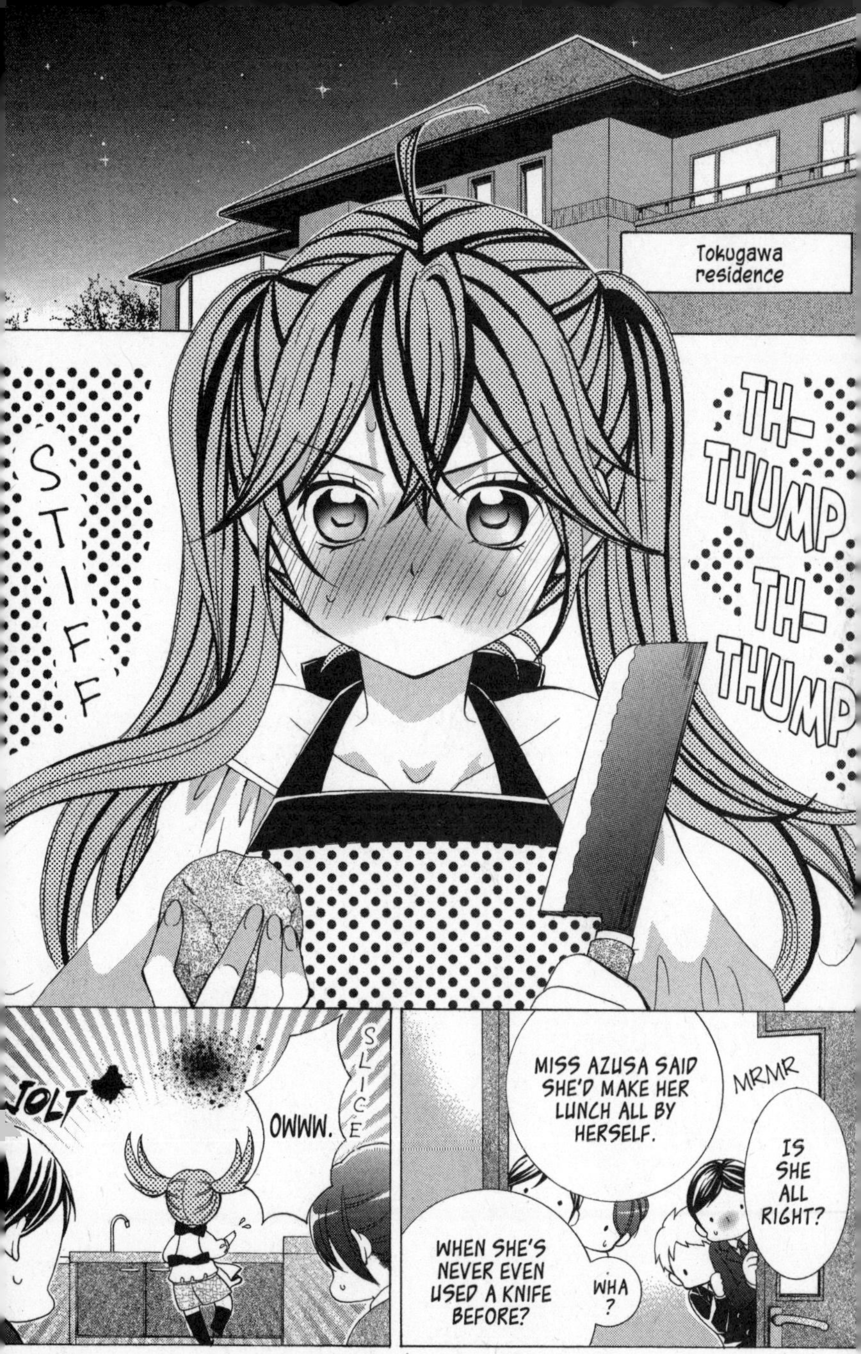
Tokugawa residence
TH-THUMP TH-THUMP
STIFF
MRMR
MISS AZUSA SAID SHE'D MAKE HER LUNCH ALL BY HERSELF.
IS SHE ALL RIGHT?
WHEN SHE'S NEVER EVEN USED A KNIFE BEFORE?
WHA?
SLICE
OWWW.
JOLT

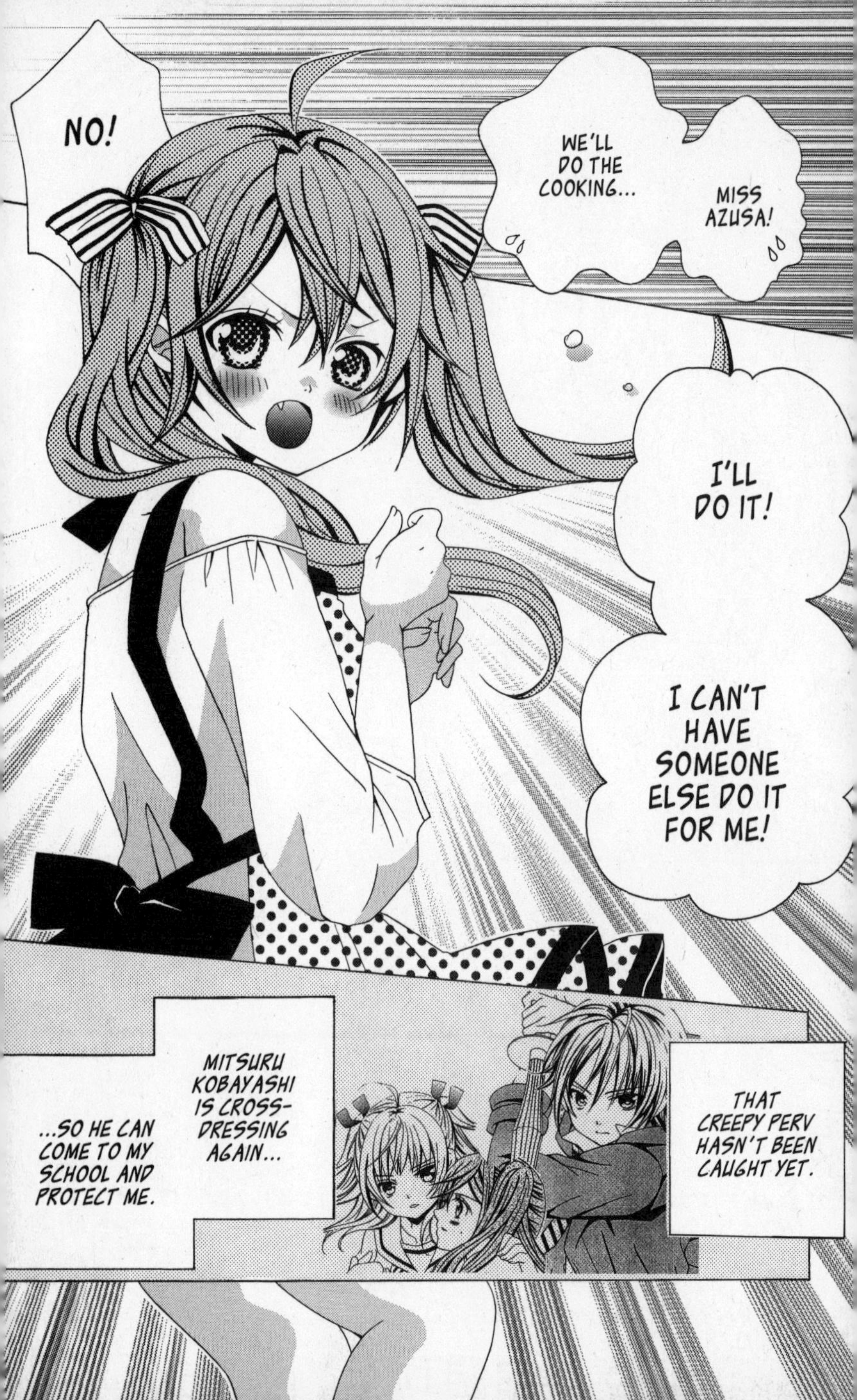
WE'LL DO THE COOKING... MISS AZUSA!
NO!
I'LL DO IT!
I CAN'T HAVE SOMEONE ELSE DO IT FOR ME!
THAT CREEPY PERV HASN'T BEEN CAUGHT YET.
MITSURU KOBAYASHI IS CROSS-DRESSING AGAIN...
...SO HE CAN COME TO MY SCHOOL AND PROTECT ME.

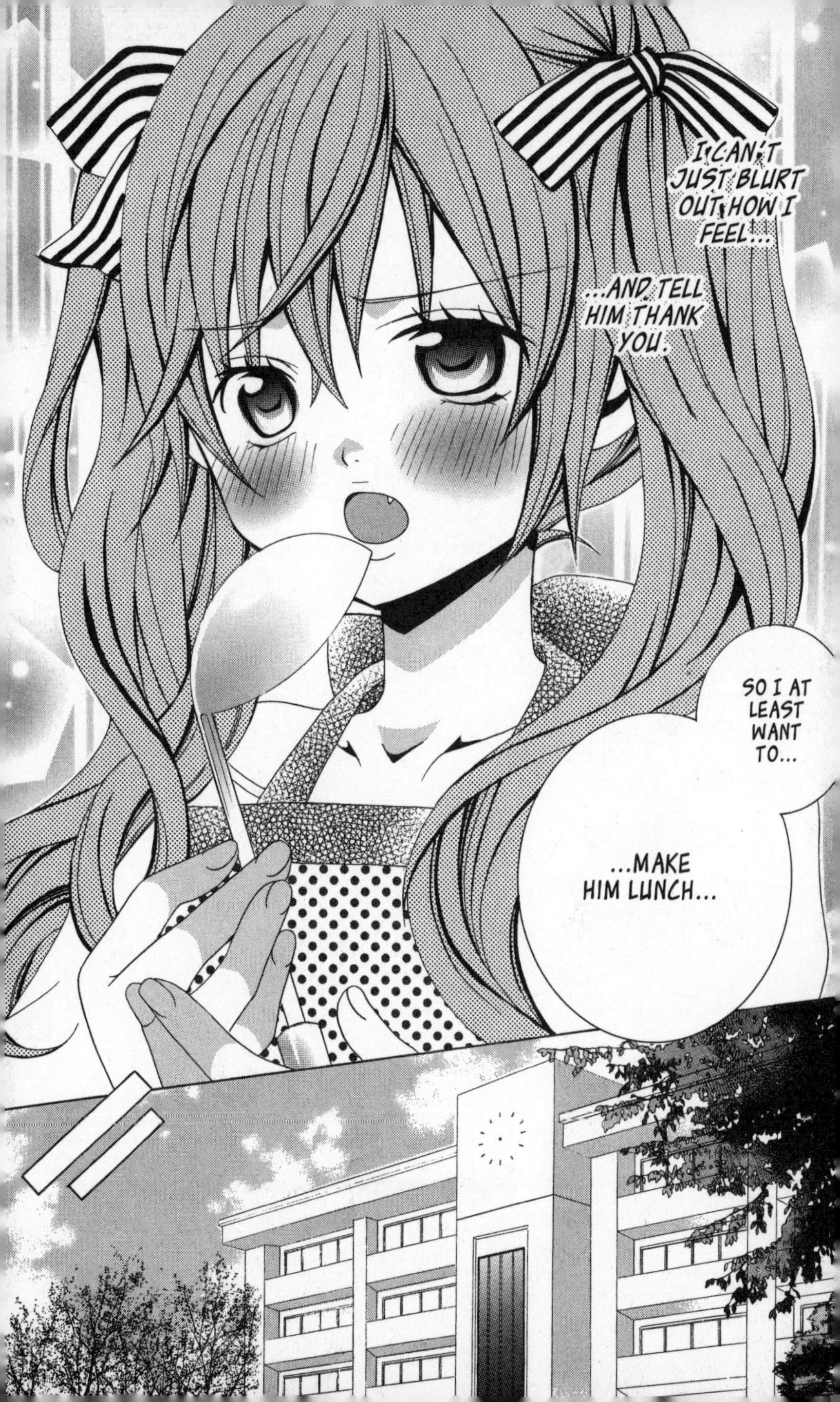
I CAN'T JUST BLURT OUT HOW I FEEL...
...AND TELL HIM THANK YOU.
SO I AT LEAST WANT TO...
...MAKE HIM LUNCH...

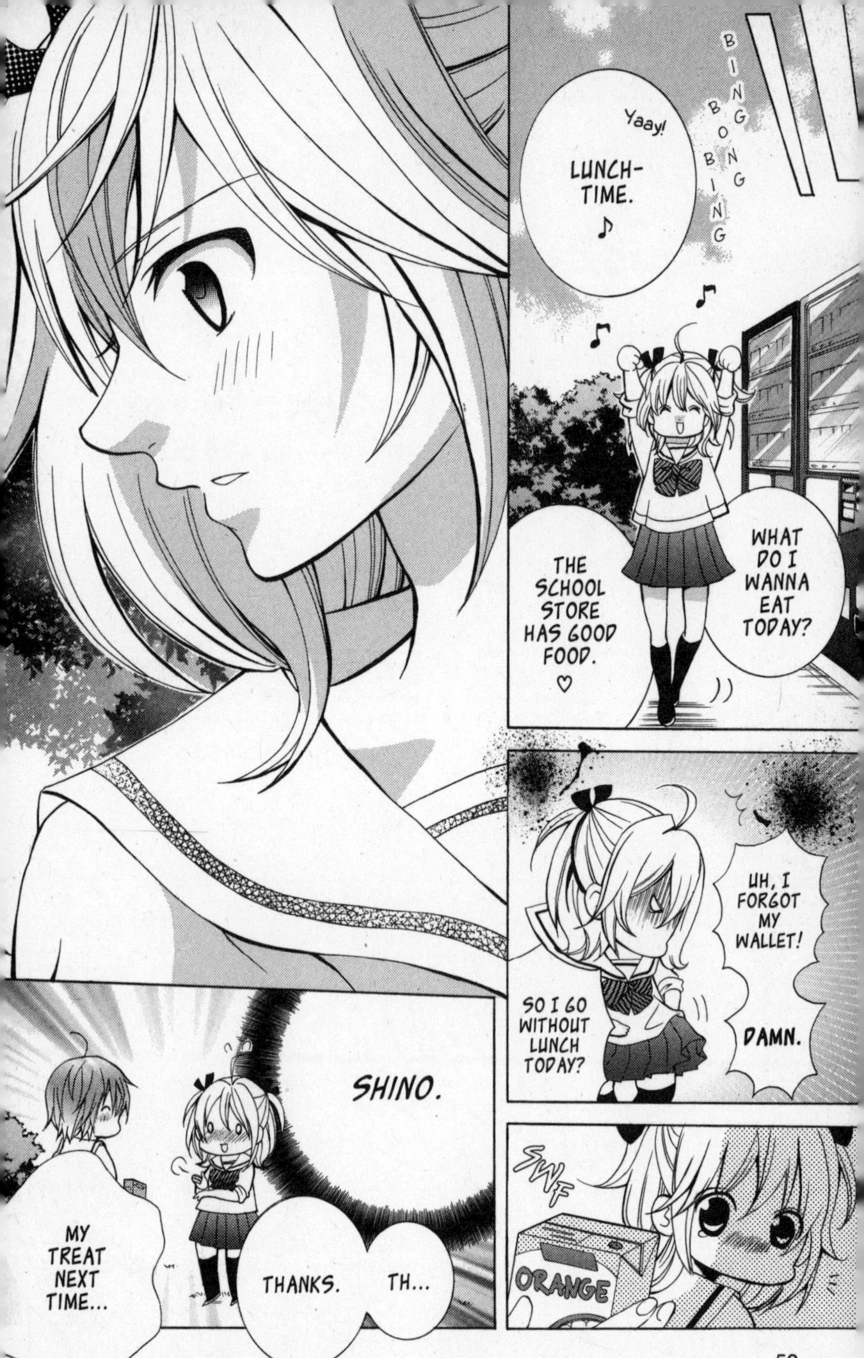
BING BONG BING BONG
Yaay!
LUNCH-TIME. ♪
WHAT DO I WANNA EAT TODAY?
THE SCHOOL STORE HAS GOOD FOOD. ♡
UH, I FORGOT MY WALLET!
DAMN.
SO I GO WITHOUT LUNCH TODAY?
SWF
ORANGE
SHINO.
THANKS.
TH...
MY TREAT NEXT TIME...

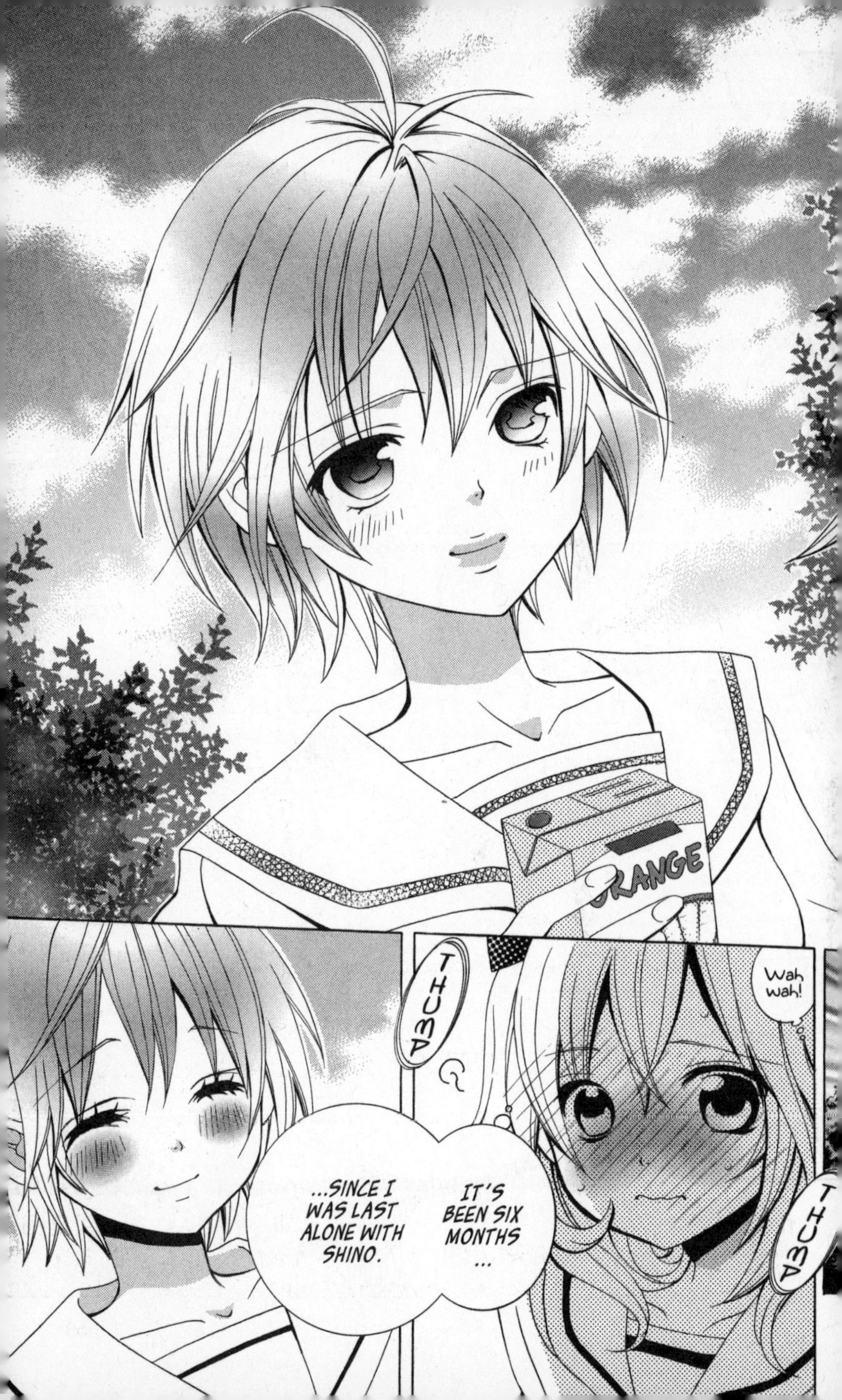
ORANGE
THUMP
Wah wah!
THUMP
IT'S BEEN SIX MONTHS ...
...SINCE I WAS LAST ALONE WITH SHINO.

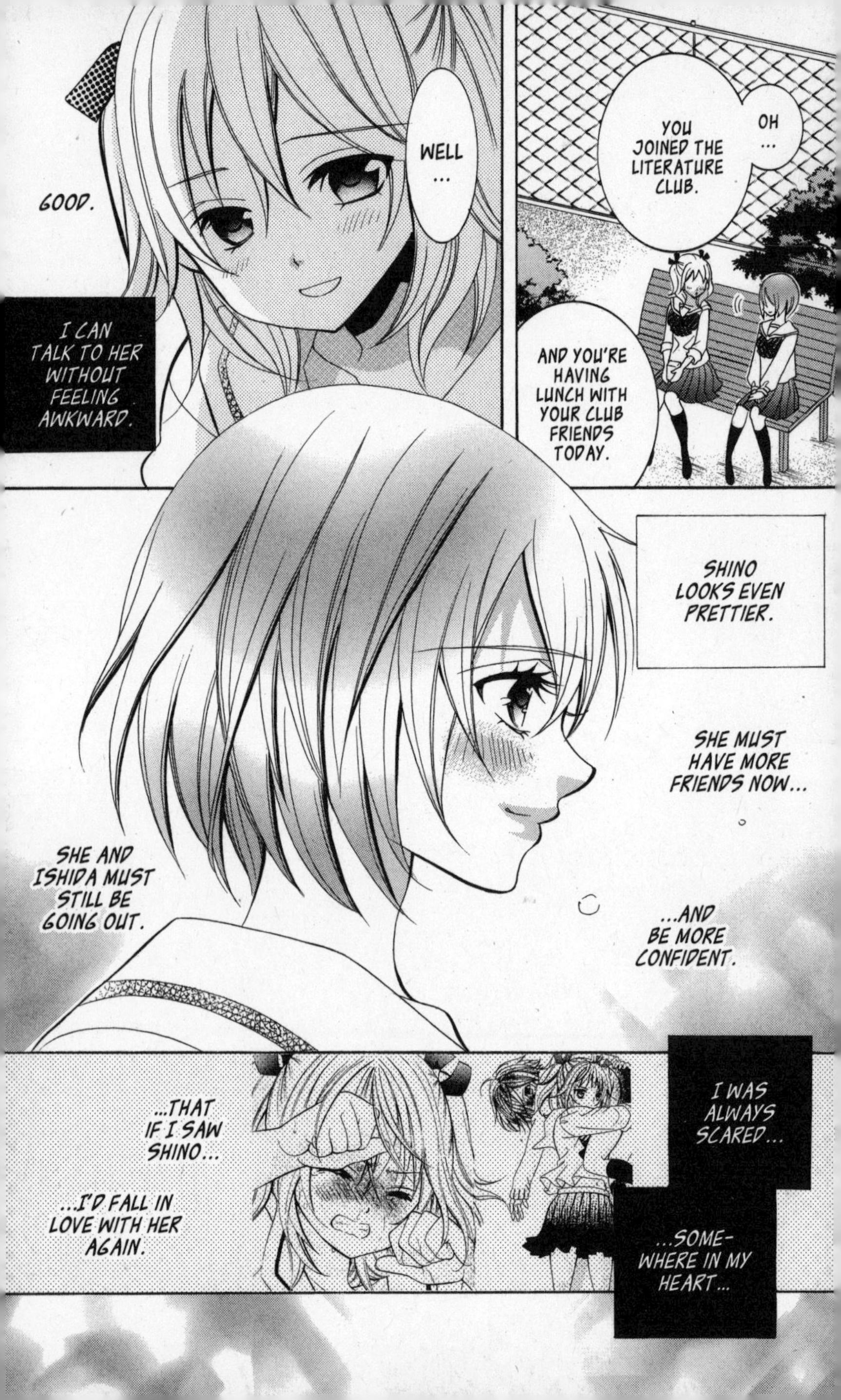
OH ...
YOU JOINED THE LITERATURE CLUB.
AND YOU'RE HAVING LUNCH WITH YOUR CLUB FRIENDS TODAY.
WELL ...
GOOD.
I CAN TALK TO HER WITHOUT FEELING AWKWARD.
SHINO LOOKS EVEN PRETTIER.
SHE MUST HAVE MORE FRIENDS NOW...
...AND BE MORE CONFIDENT.
SHE AND ISHIDA MUST STILL BE GOING OUT.
I WAS ALWAYS SCARED...
...SOME-WHERE IN MY HEART...
...THAT IF I SAW SHINO...
...I'D FALL IN LOVE WITH HER AGAIN.

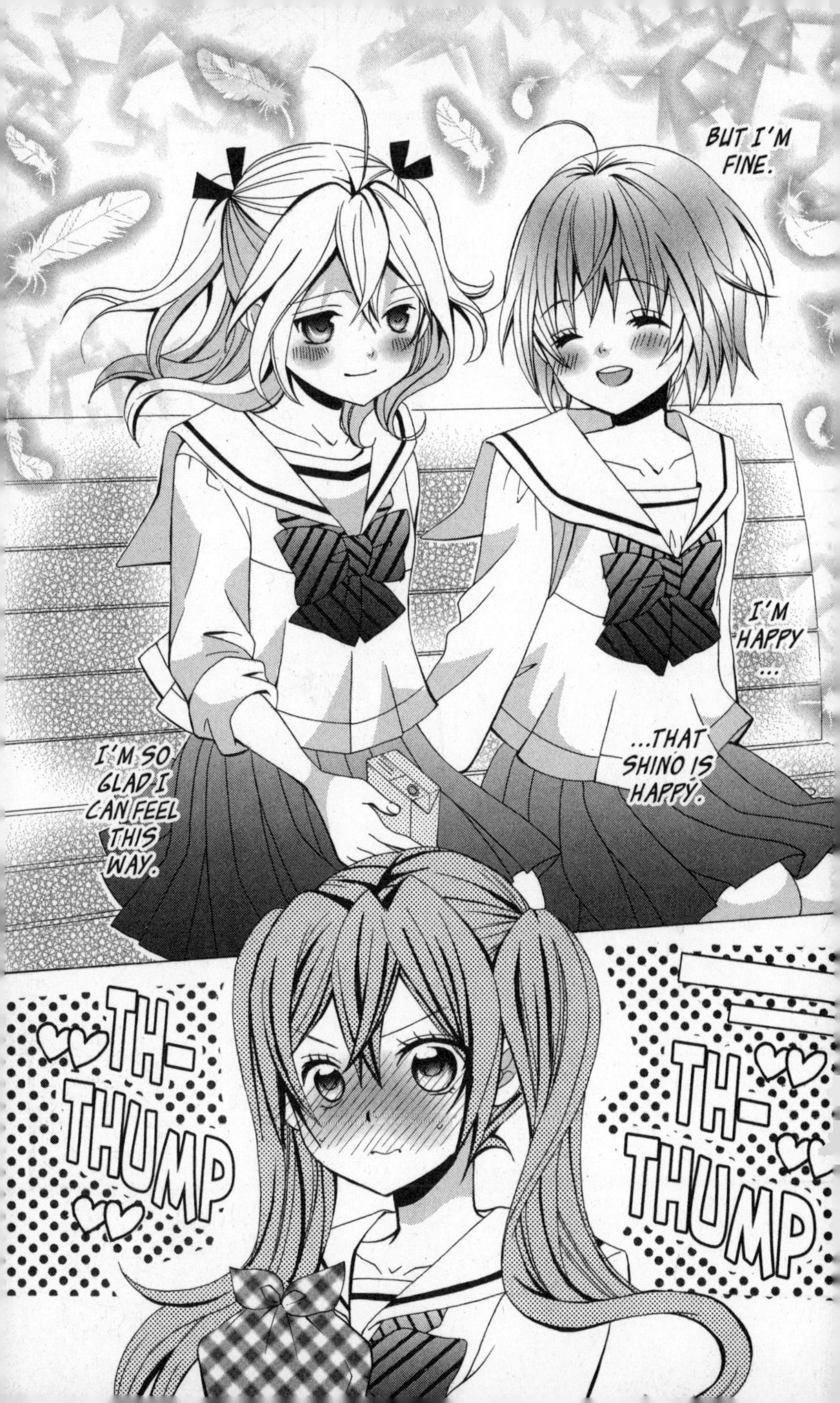
BUT I'M FINE.
I'M HAPPY...
...THAT SHINO IS HAPPY.
I'M SO GLAD I CAN FEEL THIS WAY.
TH-THUMP
TH-THUMP

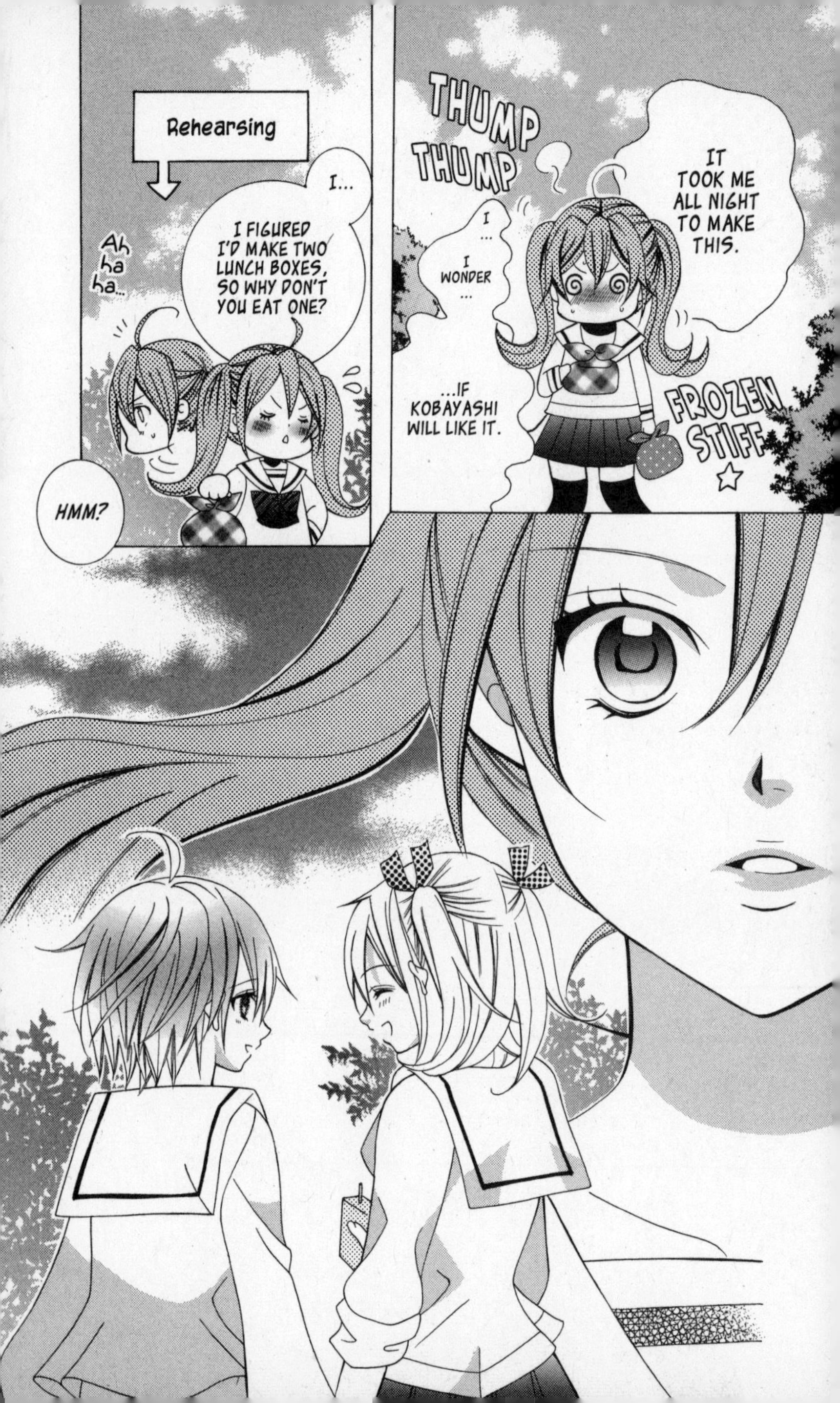
IT TOOK ME ALL NIGHT TO MAKE THIS.
THUMP THUMP
I... I WONDER...
FROZEN STIFF ☆
...IF KOBAYASHI WILL LIKE IT.
Rehearsing
I...
I FIGURED I'D MAKE TWO LUNCH BOXES, SO WHY DON'T YOU EAT ONE?
Ah ha ha...
HMM?

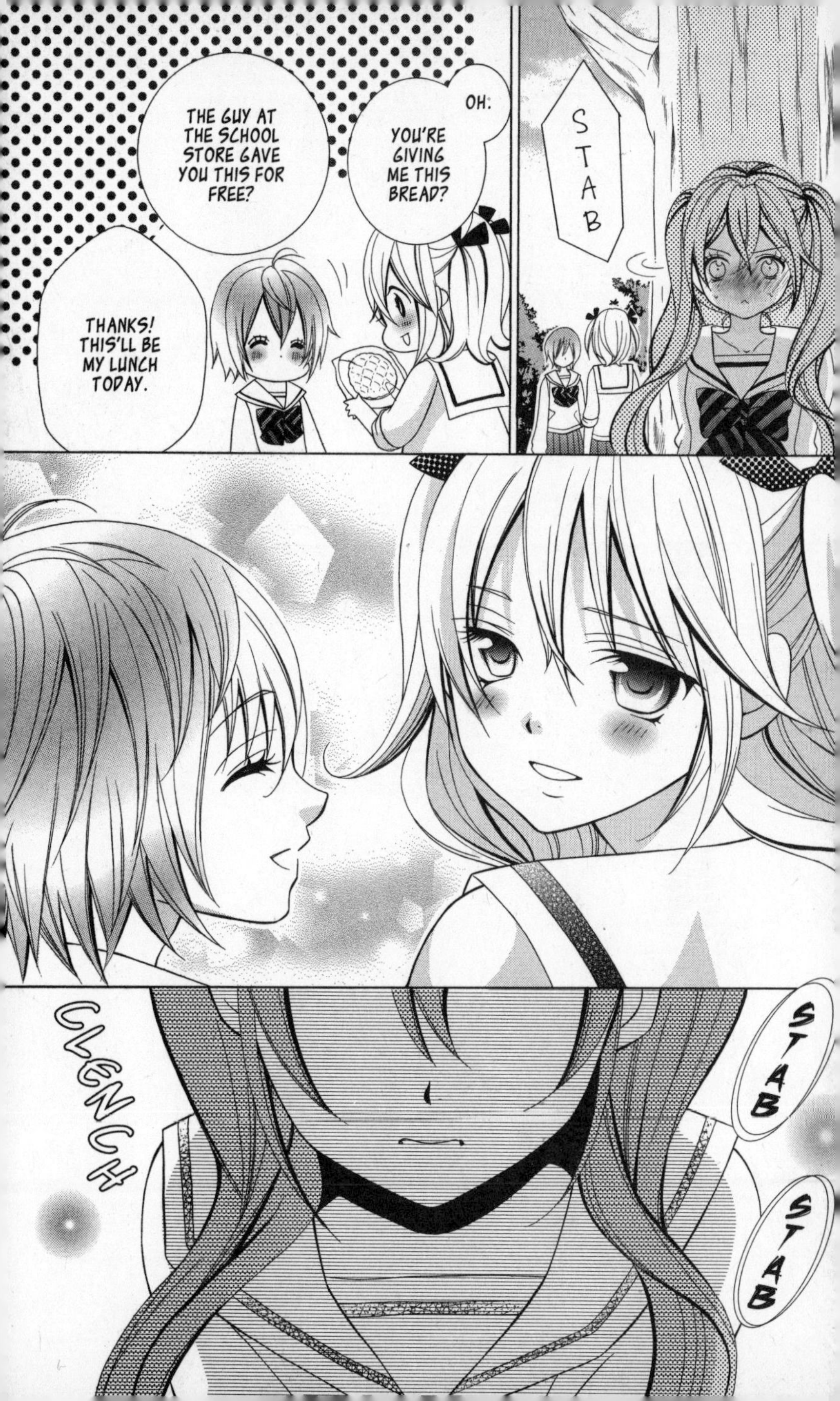
STAB
OH:
YOU'RE GIVING ME THIS BREAD?
THE GUY AT THE SCHOOL STORE GAVE YOU THIS FOR FREE?
THANKS! THIS'LL BE MY LUNCH TODAY.
STAB
STAB
CLENCH

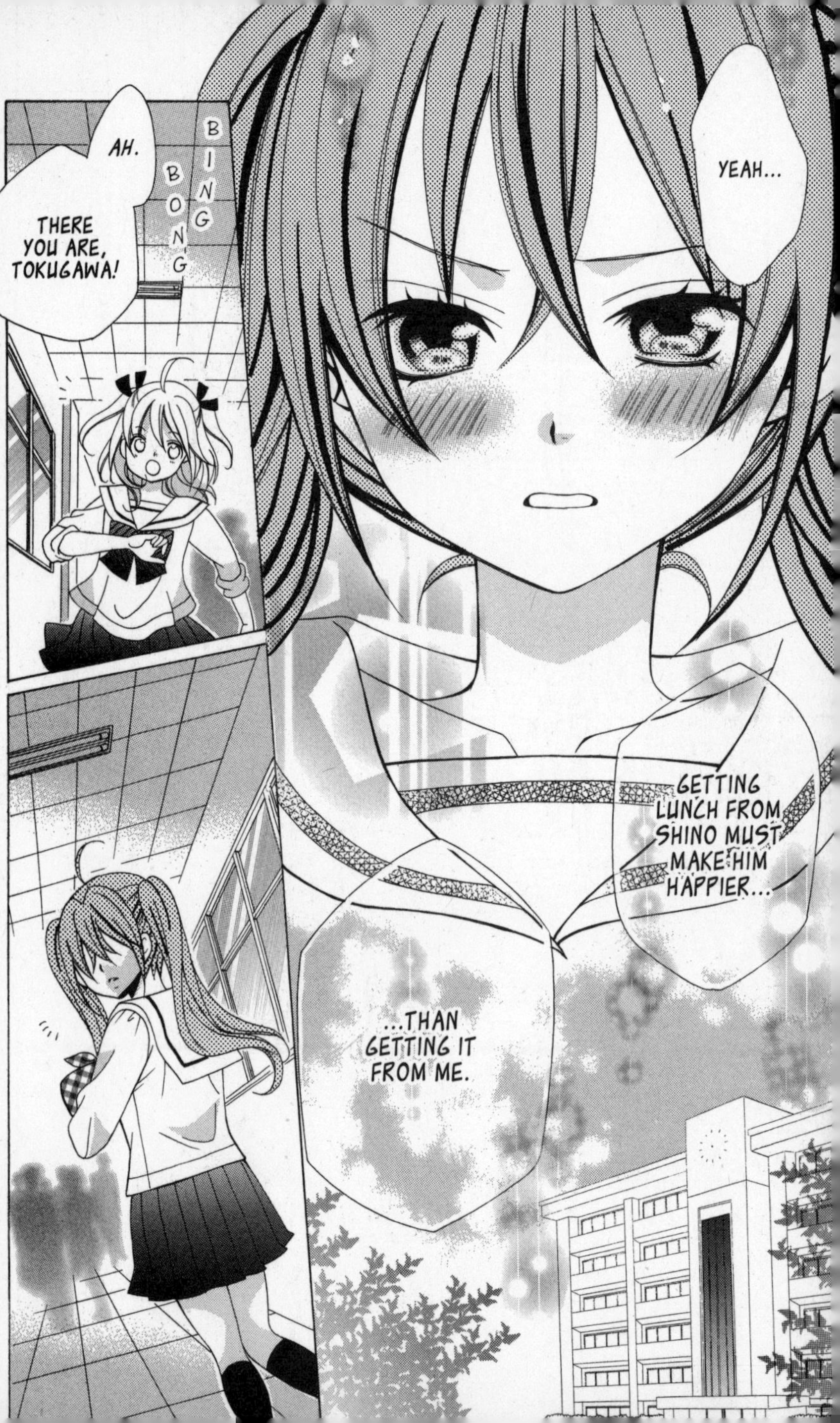
YEAH...
GETTING LUNCH FROM SHINO MUST MAKE HIM HAPPIER...
...THAN GETTING IT FROM ME.
BING BONG
AH.
THERE YOU ARE, TOKUGAWA!

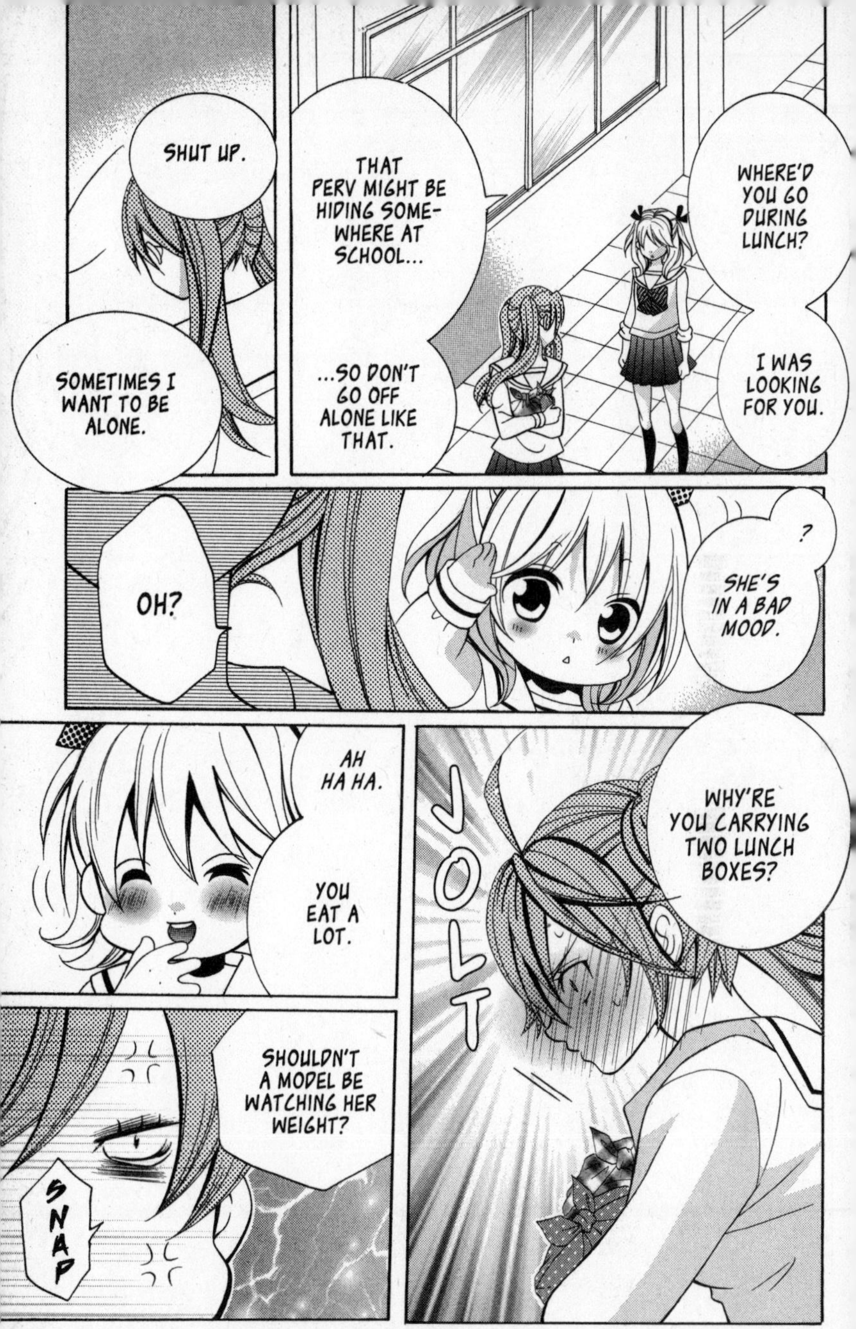
WHERE'D YOU GO DURING LUNCH?
I WAS LOOKING FOR YOU.
THAT PERV MIGHT BE HIDING SOME-WHERE AT SCHOOL...
...SO DON'T GO OFF ALONE LIKE THAT.
SHUT UP.
SOMETIMES I WANT TO BE ALONE.
?
SHE'S IN A BAD MOOD.
OH?
WHY'RE YOU CARRYING TWO LUNCH BOXES?
JOLT
AH HA HA.
YOU EAT A LOT.
SHOULDN'T A MODEL BE WATCHING HER WEIGHT?
SNAP

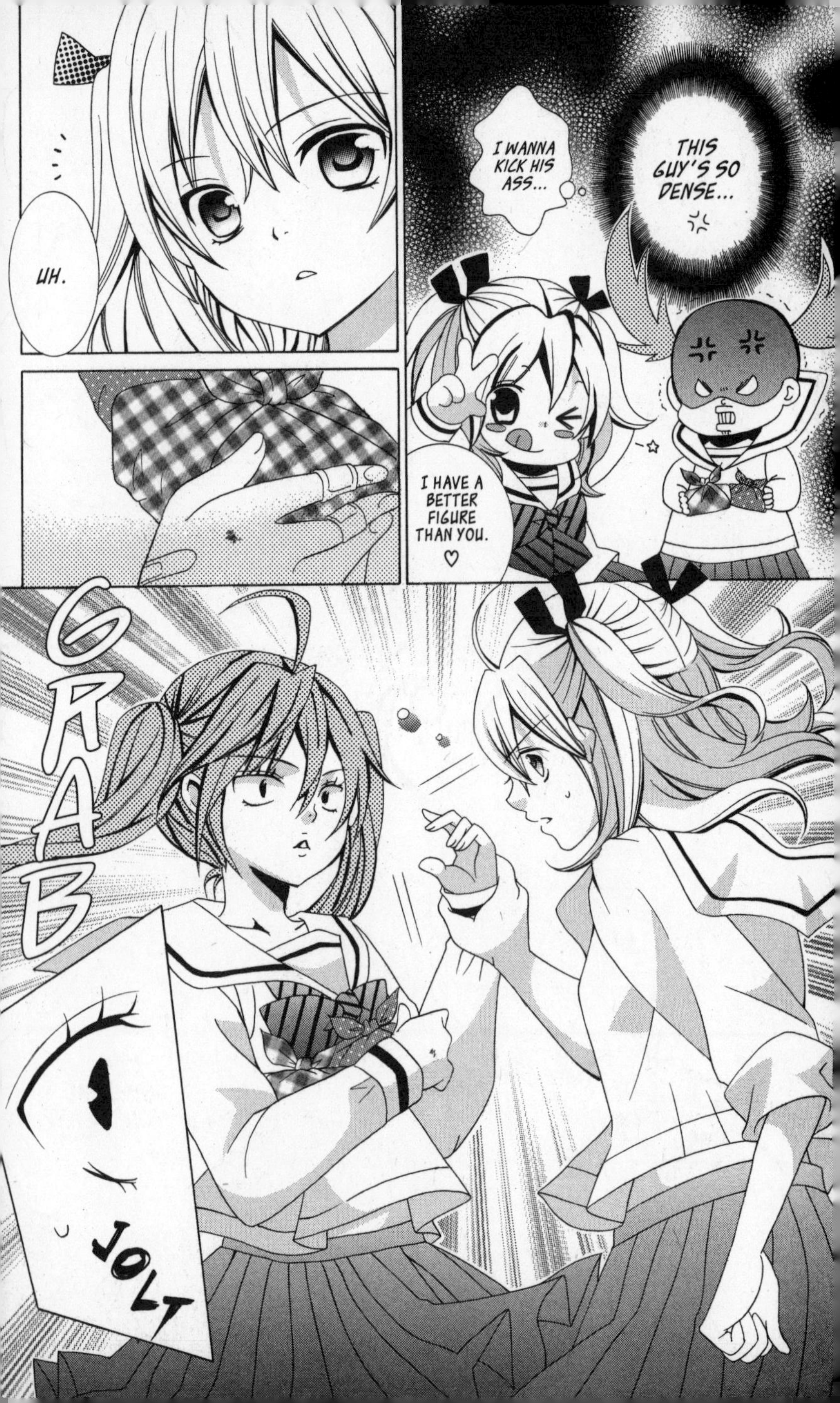
THIS GUY'S SO DENSE...
I WANNA KICK HIS ASS...
I HAVE A BETTER FIGURE THAN YOU. ♥
UH.
GRAB
JOLT

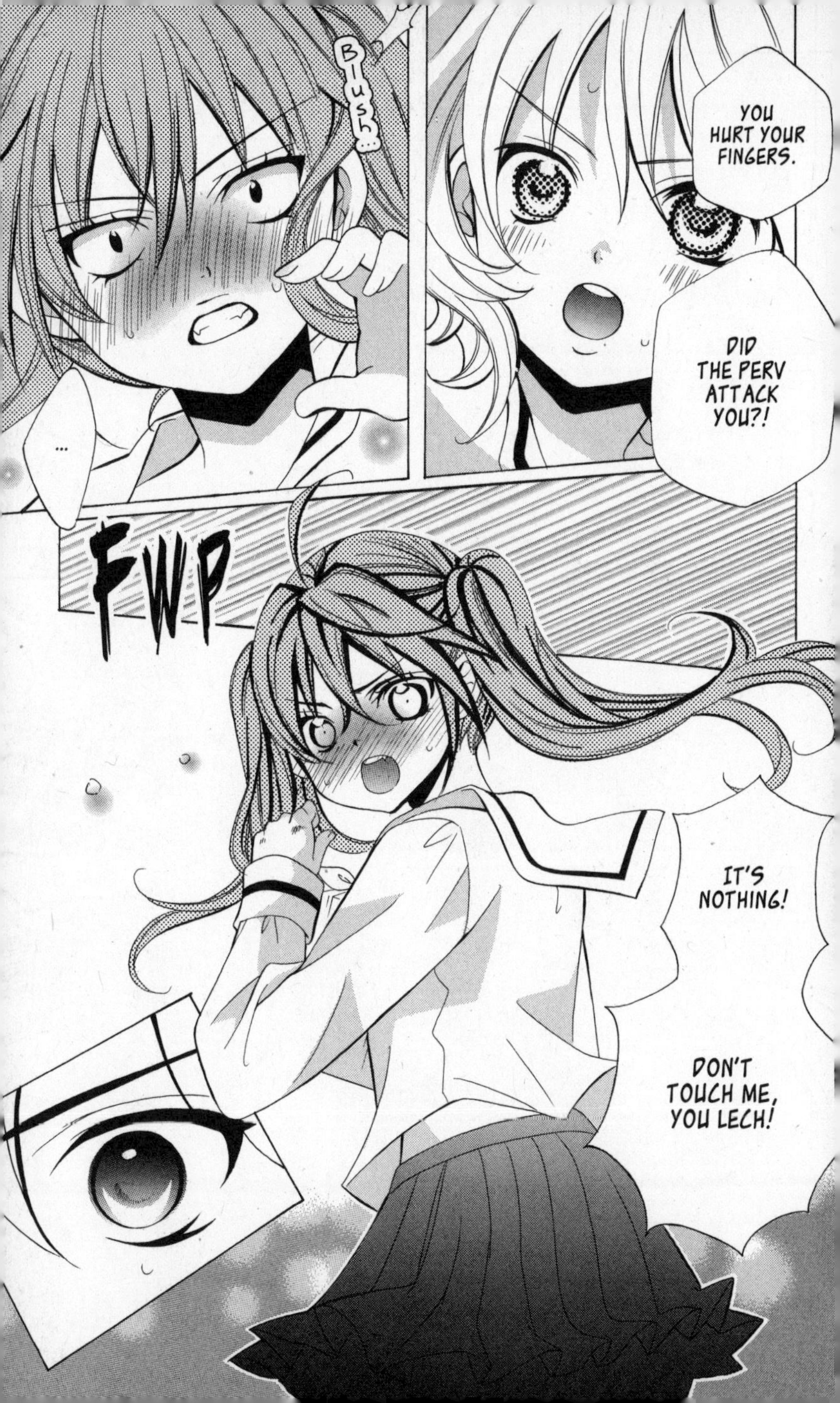
YOU HURT YOUR FINGERS.
DID THE PERV ATTACK YOU?!
Blush...
...
FWP
IT'S NOTHING!
DON'T TOUCH ME, YOU LECH!

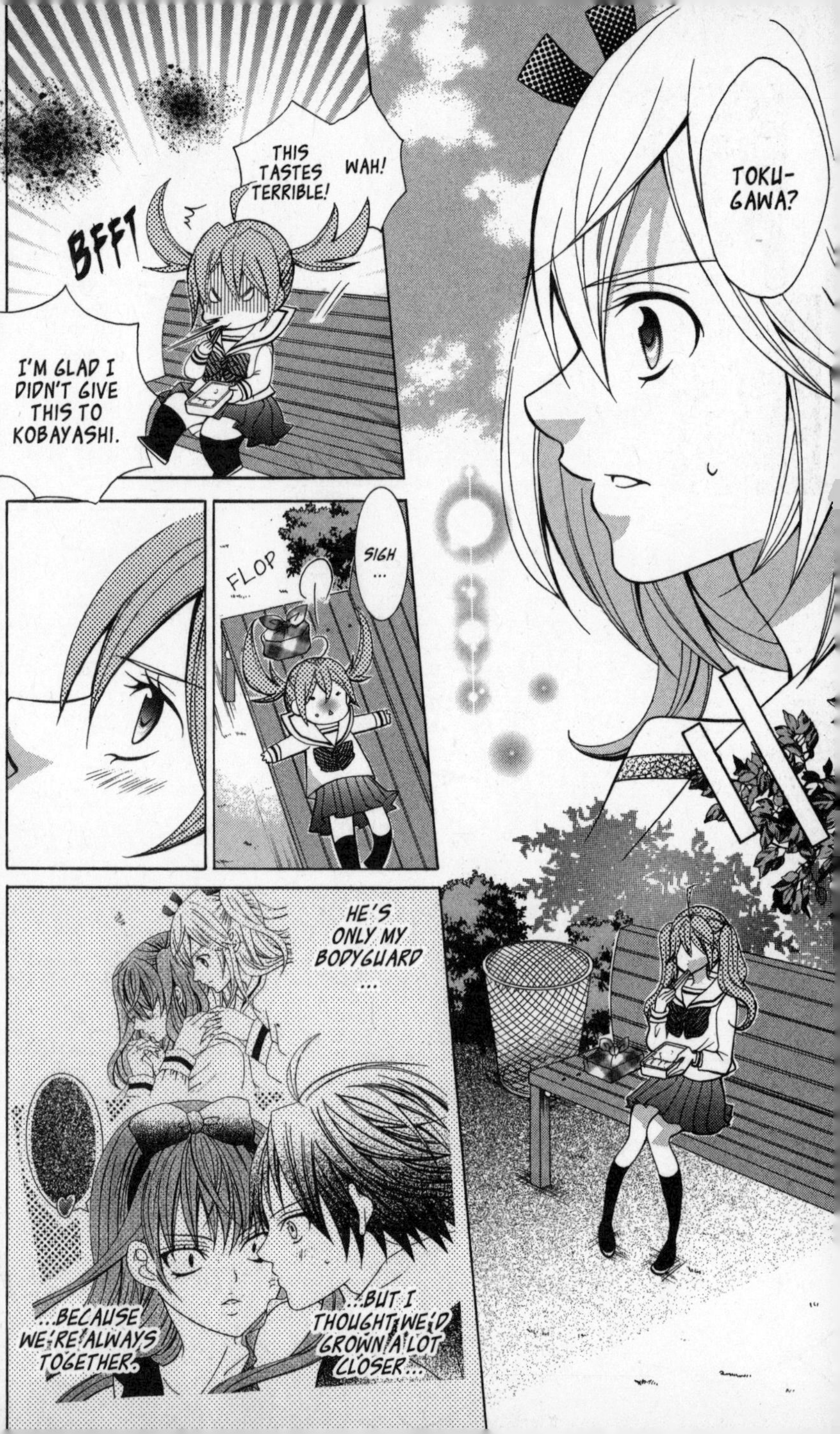
TOKU-GAWA?
WAH!
THIS TASTES TERRIBLE!
BFFT
I'M GLAD I DIDN'T GIVE THIS TO KOBAYASHI.
FLOP
SIGH...
HE'S ONLY MY BODYGUARD...
...BUT I THOUGHT WE'D GROWN A LOT CLOSER...
...BECAUSE WE'RE ALWAYS TOGETHER.

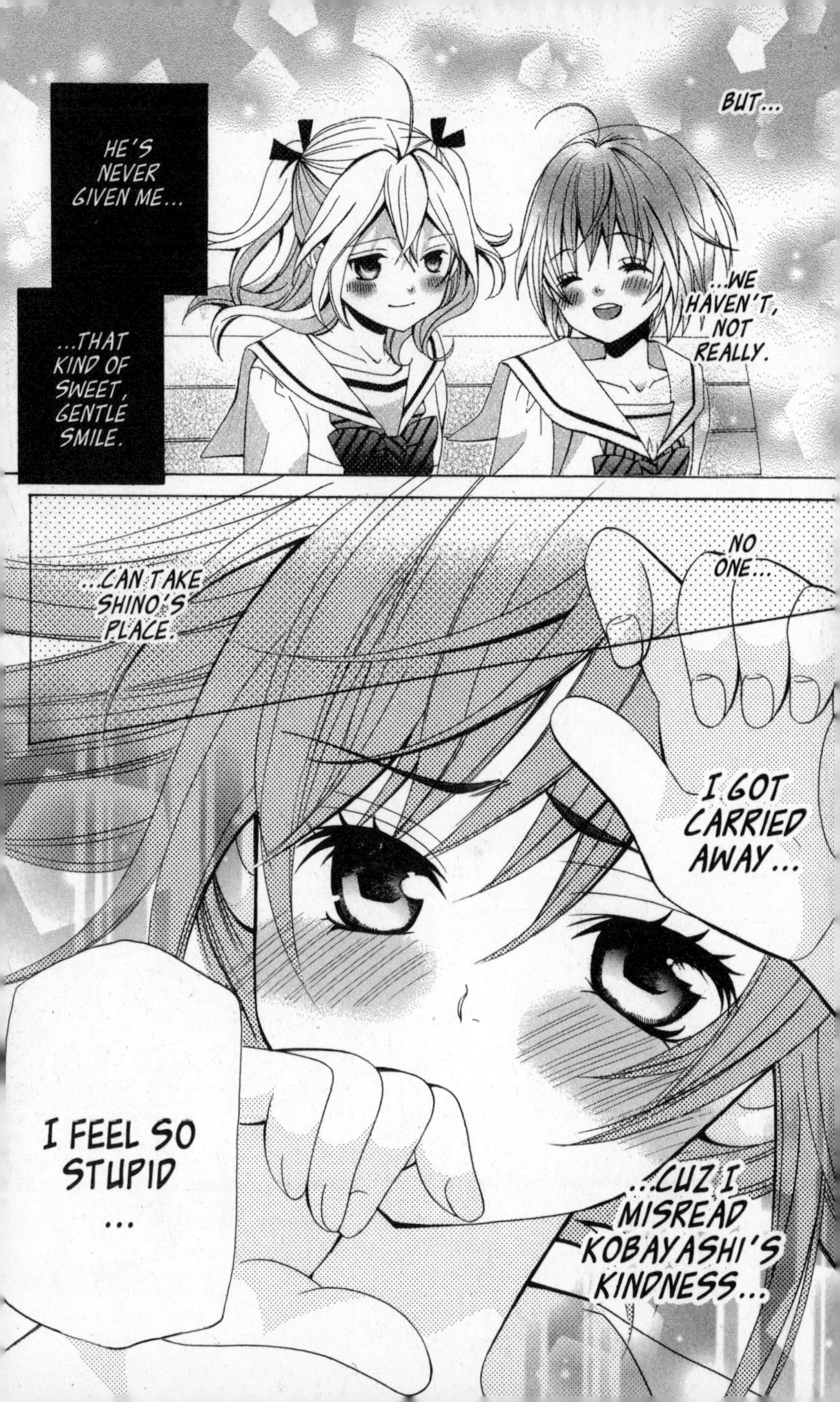
BUT...
...WE HAVEN'T, NOT REALLY.
HE'S NEVER GIVEN ME...
...THAT KIND OF SWEET, GENTLE SMILE.
NO ONE...
...CAN TAKE SHINO'S PLACE.
I GOT CARRIED AWAY...
I FEEL SO STUPID ...
...CUZ I MISREAD KOBAYASHI'S KINDNESS...

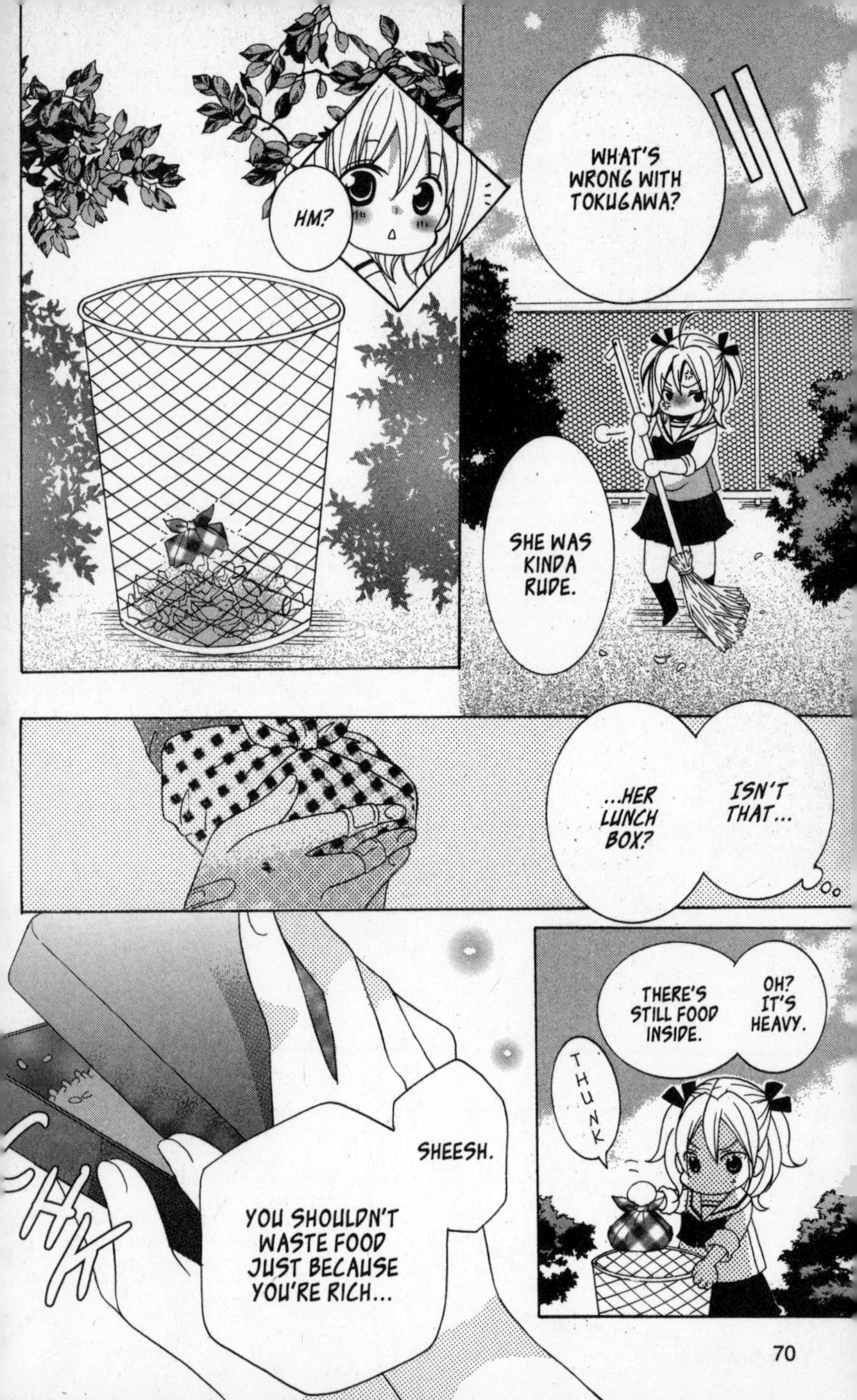
WHAT'S WRONG WITH TOKUGAWA?
SHE WAS KINDA RUDE.
HM?
ISN'T THAT...
...HER LUNCH BOX?
OH? IT'S HEAVY.
THERE'S STILL FOOD INSIDE.
THUNK
SHEESH.
YOU SHOULDN'T WASTE FOOD JUST BECAUSE YOU'RE RICH...
CHK

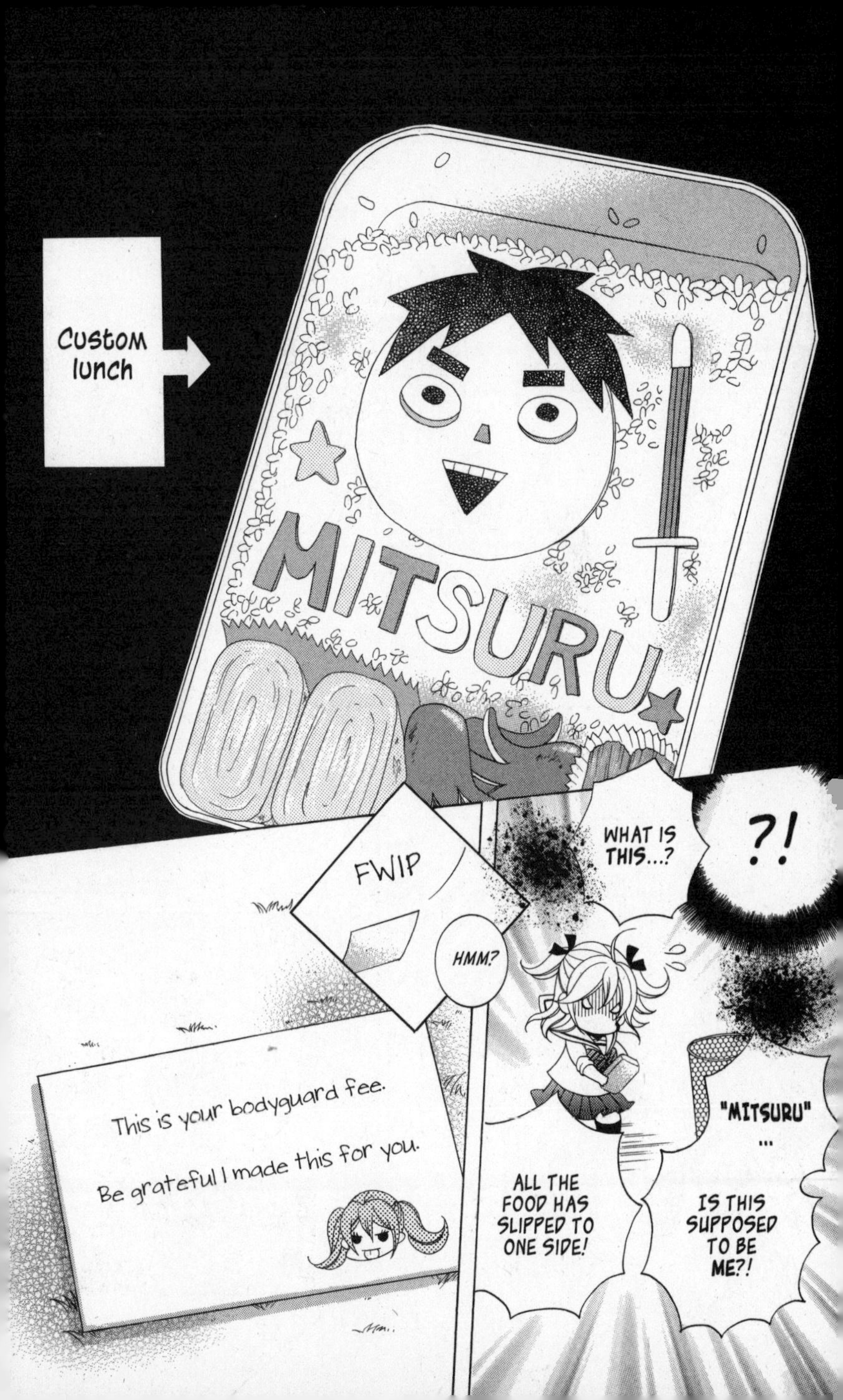
Custom lunch
MITSURU
?!
WHAT IS THIS...?
"MITSURU" ...
IS THIS SUPPOSED TO BE ME?!
ALL THE FOOD HAS SLIPPED TO ONE SIDE!
FWIP
HMM?
This is your bodyguard fee.
Be grateful I made this for you.

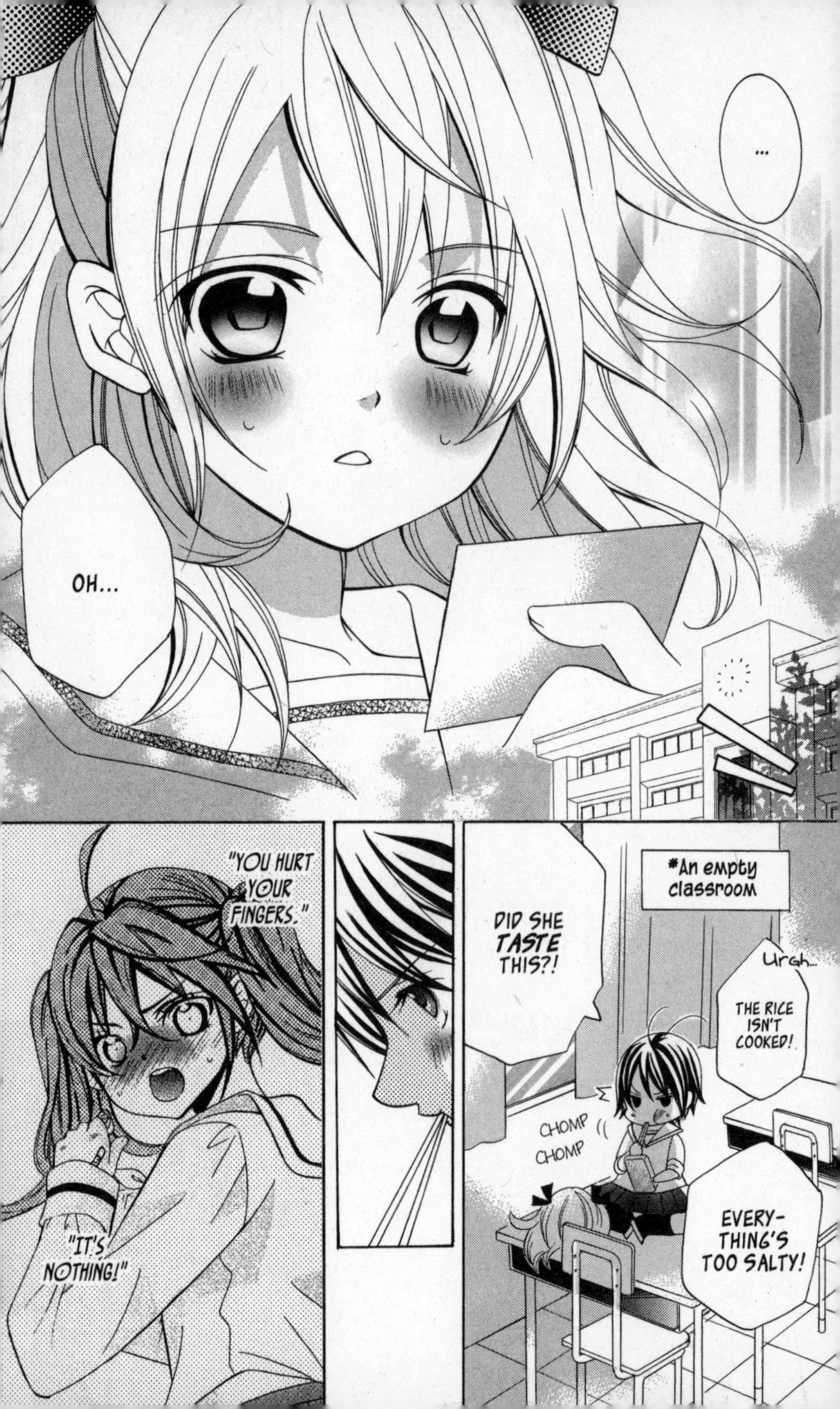
...
OH...
*An empty classroom
Urgh...
THE RICE ISN'T COOKED!
DID SHE TASTE THIS?!
CHOMP CHOMP
EVERY-THING'S TOO SALTY!
"YOU HURT YOUR FINGERS."
"IT'S NOTHING!"

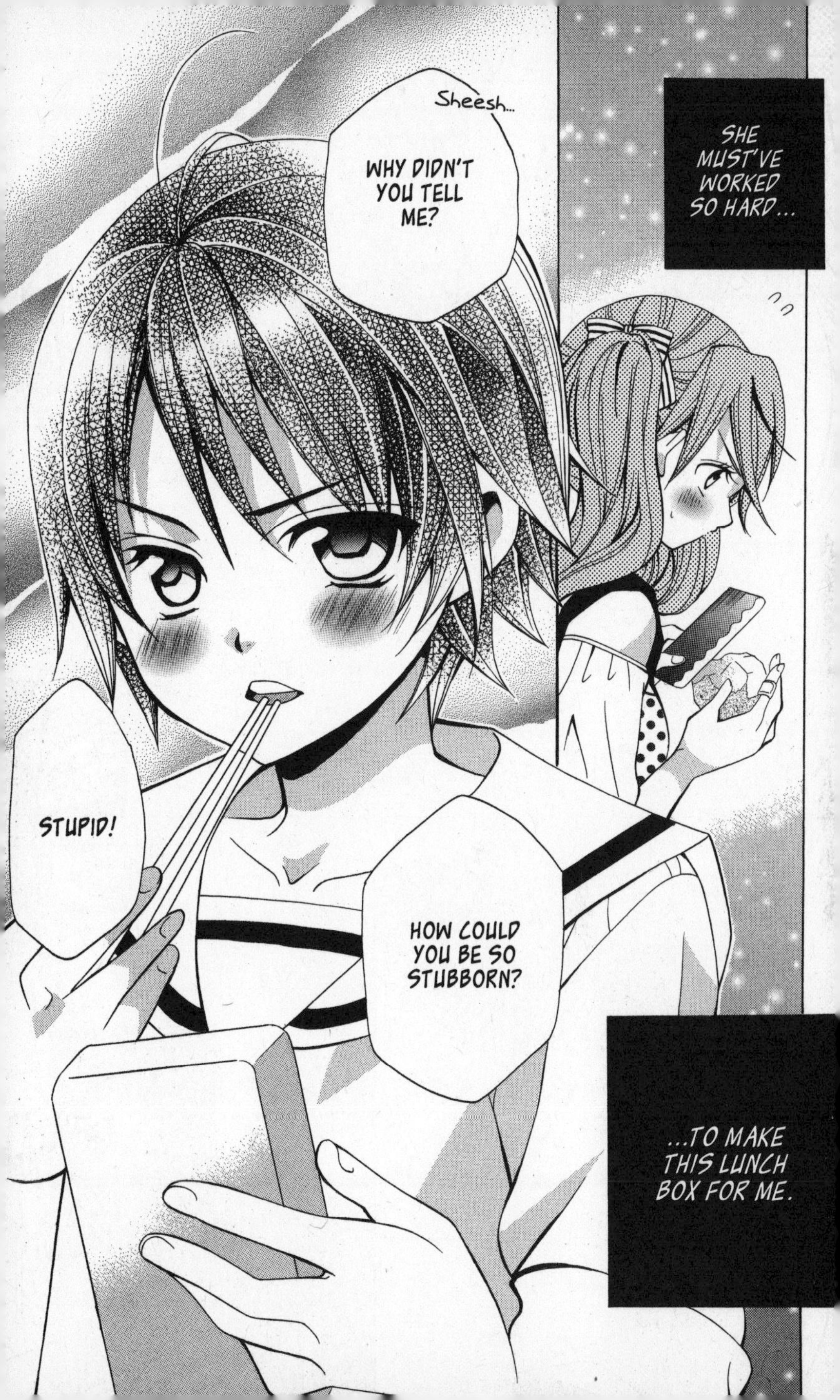
SHE MUST'VE WORKED SO HARD...
...TO MAKE THIS LUNCH BOX FOR ME.
Sheesh...
WHY DIDN'T YOU TELL ME?
STUPID!
HOW COULD YOU BE SO STUBBORN?

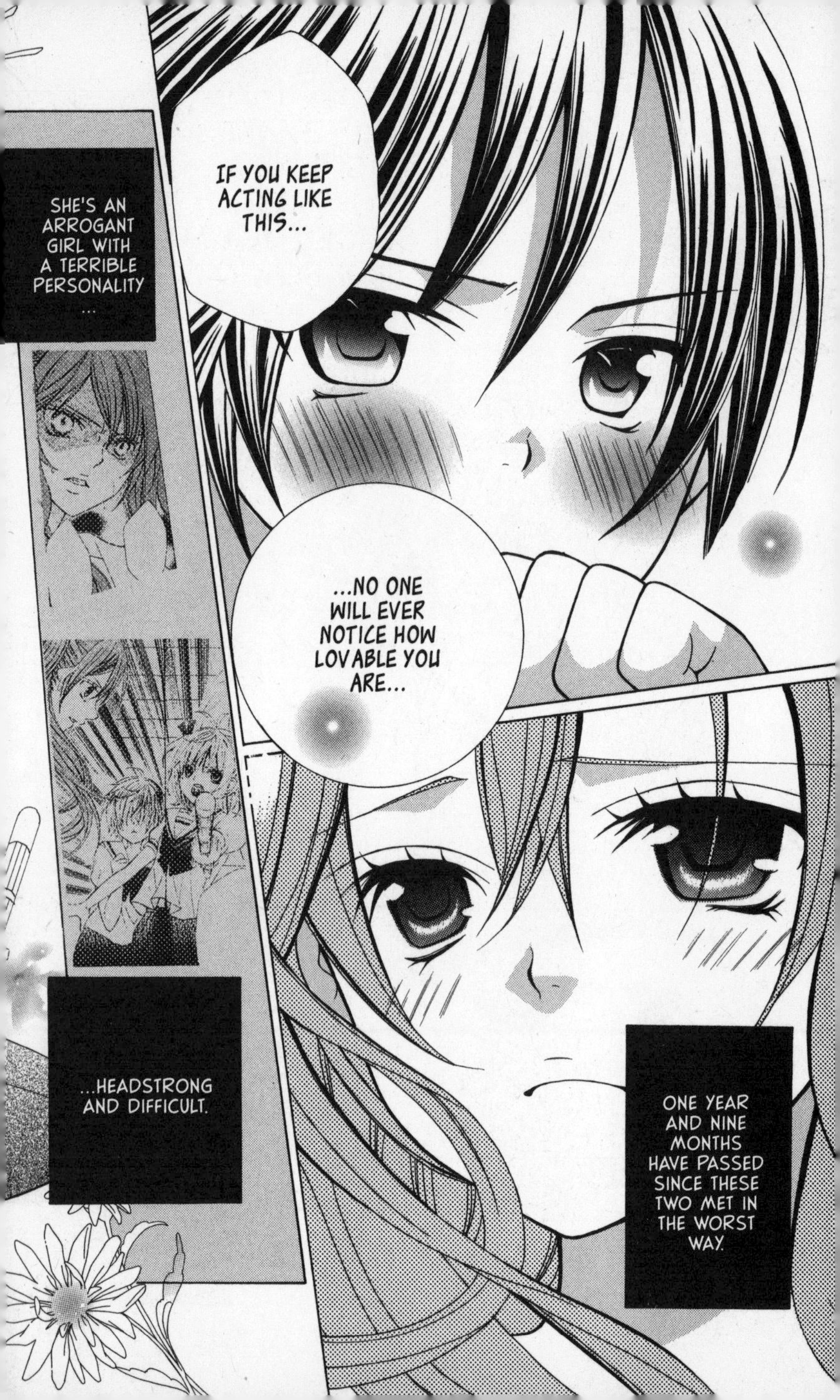
IF YOU KEEP ACTING LIKE THIS...
...NO ONE WILL EVER NOTICE HOW LOVABLE YOU ARE...
ONE YEAR AND NINE MONTHS HAVE PASSED SINCE THESE TWO MET IN THE WORST WAY.
SHE'S AN ARROGANT GIRL WITH A TERRIBLE PERSONALITY...
...HEADSTRONG AND DIFFICULT.

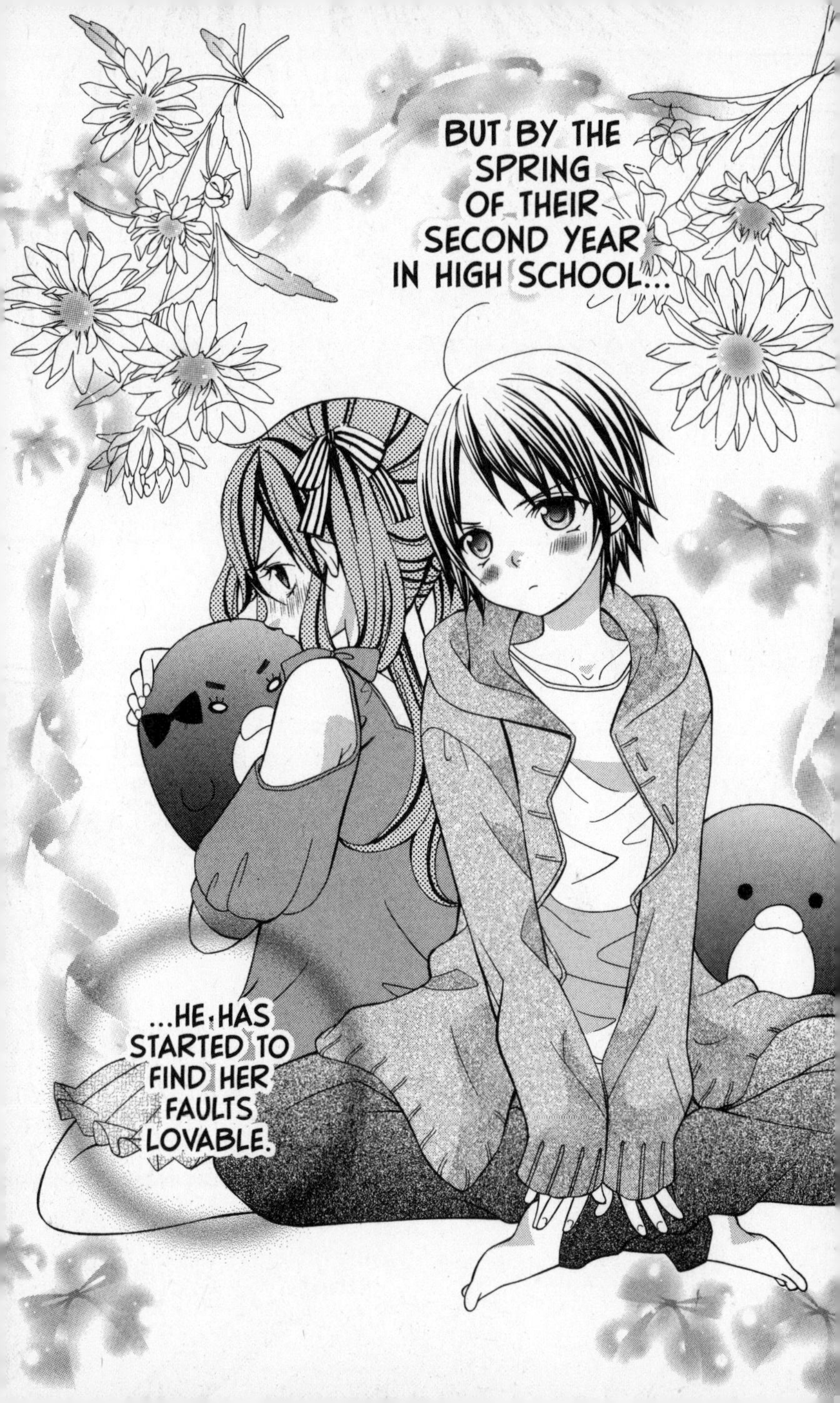
BUT BY THE SPRING OF THEIR SECOND YEAR IN HIGH SCHOOL...
...HE HAS STARTED TO FIND HER FAULTS LOVABLE.

Chapter 38

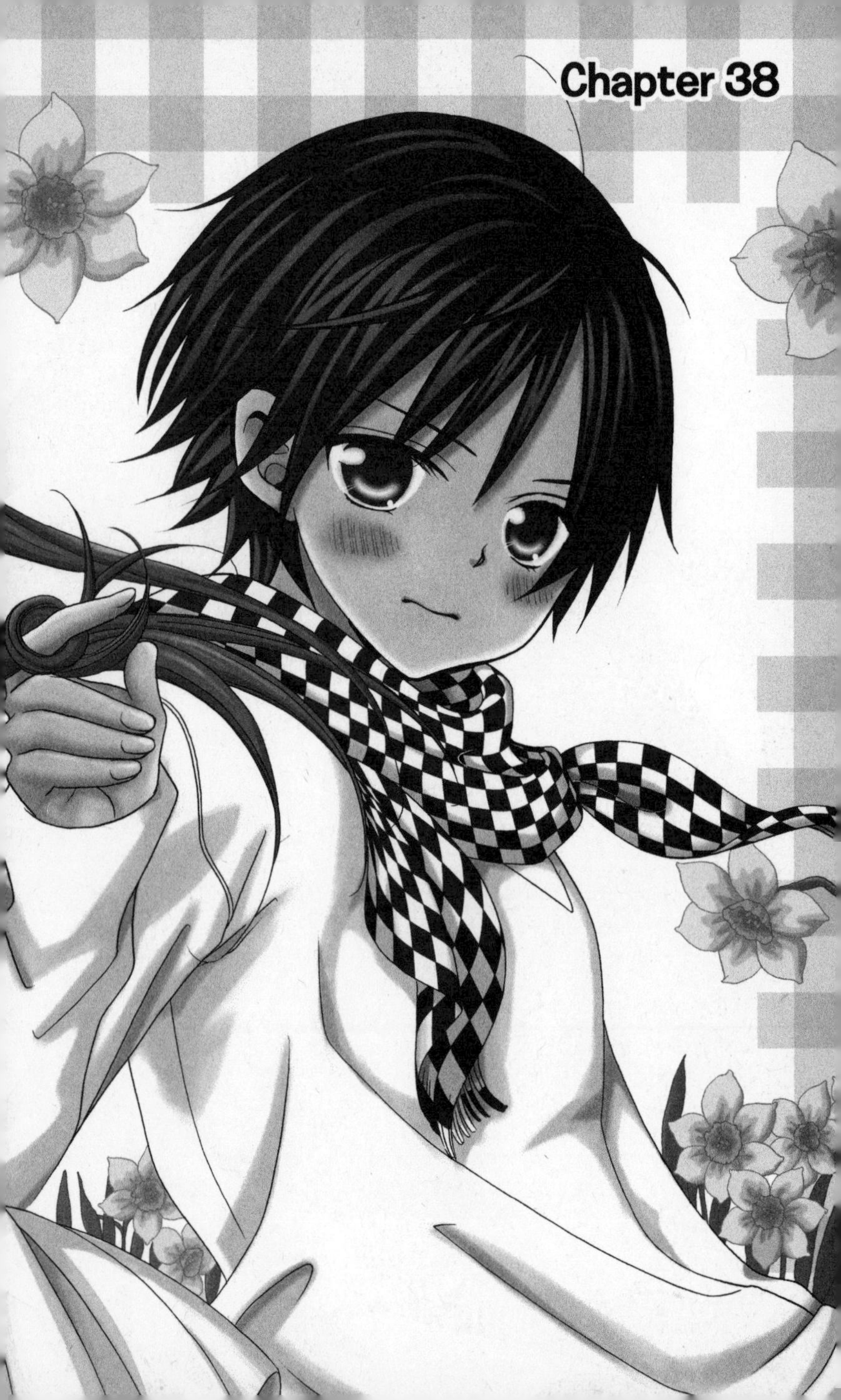

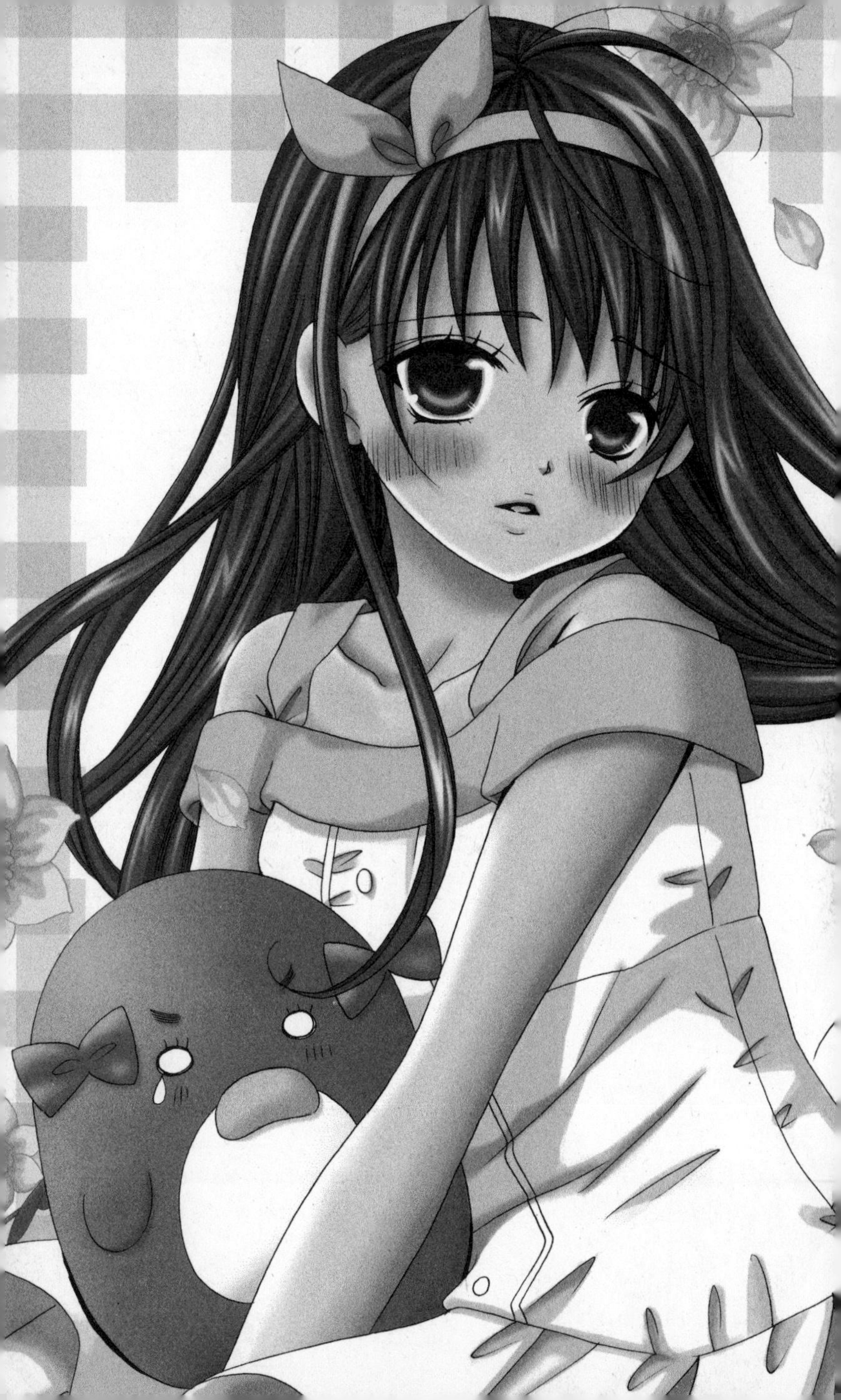

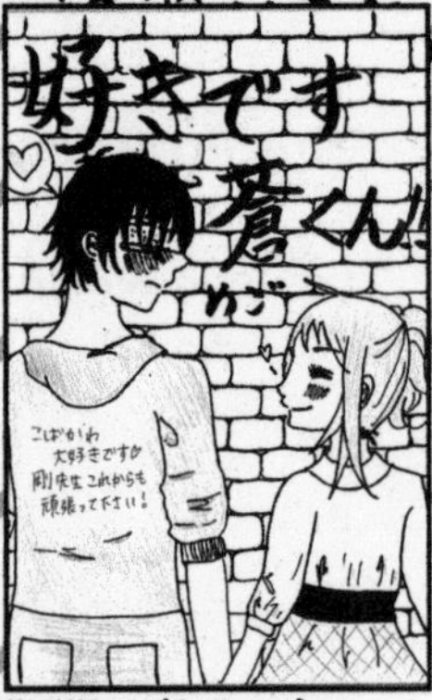
好きです蒼くん!!
めご

Mei Miura (Saitama) ↑
Ed.: I hope the two can hold hands soon...

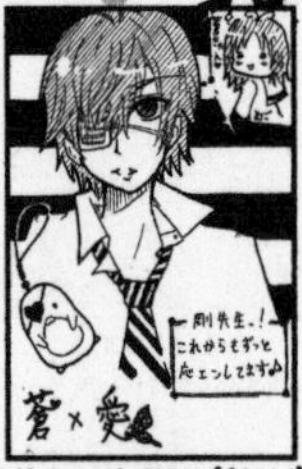
蒼 × 愛

Mayu Kajita (Aichi) ↑
Ed.: Aoi's mind is filled with Mego?!

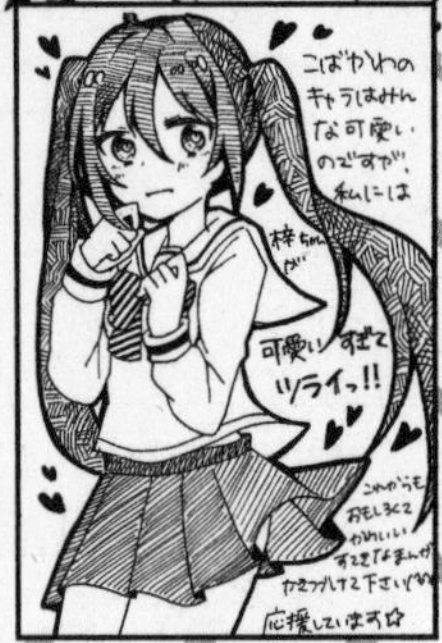
可愛いすぎてツライっ!!
応援しています☆

Tomo (Tokyo)
Ed.: Readers keep loving Azusa!
←

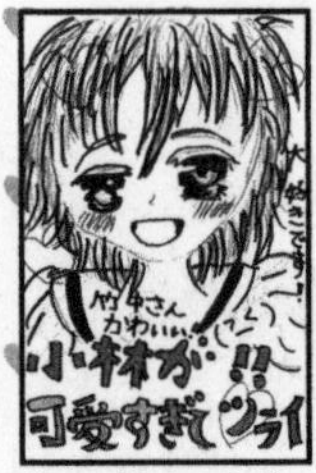
小林が!!
可愛すぎてツライ

Mayu (Shizuoka) ↑
Ed.: Shino's smile makes me smile...

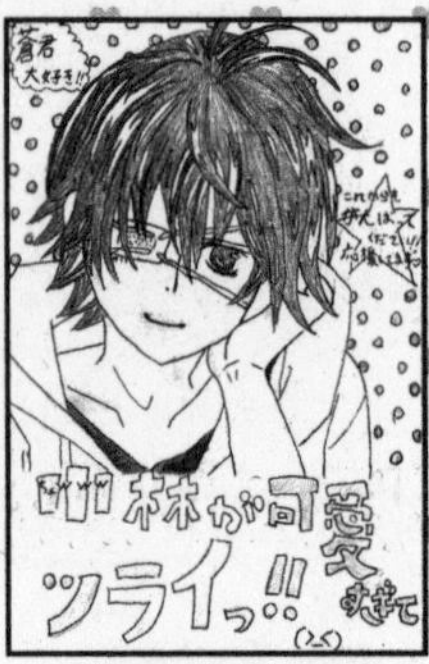
小林が可愛
ツライっ!!

Airi Tanaka (Saitama) ↑
Ed.: My heart flutters watching Aoi smile gently. ♥

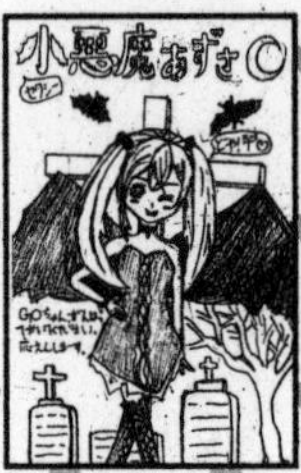
小悪魔あずさ

Marin Murayama (Kagoshima)
Ed.: Ooh, sexy.
←

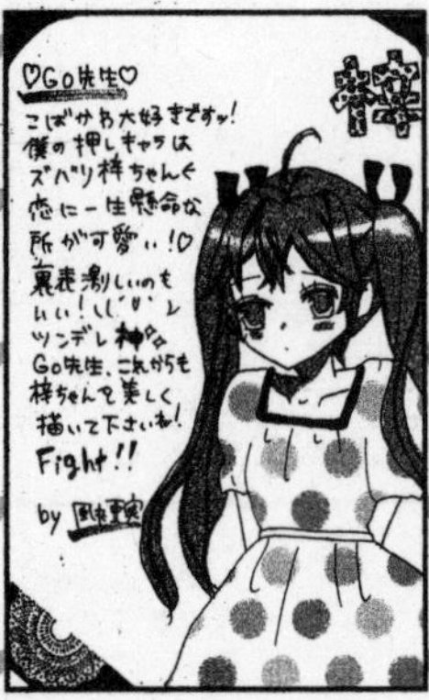
♡Go先生♡
Fight!!

Ami Kazemaru (Ehime)
Ed.: Readers love the tsundere Azusa!!
→

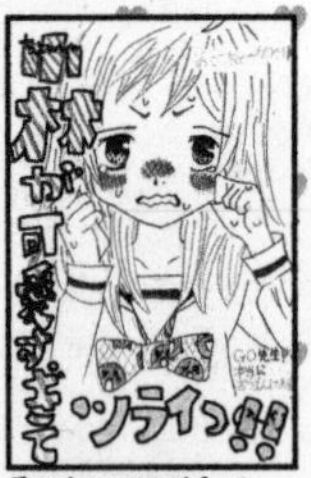
ツライっ!!

Tentoumushi ↑
(Yamaguichi)
Ed.: Mego's crying face is very powerful!!

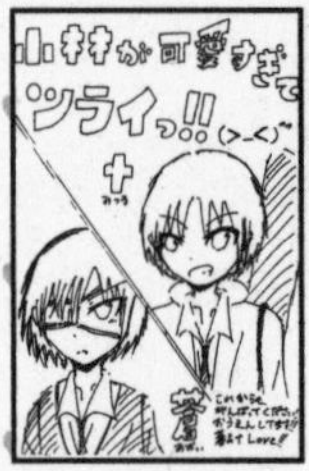
小林が可愛すぎて
ツライっ!!

Aoi & Mitsuru LOVE ♡
(Osaka)
Ed.: The two cool dudes of Akechi High!!
←

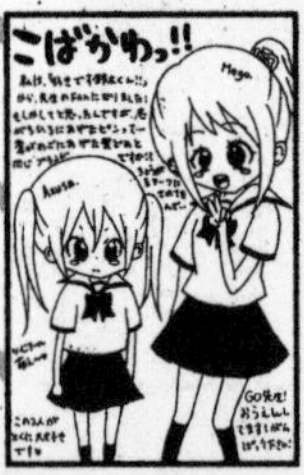
こばかわっ!!

Haruka Ueda (Ibaraki)
Ed.: Please love both of them!
←

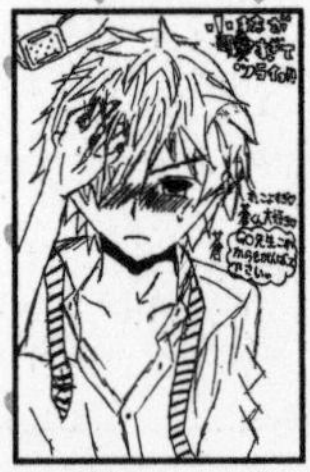

Rino Ishii (Gunma)
Ed.: Even guys fall in love with Aoi!
←

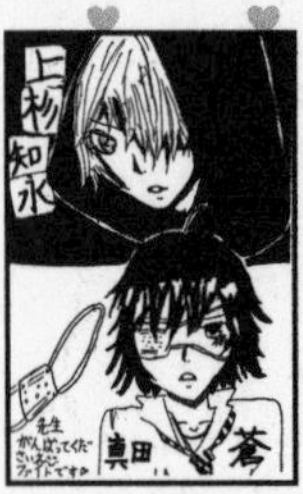
上杉知永
真田 蒼

Misaki Mikamo (Hyogo)
Ed.: We gotta keep our eyes on these two!
←

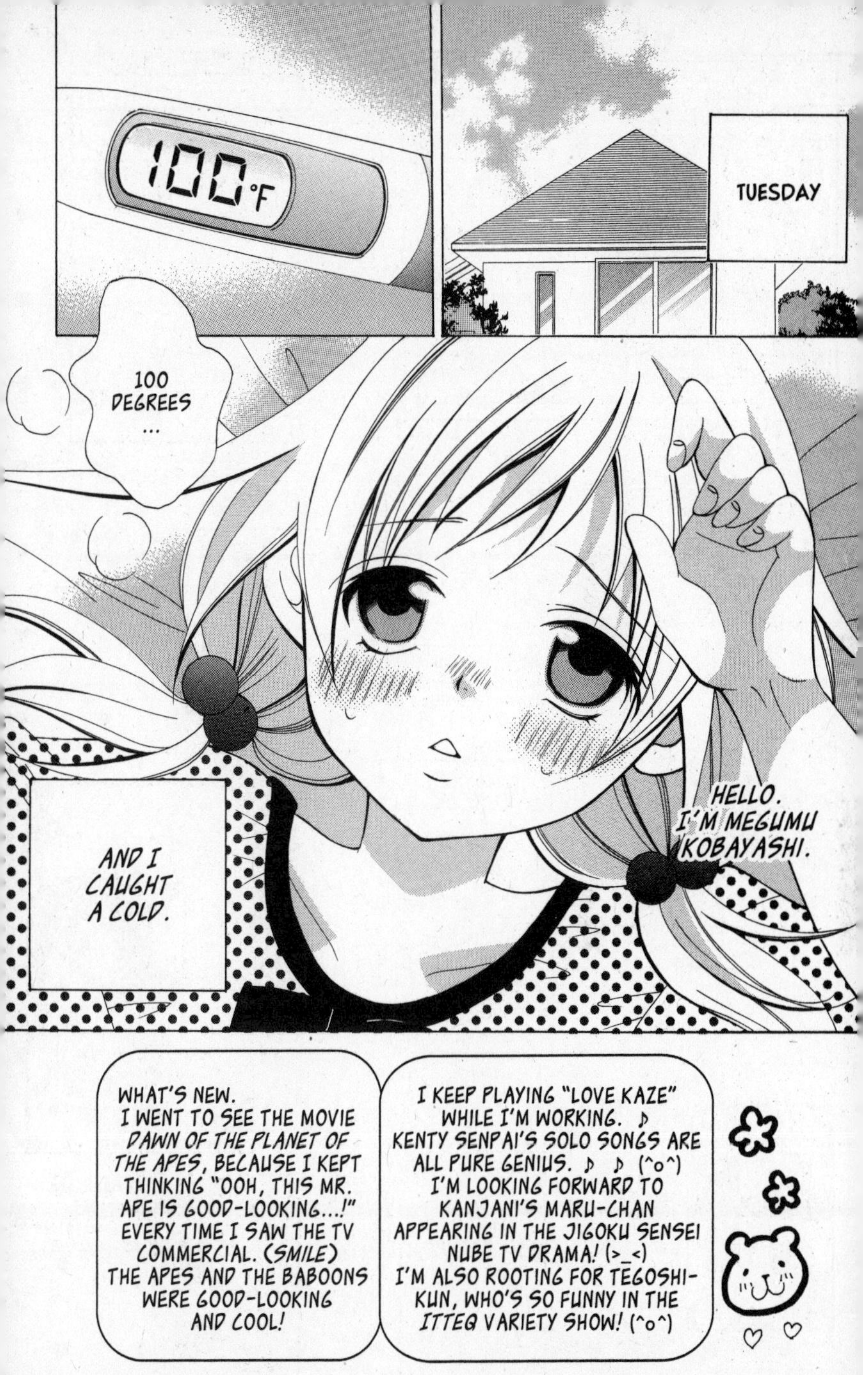
TUESDAY
100°F
100 DEGREES ...
HELLO. I'M MEGUMU KOBAYASHI.
AND I CAUGHT A COLD.

WHAT'S NEW.
I WENT TO SEE THE MOVIE *DAWN OF THE PLANET OF THE APES*, BECAUSE I KEPT THINKING "OOH, THIS MR. APE IS GOOD-LOOKING...!" EVERY TIME I SAW THE TV COMMERCIAL. (*SMILE*) THE APES AND THE BABOONS WERE GOOD-LOOKING AND COOL!

I KEEP PLAYING "LOVE KAZE" WHILE I'M WORKING. ♪ KENTY SENPAI'S SOLO SONGS ARE ALL PURE GENIUS. ♪ ♪ (^o^) I'M LOOKING FORWARD TO KANJANI'S MARU-CHAN APPEARING IN THE JIGOKU SENSEI NUBE TV DRAMA! (>_<) I'M ALSO ROOTING FOR TEGOSHI-KUN, WHO'S SO FUNNY IN THE *ITTEQ* VARIETY SHOW! (^o^)

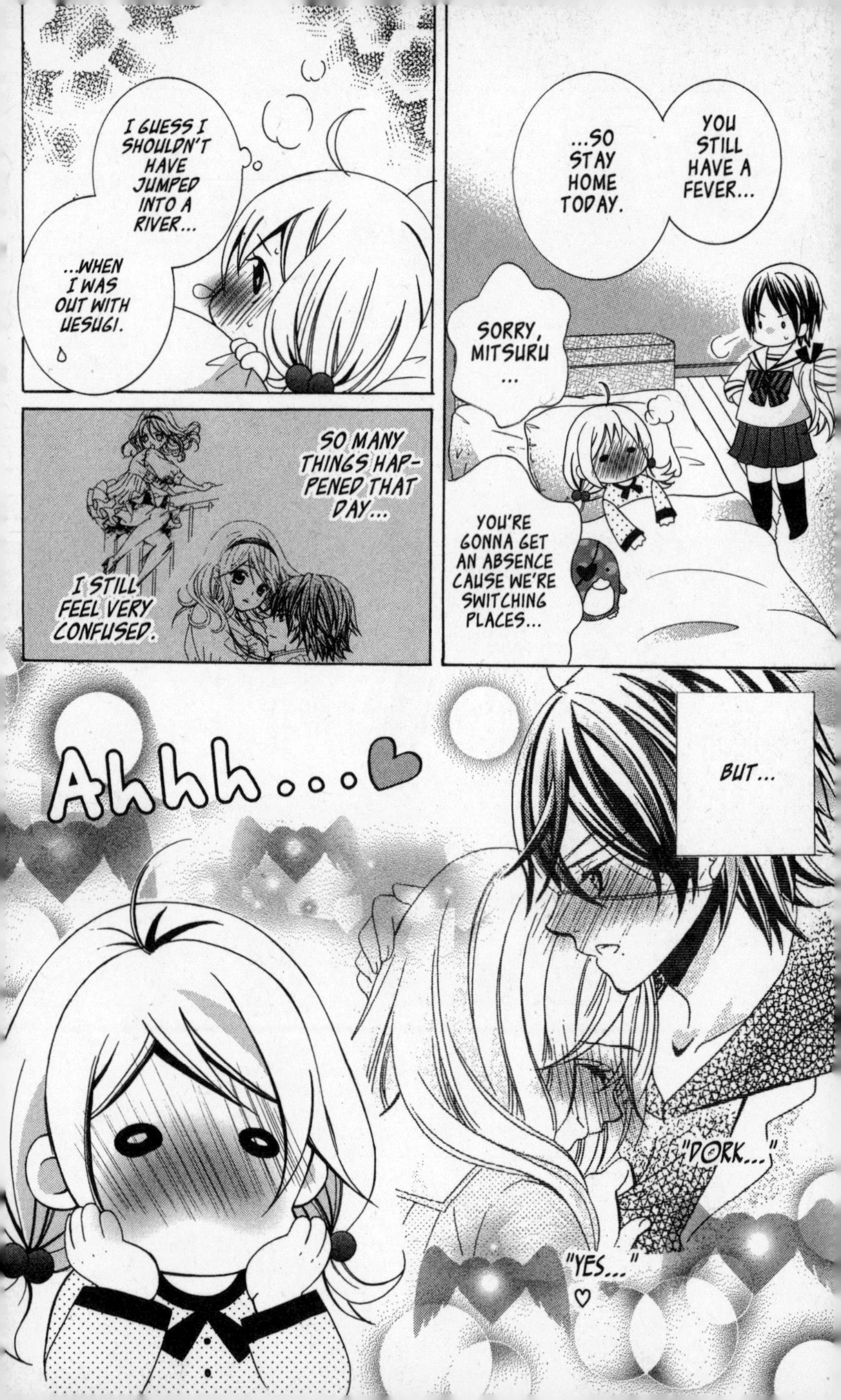
YOU STILL HAVE A FEVER...
...SO STAY HOME TODAY.
SORRY, MITSURU ...
YOU'RE GONNA GET AN ABSENCE CAUSE WE'RE SWITCHING PLACES...
I GUESS I SHOULDN'T HAVE JUMPED INTO A RIVER...
...WHEN I WAS OUT WITH UESUGI.
SO MANY THINGS HAP-PENED THAT DAY...
I STILL FEEL VERY CONFUSED.
BUT...
"DORK..."
"YES..." ♡
Ahhh...♥

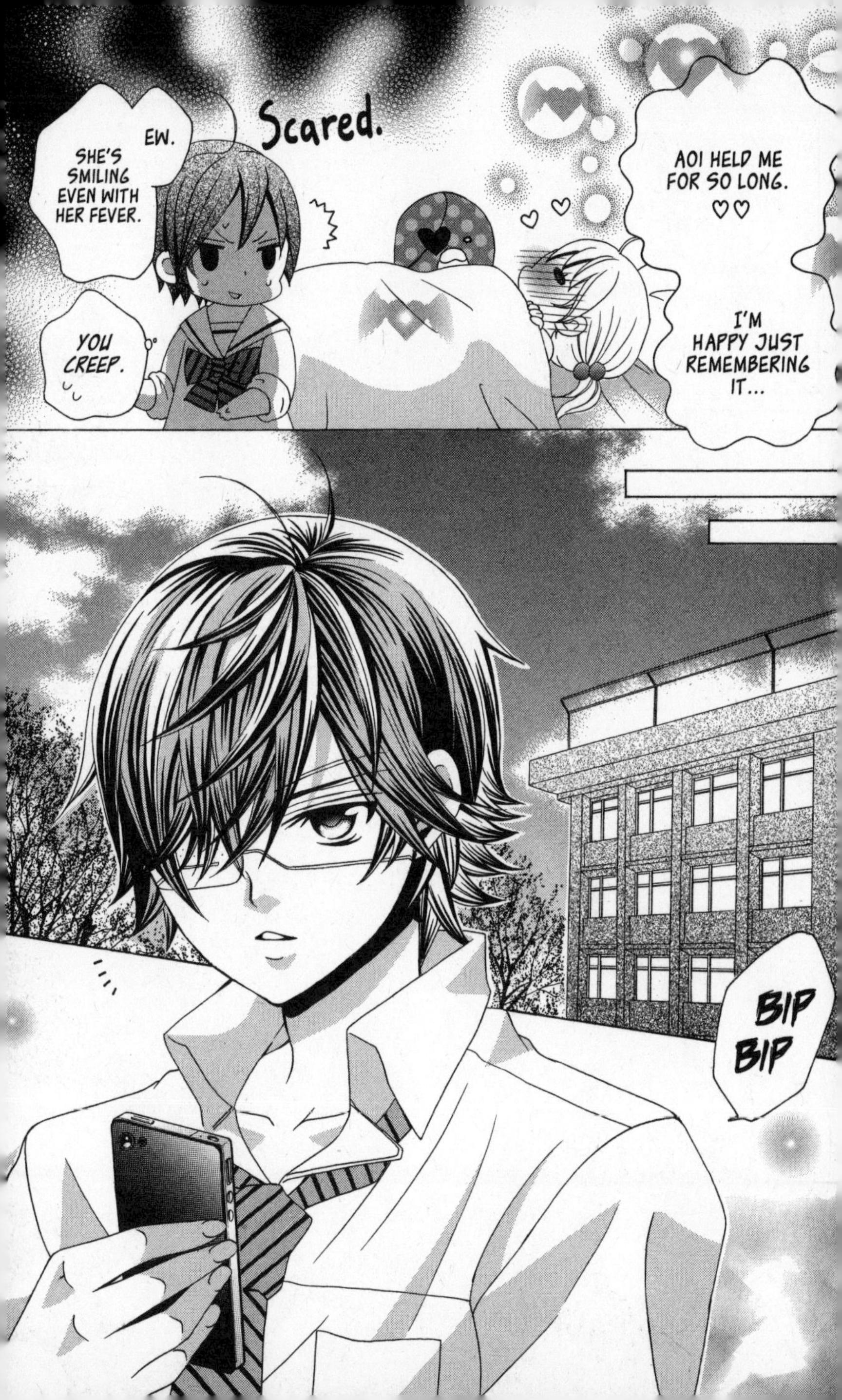
AOI HELD ME FOR SO LONG. ♡♡
I'M HAPPY JUST REMEMBERING IT...
Scared.
EW. SHE'S SMILING EVEN WITH HER FEVER.
YOU CREEP.
BIP BIP

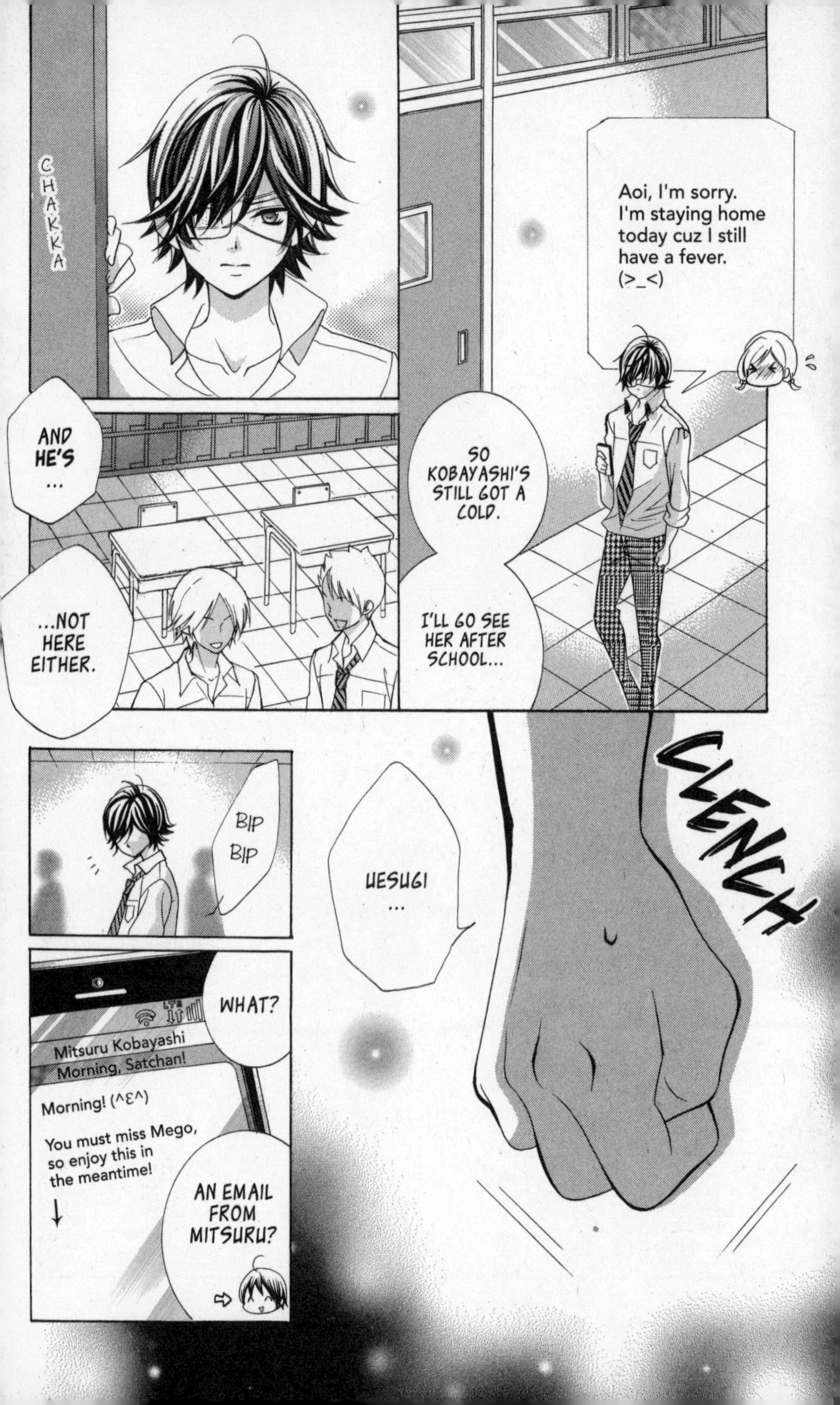
Aoi, I'm sorry. I'm staying home today cuz I still have a fever. (>_<)
SO KOBAYASHI'S STILL GOT A COLD.
I'LL GO SEE HER AFTER SCHOOL...
CHAKKA
AND HE'S...
...NOT HERE EITHER.
CLENCH
UESUGI...
BIP BIP
WHAT?
Mitsuru Kobayashi
Morning, Satchan!
Morning! (^ε^)
You must miss Mego, so enjoy this in the meantime!
↓
AN EMAIL FROM MITSURU?

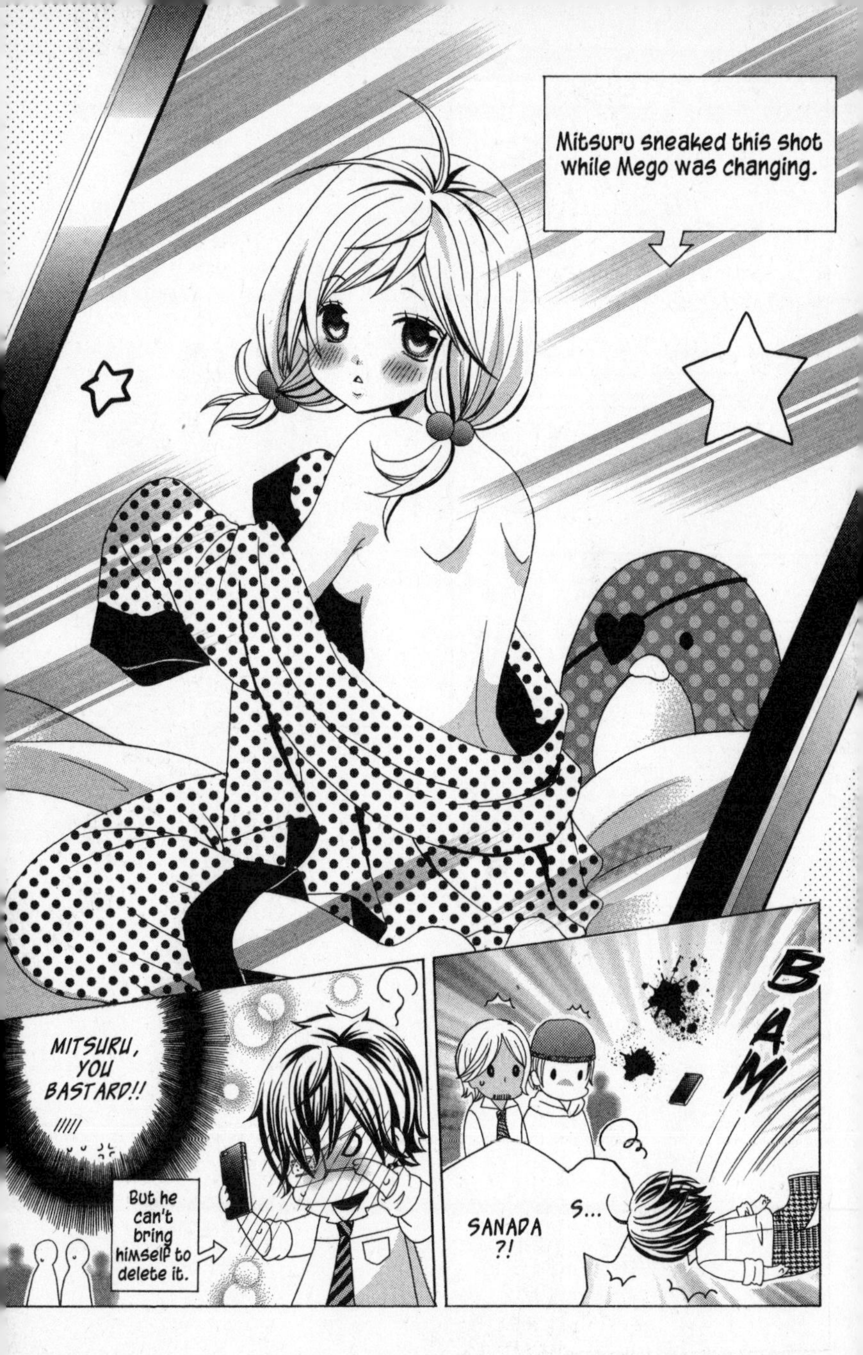
Mitsuru sneaked this shot while Mego was changing.
BAM
S...
SANADA ?!
MITSURU, YOU BASTARD!!
But he can't bring himself to delete it.

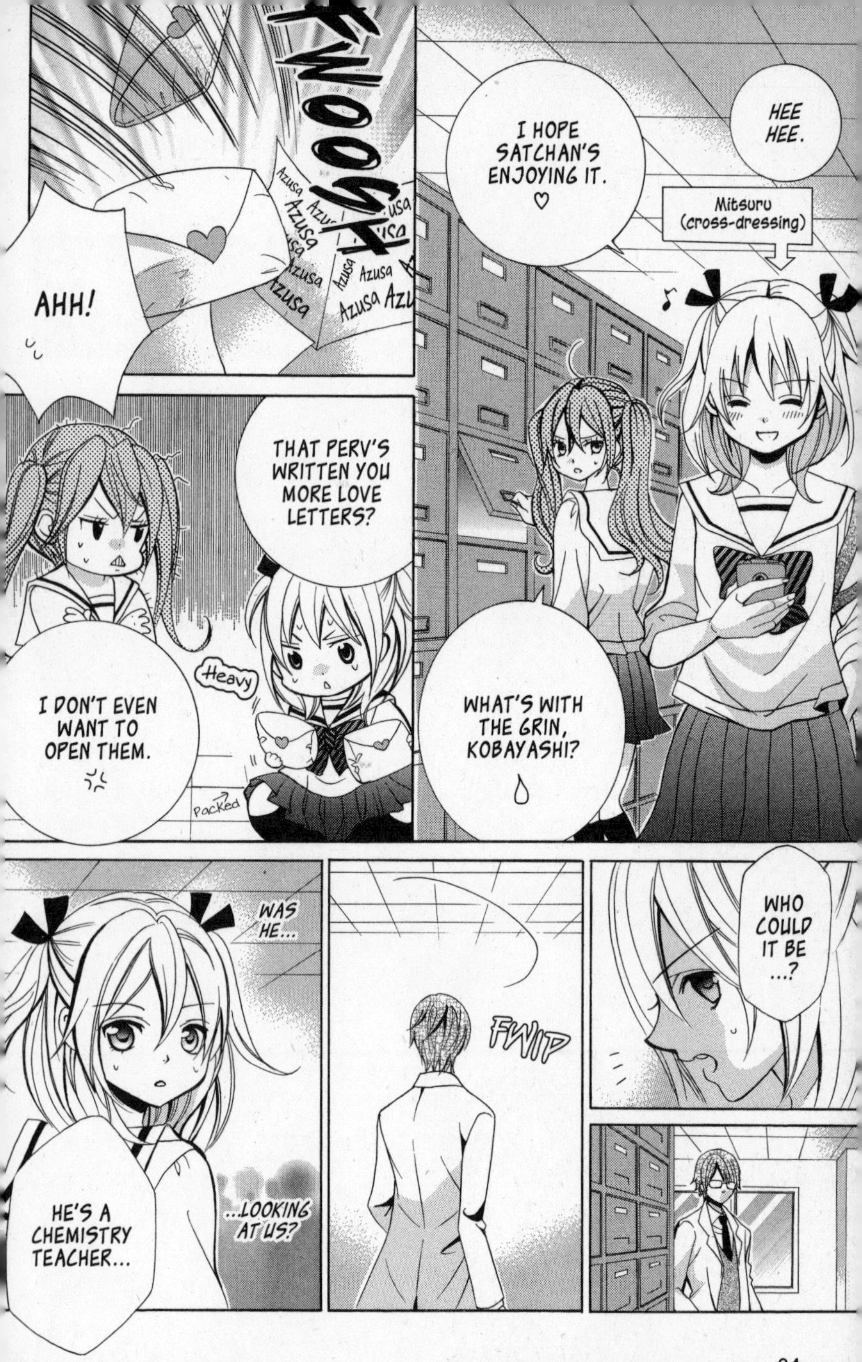
HEE HEE.
Mitsuru (cross-dressing)
I HOPE SATCHAN'S ENJOYING IT. ♡
WHAT'S WITH THE GRIN, KOBAYASHI?
FWOOSH
Azusa Azusa Azusa Azusa Azusa Azusa Azusa Azusa
AHH!
THAT PERV'S WRITTEN YOU MORE LOVE LETTERS?
Heavy
I DON'T EVEN WANT TO OPEN THEM.
Packed
WHO COULD IT BE ...?
FWIP
WAS HE...
...LOOKING AT US?
HE'S A CHEMISTRY TEACHER...

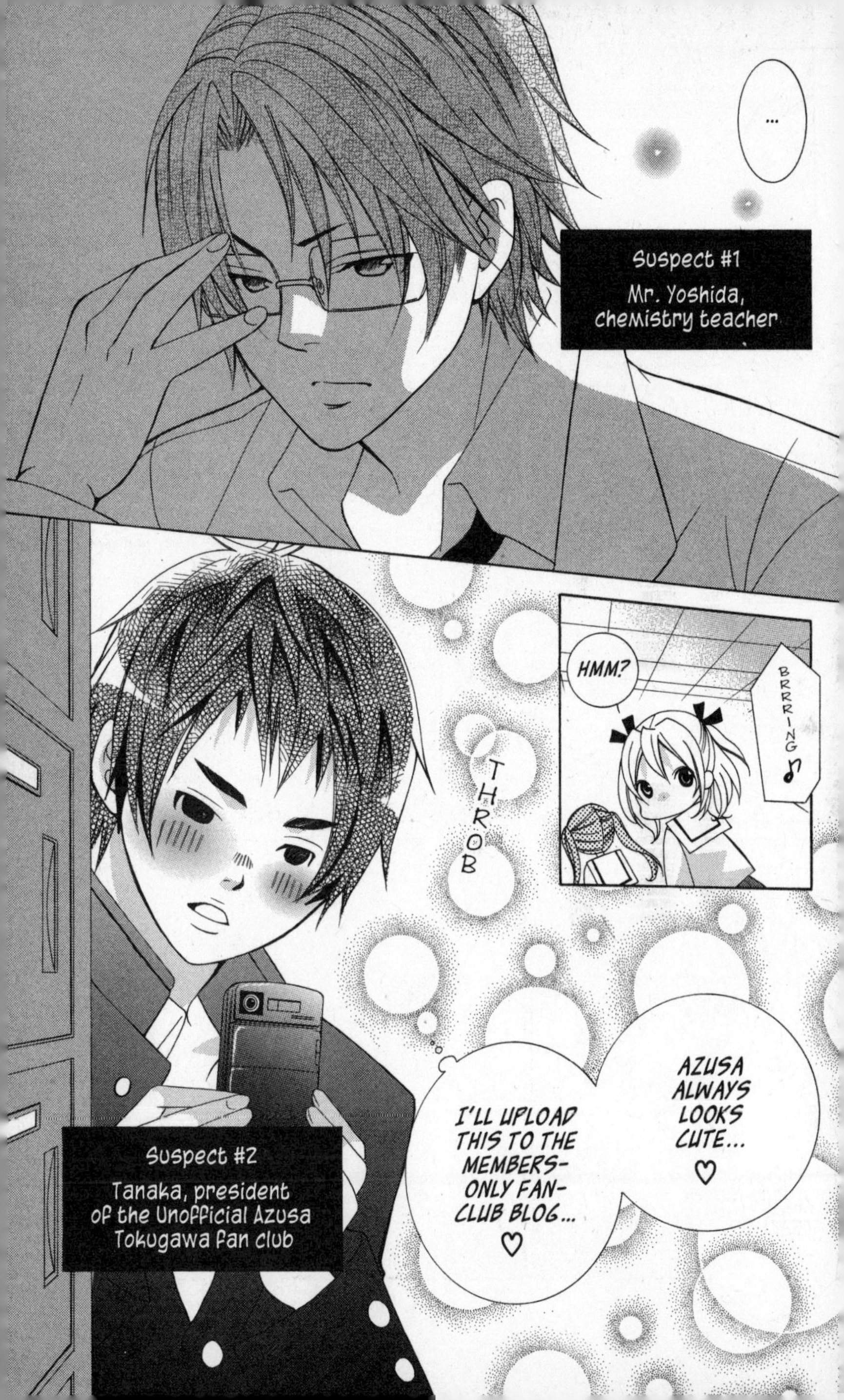
...
Suspect #1
Mr. Yoshida, chemistry teacher
HMM?
BRRRING ♪
THROB
AZUSA ALWAYS LOOKS CUTE... ♡
I'LL UPLOAD THIS TO THE MEMBERS-ONLY FAN-CLUB BLOG... ♡
Suspect #2
Tanaka, president of the Unofficial Azusa Tokugawa fan club

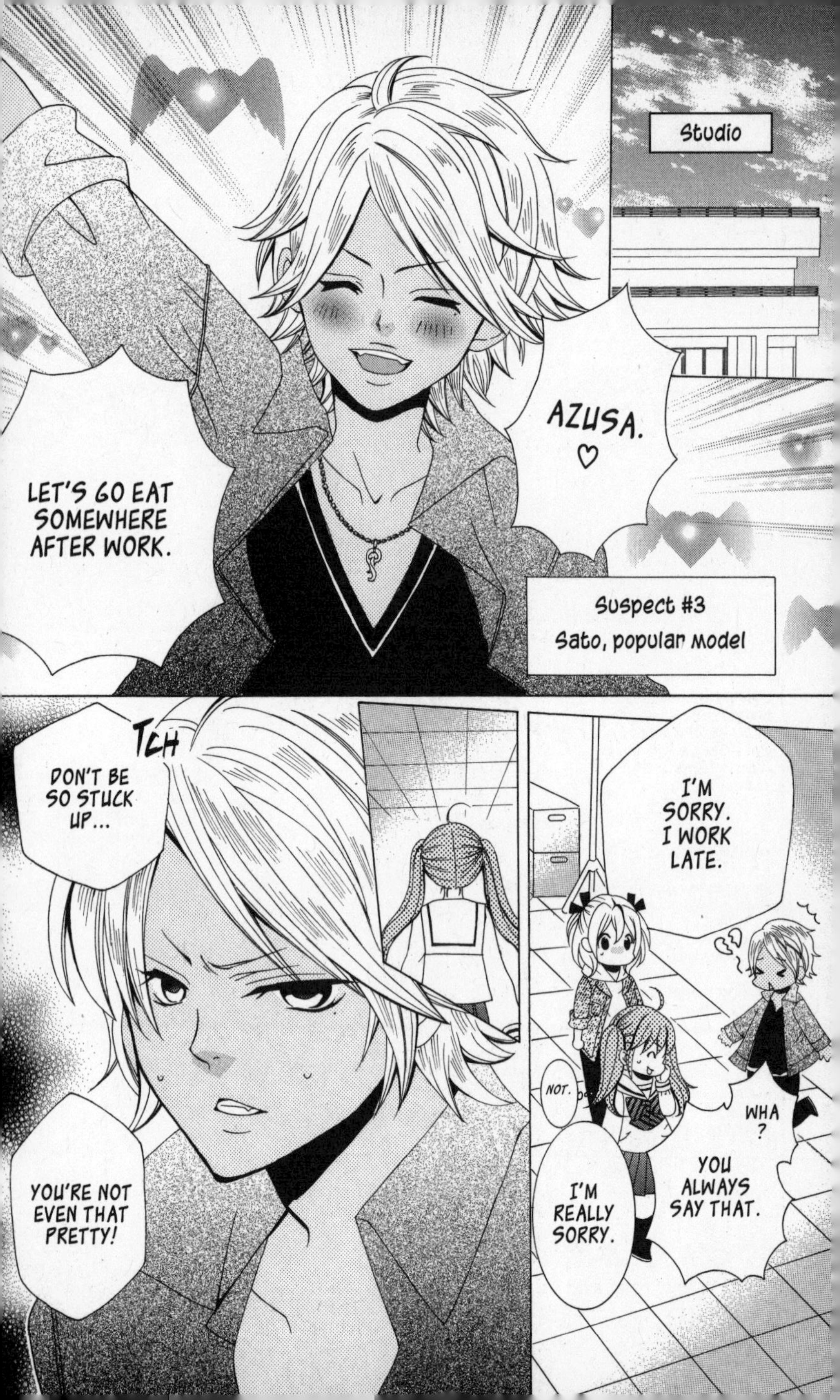
Studio
AZUSA. ♡
Suspect #3
Sato, popular model
LET'S GO EAT SOMEWHERE AFTER WORK.
I'M SORRY. I WORK LATE.
WHA ?
YOU ALWAYS SAY THAT.
NOT.
I'M REALLY SORRY.
TCH
DON'T BE SO STUCK UP...
YOU'RE NOT EVEN THAT PRETTY!

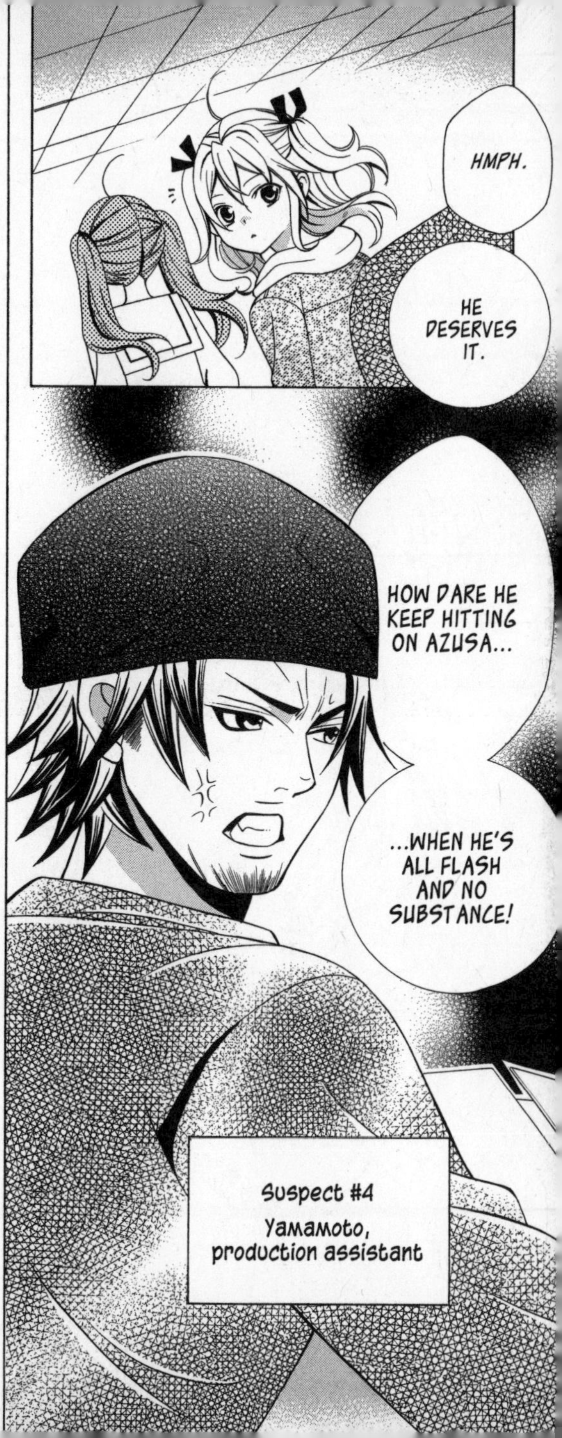
HMPH.
HE DESERVES IT.
HOW DARE HE KEEP HITTING ON AZUSA...
...WHEN HE'S ALL FLASH AND NO SUBSTANCE!
Suspect #4
Yamamoto, production assistant

SPECIAL THANKS

Yuka Ito-sama,
Rieko Hirai-sama,
Kayoko Takahashi-sama,
Kawasaki-sama,
Nagisa Sato Sensei.

Rei Nanase Sensei,
Arisu Fujishiro Sensei,
Mumi Mimura Sensei,
Masayo Nagata-sama,
Naochan-sama,
Asuka Sakura Sensei
and many others.

Bookstore Dan Kinshicho Branch, Kinokuniya Shinjuku Branch, LIBRO Ikebukuro Branch, Kinokuniya Hankyu 32-Bangai Branch.

Sendai Hachimonjiya Bookstore, Books HOSHINO Kintetsu Pass'e Branch, Asahiya Tennnoji MiO Branch, Kurashiki Kikuya Bookstore.

Salesperson:
Mizusawa-sama

Previous salesperson:
Honma-sama

Previous editor:
Nakata-sama

Current editor:
Shoji-sama

I also sincerely express my gratitude to everyone who picked up this volume.

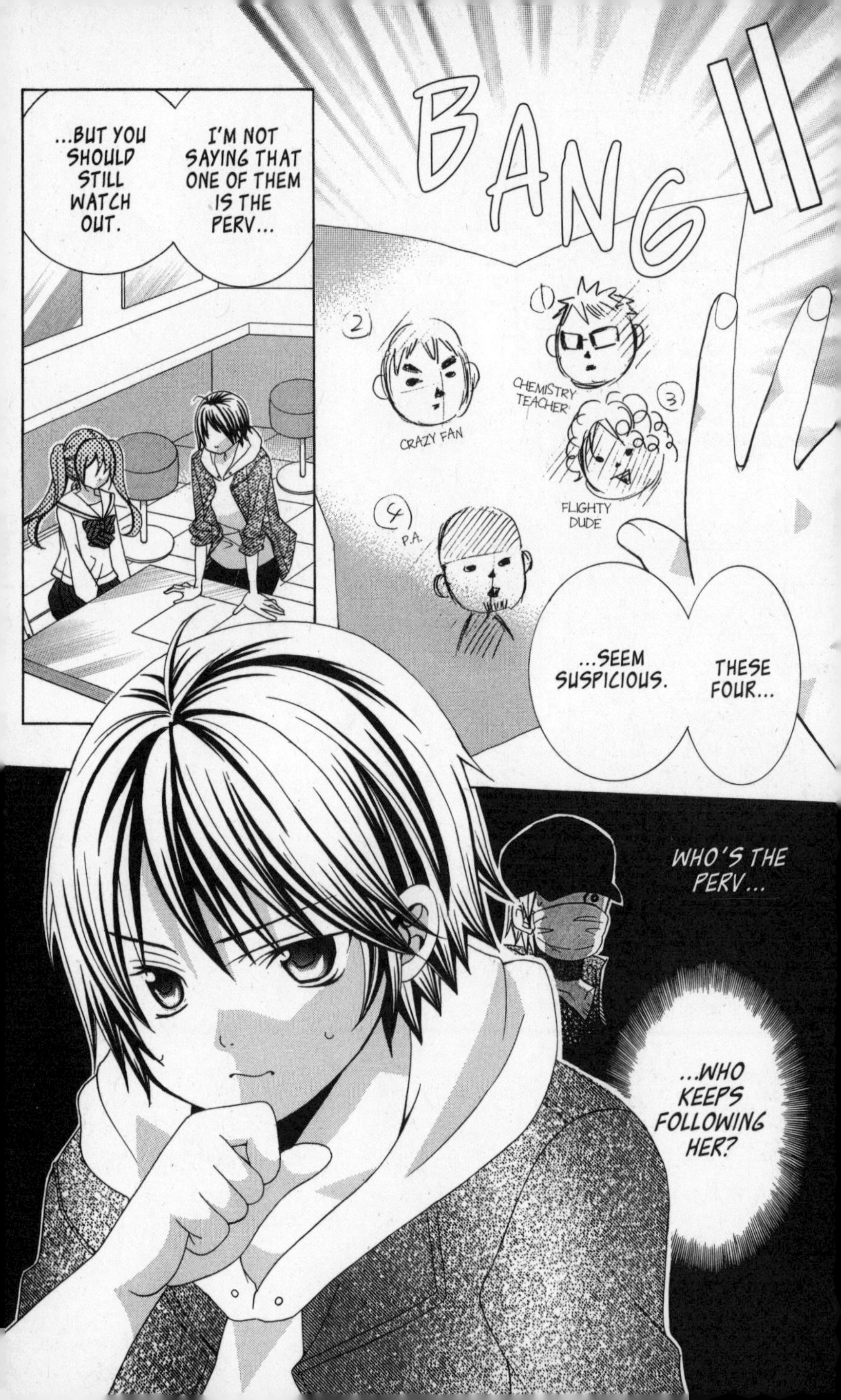

BANG!!
1
CHEMISTRY TEACHER
2
CRAZY FAN
3
FLIGHTY DUDE
4
P.A.
THESE FOUR...
...SEEM SUSPICIOUS.
I'M NOT SAYING THAT ONE OF THEM IS THE PERV...
...BUT YOU SHOULD STILL WATCH OUT.
WHO'S THE PERV...
...WHO KEEPS FOLLOWING HER?

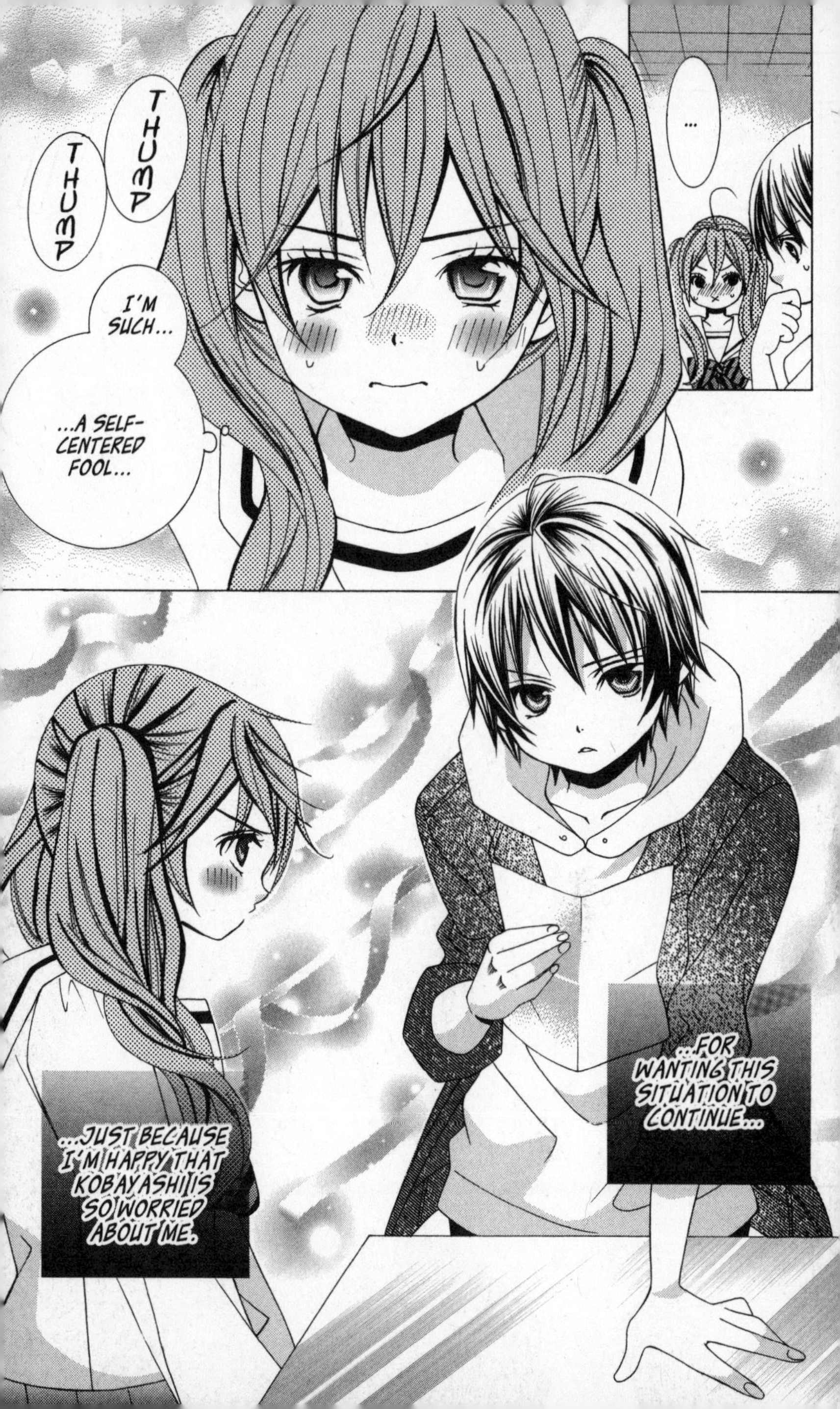
...
THUMP
THUMP
I'M SUCH...
...A SELF-CENTERED FOOL...
...FOR WANTING THIS SITUATION TO CONTINUE...
...JUST BECAUSE I'M HAPPY THAT KOBAYASHI IS SO WORRIED ABOUT ME.

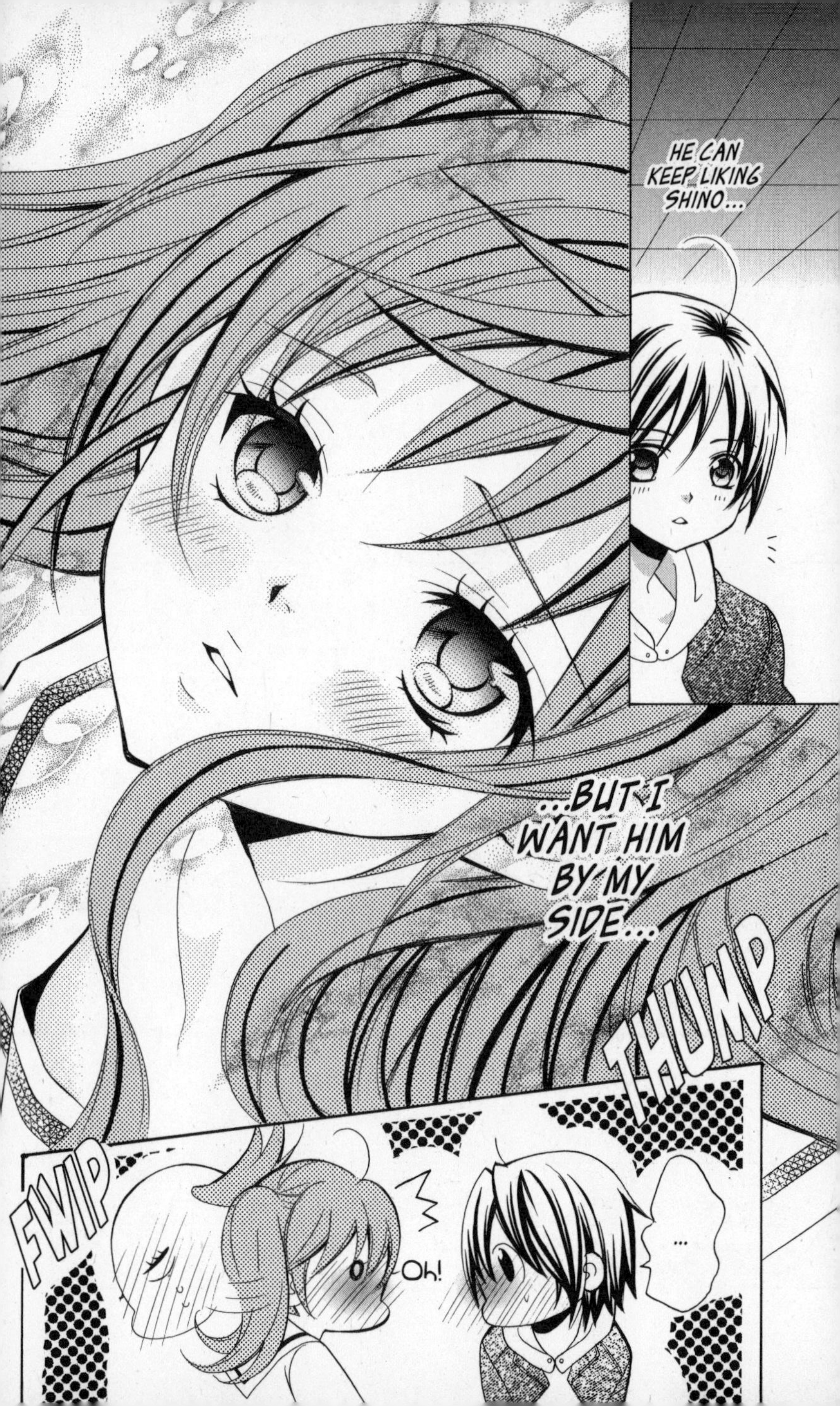

HE CAN KEEP LIKING SHINO...
...BUT I WANT HIM BY MY SIDE...
THUMP
...
Oh!
FWIP

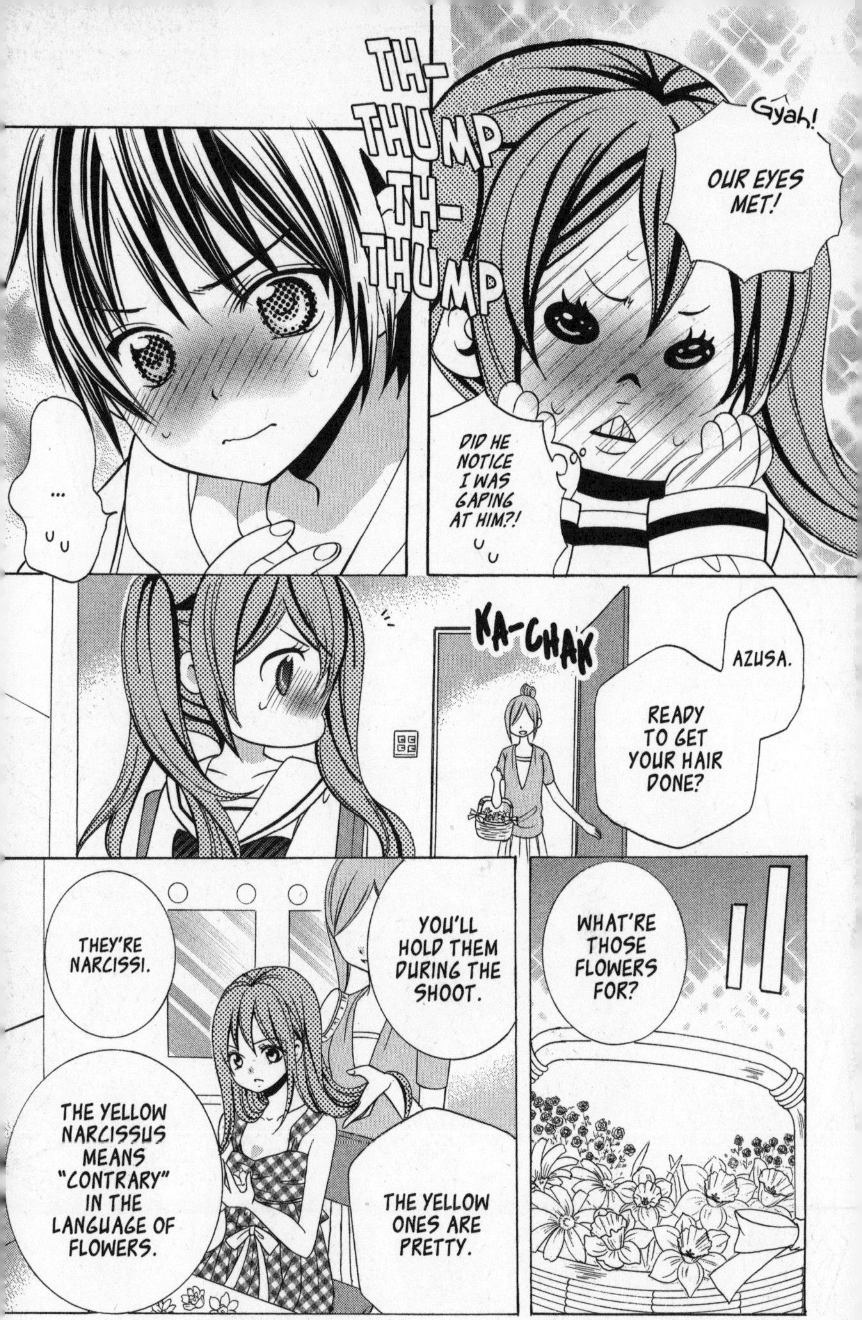
TH-THUMP TH-THUMP
Gyah!
OUR EYES MET!
DID HE NOTICE I WAS GAPING AT HIM?!
...
KA-CHAK
AZUSA.
READY TO GET YOUR HAIR DONE?
WHAT'RE THOSE FLOWERS FOR?
YOU'LL HOLD THEM DURING THE SHOOT.
THEY'RE NARCISSI.
THE YELLOW ONES ARE PRETTY.
THE YELLOW NARCISSUS MEANS "CONTRARY" IN THE LANGUAGE OF FLOWERS.

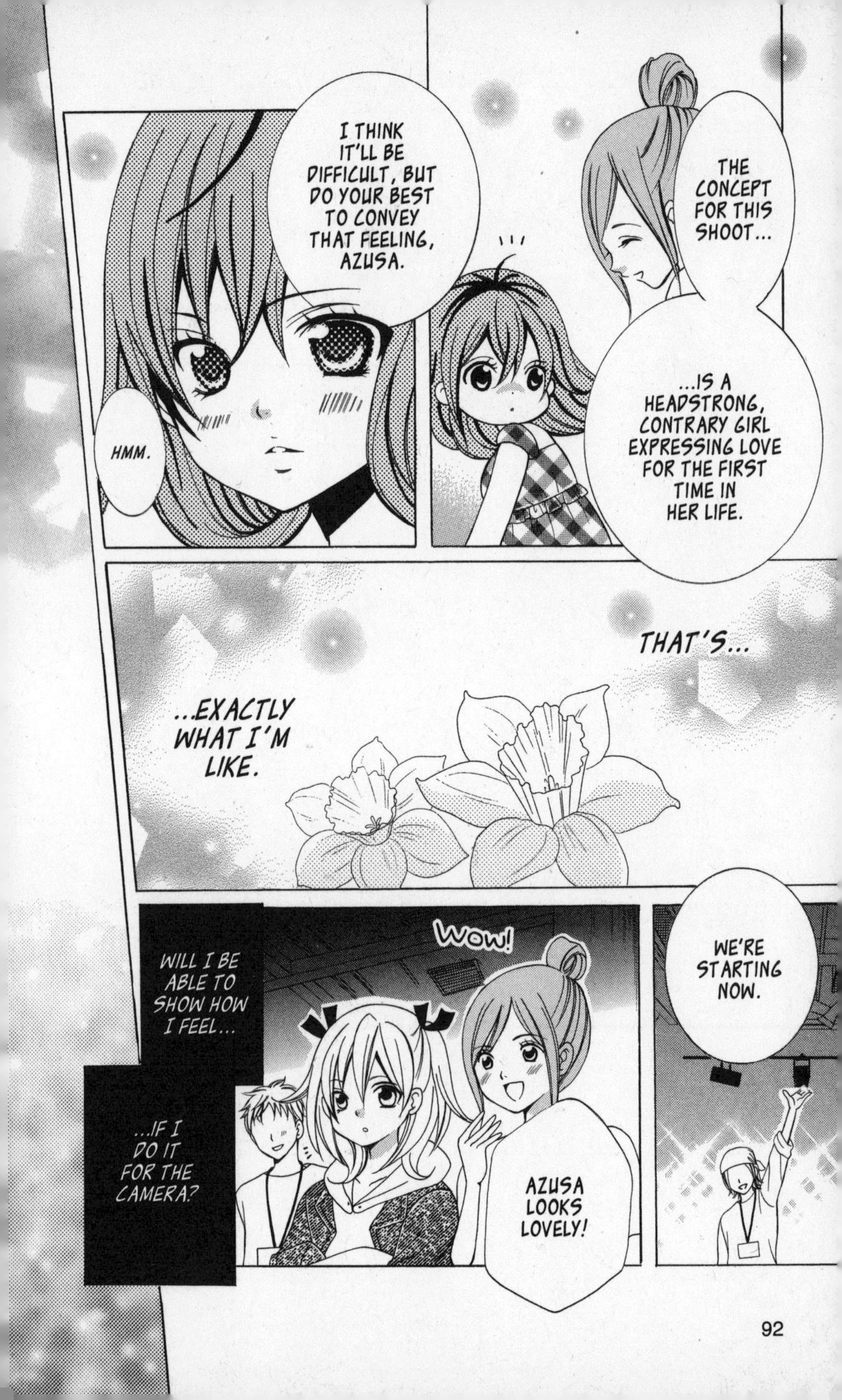
THE CONCEPT FOR THIS SHOOT...
...IS A HEADSTRONG, CONTRARY GIRL EXPRESSING LOVE FOR THE FIRST TIME IN HER LIFE.
I THINK IT'LL BE DIFFICULT, BUT DO YOUR BEST TO CONVEY THAT FEELING, AZUSA.
HMM.
THAT'S...
...EXACTLY WHAT I'M LIKE.
WE'RE STARTING NOW.
WOW!
AZUSA LOOKS LOVELY!
WILL I BE ABLE TO SHOW HOW I FEEL...
...IF I DO IT FOR THE CAMERA?

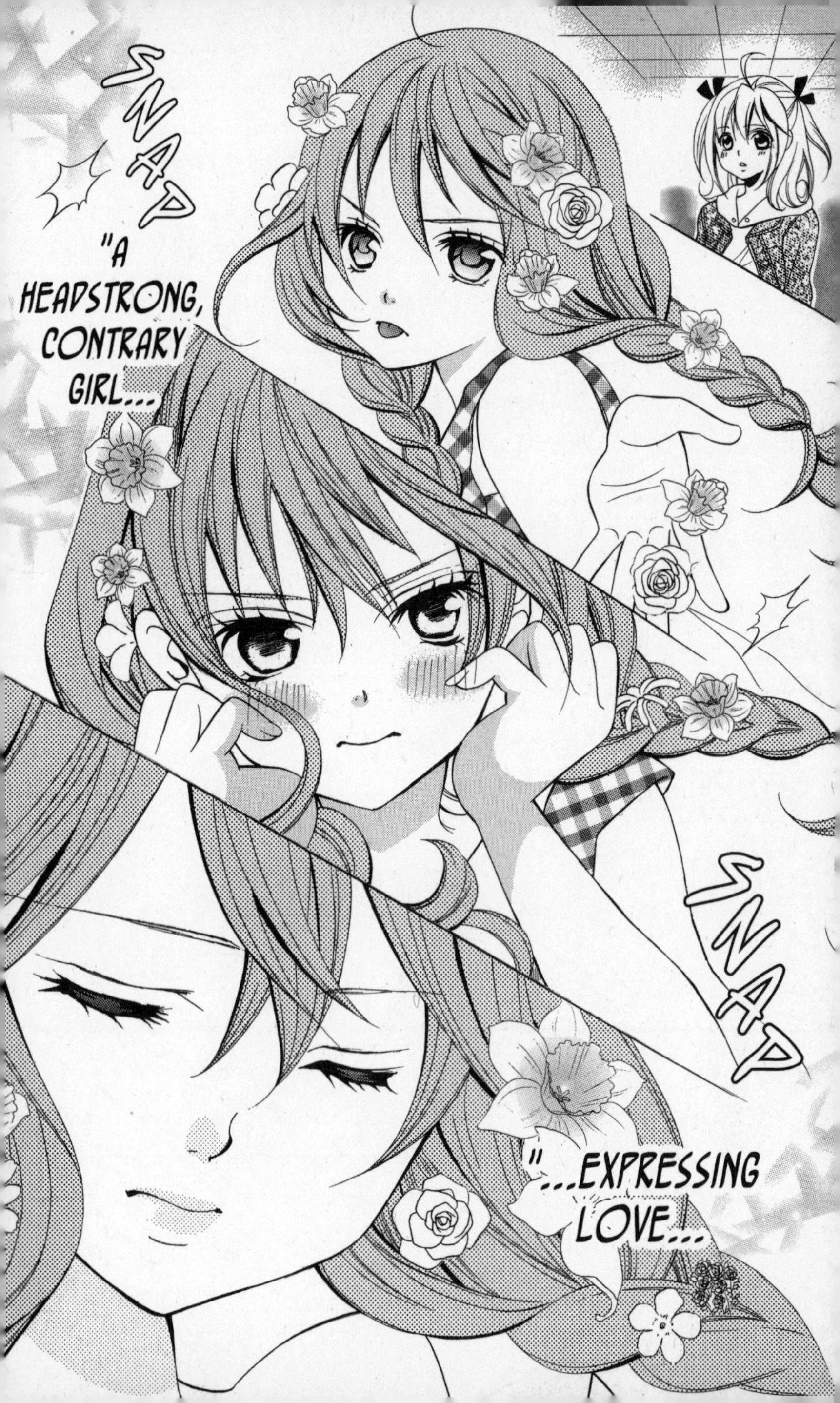
SNAP
"A HEADSTRONG, CONTRARY GIRL...
SNAP
"...EXPRESSING LOVE...

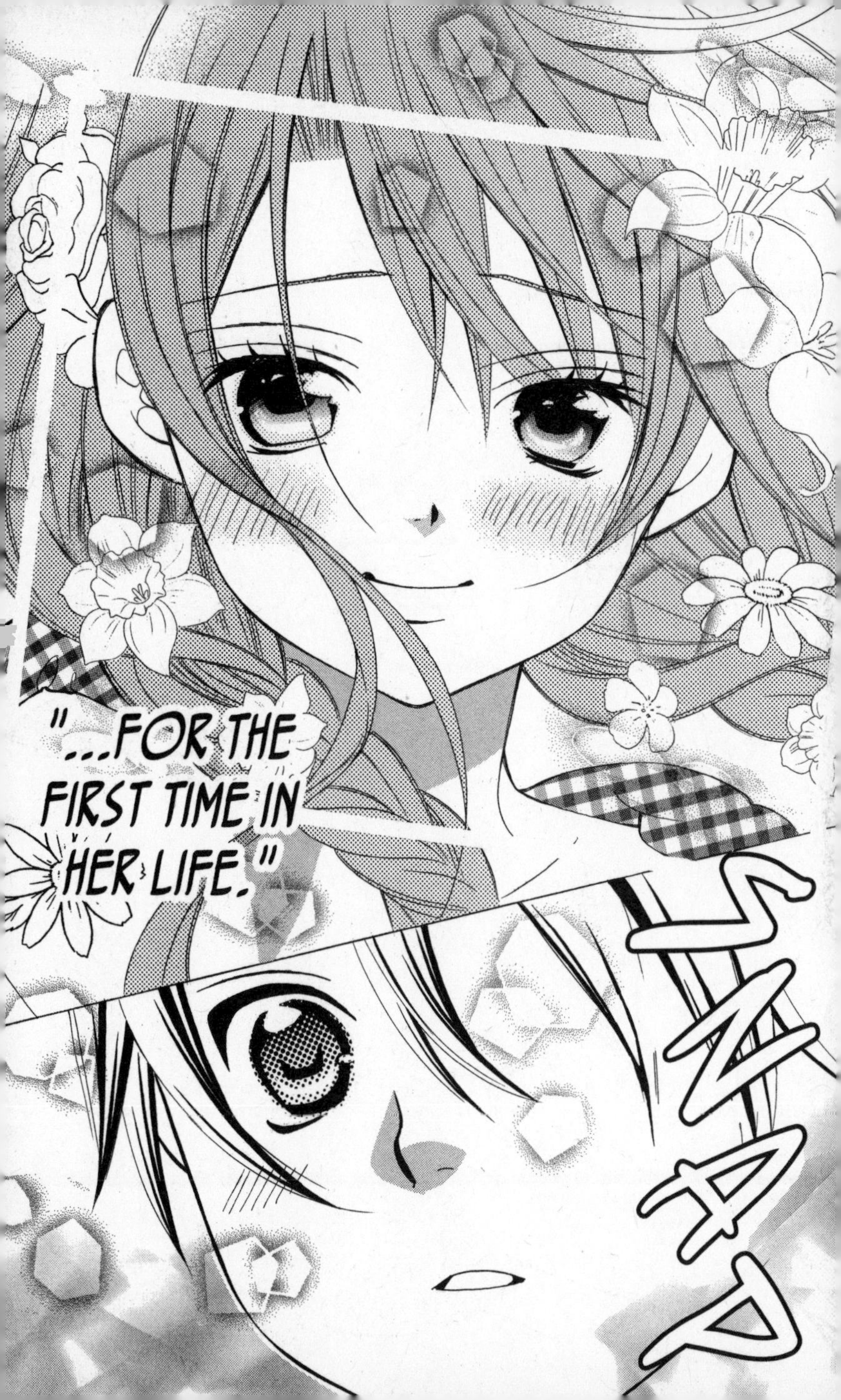
"...FOR THE FIRST TIME IN HER LIFE."
SNAP

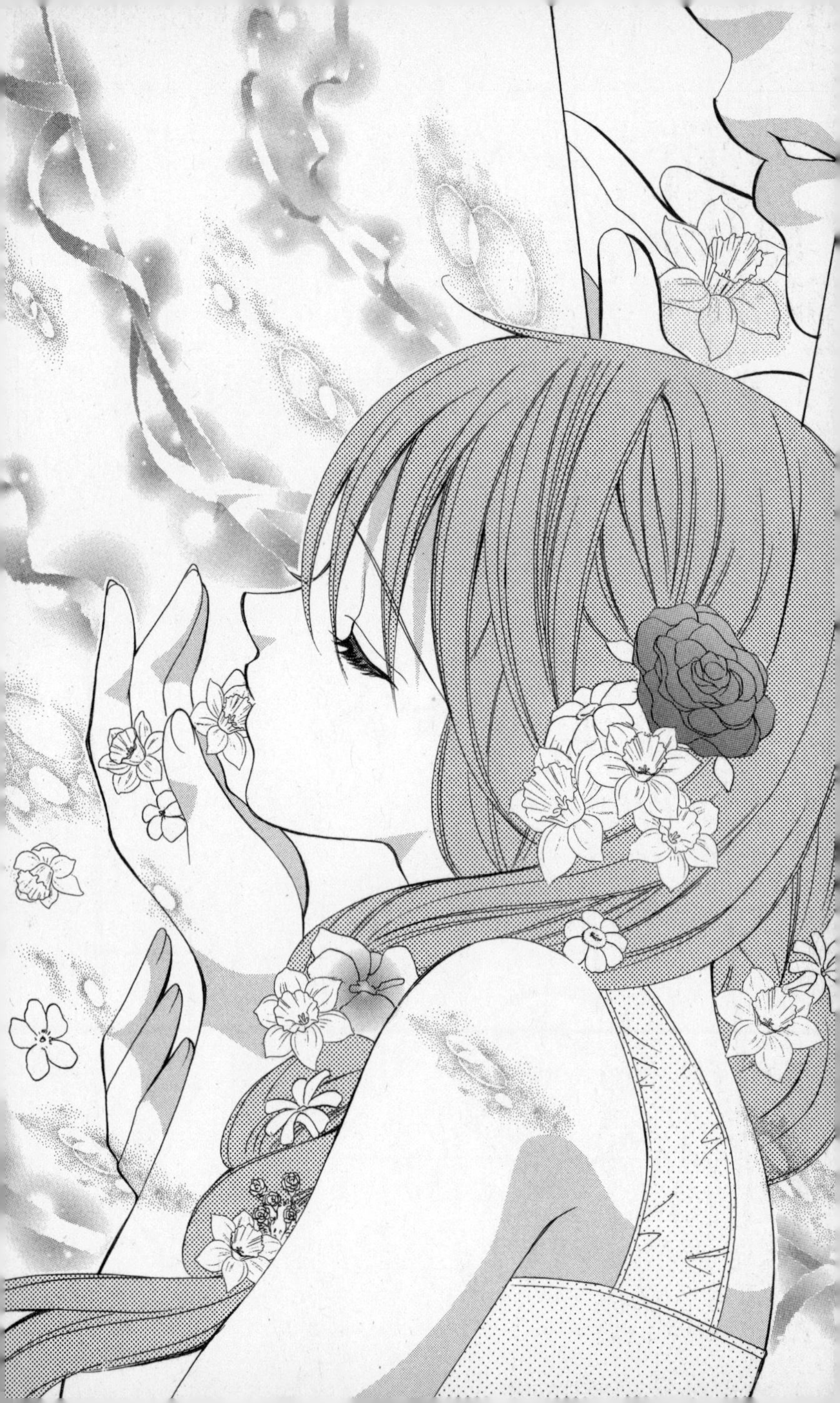

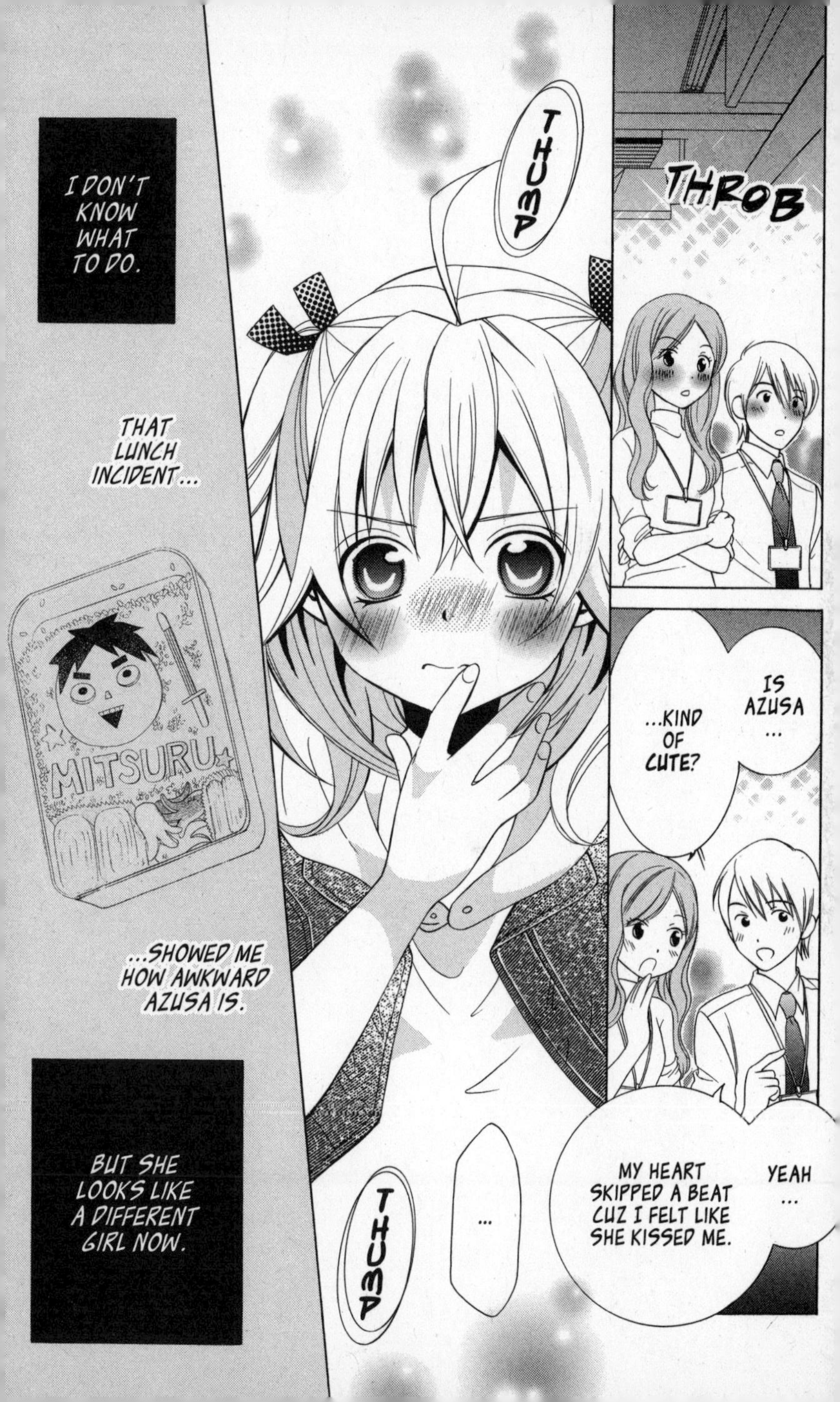
THROB
IS AZUSA ...
...KIND OF CUTE?
YEAH ...
MY HEART SKIPPED A BEAT CUZ I FELT LIKE SHE KISSED ME.
THUMP
...
THUMP
I DON'T KNOW WHAT TO DO.
THAT LUNCH INCIDENT ...
MITSURU
...SHOWED ME HOW AWKWARD AZUSA IS.
BUT SHE LOOKS LIKE A DIFFERENT GIRL NOW.

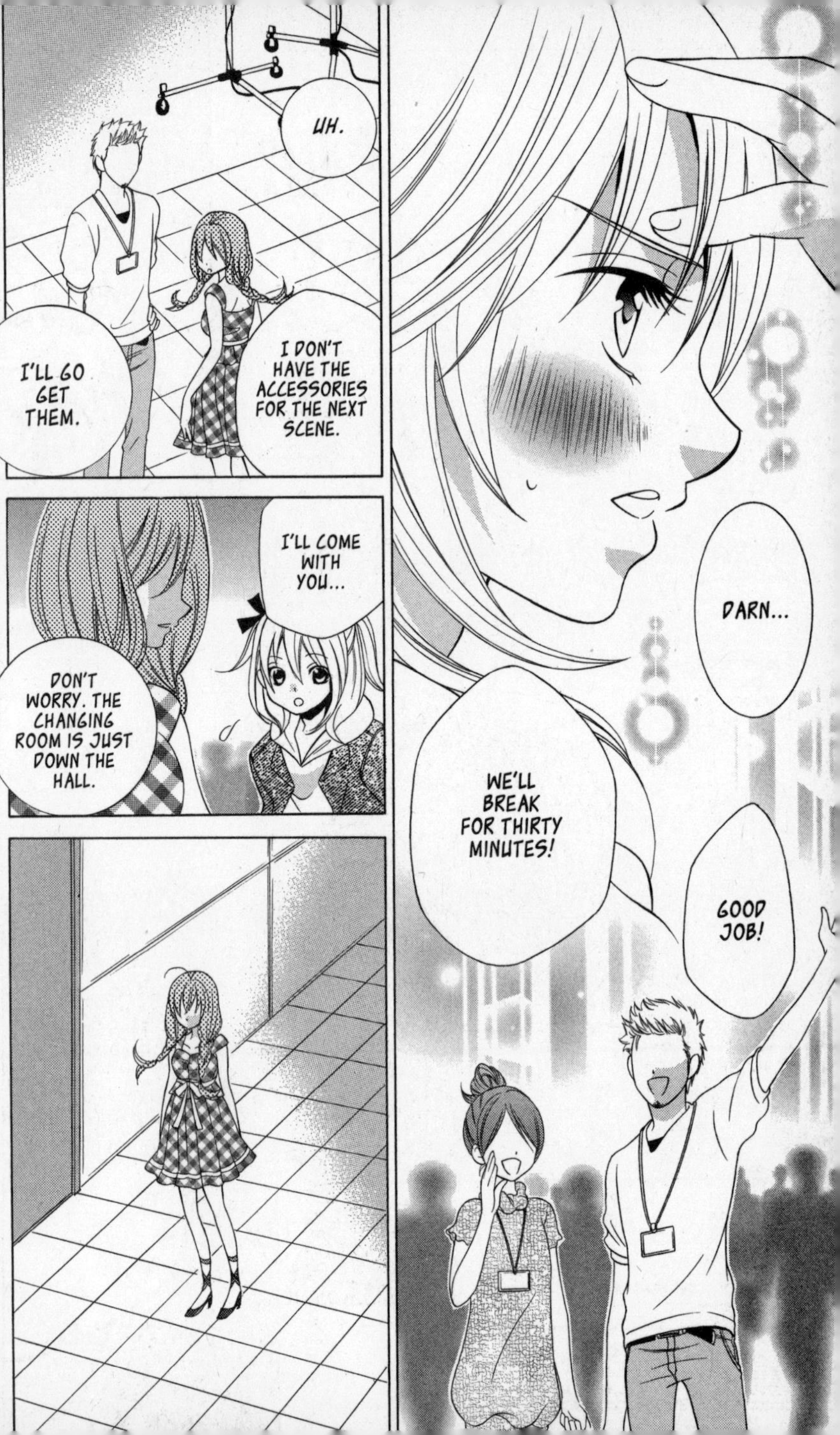
DARN...
GOOD JOB!
WE'LL BREAK FOR THIRTY MINUTES!
UH.
I DON'T HAVE THE ACCESSORIES FOR THE NEXT SCENE.
I'LL GO GET THEM.
I'LL COME WITH YOU...
DON'T WORRY. THE CHANGING ROOM IS JUST DOWN THE HALL.

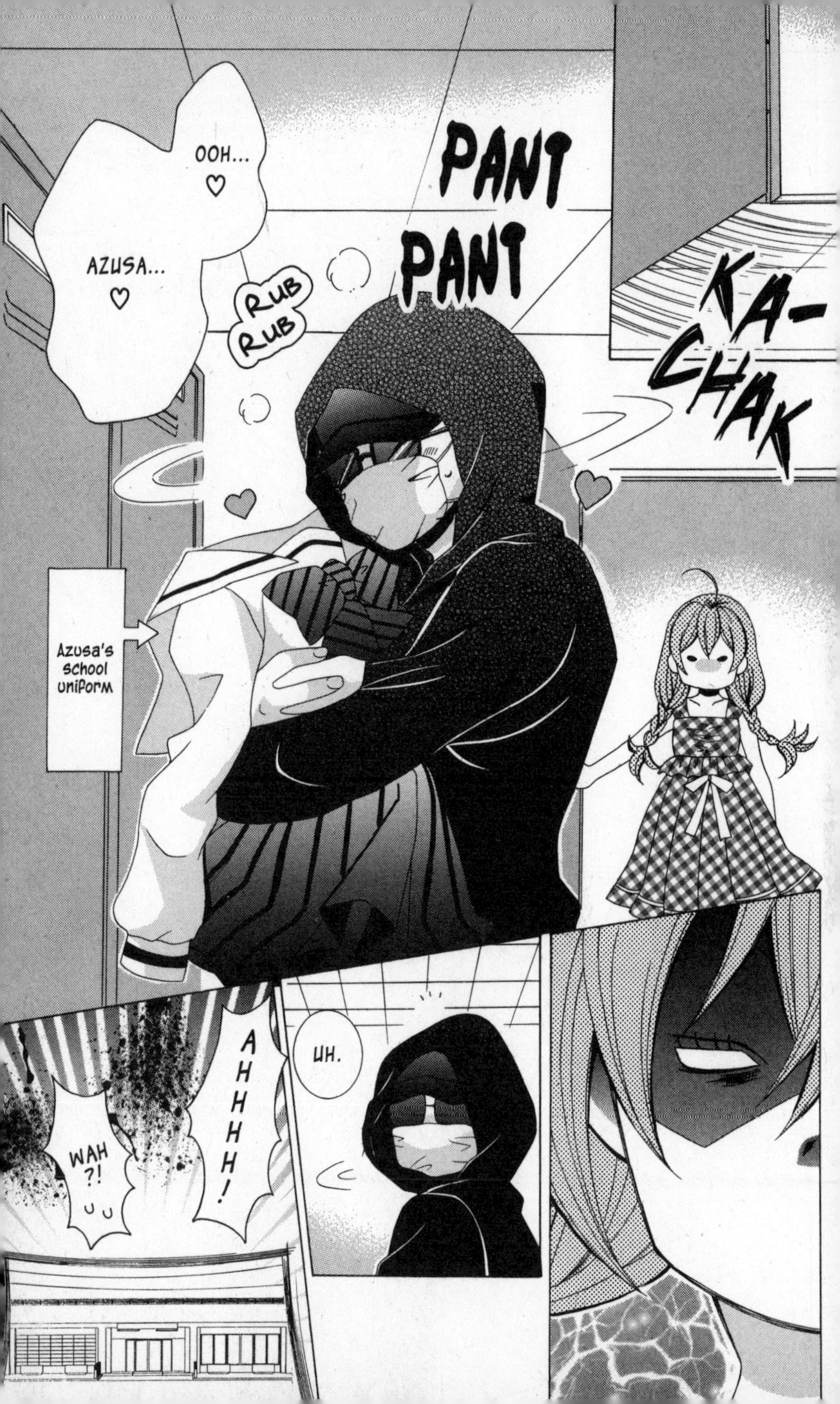

KA-CHAK
PANT PANT
RUB RUB
OOH... ♡
AZUSA... ♡
Azusa's school uniform
UH.
AHHHHH!
WAH?!

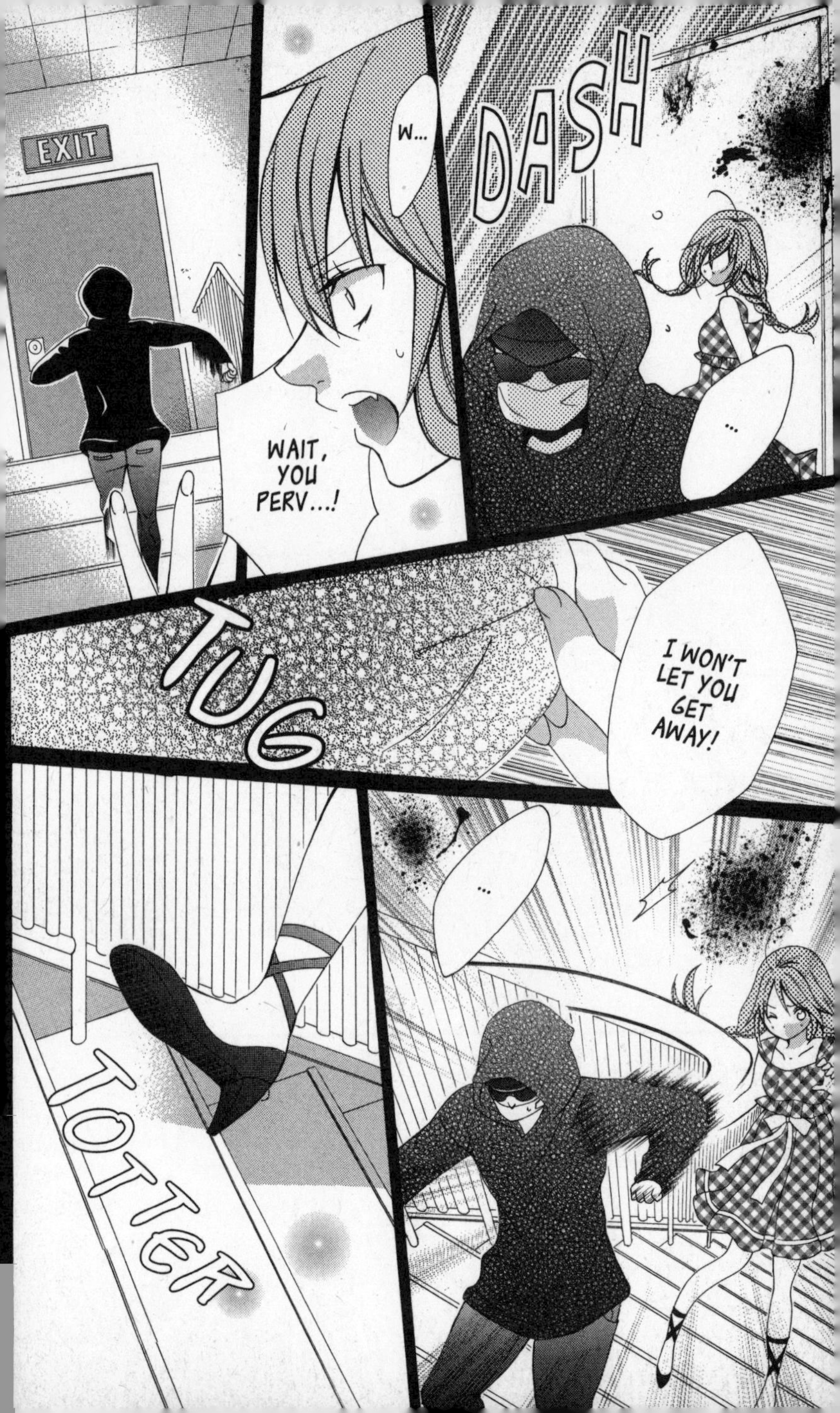
DASH
...
W...
WAIT, YOU PERV...!
EXIT
I WON'T LET YOU GET AWAY!
TUG
...
TOTTER

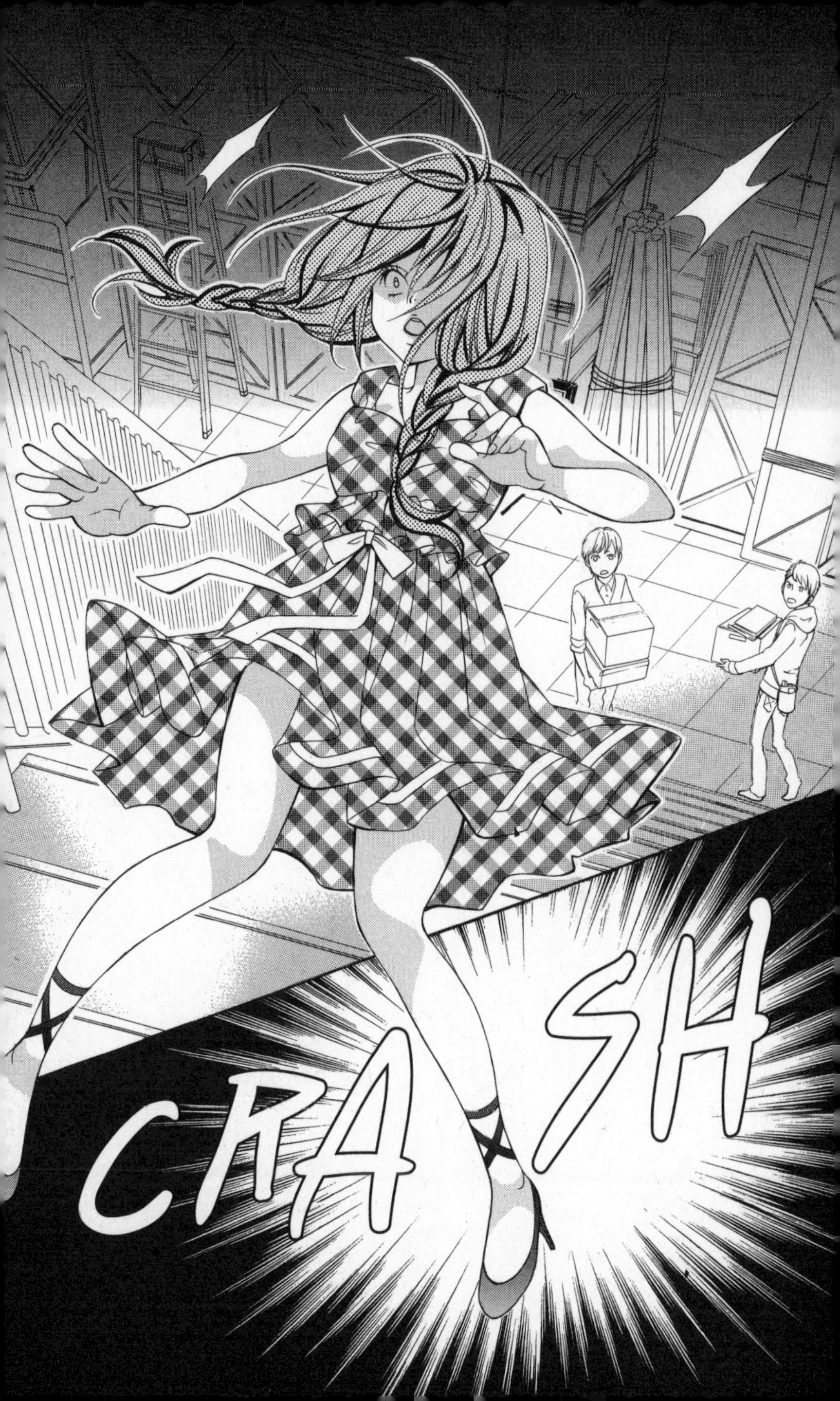
CRASH

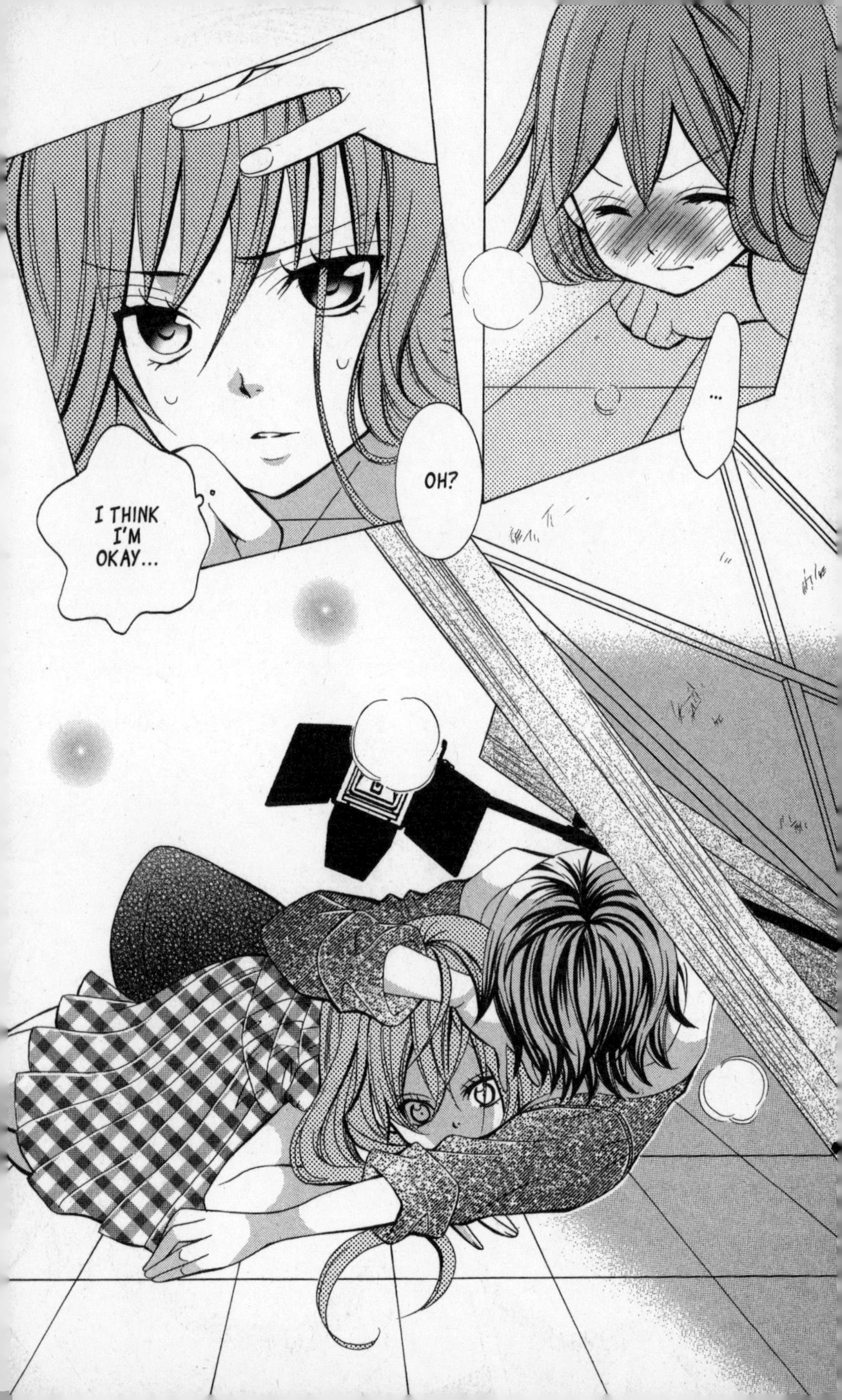
...
OH?
I THINK I'M OKAY...

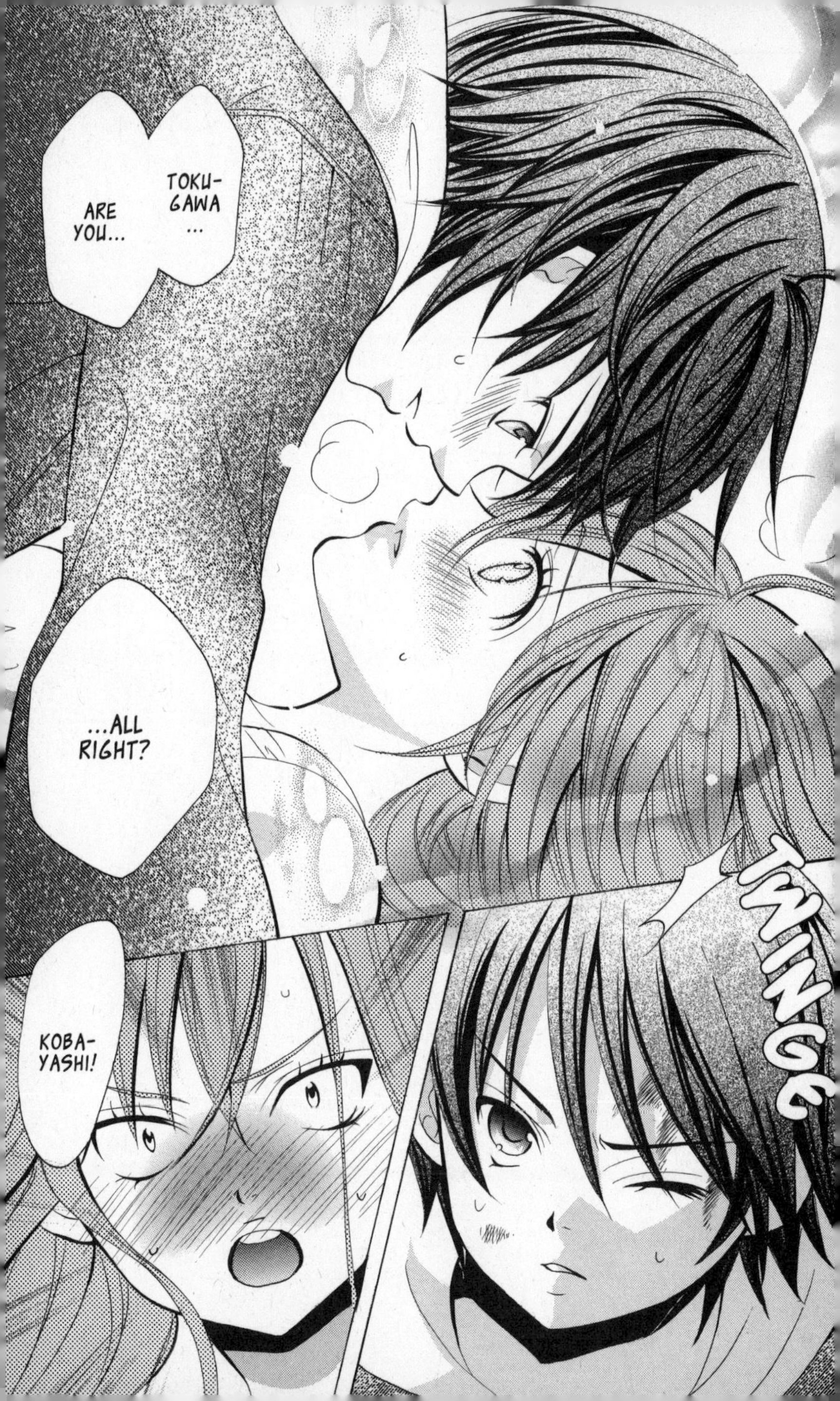
TOKU-GAWA...
ARE YOU...
...ALL RIGHT?
TWINGE
KOBA-YASHI!

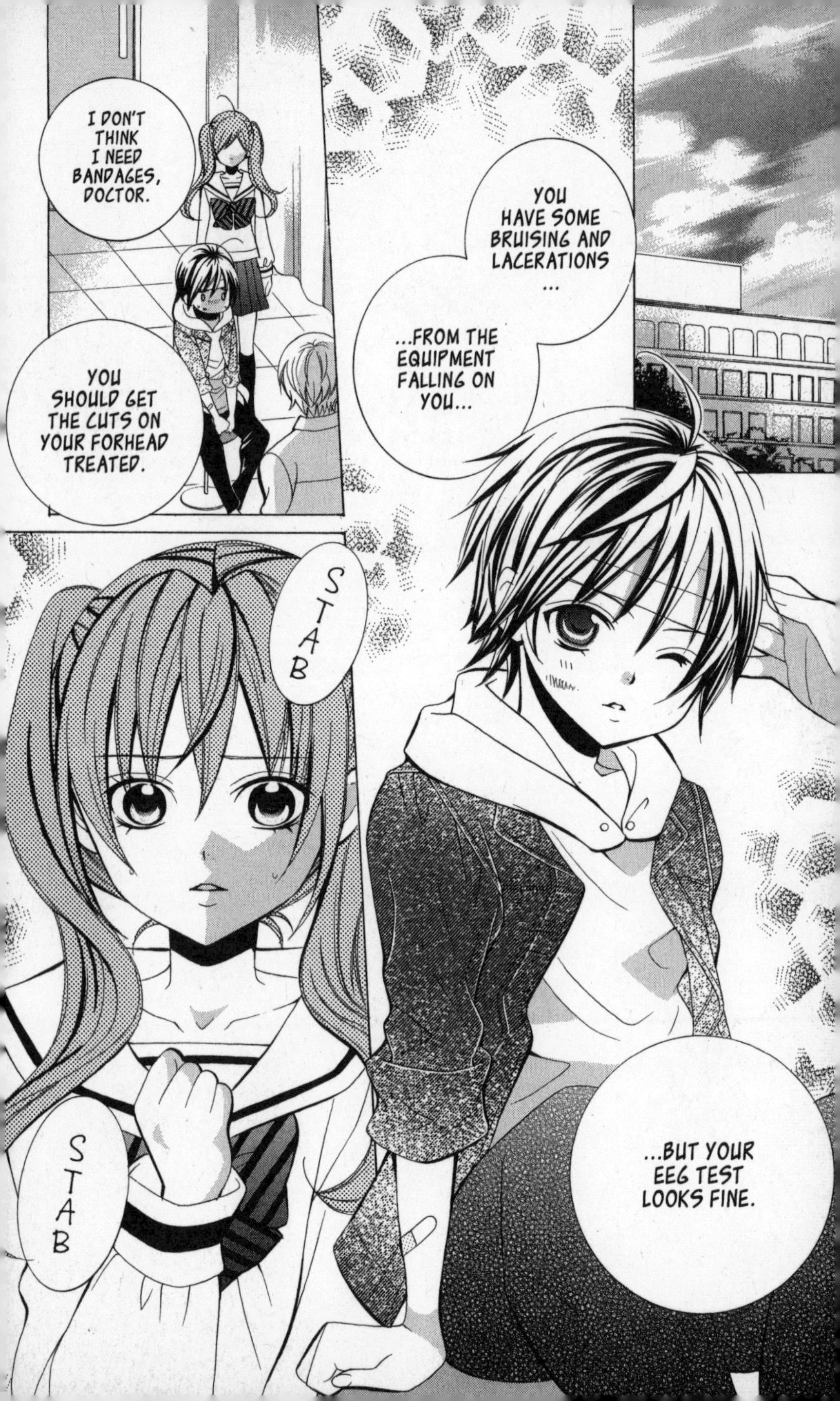
YOU HAVE SOME BRUISING AND LACERATIONS...
...FROM THE EQUIPMENT FALLING ON YOU...
...BUT YOUR EEG TEST LOOKS FINE.
I DON'T THINK I NEED BANDAGES, DOCTOR.
YOU SHOULD GET THE CUTS ON YOUR FORHEAD TREATED.
STAB
STAB

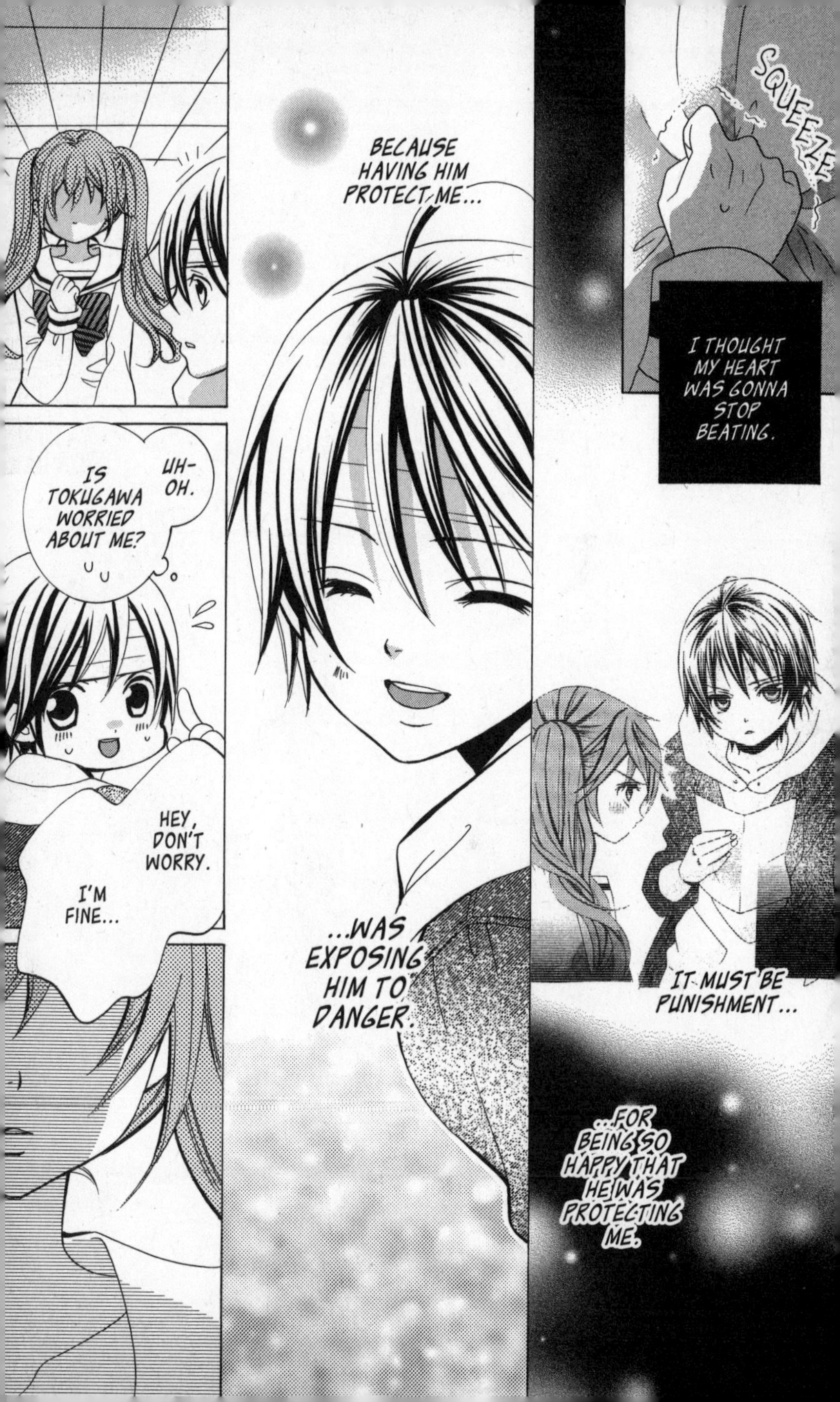
SQUEEZE
I THOUGHT MY HEART WAS GONNA STOP BEATING.
IT MUST BE PUNISHMENT...
...FOR BEING SO HAPPY THAT HE WAS PROTECTING ME.
BECAUSE HAVING HIM PROTECT ME...
...WAS EXPOSING HIM TO DANGER.
UH-OH.
IS TOKUGAWA WORRIED ABOUT ME?
HEY, DON'T WORRY.
I'M FINE...

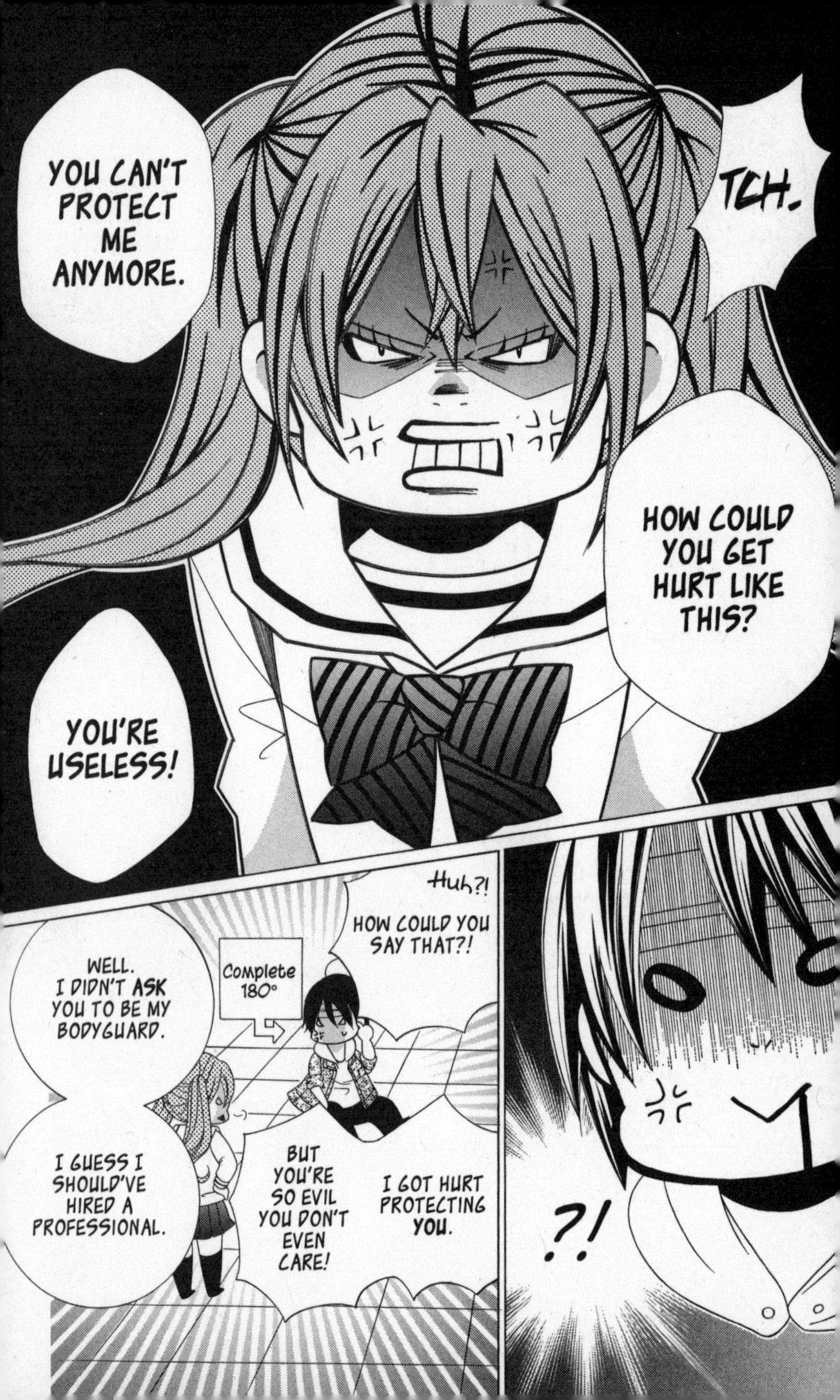
TCH.
HOW COULD YOU GET HURT LIKE THIS?
YOU CAN'T PROTECT ME ANYMORE.
YOU'RE USELESS!
?!
Huh?!
HOW COULD YOU SAY THAT?!
Complete 180°
I GOT HURT PROTECTING YOU.
BUT YOU'RE SO EVIL YOU DON'T EVEN CARE!
WELL. I DIDN'T ASK YOU TO BE MY BODYGUARD.
I GUESS I SHOULD'VE HIRED A PROFESSIONAL.

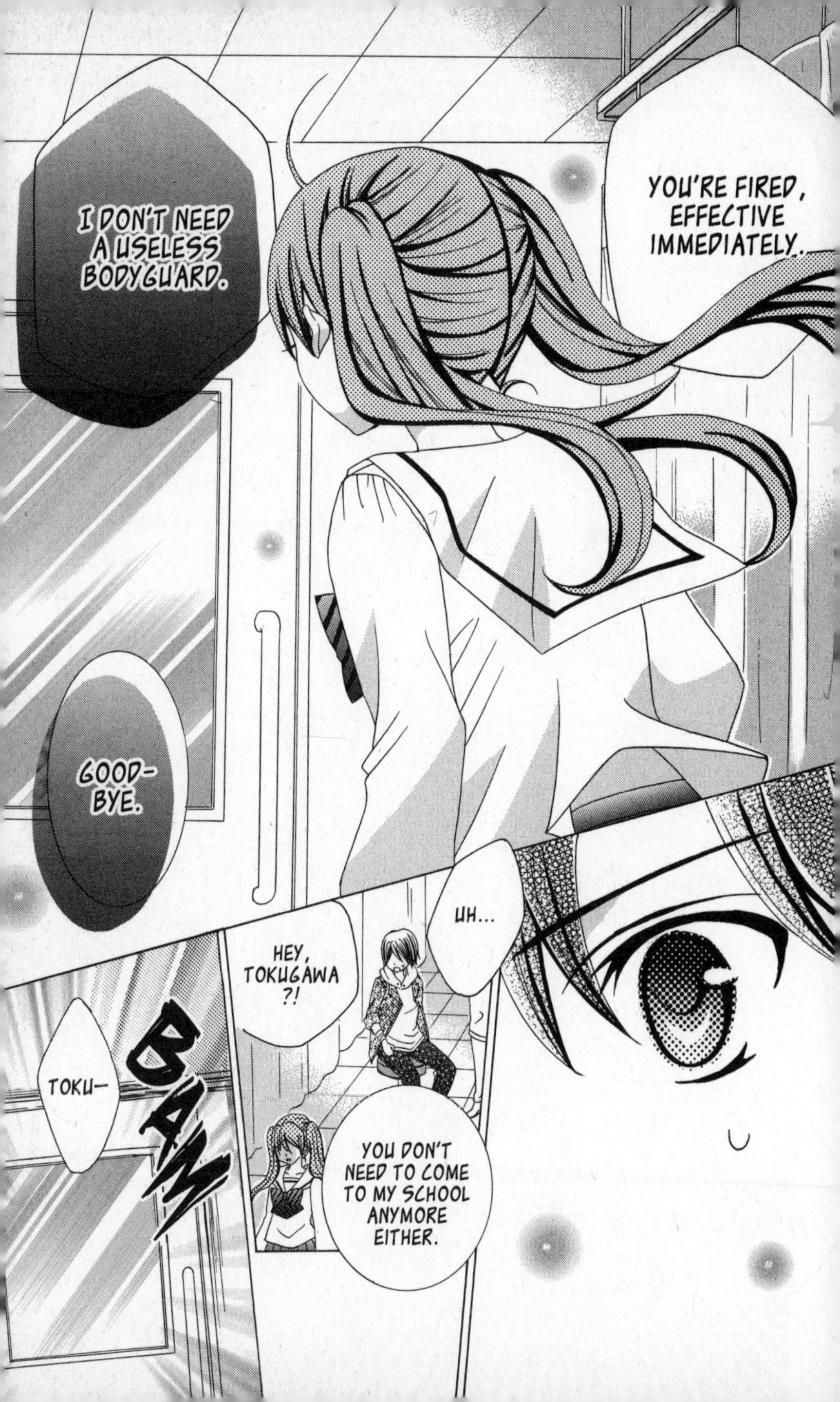
YOU'RE FIRED, EFFECTIVE IMMEDIATELY.
I DON'T NEED A USELESS BODYGUARD.
GOOD-BYE.
YOU DON'T NEED TO COME TO MY SCHOOL ANYMORE EITHER.
UH...
HEY, TOKUGAWA?!
TOKU-
BAM

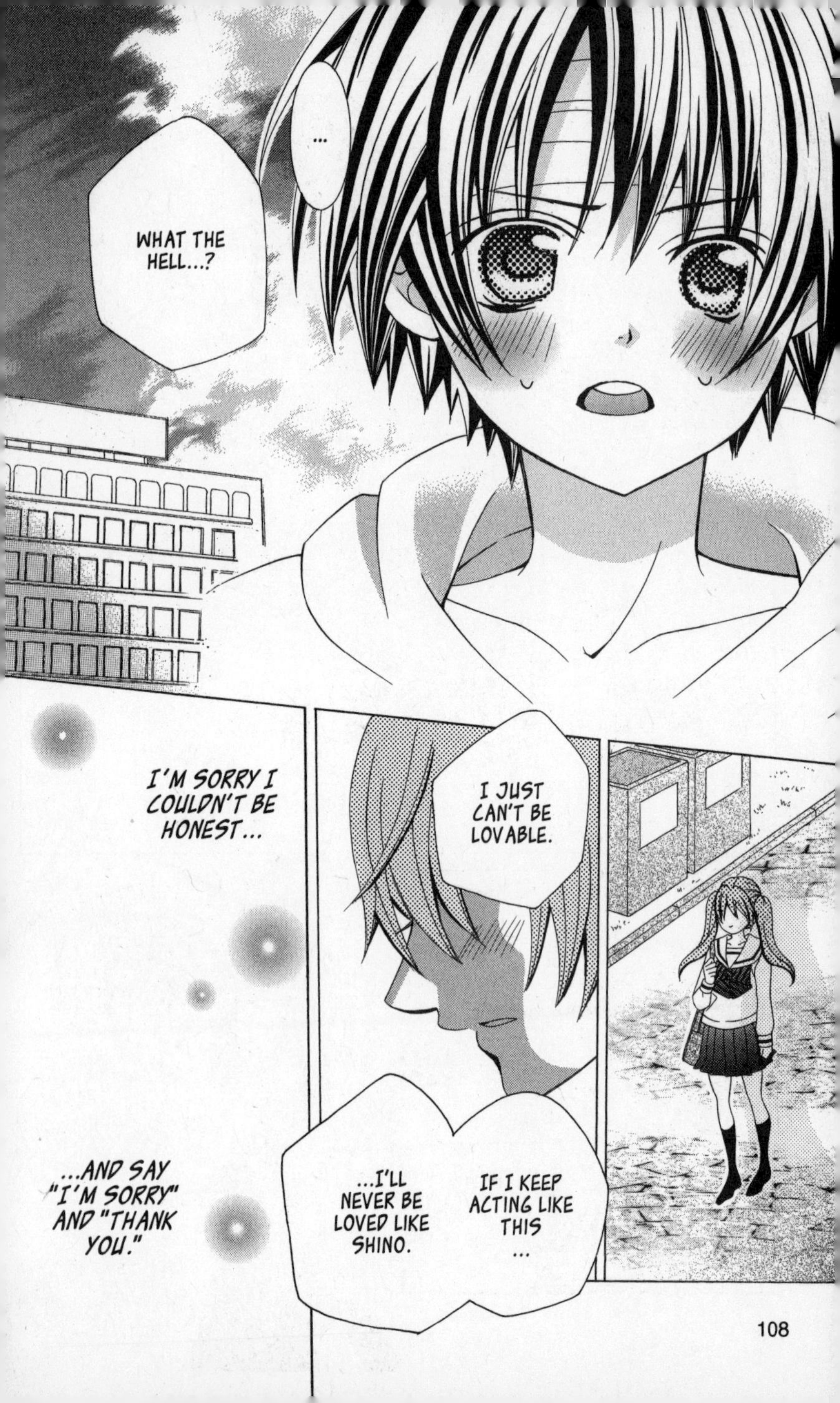
...
WHAT THE HELL...?
I JUST CAN'T BE LOVABLE.
IF I KEEP ACTING LIKE THIS ...
...I'LL NEVER BE LOVED LIKE SHINO.
I'M SORRY I COULDN'T BE HONEST...
...AND SAY "I'M SORRY" AND "THANK YOU."

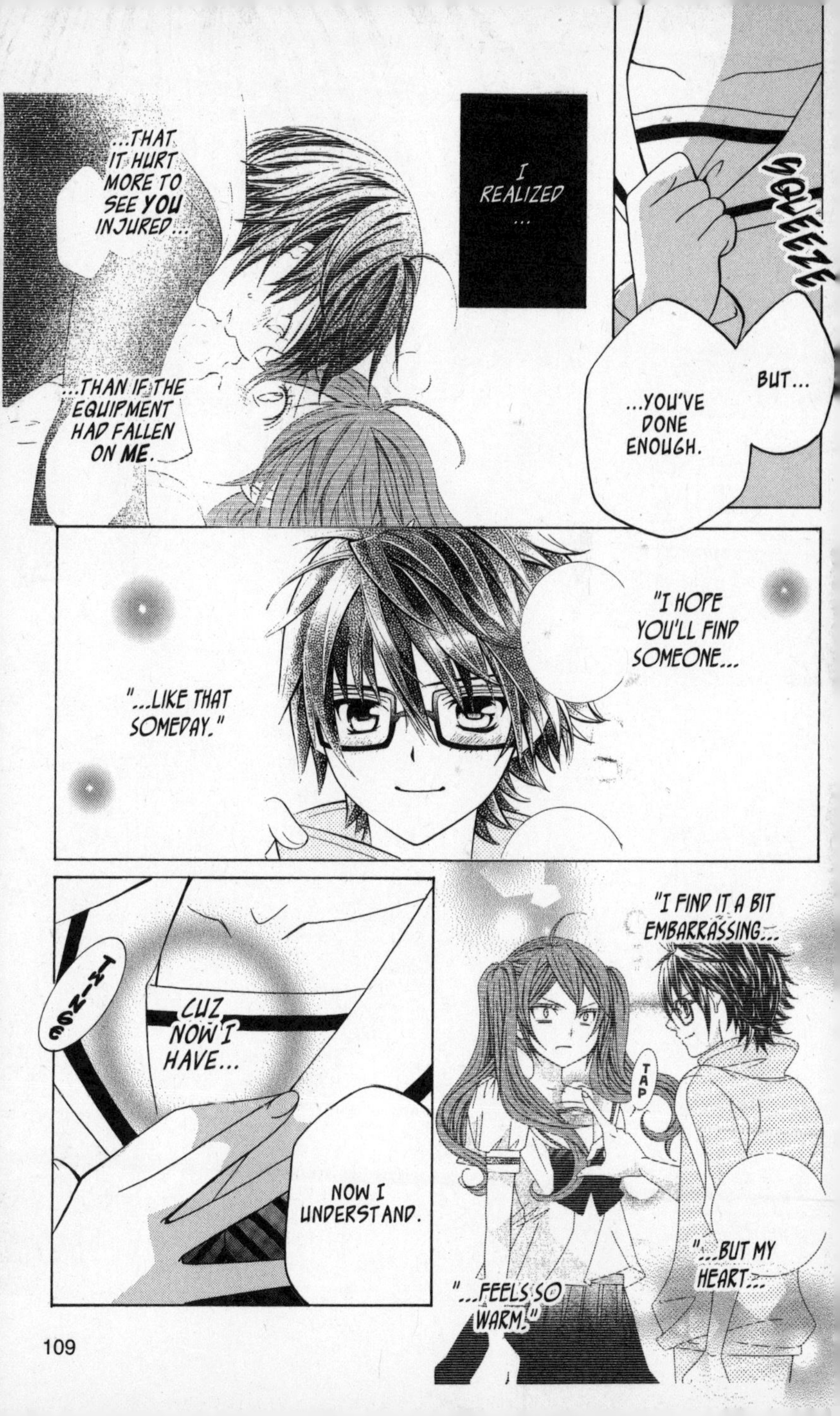
SQUEEZE
BUT...
...YOU'VE DONE ENOUGH.
I REALIZED ...
...THAT IT HURT MORE TO SEE YOU INJURED...
...THAN IF THE EQUIPMENT HAD FALLEN ON ME.
"I HOPE YOU'LL FIND SOMEONE...
"...LIKE THAT SOMEDAY."
"I FIND IT A BIT EMBARRASSING...
TAP
"...BUT MY HEART...
"...FEELS SO WARM."
TWINGE
CUZ NOW I HAVE...
NOW I UNDERSTAND.

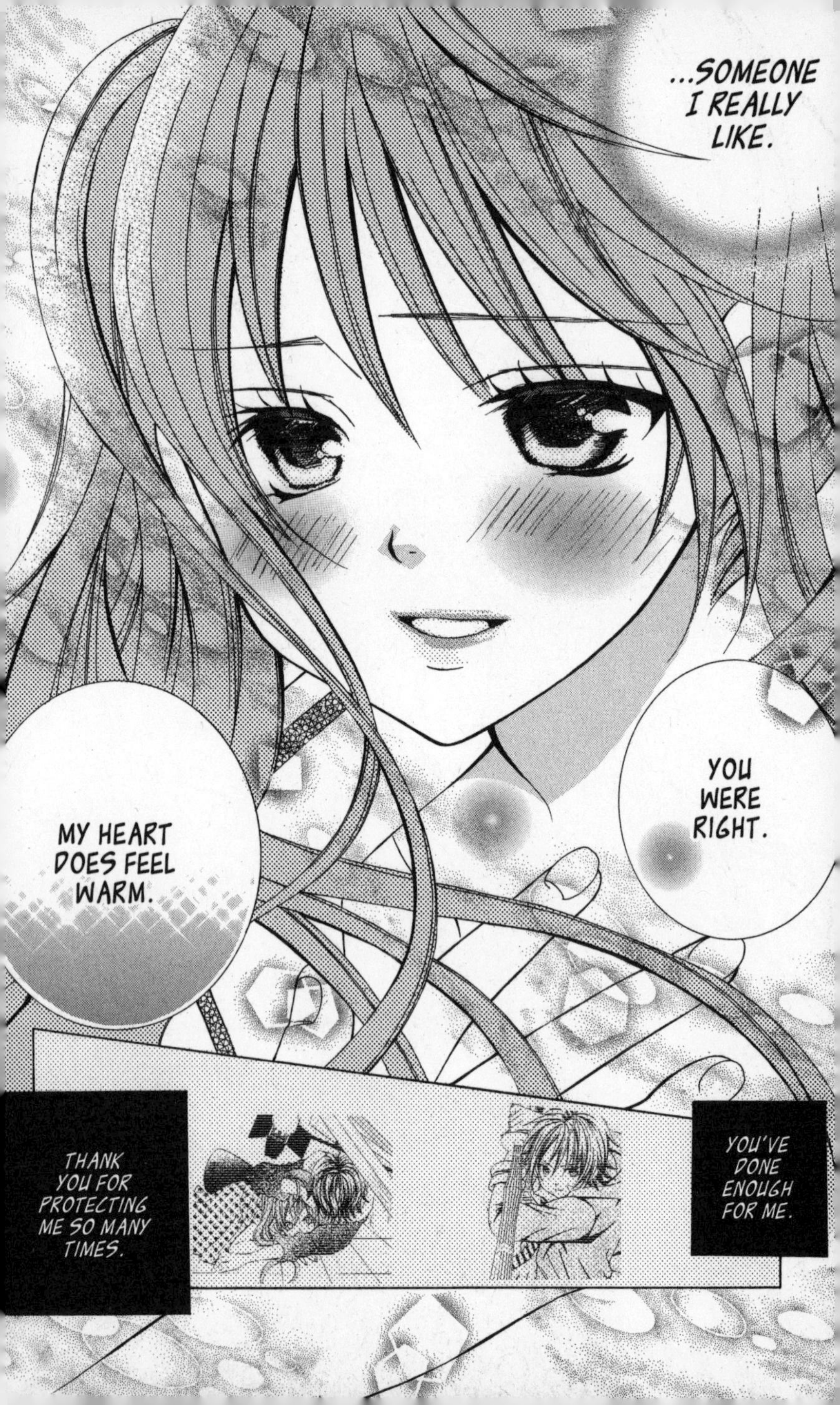
...SOMEONE I REALLY LIKE.
YOU WERE RIGHT.
MY HEART DOES FEEL WARM.
YOU'VE DONE ENOUGH FOR ME.
THANK YOU FOR PROTECTING ME SO MANY TIMES.

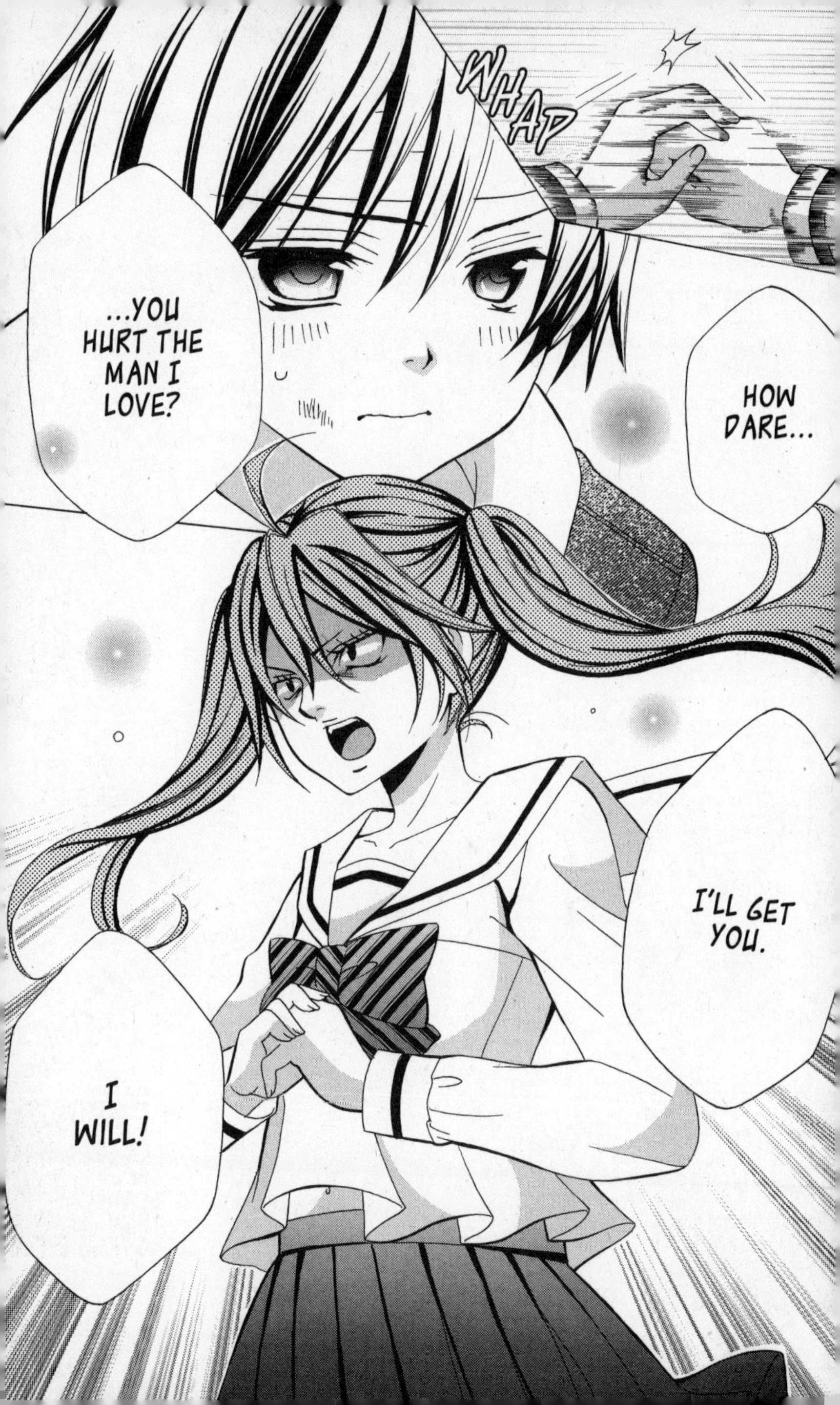
WHAP
HOW DARE...
...YOU HURT THE MAN I LOVE?
I'LL GET YOU.
I WILL!

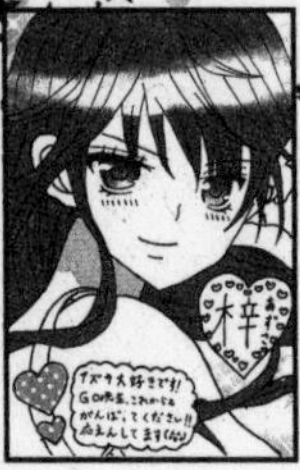
梓

Shiori Mori (Fukuoka)
Ed.: Azusa! You're beautiful... (sweats) ←

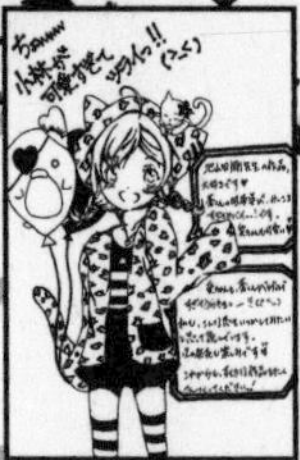

Ichigo Momo (Tochigi) ↑
Ed.: Leopard ears?! They're amazingly cute!!

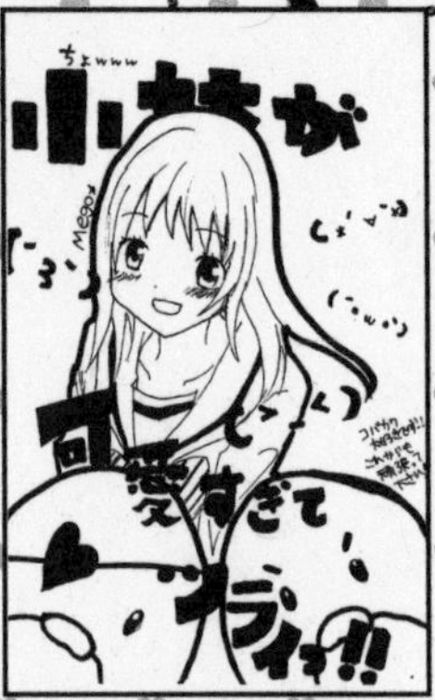
ちょwww
小林が
Mego
可愛すぎて
ツライ!!

Kona Terami (Osaka)
Ed.: Mego and the penguins make me smile!! →

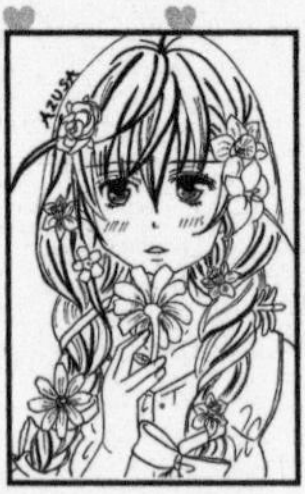
AZUSA

Manami Saito (Oita)
Ed.: Azusa has gotten more beautiful after she's fallen in love! ←

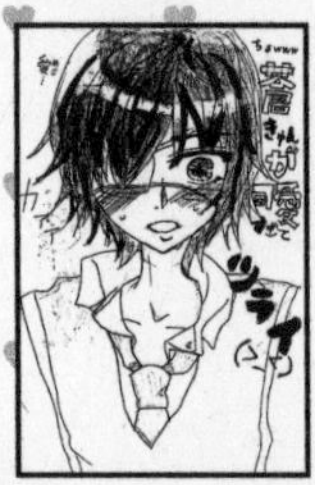
ちょwww
ツライ

Nyahorabii (Tokyo)
Ed.: Readers love Aoi's sweet face!! ←

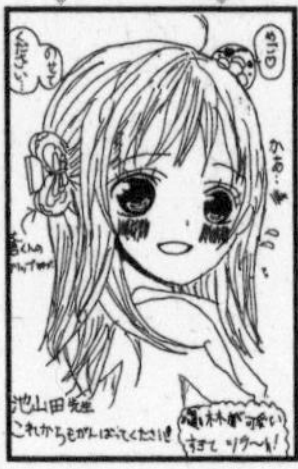

Hina Kouno (Saitama)
Ed.: A mature-looking Mego... is beautiful!! →

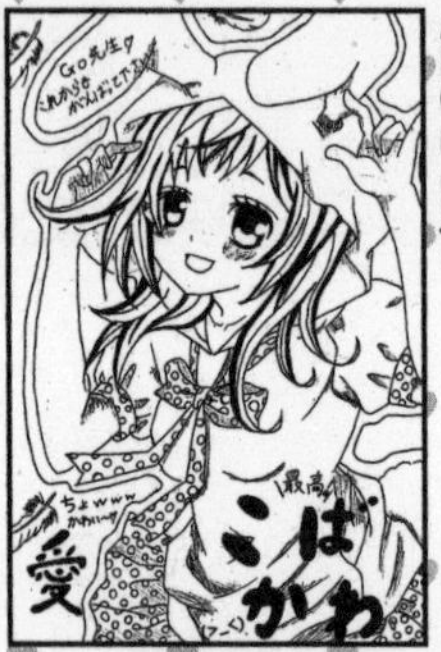
最高
こばかわ
愛

Mana Hattori (Gifu)
Ed.: Animal ears are justice!! ←

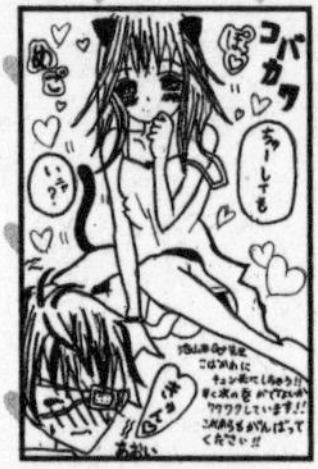
コバカワ

Kana Yamamoto (Okayama)
Ed.: Mego's gonna kill me with her cat ears!! ←

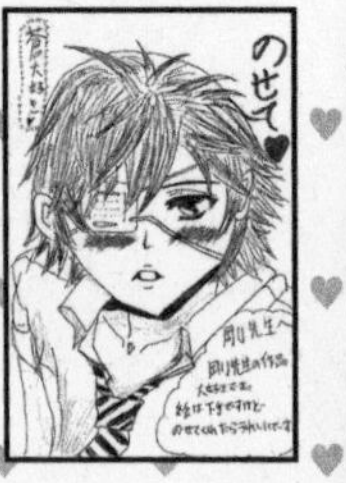
のせて♥

Yuichigo☆ (Okayama)
Ed.: Aoi with crimson cheeks... My nose is gonna bleed... →

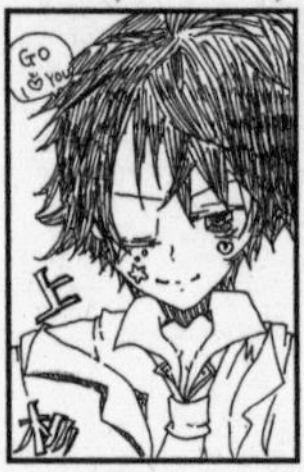
GO
上

Hana Takeda (Niigata)
Ed.: I was waiting for Uesugi!! ←

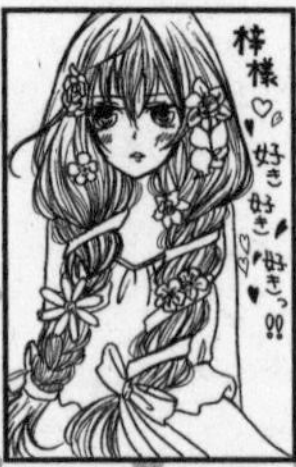
梓様♡
好き
好き
好きっ!!

Yukie Tada (Aichi) ↑
Ed.: This drawing is full of Azusa's charms!!

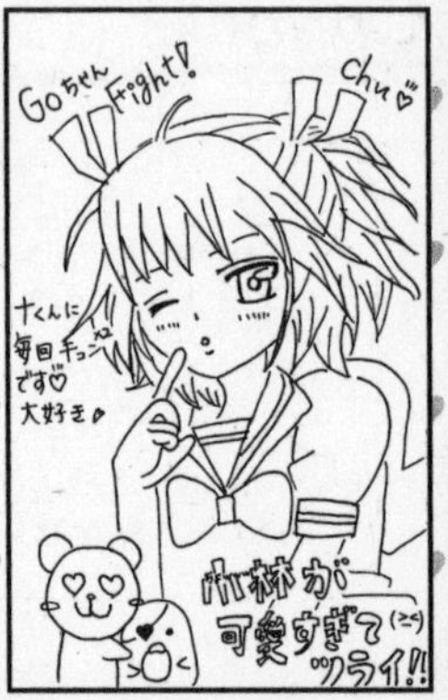
Goちゃん Fight!
Chu♡
十くんに
毎回キュン♡です♡
大好き♪
小林が
可愛すぎて(こ)
ツライ!!

Yuika Uchida (Saitama)
Ed.: This is a classic! →

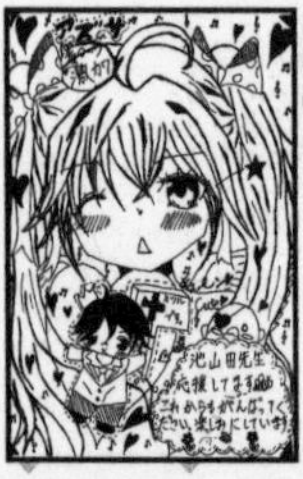

Hana Suzuki (Tochigi)
Ed.: Azusa is cute!! ←

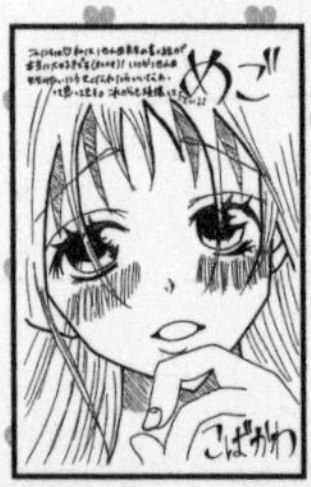
めご
こばかわ

Fuuna Iwai (Osaka)
Ed.: Mego's pretty and makes my heart thump! ←

Chapter 39

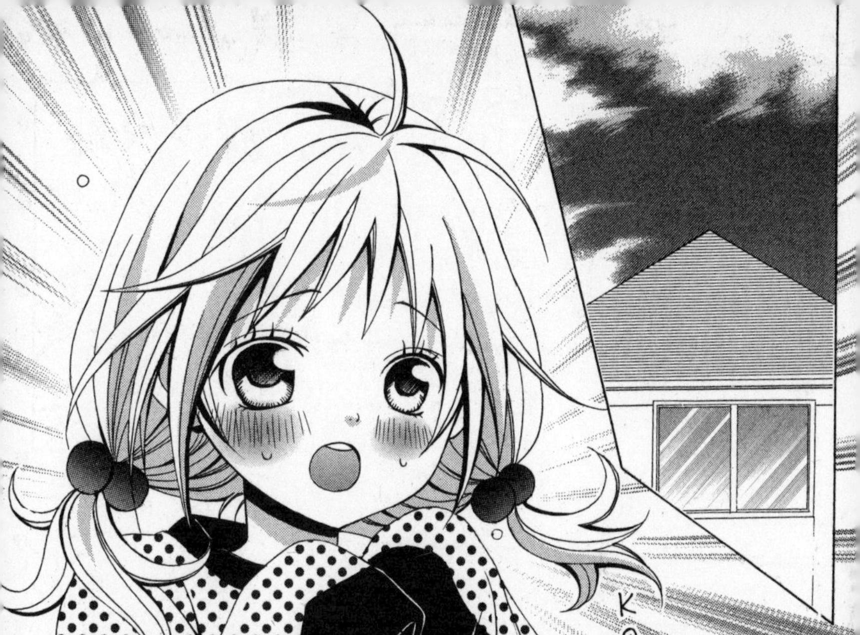
KOFF
MITSURU ?!
WHAT HAPPENED TO YOU?!

THE *HAIKYU!!* ANIME WAS SO PASSIONATE! KAGEYAMA-KUN AND OIKAWA-SAN WERE SO COOL...! I WASN'T SURE WHO I SHOULD ROOT FOR IN THE END. (>_<) I ENJOY THE *SEVEN DEADLY SINS* ANIME TOO! I LOVE THE MANGA, SO I'M IMPRESSED BY THE QUALITY OF THE ANIME WITH THE BEAUTIFUL DRAWINGS AND MUSIC. ♡♡

I'LL MISS *VANGUARD*, SINCE THE ANIME SEEMS TO BE ENDING SOON. (>_<) WILL KAI-KUN GRADUATE FROM HIGH SCHOOL? I'M LOOKING FORWARD TO THE NEW SERIES BECAUSE I THINK THE GROWN-UP VERSION OF AICHI-KUN AND COMPANY WILL APPEAR! I HOPE KAI-KUN HAS TURNED INTO A GOOD-LOOKING GUY! (*SMILE*)

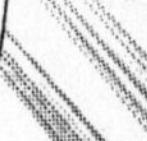

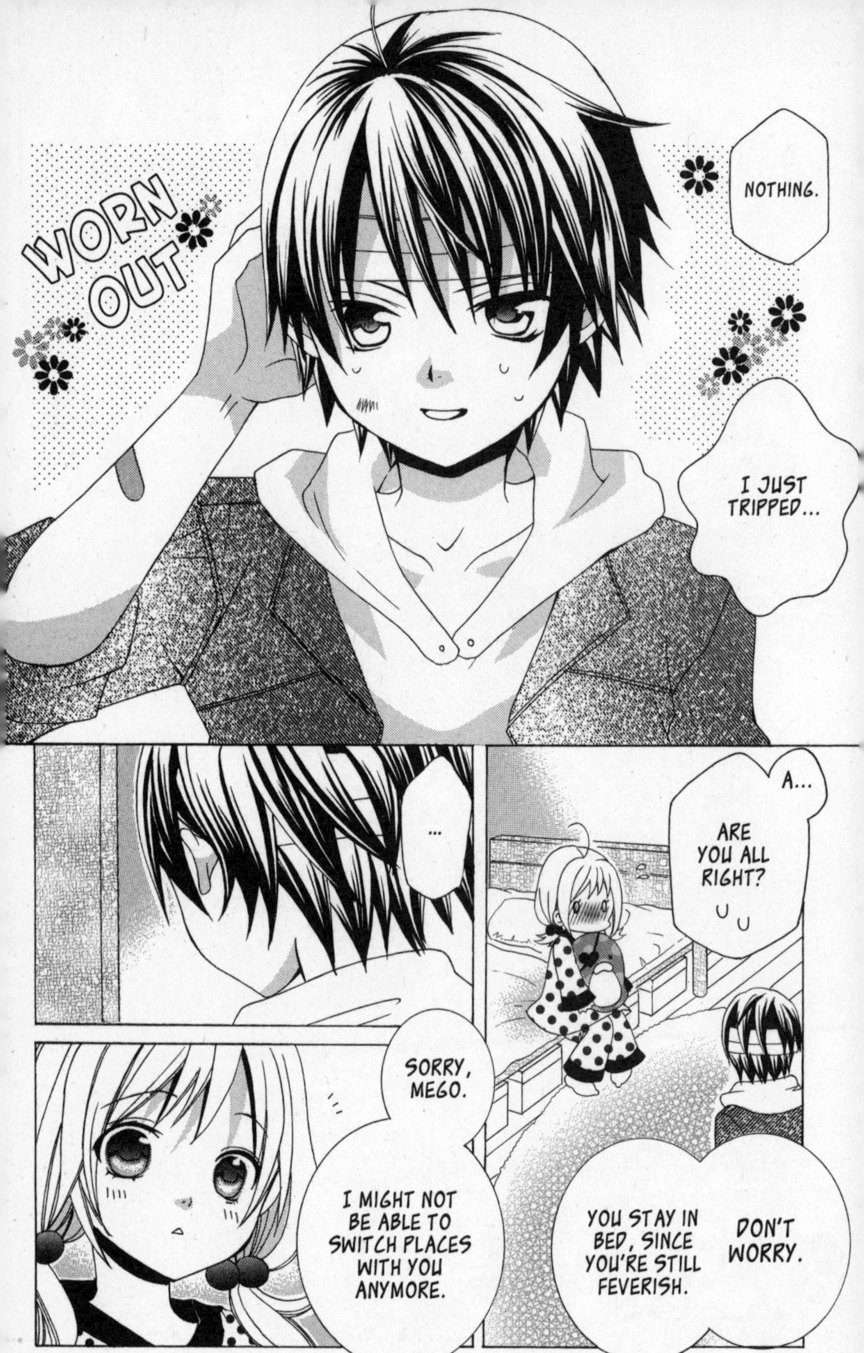
NOTHING.
WORN OUT
I JUST TRIPPED...
A...
ARE YOU ALL RIGHT?
DON'T WORRY.
YOU STAY IN BED, SINCE YOU'RE STILL FEVERISH.
...
SORRY, MEGO.
I MIGHT NOT BE ABLE TO SWITCH PLACES WITH YOU ANYMORE.

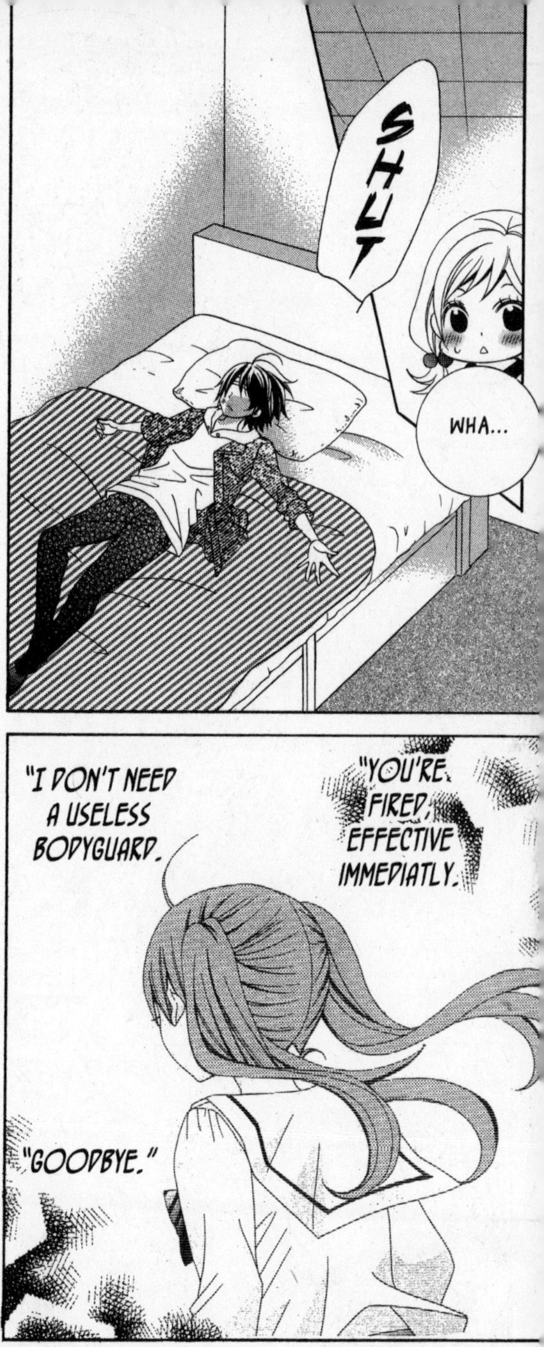
SHUT
WHA...
"YOU'RE FIRED, EFFECTIVE IMMEDIATLY.
"I DON'T NEED A USELESS BODYGUARD.
"GOODBYE."

So Cute It Hurts!!

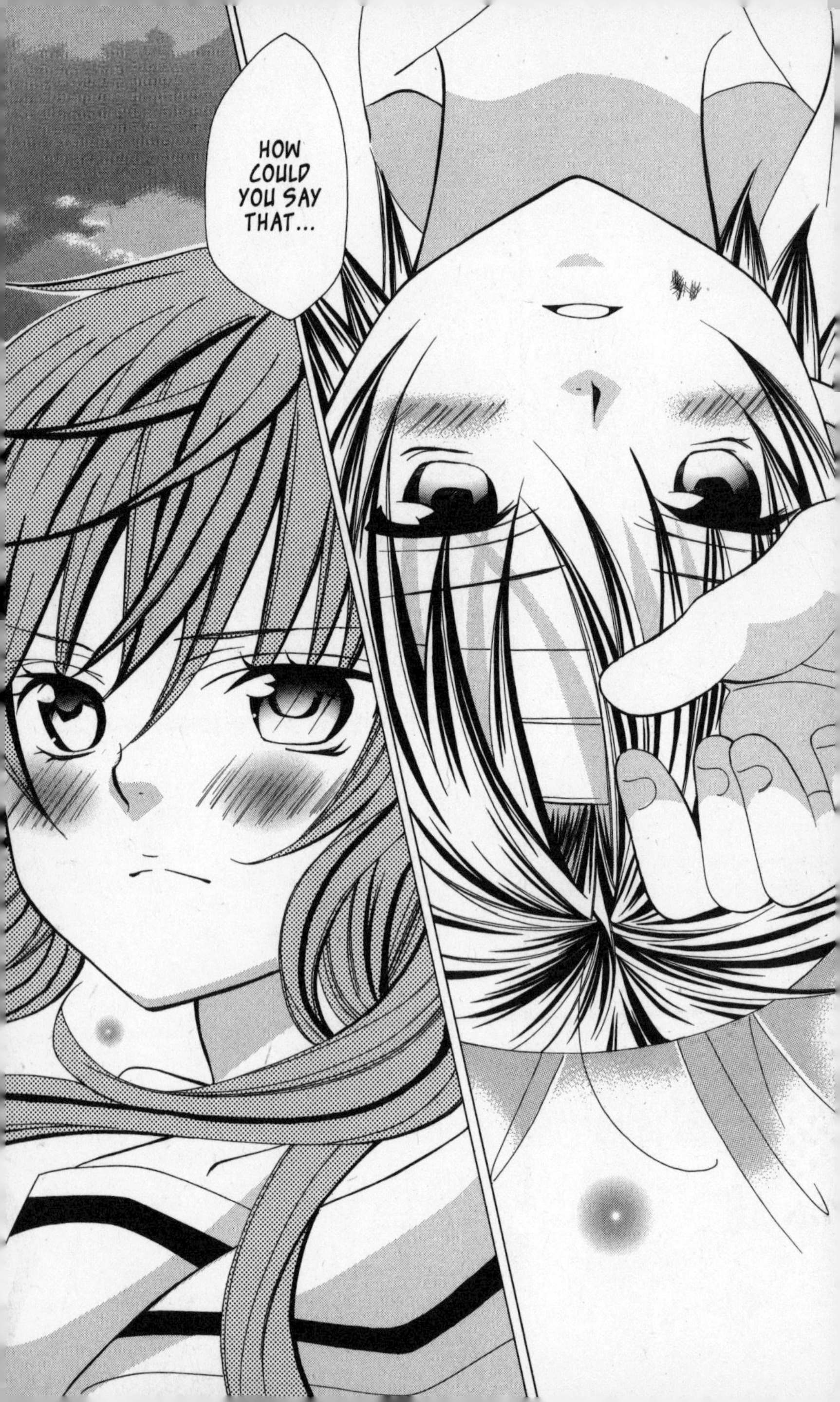
HOW COULD YOU SAY THAT...

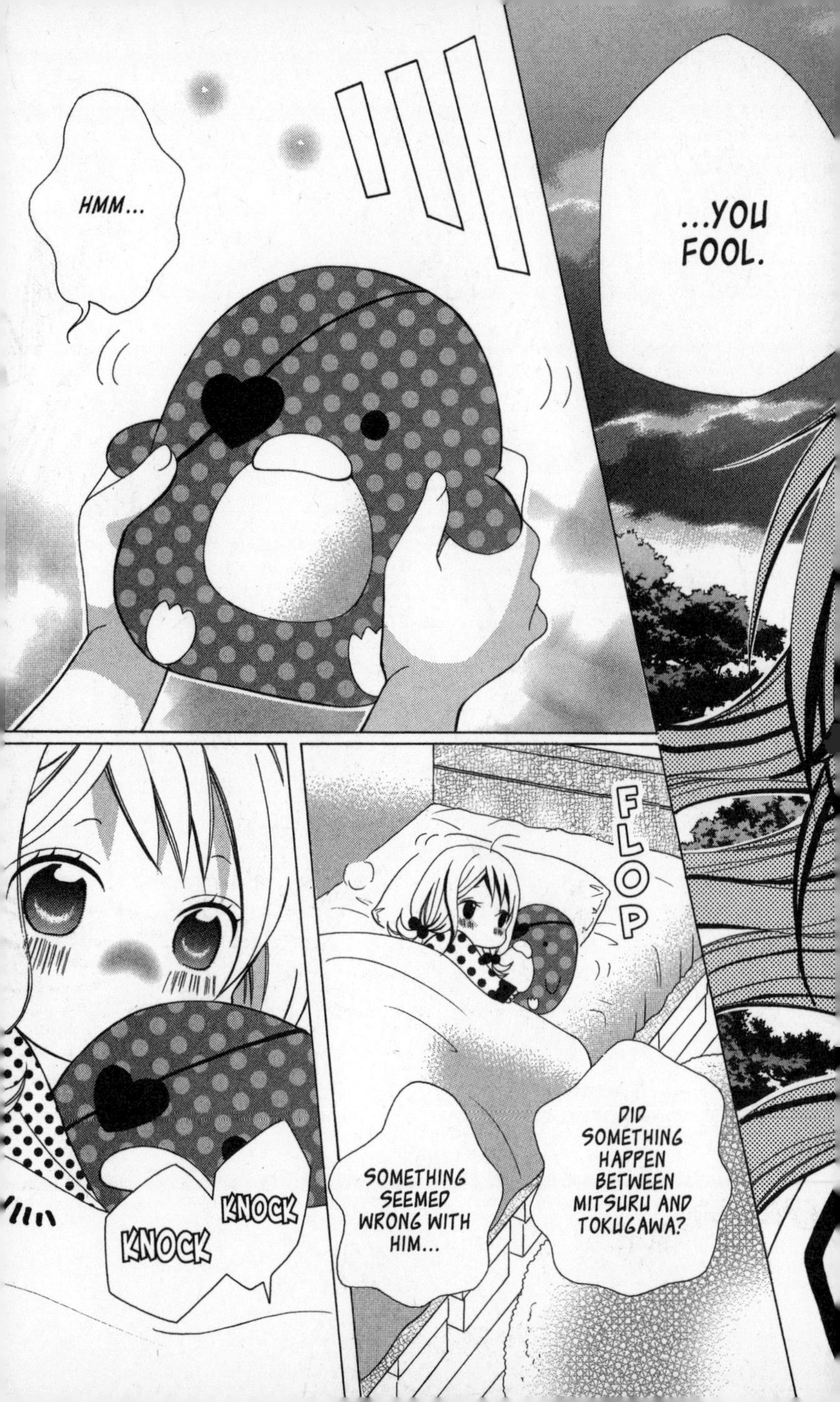
...YOU FOOL.
HMM...
FLOP
DID SOMETHING HAPPEN BETWEEN MITSURU AND TOKUGAWA?
SOMETHING SEEMED WRONG WITH HIM...
KNOCK
KNOCK

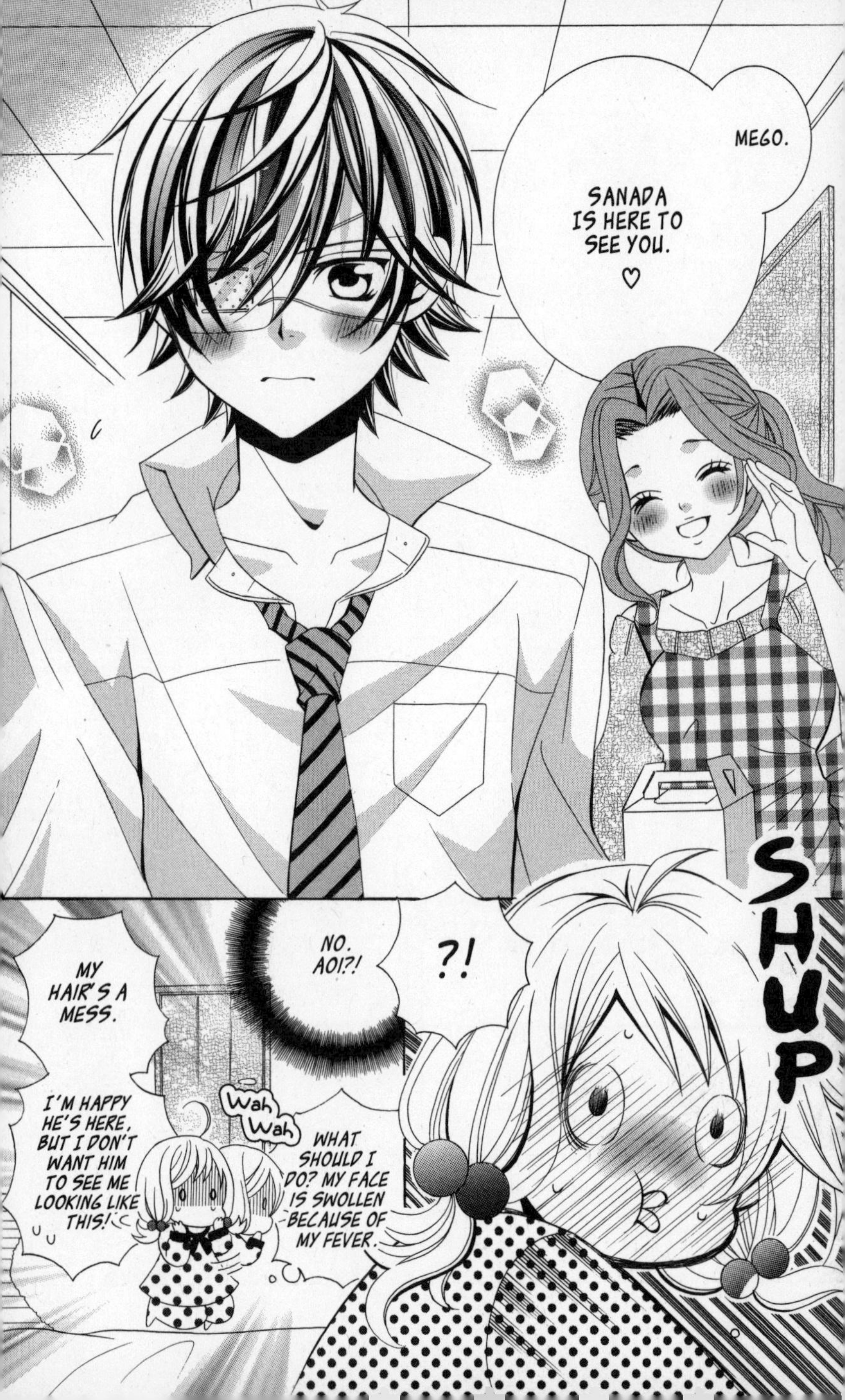
MEGO.
SANADA IS HERE TO SEE YOU. ♡
SHUP
?!
NO. AOI!?!
MY HAIR'S A MESS.
WHAT SHOULD I DO? MY FACE IS SWOLLEN BECAUSE OF MY FEVER.
Wah Wah
I'M HAPPY HE'S HERE, BUT I DON'T WANT HIM TO SEE ME LOOKING LIKE THIS!

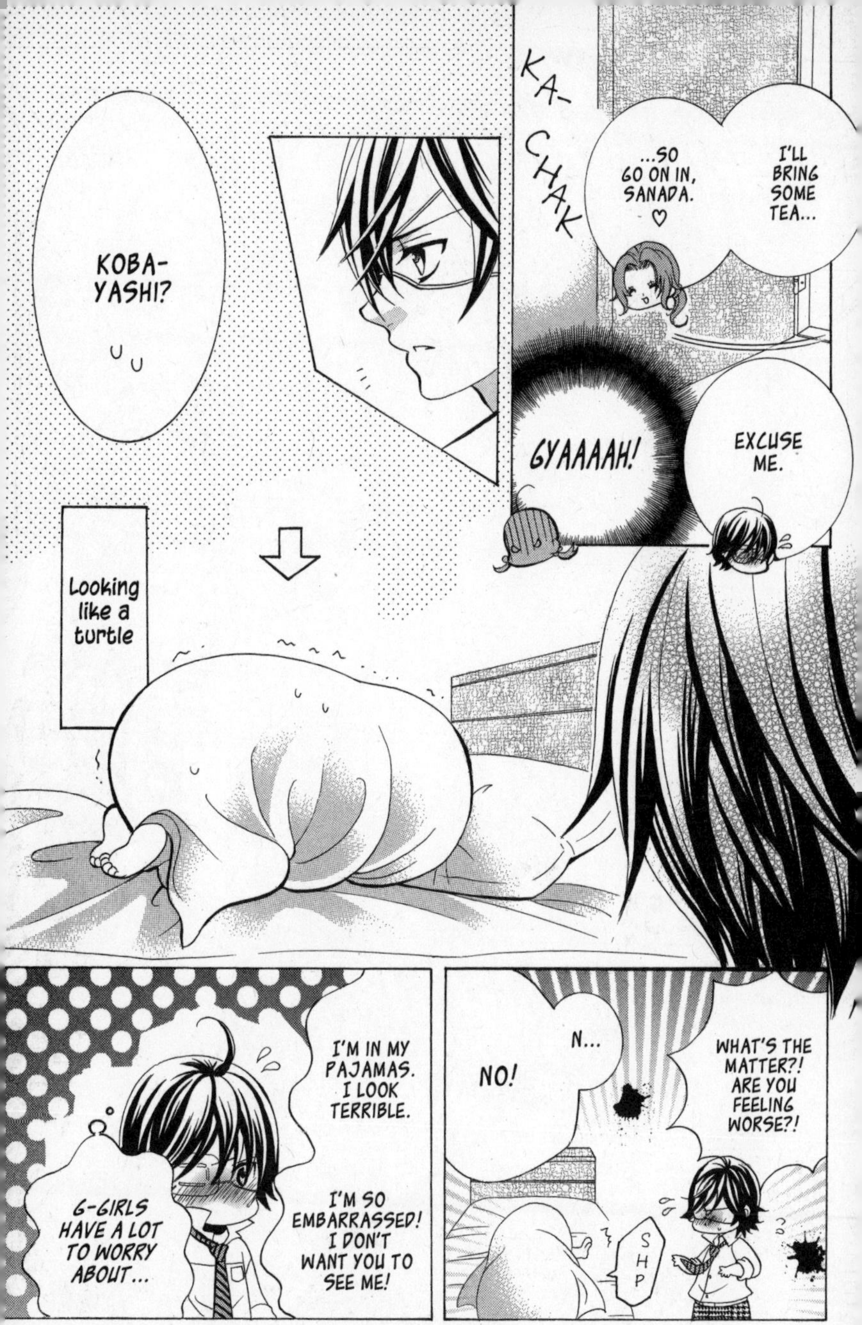
KA-CHAK
I'LL BRING SOME TEA...
...SO GO ON IN, SANADA. ♡
EXCUSE ME.
GYAAAAH!
KOBA-YASHI?
Looking like a turtle
WHAT'S THE MATTER?! ARE YOU FEELING WORSE?!
N...
NO!
SHP
I'M IN MY PAJAMAS. I LOOK TERRIBLE.
I'M SO EMBARRASSED! I DON'T WANT YOU TO SEE ME!
G-GIRLS HAVE A LOT TO WORRY ABOUT...

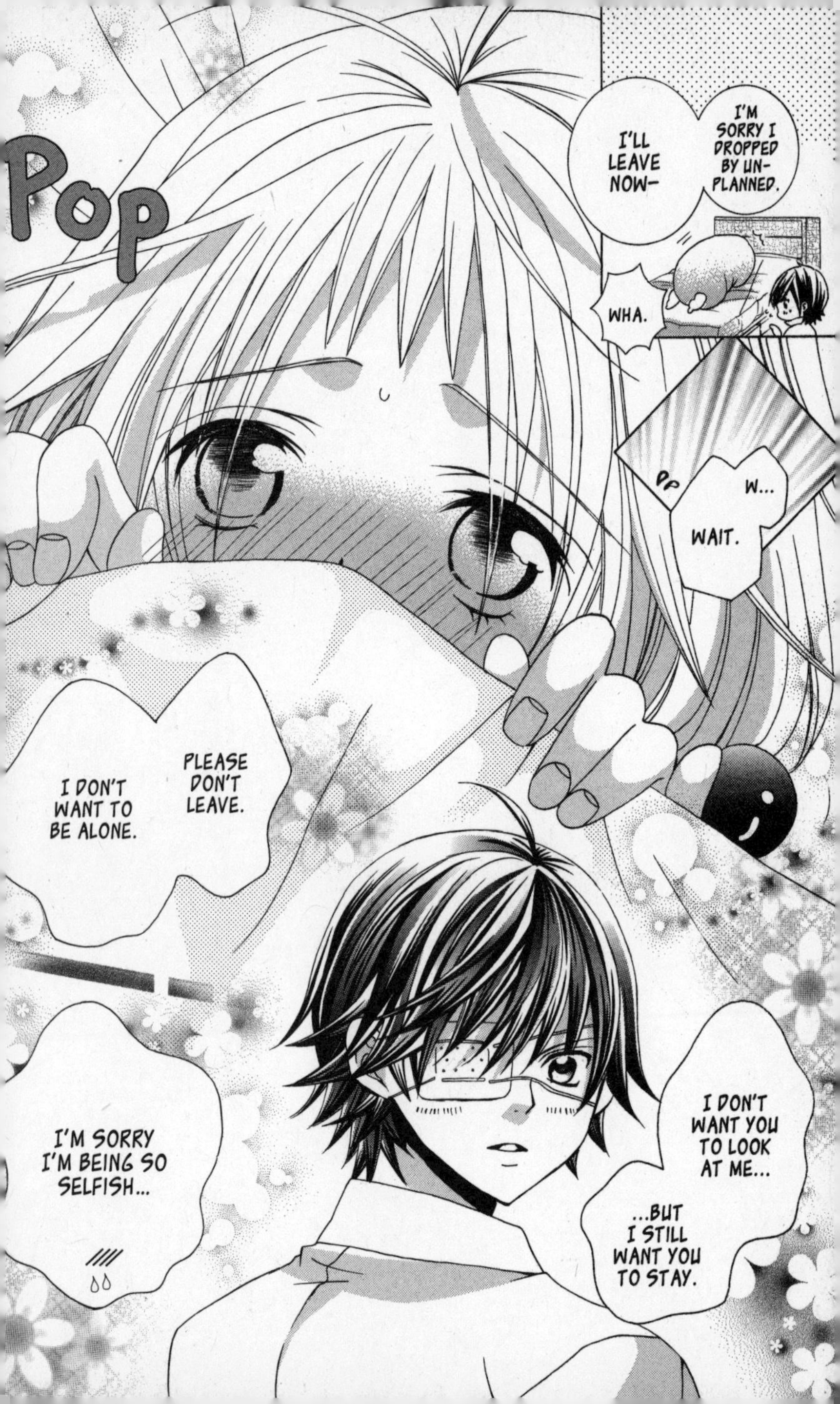
I'M SORRY I DROPPED BY UN-PLANNED.
I'LL LEAVE NOW—
WHA.
W... WAIT.
POP
PLEASE DON'T LEAVE.
I DON'T WANT TO BE ALONE.
I DON'T WANT YOU TO LOOK AT ME...
...BUT I STILL WANT YOU TO STAY.
I'M SORRY I'M BEING SO SELFISH...

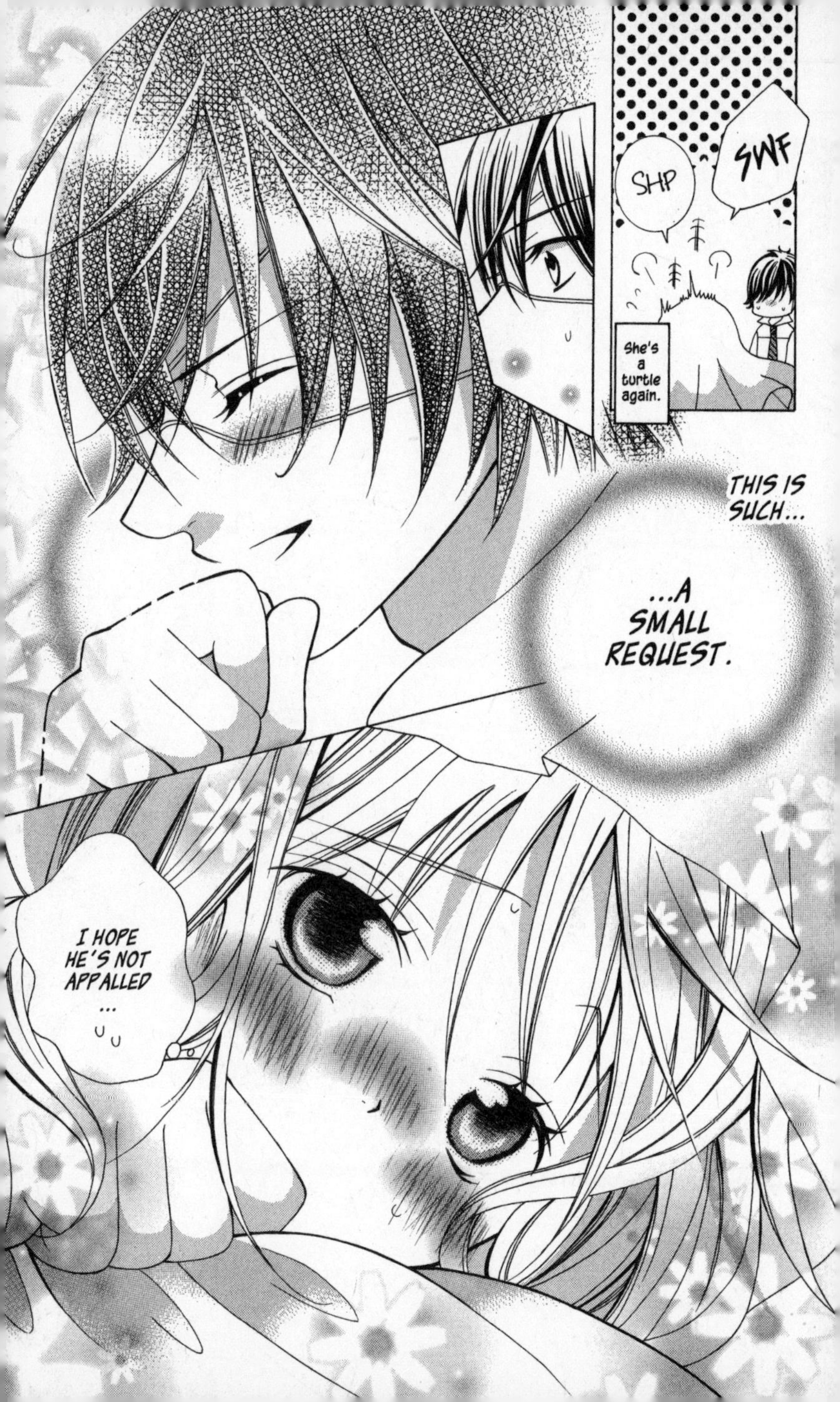
SWF
SHP
She's a turtle again.
THIS IS SUCH...
...A SMALL REQUEST.
I HOPE HE'S NOT APPALLED ...

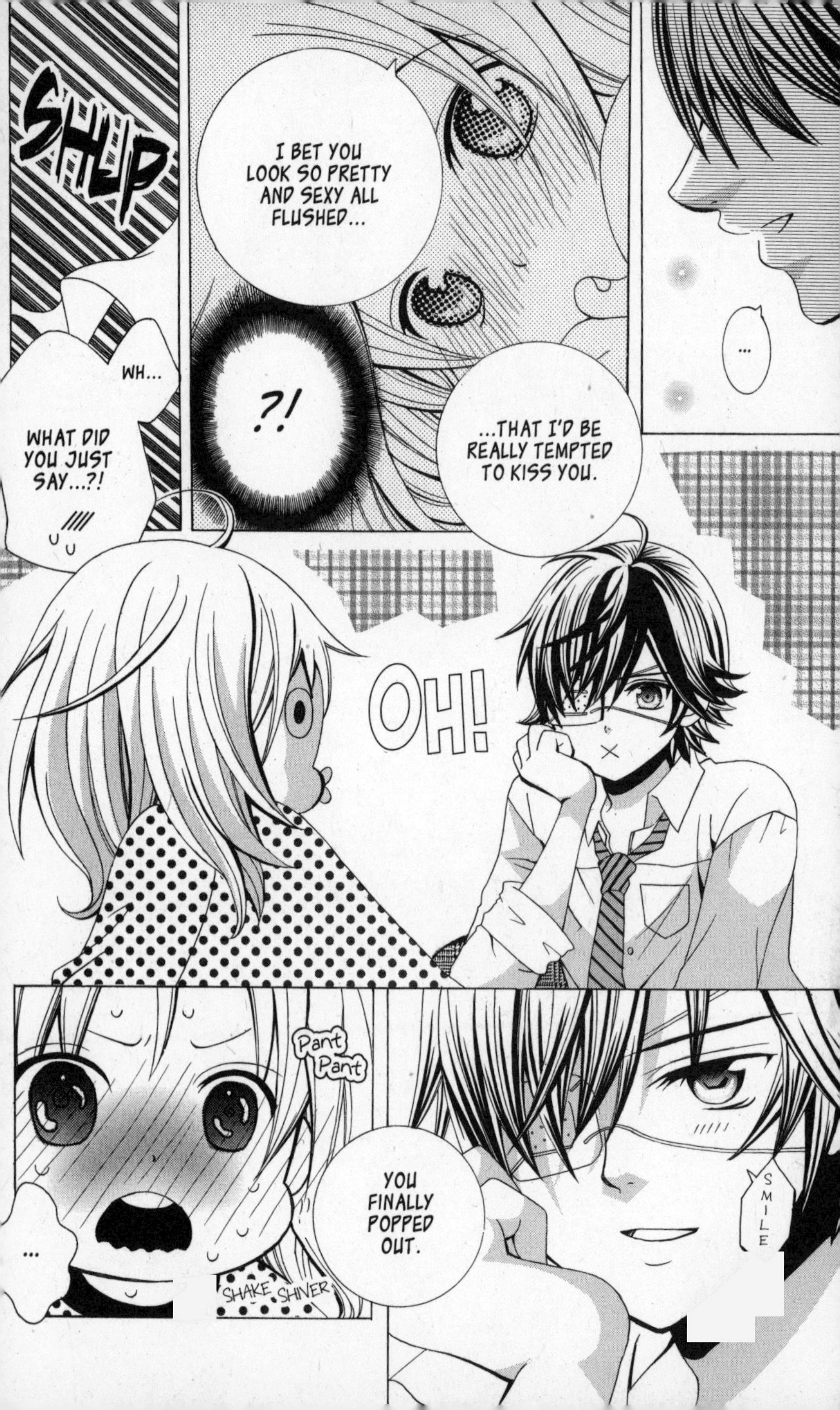
...
I BET YOU LOOK SO PRETTY AND SEXY ALL FLUSHED...
...THAT I'D BE REALLY TEMPTED TO KISS YOU.
?!
SHUP
WH...
WHAT DID YOU JUST SAY...?!
OH!
YOU FINALLY POPPED OUT.
SMILE
Pant Pant
...
SHAKE SHIVER

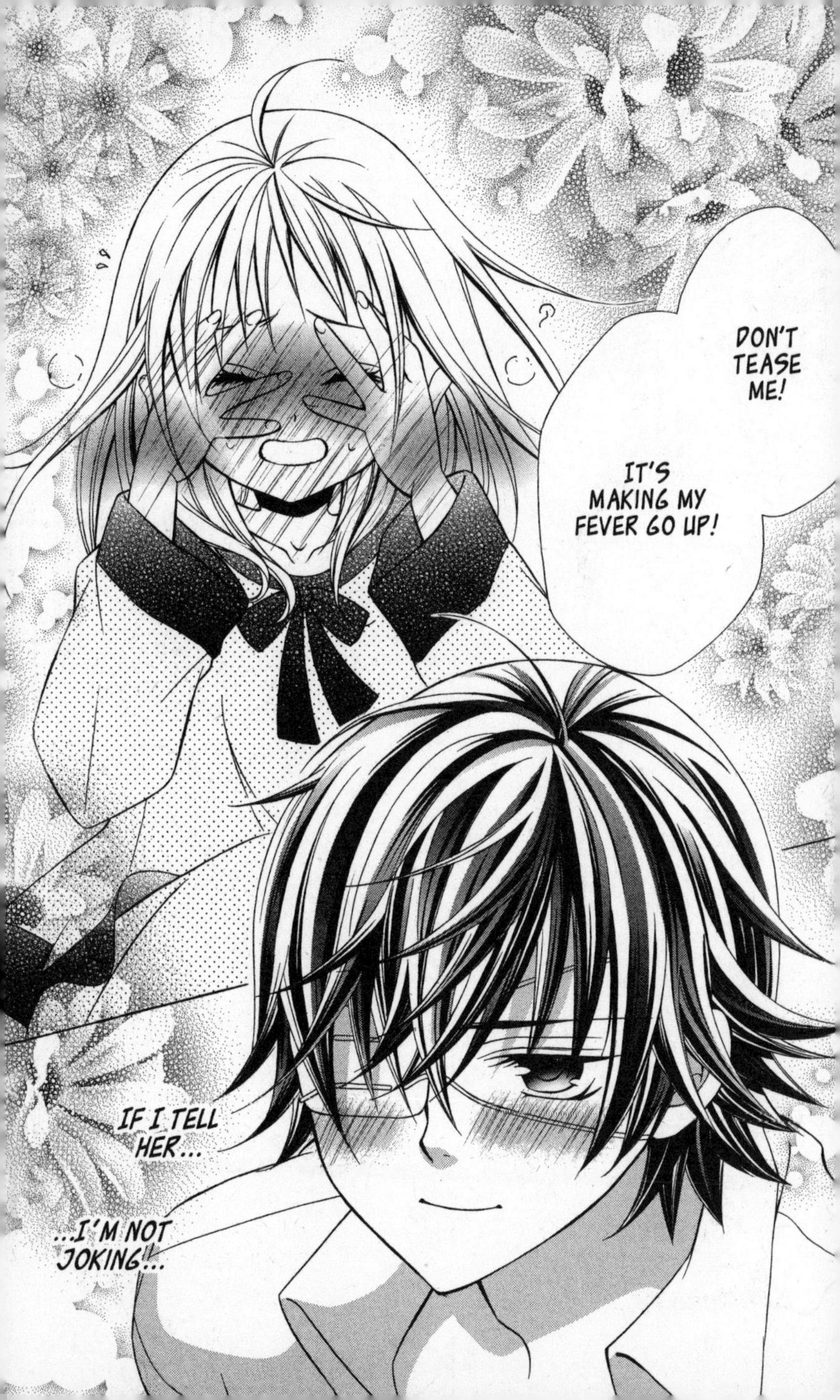
DON'T TEASE ME!
IT'S MAKING MY FEVER GO UP!
IF I TELL HER...
...I'M NOT JOKING...

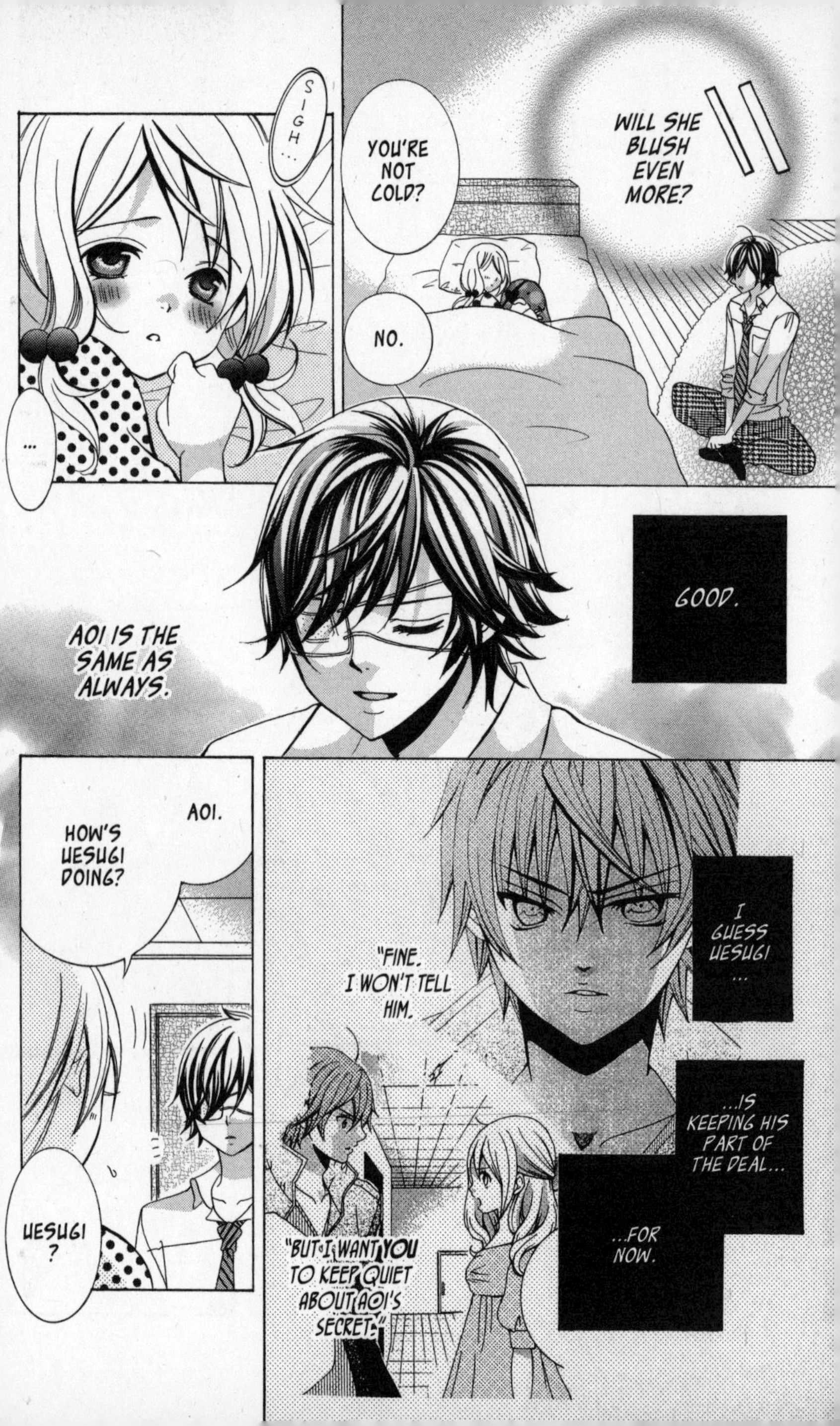
WILL SHE BLUSH EVEN MORE?
YOU'RE NOT COLD?
NO.
SIGH...
...
GOOD.
AOI IS THE SAME AS ALWAYS.
I GUESS UESUGI ...
"FINE. I WON'T TELL HIM.
...IS KEEPING HIS PART OF THE DEAL...
"BUT I WANT YOU TO KEEP QUIET ABOUT AOI'S SECRET."
...FOR NOW.
AOI.
HOW'S UESUGI DOING?
UESUGI?

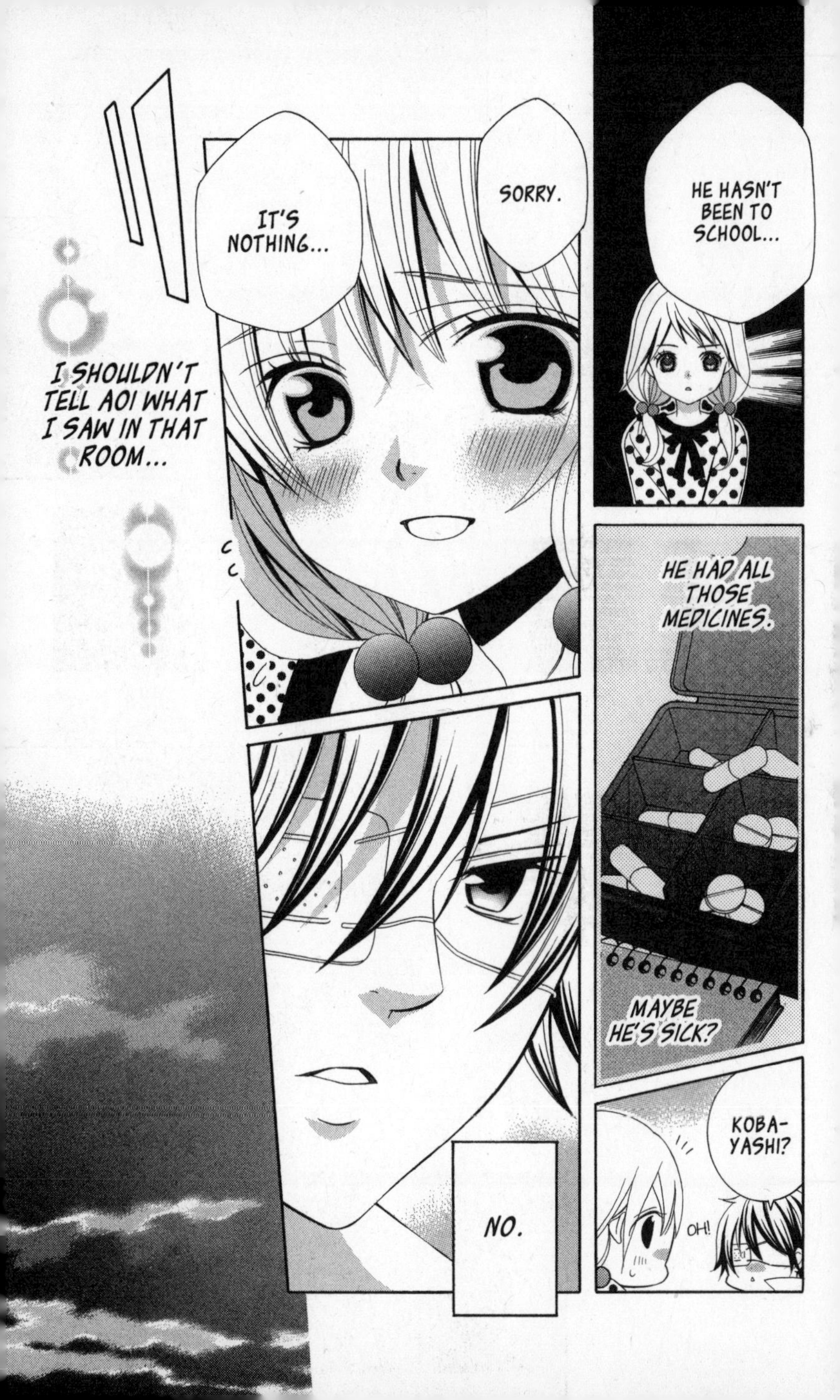
HE HASN'T BEEN TO SCHOOL...
HE HAD ALL THOSE MEDICINES.
MAYBE HE'S SICK?
KOBA-YASHI?
OH!
SORRY.
IT'S NOTHING...
NO.
I SHOULDN'T TELL AOI WHAT I SAW IN THAT ROOM...

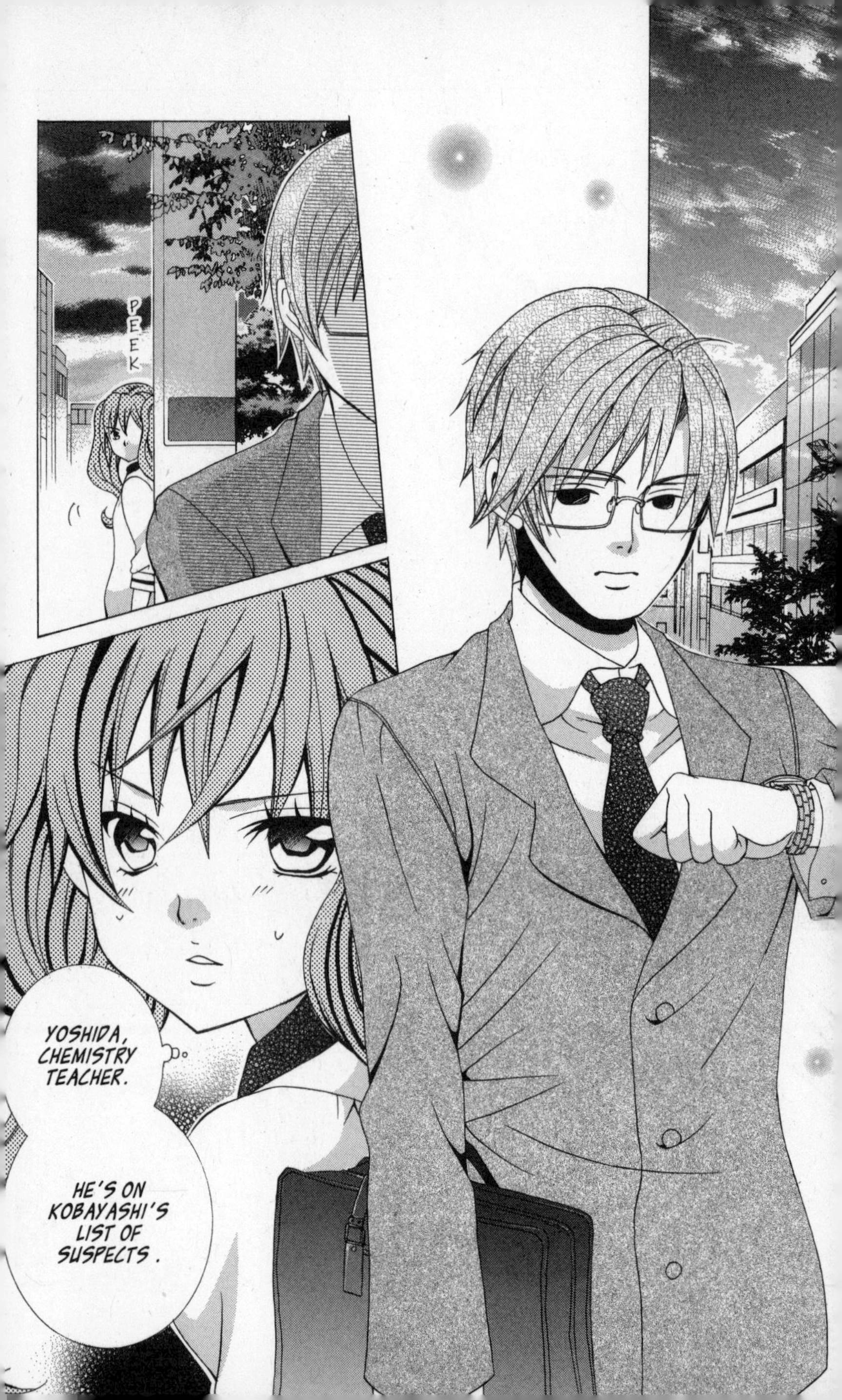
PEEK
YOSHIDA, CHEMISTRY TEACHER.
HE'S ON KOBAYASHI'S LIST OF SUSPECTS.

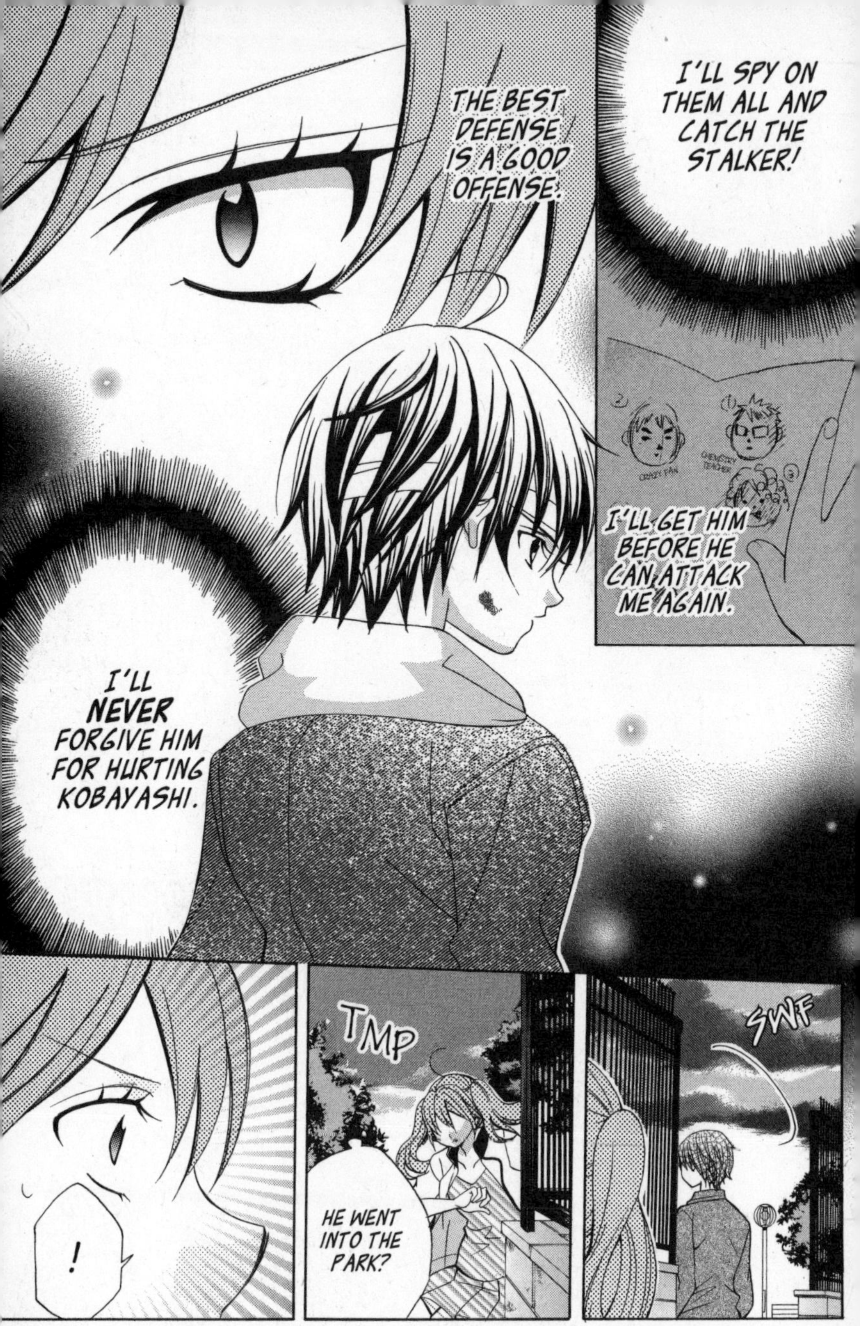
I'LL SPY ON THEM ALL AND CATCH THE STALKER!
THE BEST DEFENSE IS A GOOD OFFENSE.
CHEMISTRY TEACHER
CRAZY FAN
I'LL GET HIM BEFORE HE CAN ATTACK ME AGAIN.
I'LL **NEVER** FORGIVE HIM FOR HURTING KOBAYASHI.
SWF
TMP
HE WENT INTO THE PARK?
!

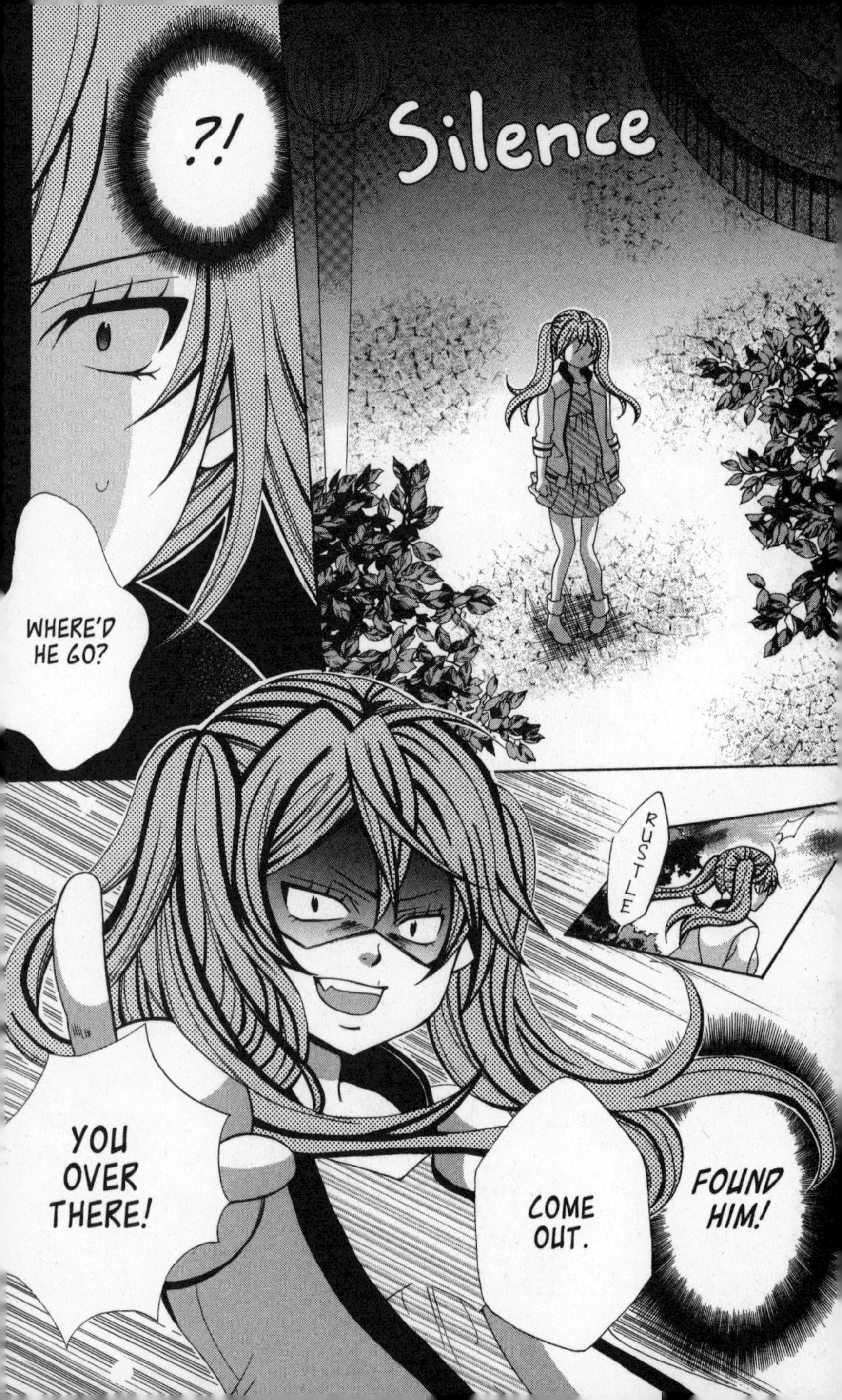
Silence
?!
WHERE'D HE GO?
RUSTLE
FOUND HIM!
COME OUT.
YOU OVER THERE!

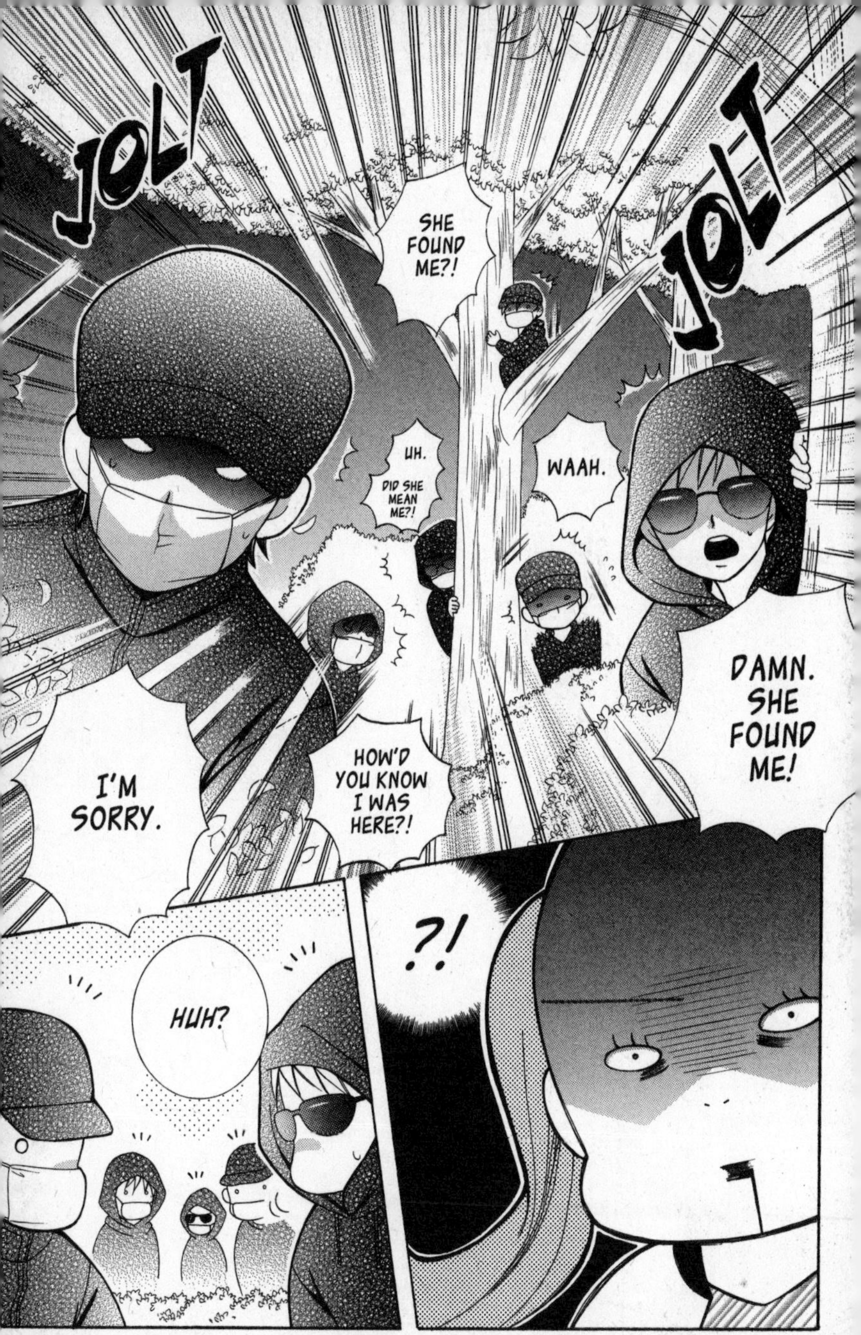
JOLT
SHE FOUND ME?!
JOLT
WAAH.
UH. DID SHE MEAN ME?!
DAMN. SHE FOUND ME!
HOW'D YOU KNOW I WAS HERE?!
I'M SORRY.
?!
HUH?

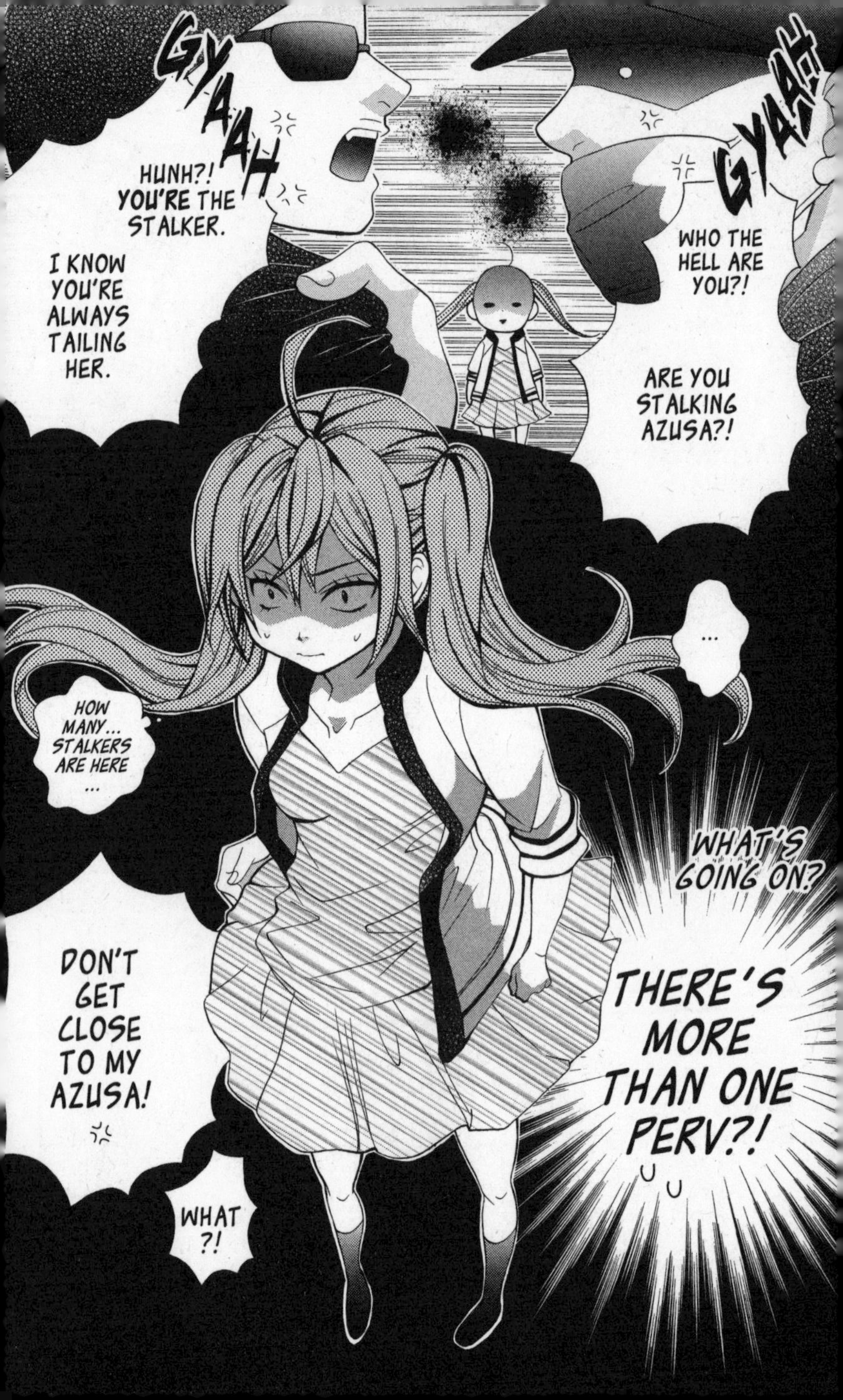
GYAAH
WHO THE HELL ARE YOU?!
ARE YOU STALKING AZUSA?!
GYAAAH
HUNH?! YOU'RE THE STALKER.
I KNOW YOU'RE ALWAYS TAILING HER.
...
HOW MANY... STALKERS ARE HERE ...
WHAT'S GOING ON?
THERE'S MORE THAN ONE PERV?!
DON'T GET CLOSE TO MY AZUSA!
WHAT?!

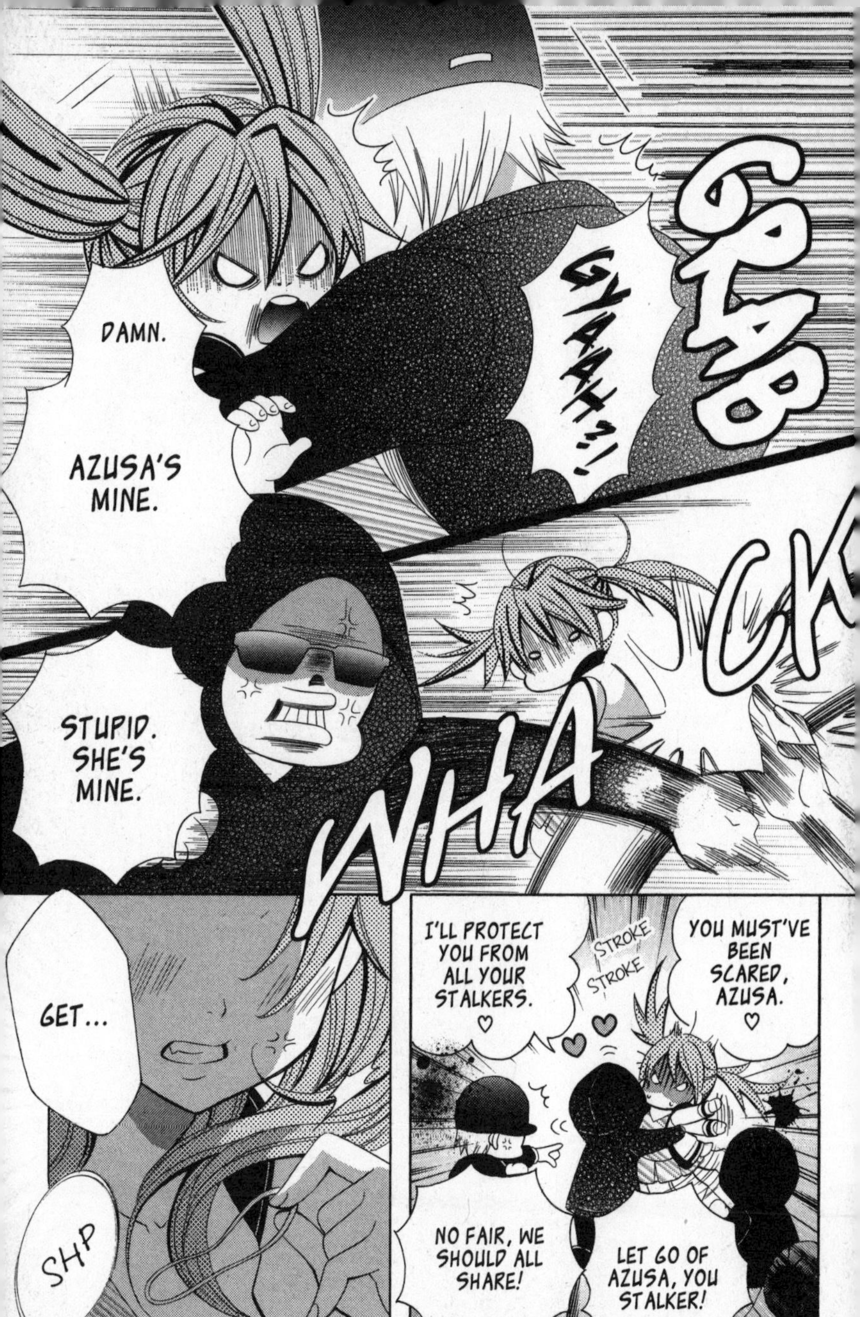
GRAB
GYAAAH?!
DAMN.
AZUSA'S MINE.
WHACK
STUPID. SHE'S MINE.
YOU MUST'VE BEEN SCARED, AZUSA. ♡
STROKE STROKE
I'LL PROTECT YOU FROM ALL YOUR STALKERS. ♡
LET GO OF AZUSA, YOU STALKER!
NO FAIR, WE SHOULD ALL SHARE!
GET...
SHP

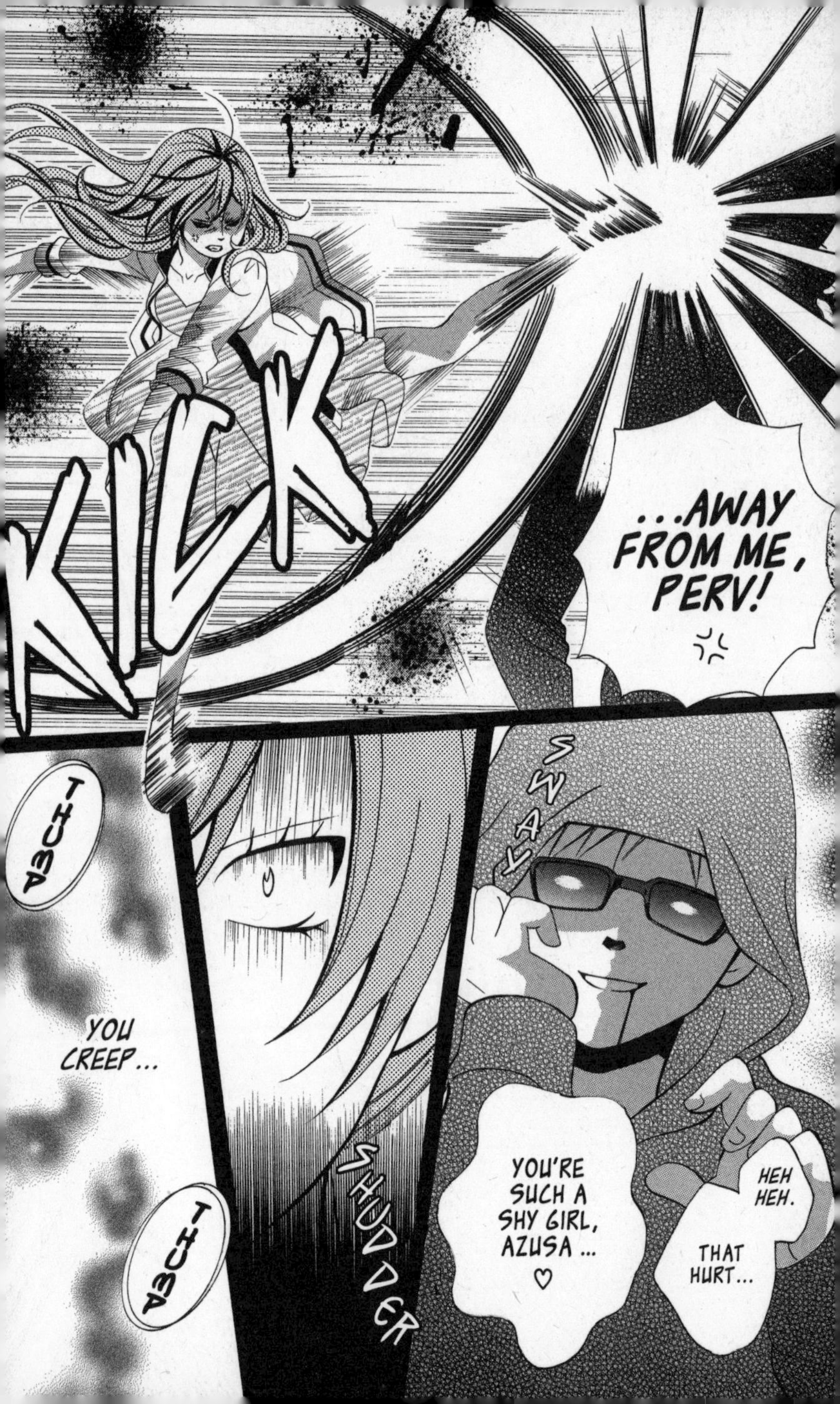
...AWAY FROM ME, PERV!
KICK
SWAY
HEH HEH.
THAT HURT...
YOU'RE SUCH A SHY GIRL, AZUSA ... ♡
SHUDDER
THUMP
YOU CREEP...
THUMP

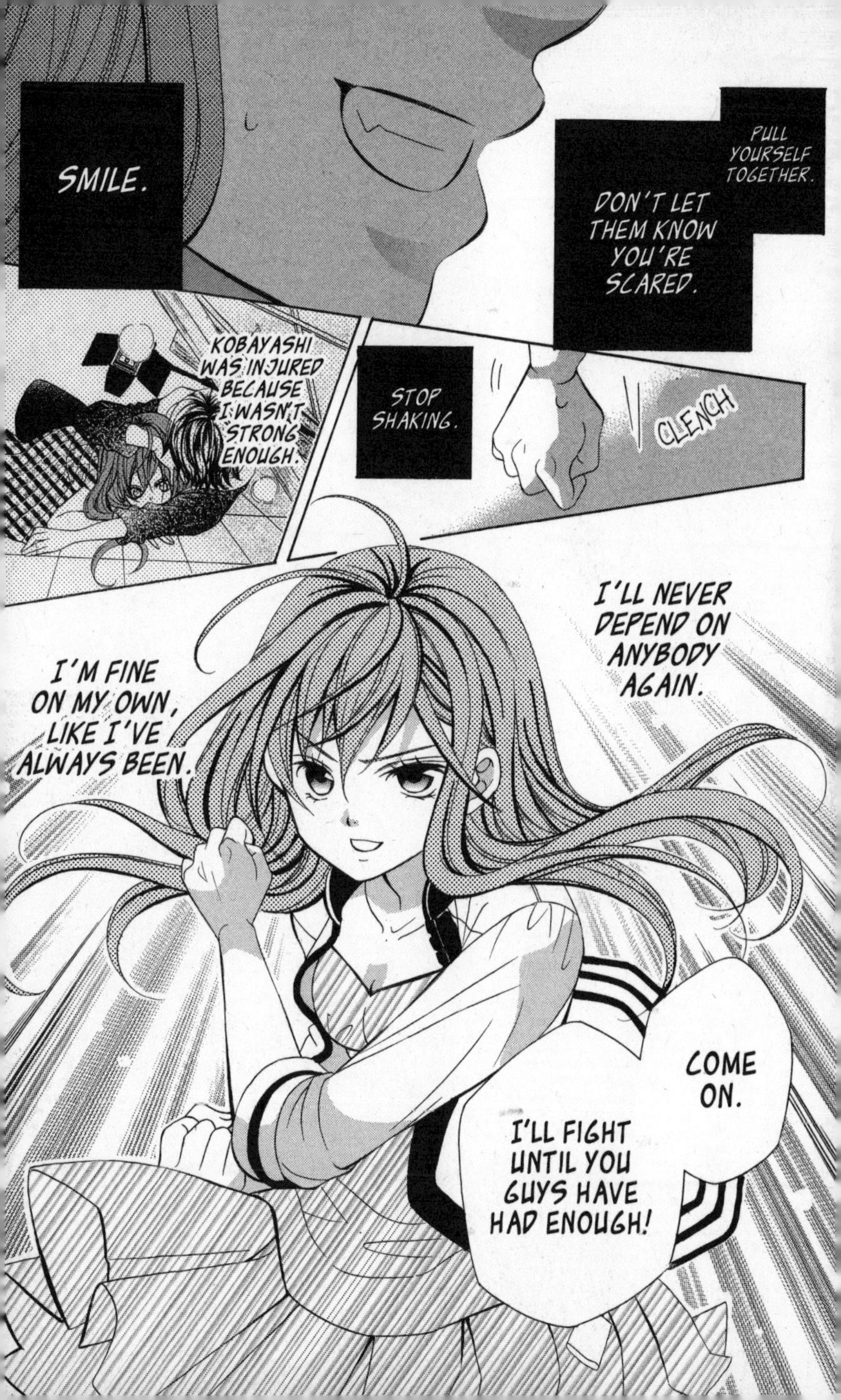
PULL YOURSELF TOGETHER.
DON'T LET THEM KNOW YOU'RE SCARED.
SMILE.
CLENCH
STOP SHAKING.
KOBAYASHI WAS INJURED BECAUSE I WASN'T STRONG ENOUGH.
I'LL NEVER DEPEND ON ANYBODY AGAIN.
I'M FINE ON MY OWN, LIKE I'VE ALWAYS BEEN.
COME ON.
I'LL FIGHT UNTIL YOU GUYS HAVE HAD ENOUGH!

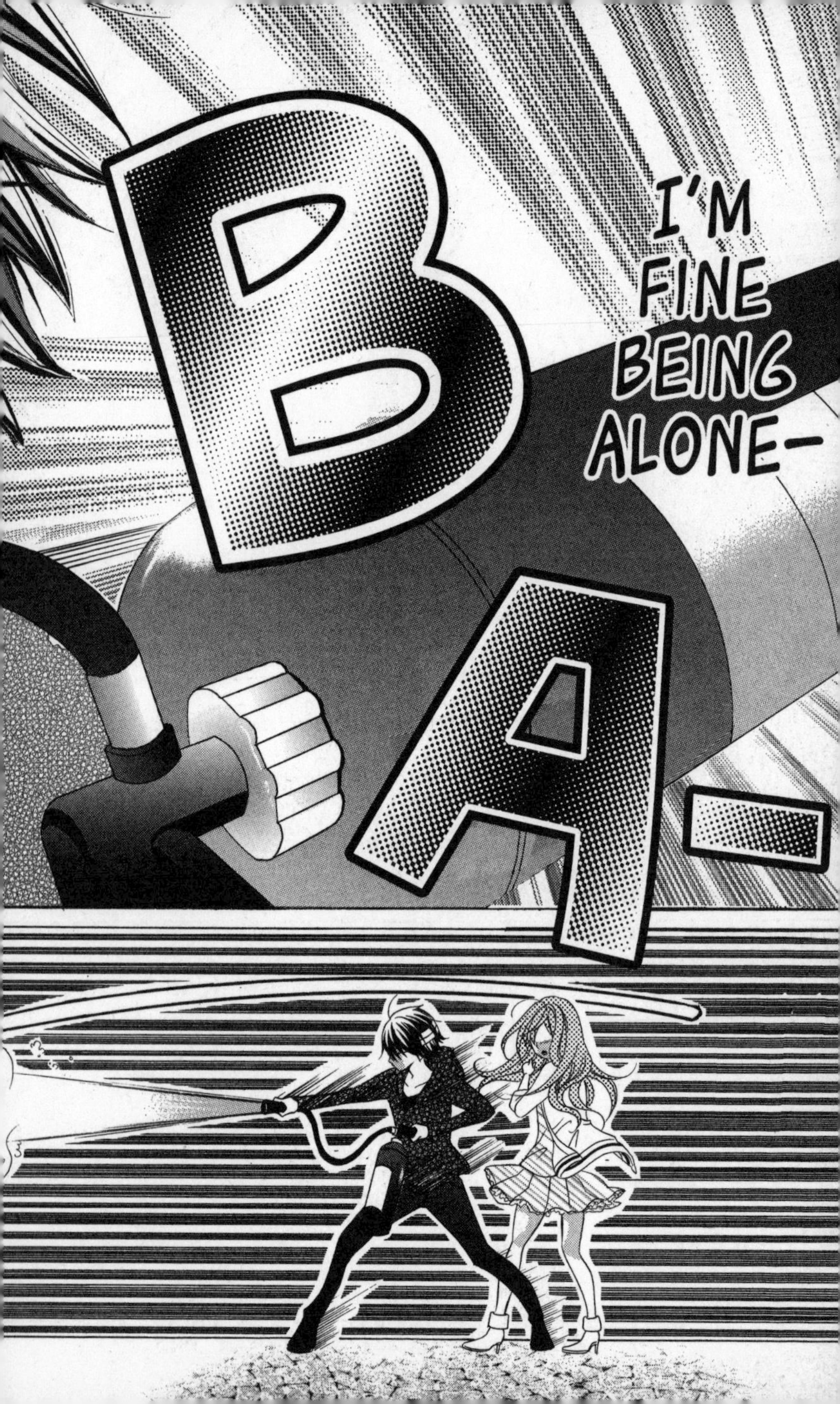
I'M FINE BEING ALONE-
BA-

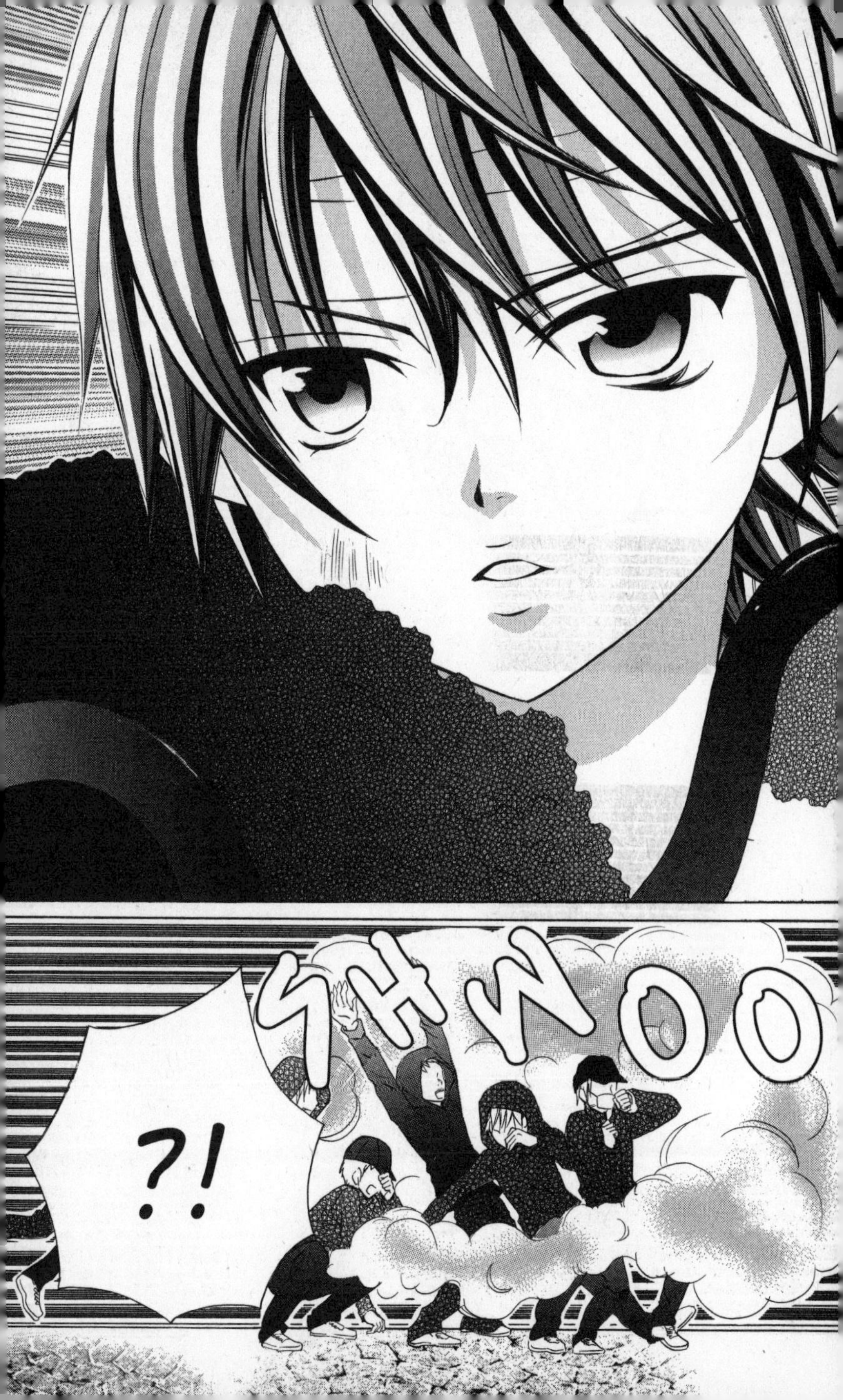
SHWOO
?!

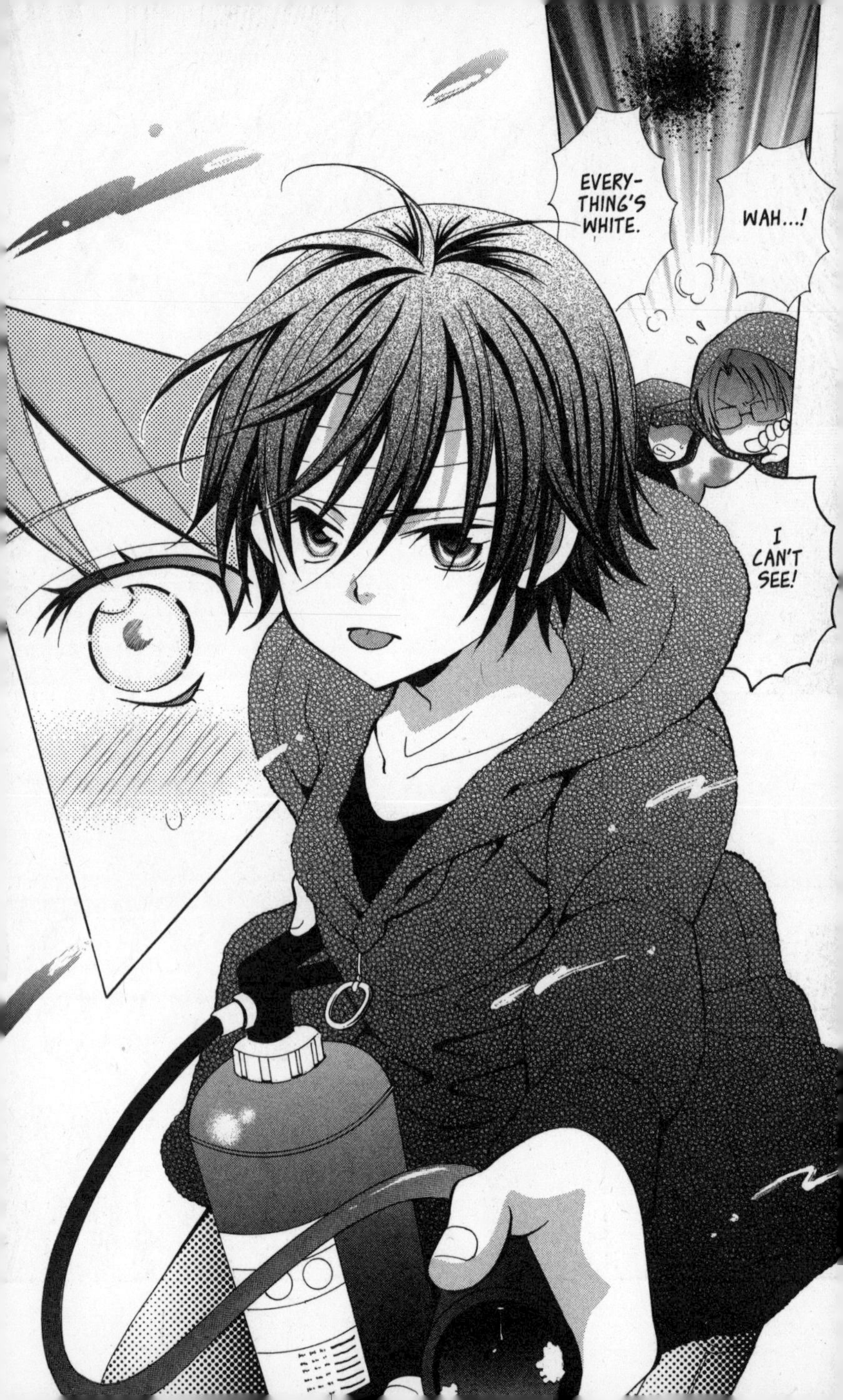
WAH...!
EVERY-THING'S WHITE.
I CAN'T SEE!

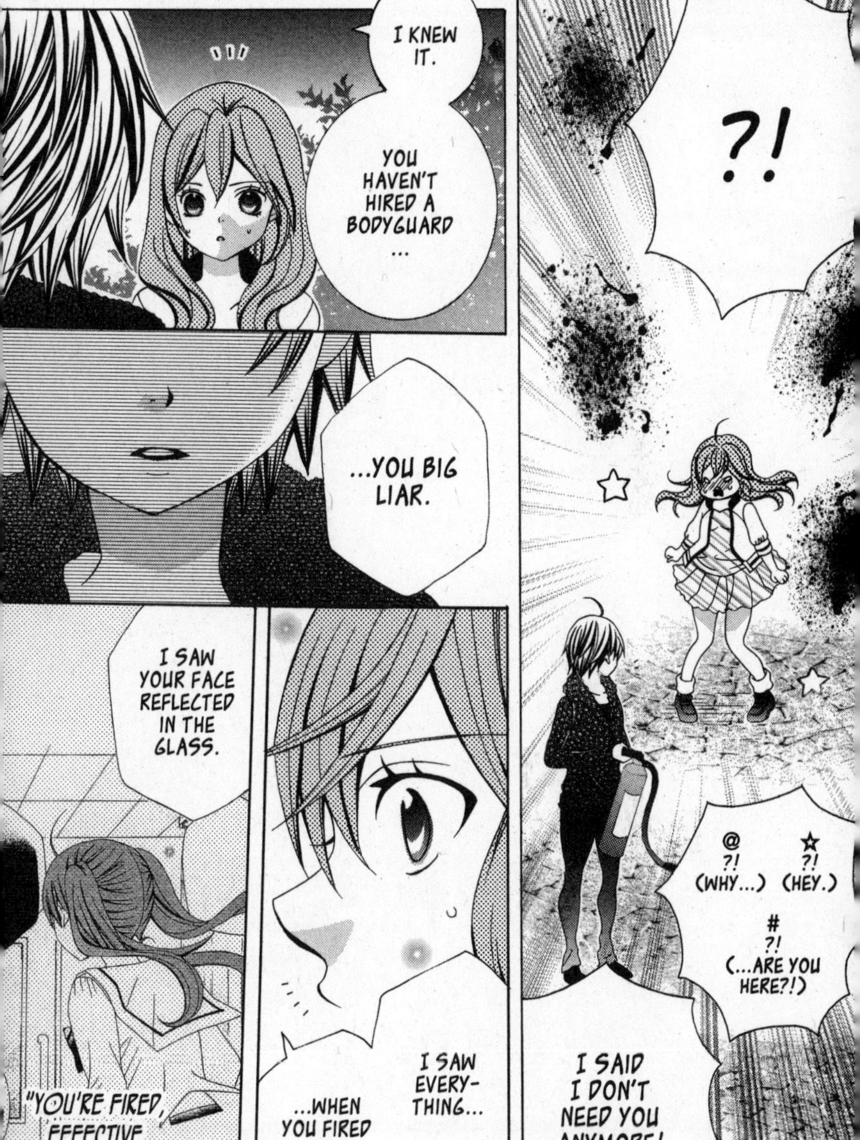
?!
@ ?! (WHY...) ☆ ?! (HEY.) # ?! (...ARE YOU HERE?!)
I SAID I DON'T NEED YOU ANYMORE!
I KNEW IT.
YOU HAVEN'T HIRED A BODYGUARD...
...YOU BIG LIAR.
I SAW EVERYTHING...
...WHEN YOU FIRED ME.
I SAW YOUR FACE REFLECTED IN THE GLASS.
"YOU'RE FIRED, EFFECTIVE IMMEDIATELY."

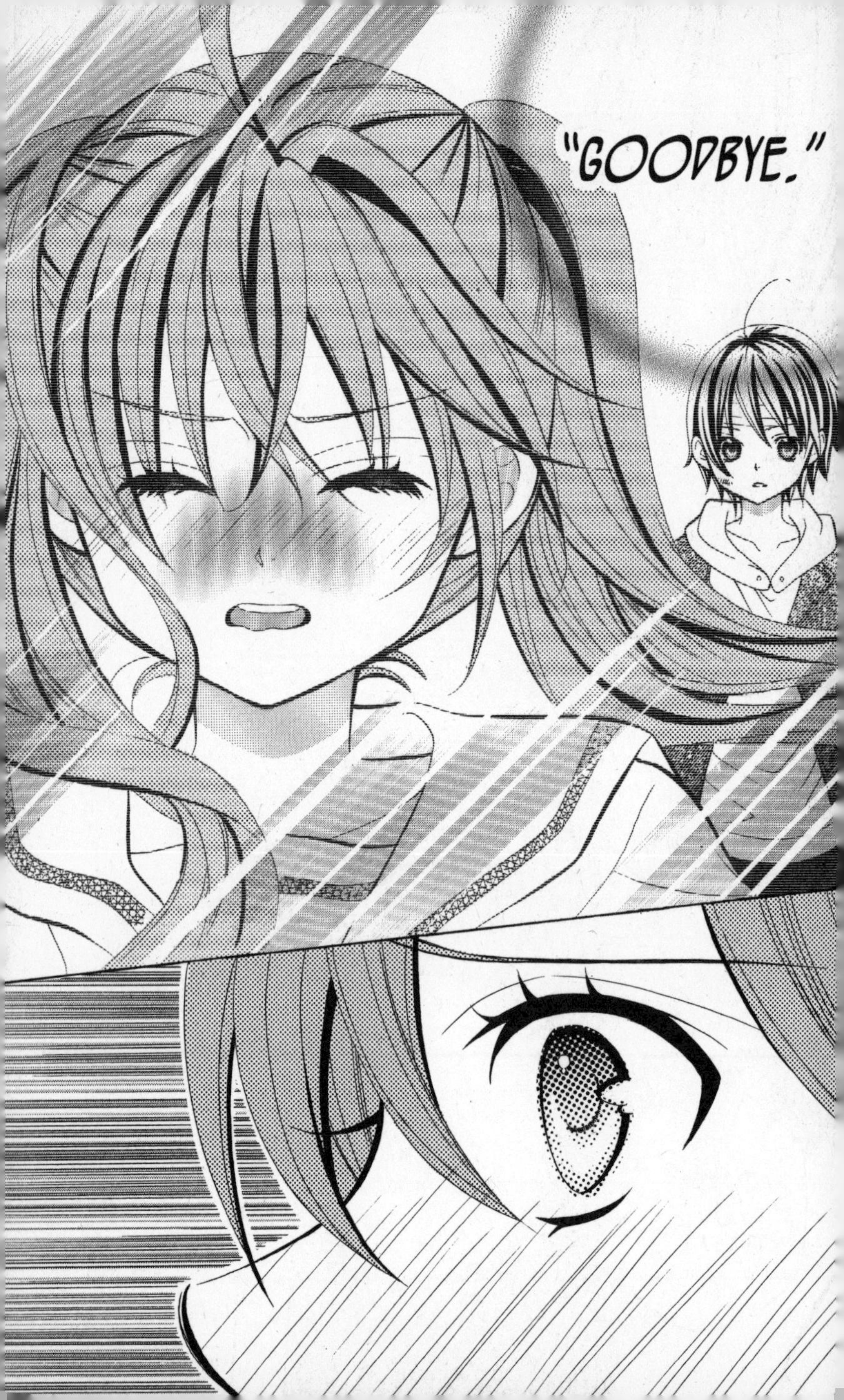
"GOODBYE."

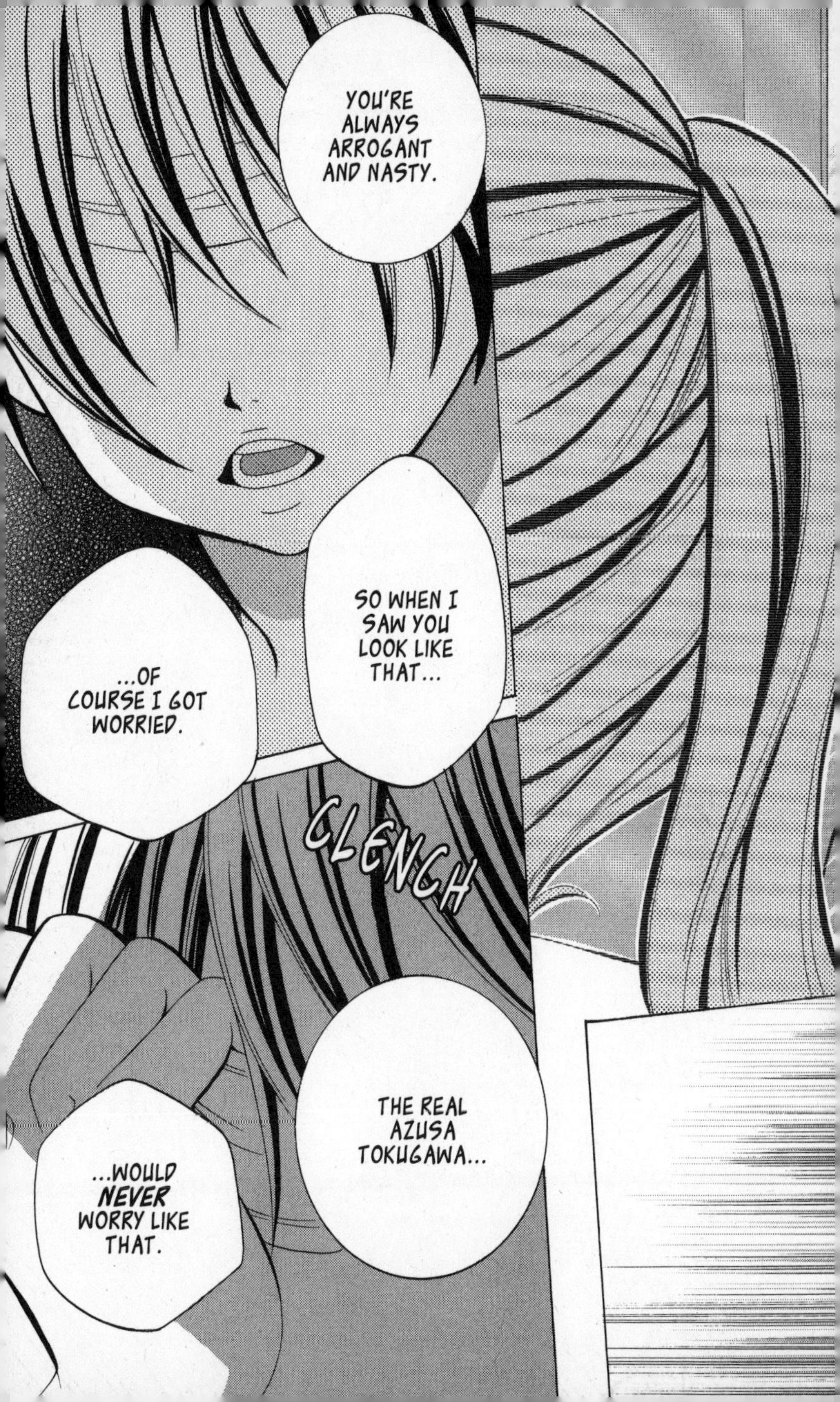
YOU'RE ALWAYS ARROGANT AND NASTY.
SO WHEN I SAW YOU LOOK LIKE THAT...
...OF COURSE I GOT WORRIED.
CLENCH
THE REAL AZUSA TOKUGAWA...
...WOULD ***NEVER*** WORRY LIKE THAT.

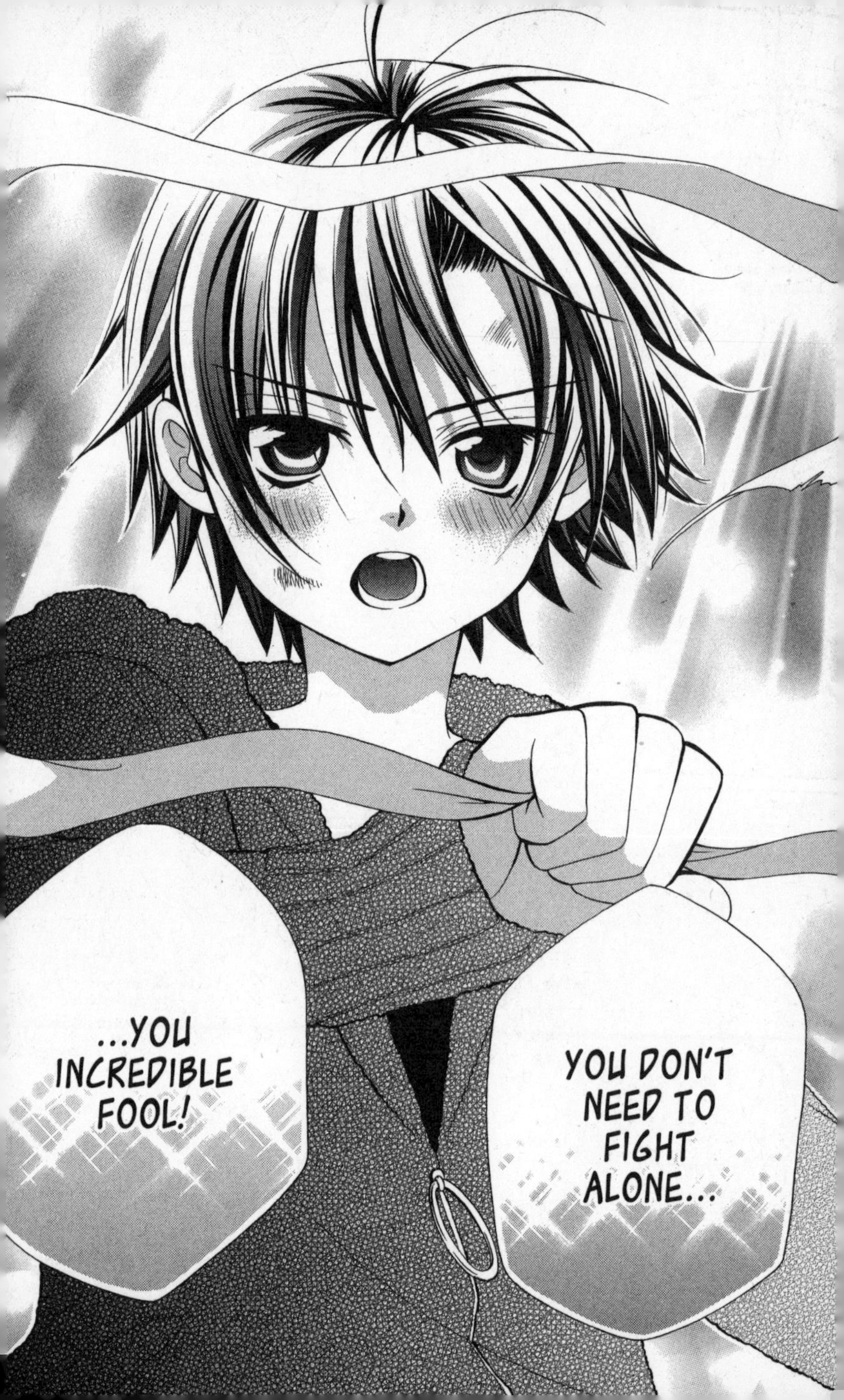
YOU DON'T NEED TO FIGHT ALONE...
...YOU INCREDIBLE FOOL!

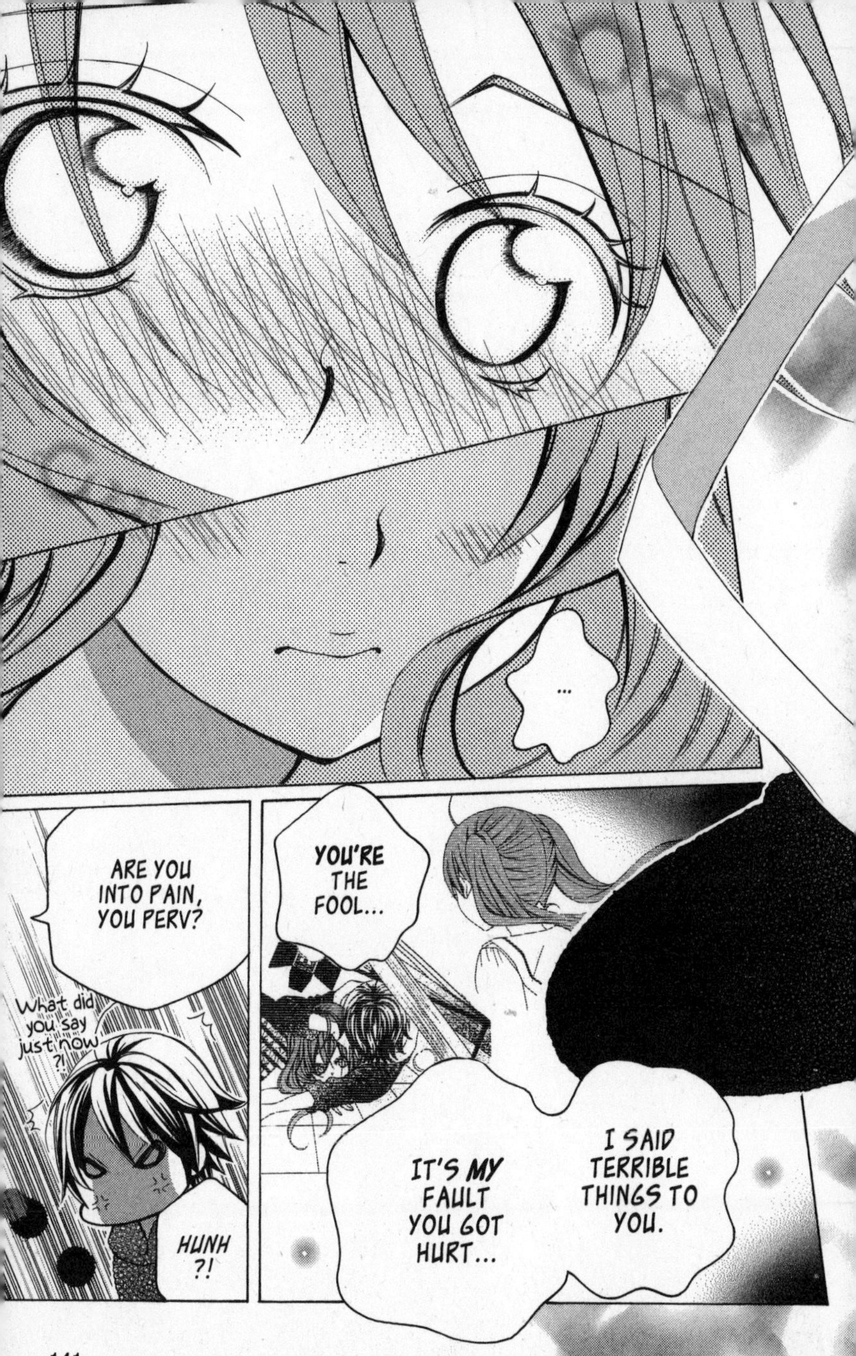
...
YOU'RE THE FOOL...
I SAID TERRIBLE THINGS TO YOU.
IT'S MY FAULT YOU GOT HURT...
ARE YOU INTO PAIN, YOU PERV?
What did you say just now?!
HUNH?!

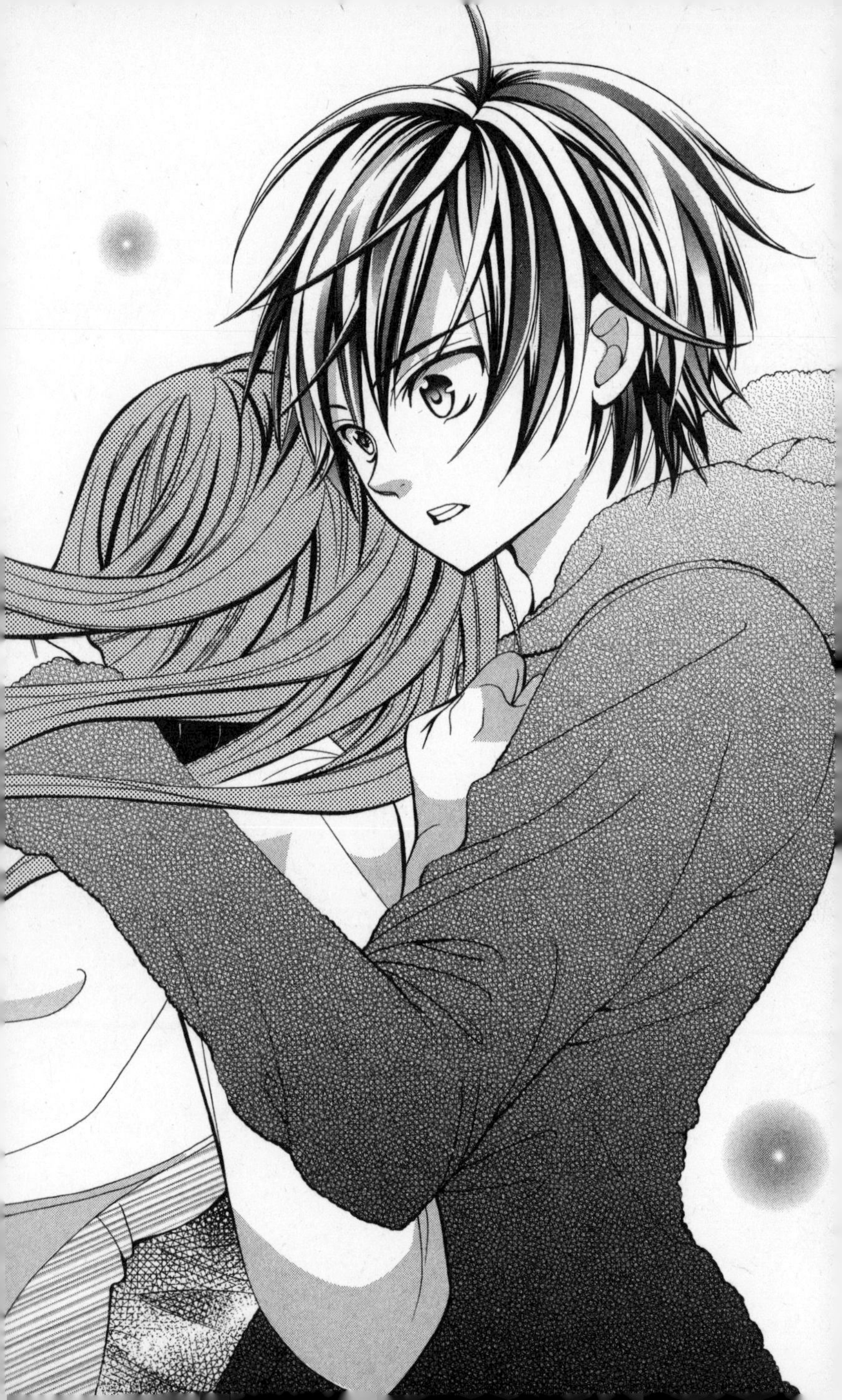

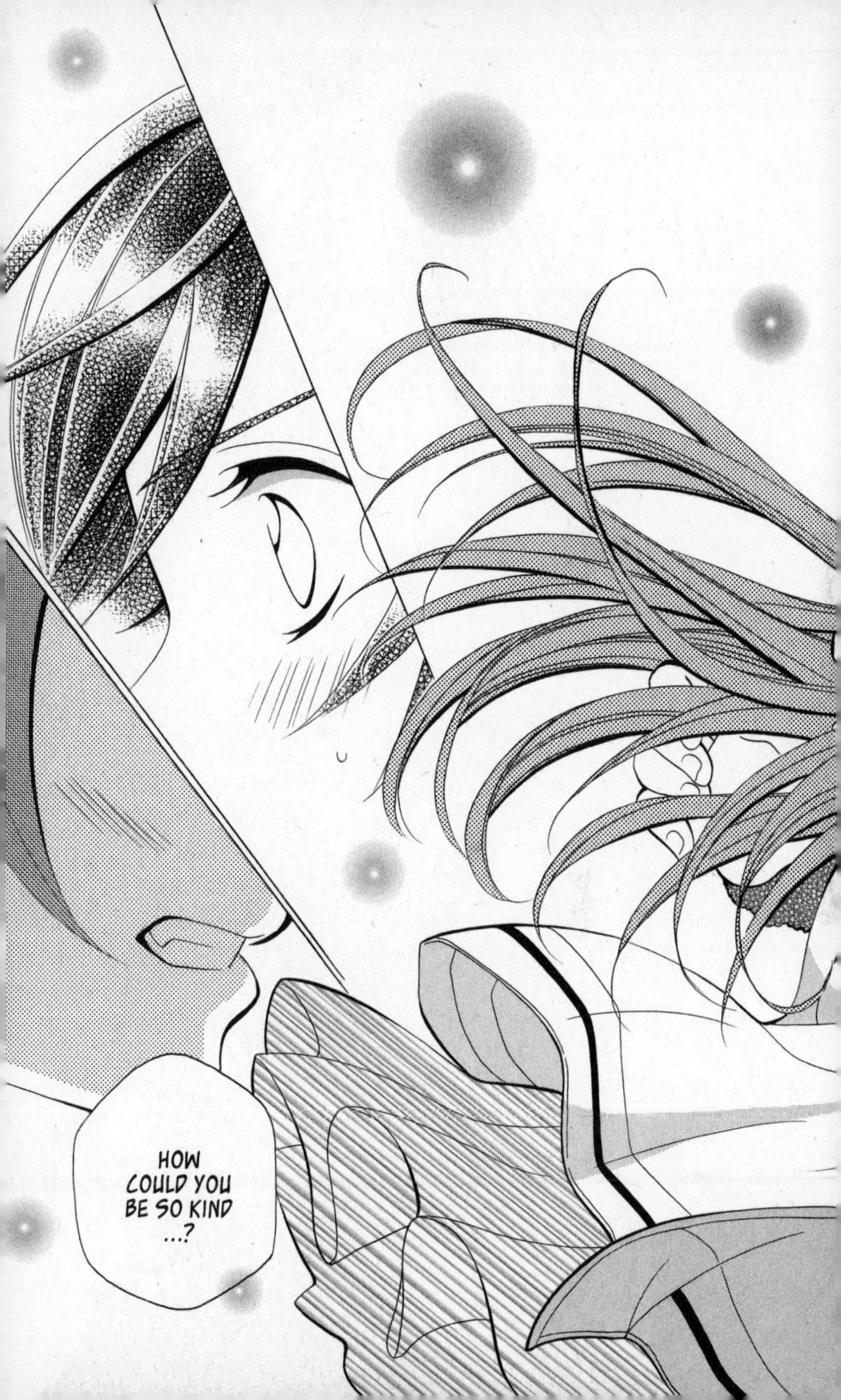
HOW COULD YOU BE SO KIND ...?

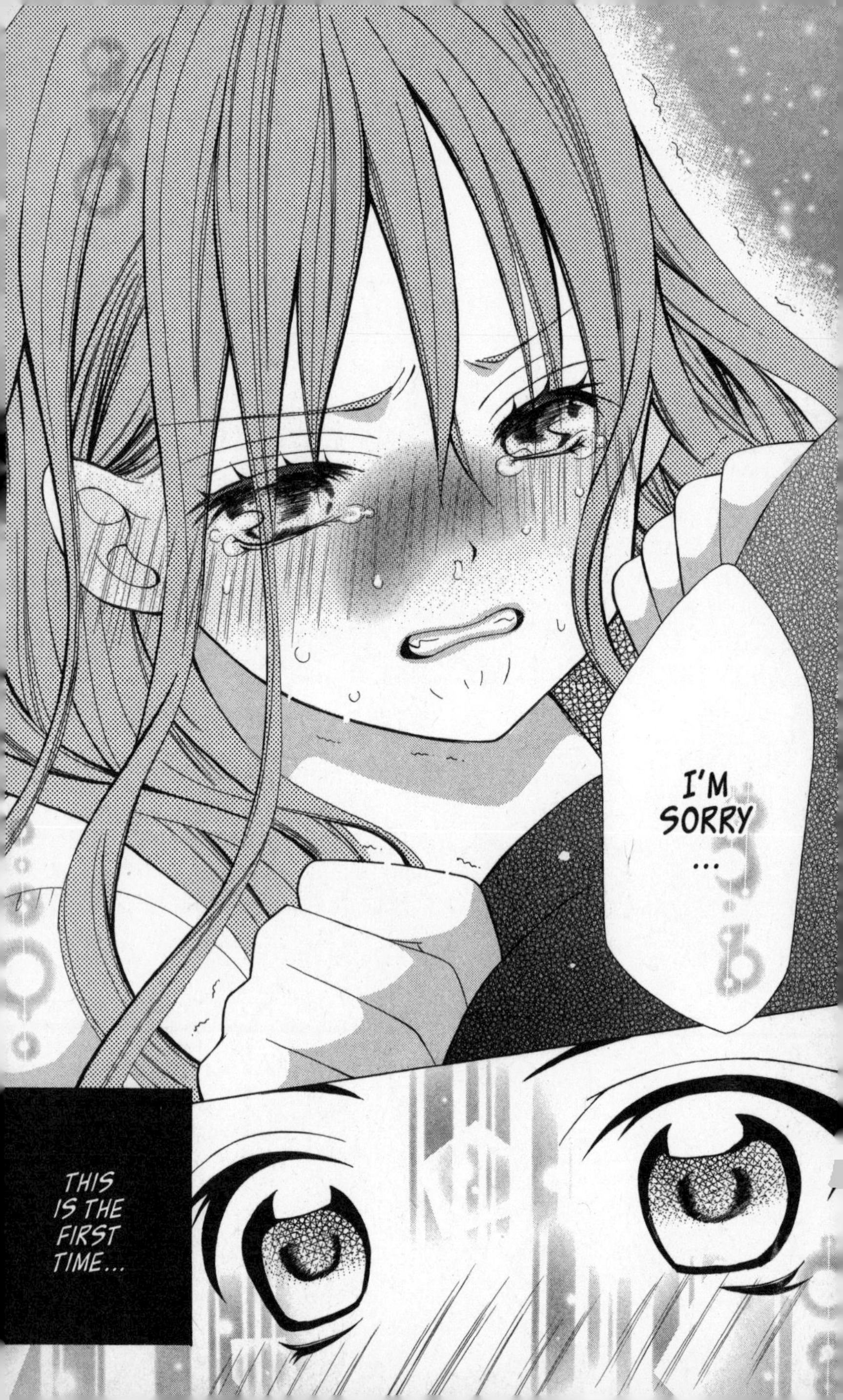
I'M SORRY ...
THIS IS THE FIRST TIME...

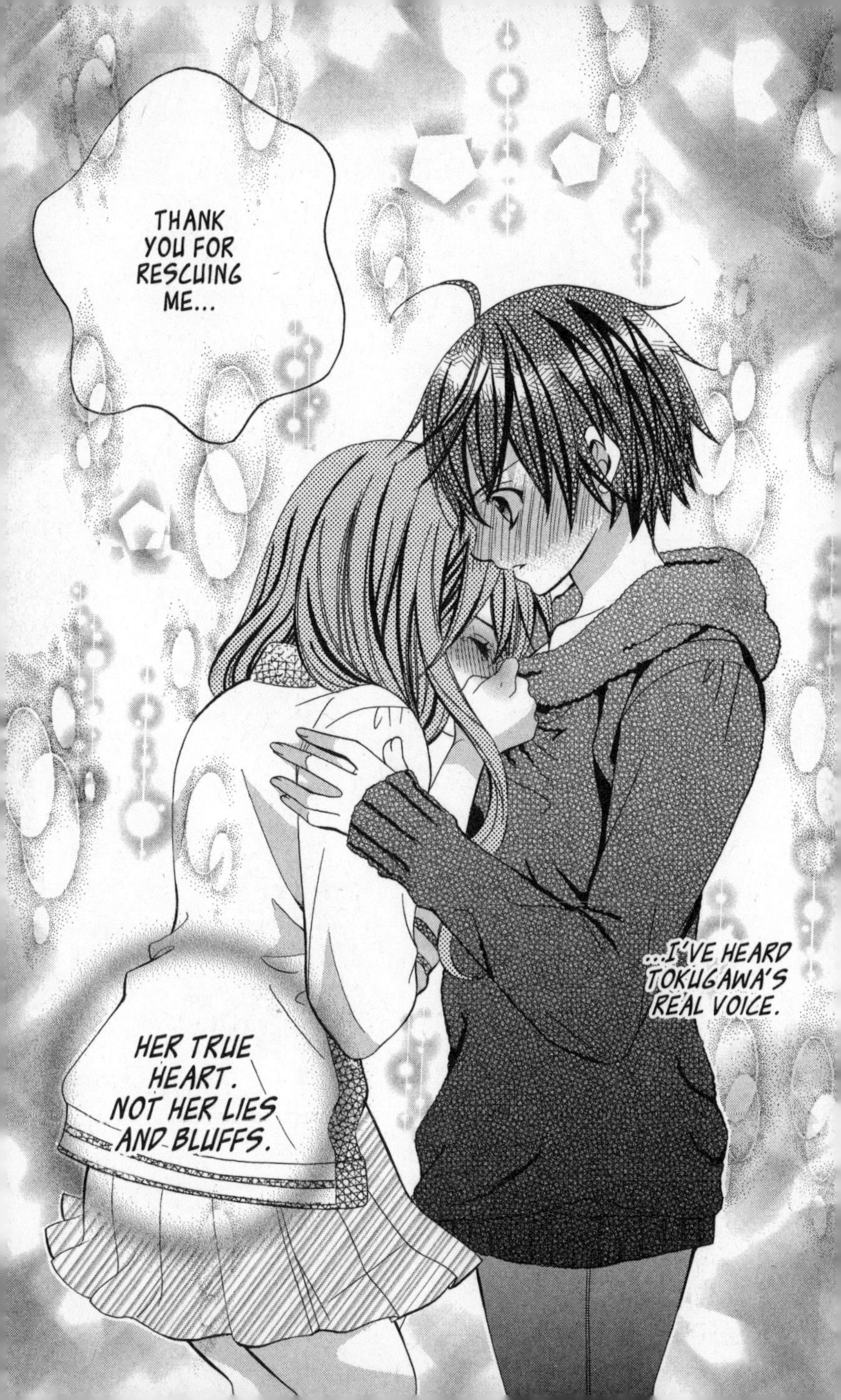
THANK YOU FOR RESCUING ME...
...I'VE HEARD TOKUGAWA'S REAL VOICE.
HER TRUE HEART. NOT HER LIES AND BLUFFS.

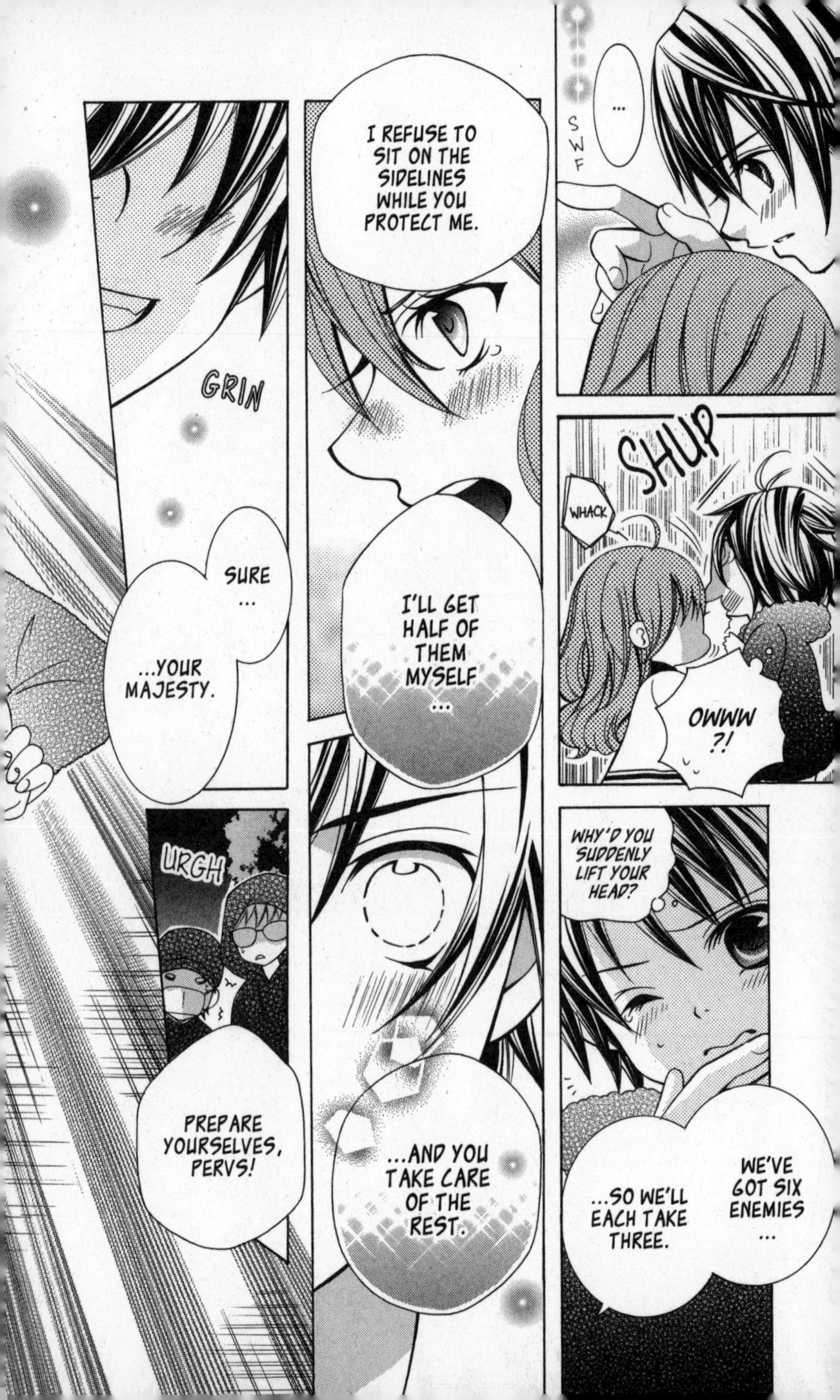
...
SWF
SHUP
WHACK
OWWW?!
WHY'D YOU SUDDENLY LIFT YOUR HEAD?
WE'VE GOT SIX ENEMIES...
...SO WE'LL EACH TAKE THREE.
I REFUSE TO SIT ON THE SIDELINES WHILE YOU PROTECT ME.
I'LL GET HALF OF THEM MYSELF...
...AND YOU TAKE CARE OF THE REST.
GRIN
SURE...
...YOUR MAJESTY.
URGH
PREPARE YOURSELVES, PERVS!

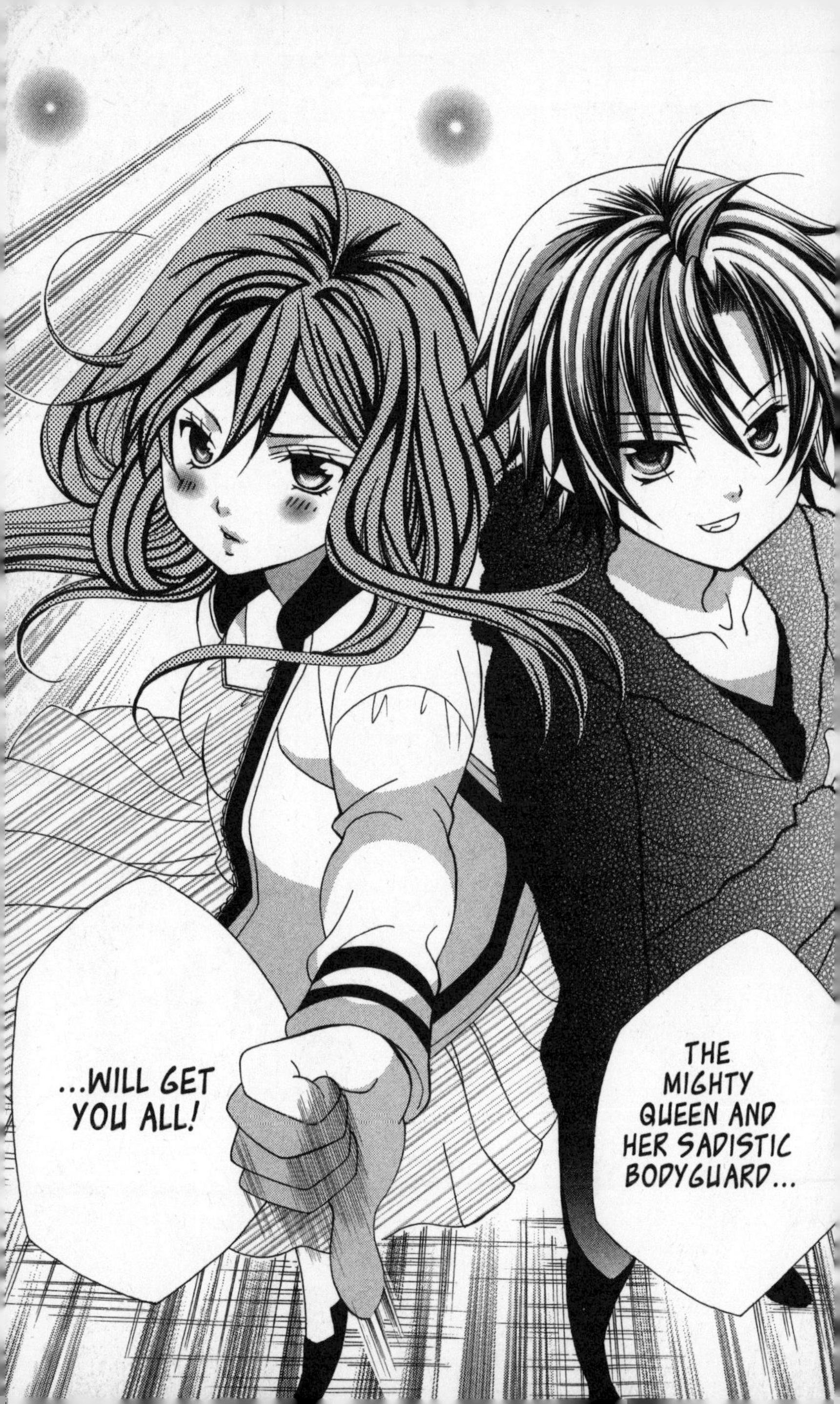
THE MIGHTY QUEEN AND HER SADISTIC BODYGUARD...
...WILL GET YOU ALL!

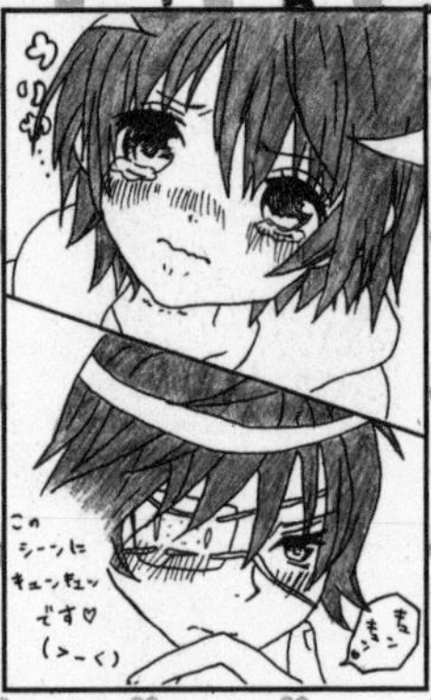
このシーンにキュンキュンです♡
(>_<)

Dokuganryu Masamune Date (Saitama) →

Ed.: Same here!!

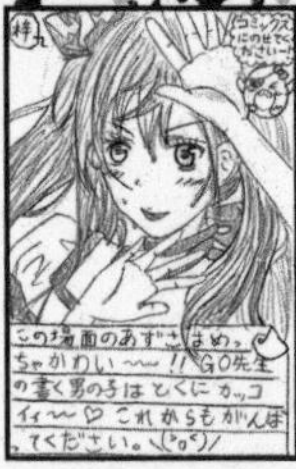
この場面のあずさはめっちゃかわい〜!! GO先生の書く男の子はとくにカッコイィ〜♡ これからもがんばってください。

Maaya Narita (Aomori) ↑

Ed.: Azusa heart-fluttering scene. ♥

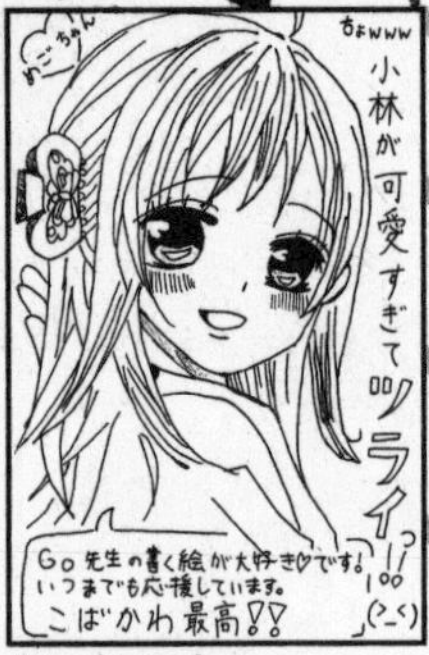
めごちゃん
ちょwww
小林が可愛すぎてツライっ!!
Go先生の書く絵が大好き♡です! いつまでも応援しています。
こばかわ最高!!

Mina (Tokyo) ↑

Ed.: This Mego makes my heart flutter!

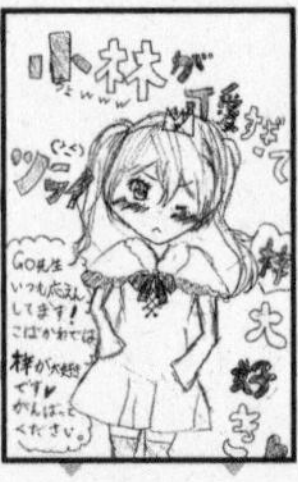
小林が可愛すぎてツライ
GO先生いつも応援してます! こばかわでは梓が大好きです がんばってください。
梓大好き

Satchan (Gifu) ←

Ed.: The tsundere Azusa is super cute!

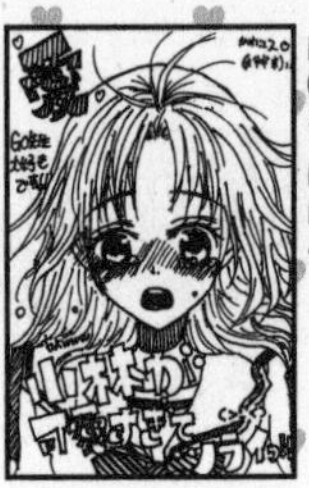
小林が可愛すぎてツライっ

Kaori Arimitsu (Kochi) ←

Ed.: Mego is always honest and straightforward!

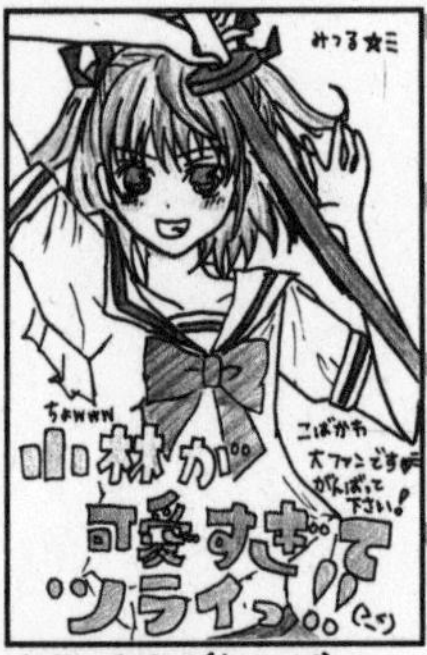
みつる☆ミ
ちょwww
小林が可愛すぎてツライっ!!
こばかわ大ファンです! がんばって下さい!

Shiho Saito (Aomori) ↑

Ed.: Here's Mitsuru's killer pose. ♪

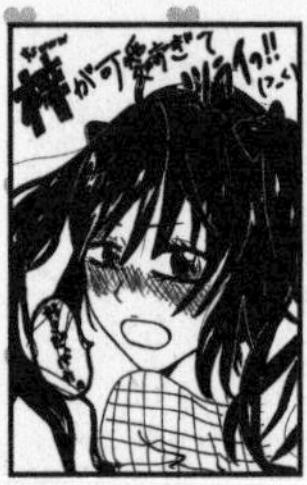
梓が可愛すぎてツライっ!!

Nijiiro no Kumo (Niigata) ←

Ed.: Thanks for Azusa's sweet expression!

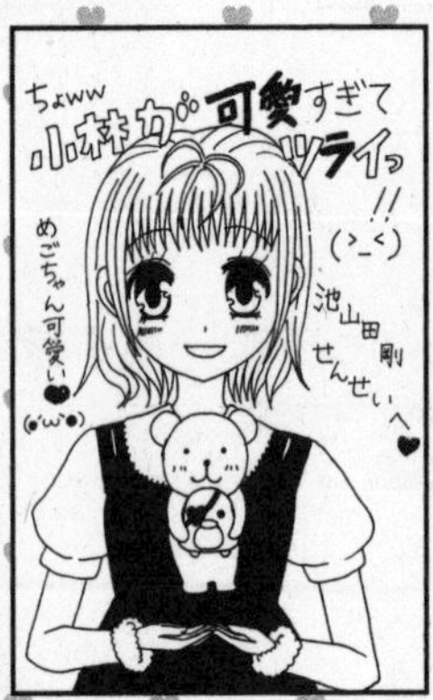
ちょww
小林が可愛すぎてツライっ!!
めごちゃん可愛い
池山田剛せんせいへ

Nekozukin (Hokkaido) →

Ed.: Mego + Go-chan + eye-patch penguin combo is amazingly cute!

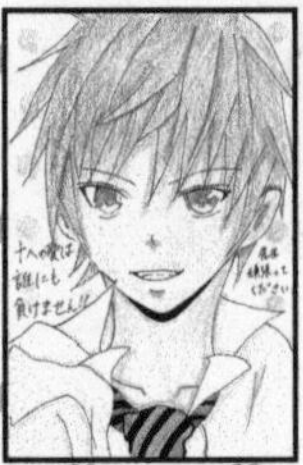

Chihiro Kikuta (Osaka) ←

Ed.: This drawing is full of love for Mitsuru!!

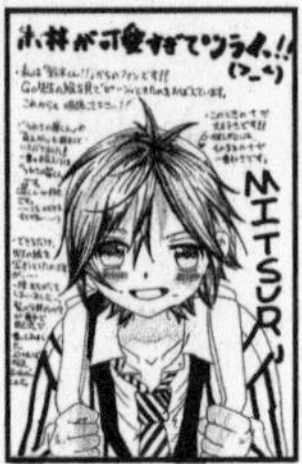
小林が可愛すぎてツライ!!
MITSURU

Kaede (Kyoto) ↑

Ed.: Mitsuru looked so cute back then. (Faraway look)

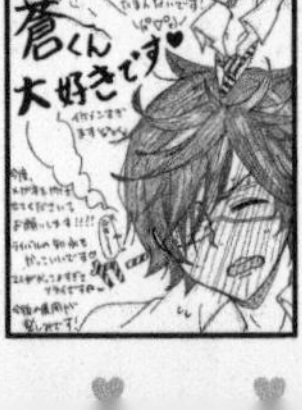
蒼くん大好きです♥

Miu (Niigata) ←

Ed.: I just love the blushing Aoi!

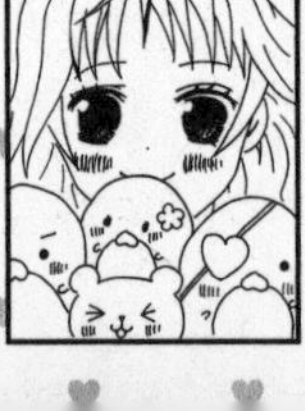

Kotomi Sakata (Saitama) ←

Ed.: All these penguins are cuuute! ♥

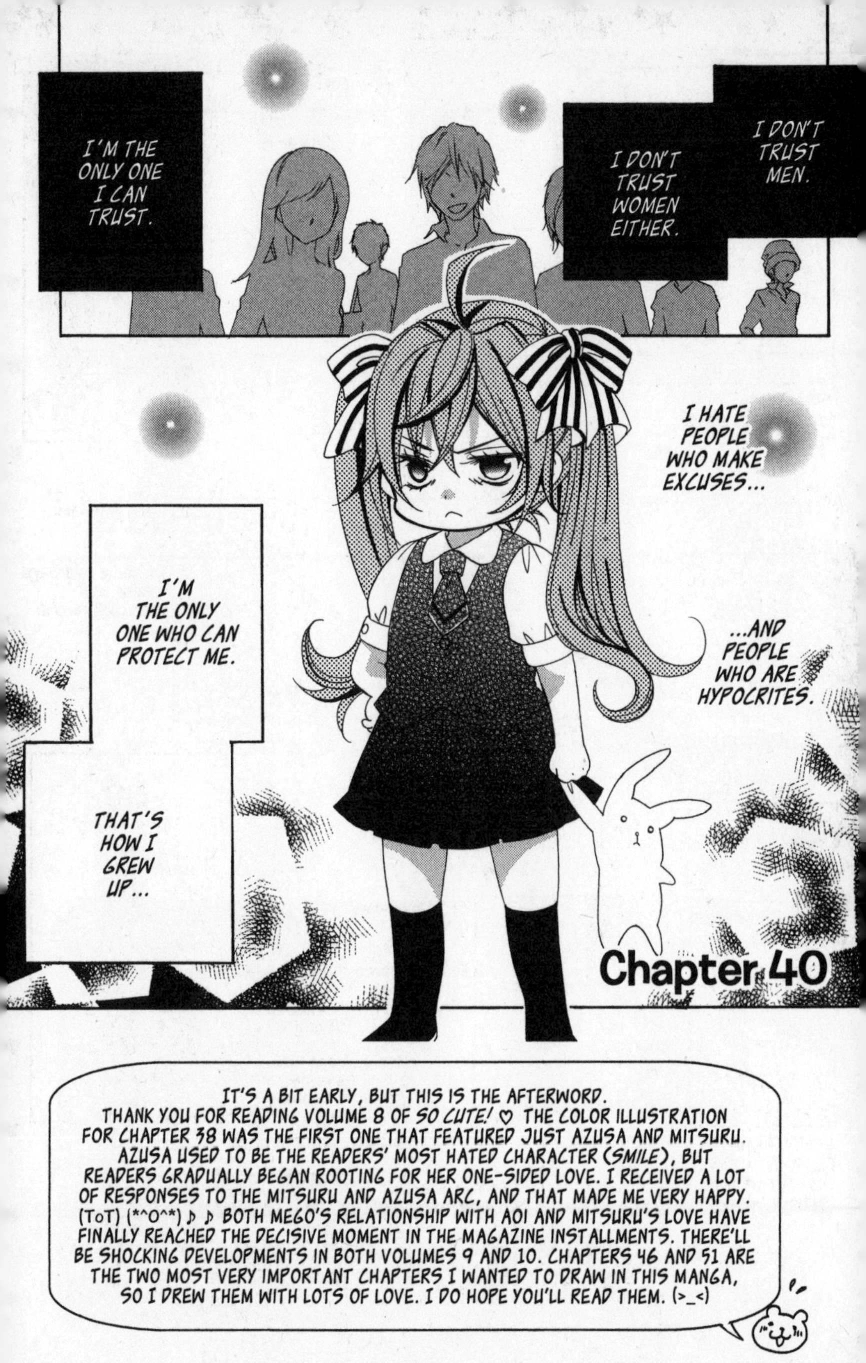
I DON'T TRUST MEN.
I DON'T TRUST WOMEN EITHER.
I'M THE ONLY ONE I CAN TRUST.
I HATE PEOPLE WHO MAKE EXCUSES...
...AND PEOPLE WHO ARE HYPOCRITES.
I'M THE ONLY ONE WHO CAN PROTECT ME.
THAT'S HOW I GREW UP...
Chapter 40

IT'S A BIT EARLY, BUT THIS IS THE AFTERWORD. THANK YOU FOR READING VOLUME 8 OF *SO CUTE!* ♡ THE COLOR ILLUSTRATION FOR CHAPTER 38 WAS THE FIRST ONE THAT FEATURED JUST AZUSA AND MITSURU. AZUSA USED TO BE THE READERS' MOST HATED CHARACTER (*SMILE*), BUT READERS GRADUALLY BEGAN ROOTING FOR HER ONE-SIDED LOVE. I RECEIVED A LOT OF RESPONSES TO THE MITSURU AND AZUSA ARC, AND THAT MADE ME VERY HAPPY. (ToT) (*^O^*) ♪ ♪ BOTH MEGO'S RELATIONSHIP WITH AOI AND MITSURU'S LOVE HAVE FINALLY REACHED THE DECISIVE MOMENT IN THE MAGAZINE INSTALLMENTS. THERE'LL BE SHOCKING DEVELOPMENTS IN BOTH VOLUMES 9 AND 10. CHAPTERS 46 AND 51 ARE THE TWO MOST VERY IMPORTANT CHAPTERS I WANTED TO DRAW IN THIS MANGA, SO I DREW THEM WITH LOTS OF LOVE. I DO HOPE YOU'LL READ THEM. (>_<)

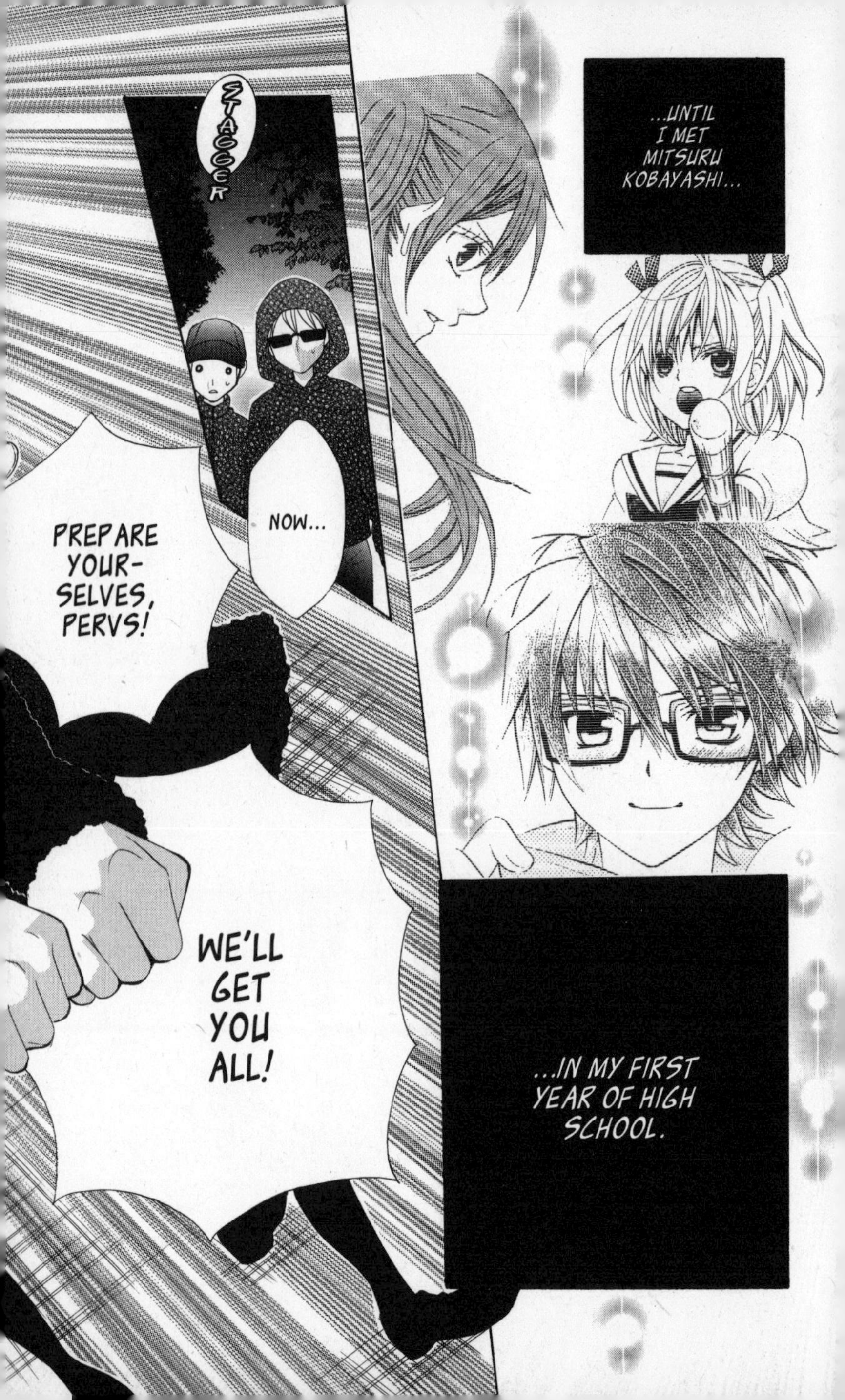
...UNTIL I MET MITSURU KOBAYASHI...
...IN MY FIRST YEAR OF HIGH SCHOOL.
STAGGER
NOW...
PREPARE YOUR-SELVES, PERVS!
WE'LL GET YOU ALL!

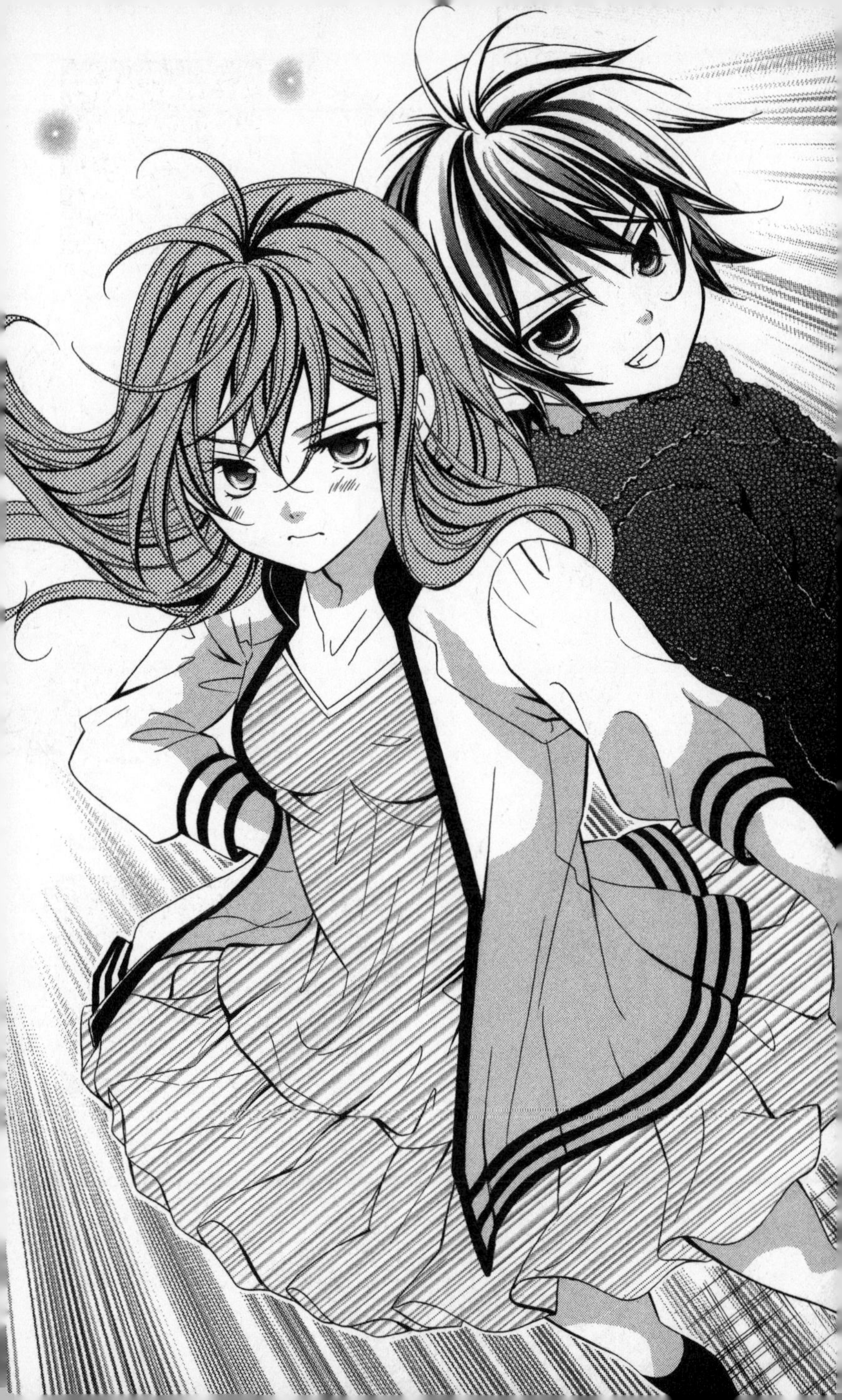

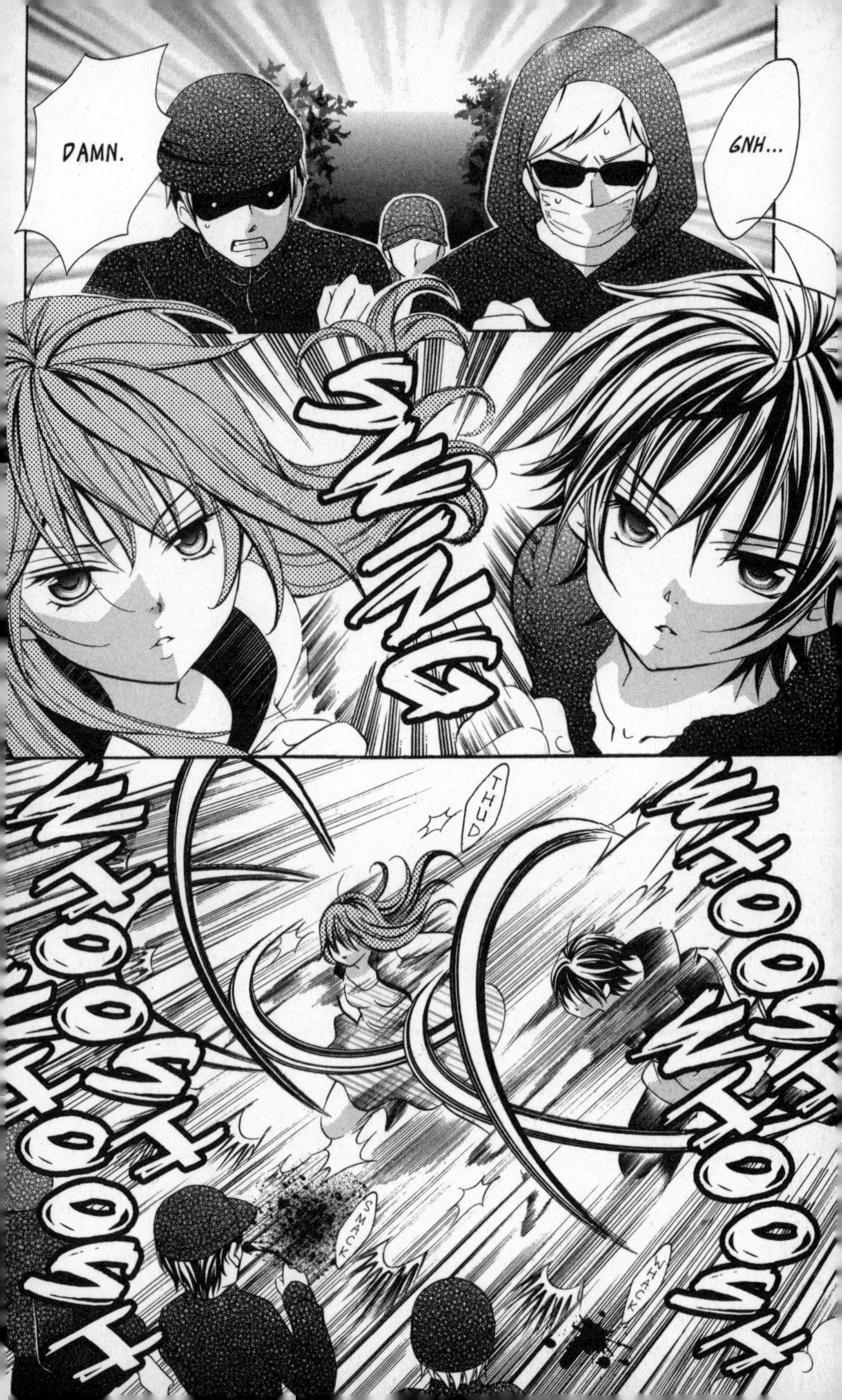
GNH...
DAMN.
SWING
WHOOSH WHOOSH
THUD
WHACK
SMACK
WHOOSH WHOOSH

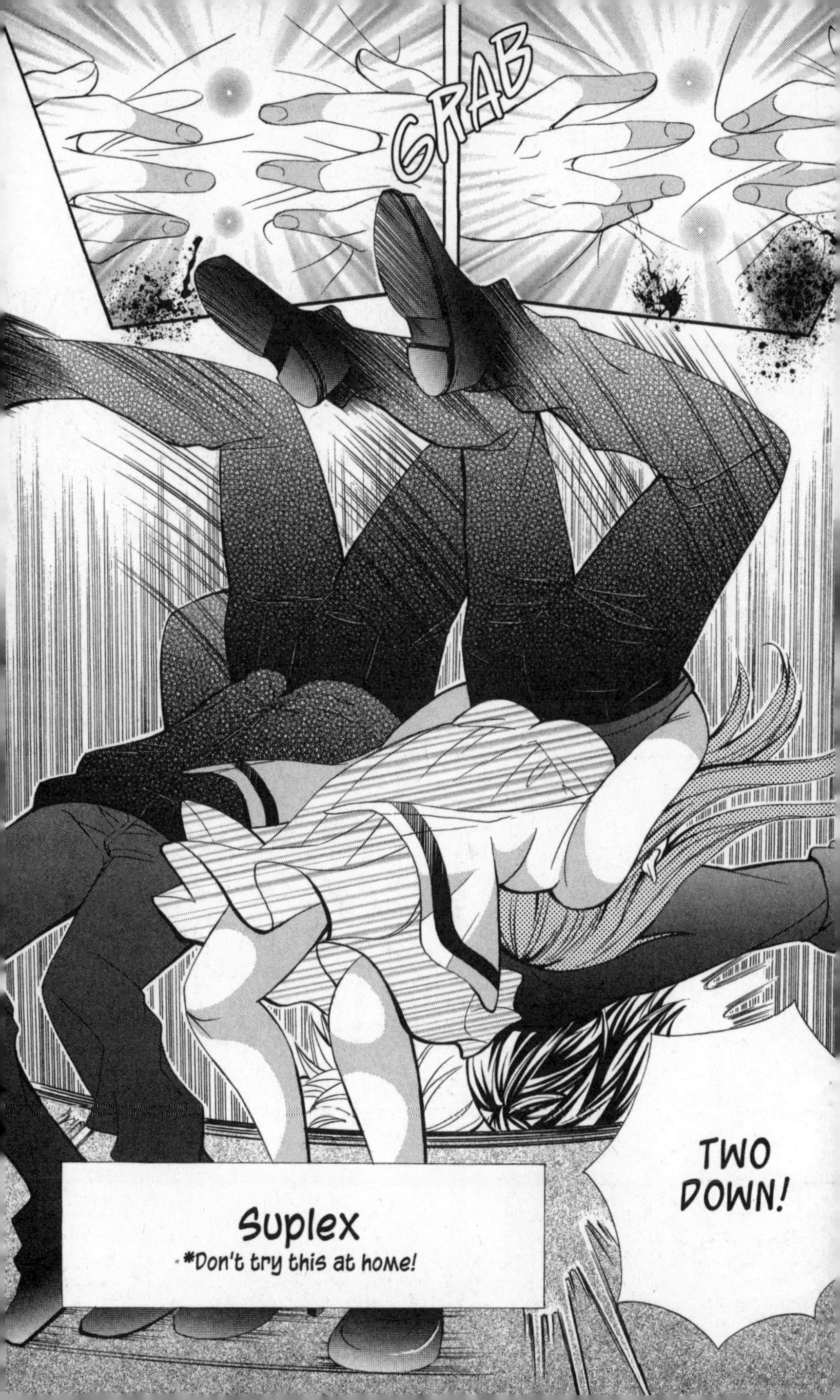
GRAB
TWO DOWN!
Suplex
*Don't try this at home!

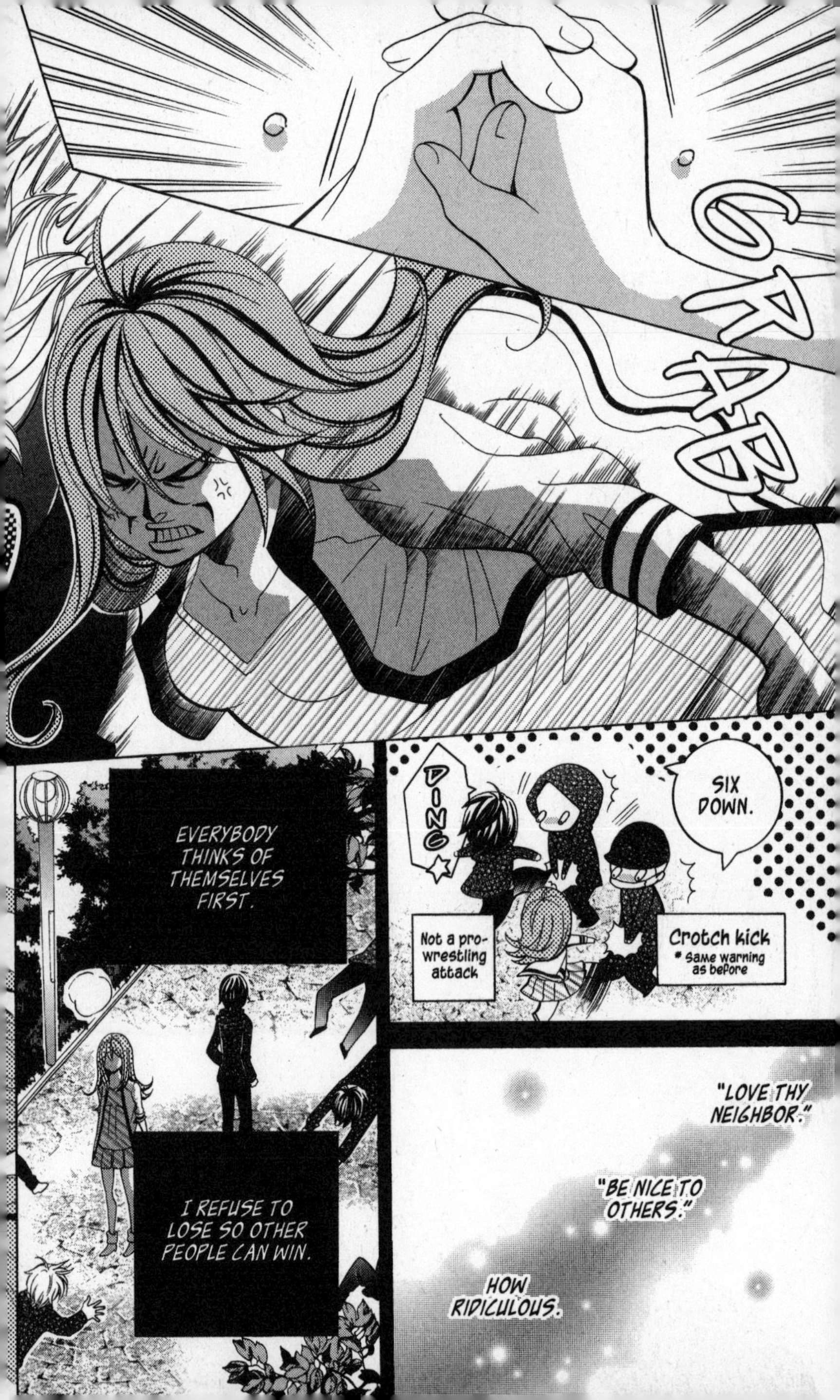
GRAB
DING
SIX DOWN.
Crotch kick
* Same warning as before
Not a pro-wrestling attack
"LOVE THY NEIGHBOR."
"BE NICE TO OTHERS."
HOW RIDICULOUS.
EVERYBODY THINKS OF THEMSELVES FIRST.
I REFUSE TO LOSE SO OTHER PEOPLE CAN WIN.

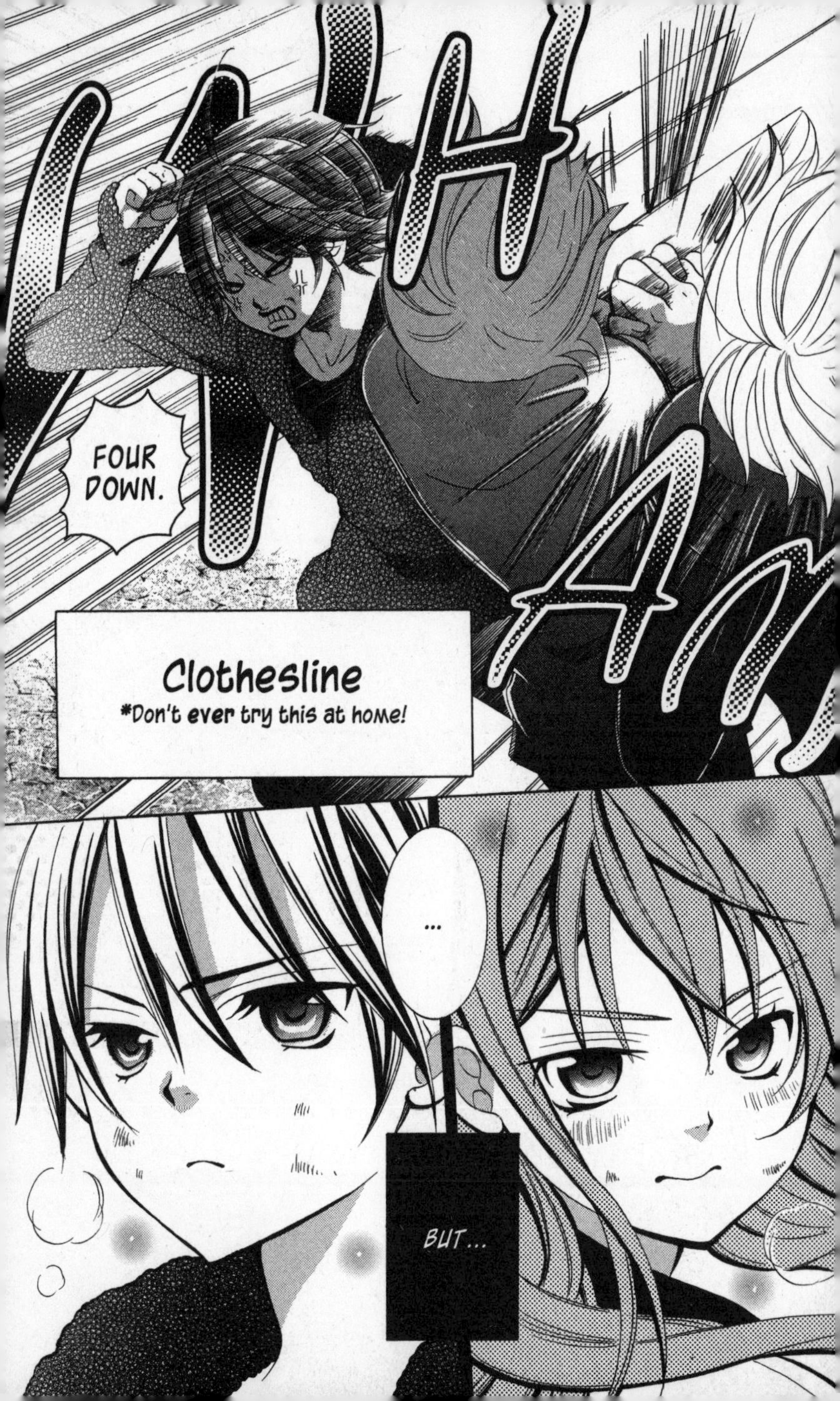
FOUR DOWN.
Clothesline
*Don't ever try this at home!
...
BUT...

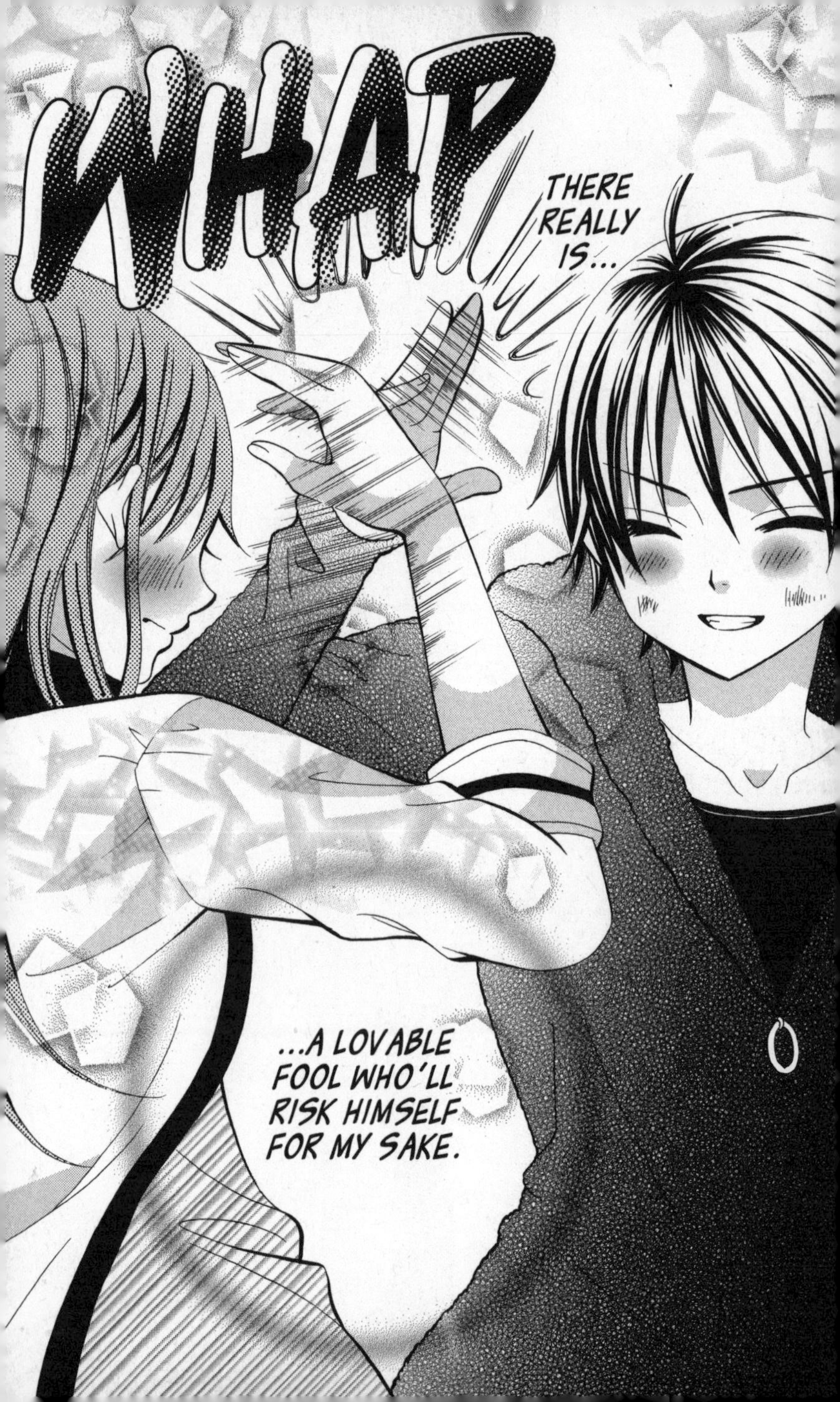
WHAP
THERE REALLY IS...
...A LOVABLE FOOL WHO'LL RISK HIMSELF FOR MY SAKE.

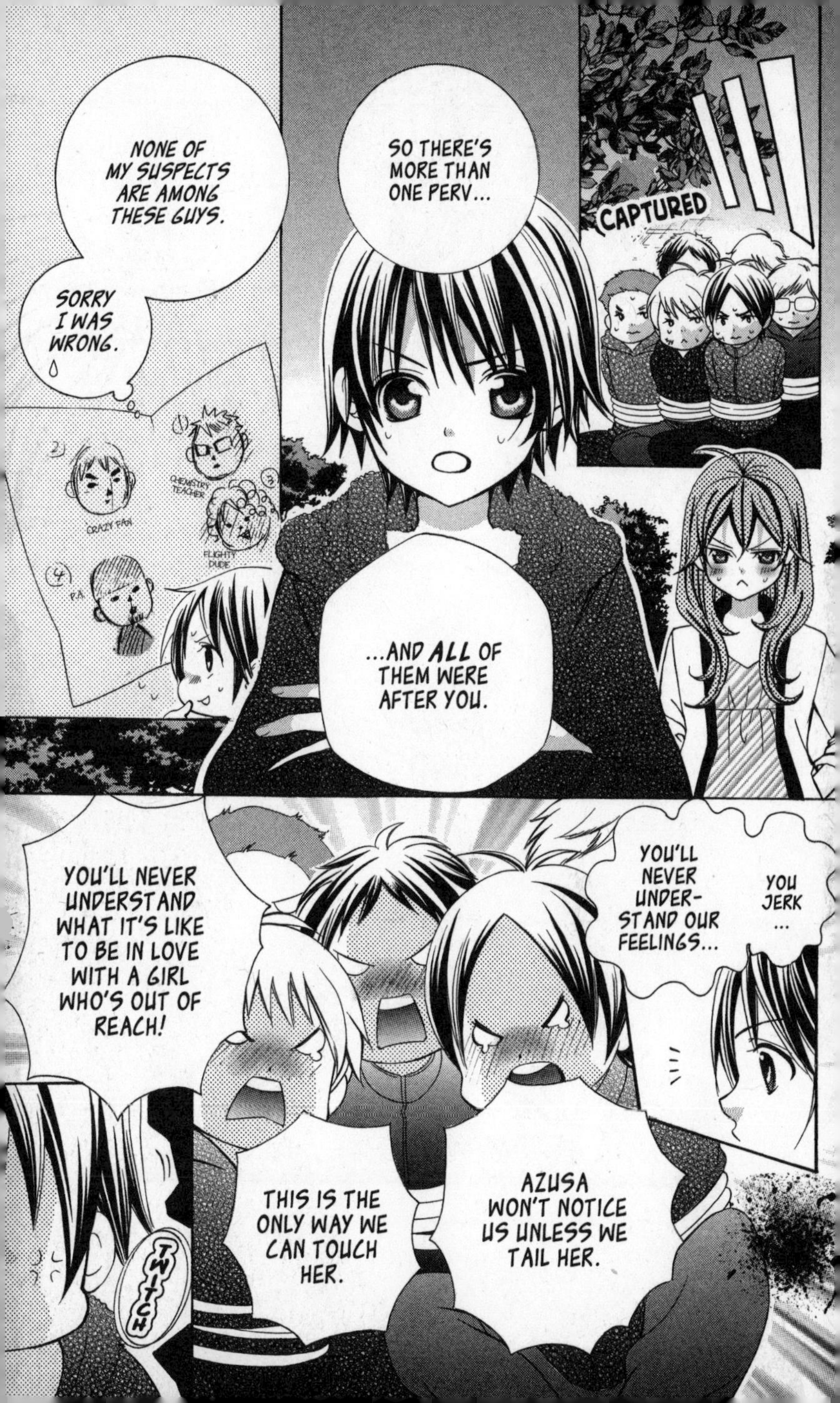
CAPTURED
SO THERE'S MORE THAN ONE PERV...
...AND ALL OF THEM WERE AFTER YOU.
NONE OF MY SUSPECTS ARE AMONG THESE GUYS.
SORRY I WAS WRONG.
1 CHEMISTRY TEACHER
2 CRAZY FAN
3 FLIGHTY DUDE
4 P.A.
YOU JERK ...
YOU'LL NEVER UNDER-STAND OUR FEELINGS...
YOU'LL NEVER UNDERSTAND WHAT IT'S LIKE TO BE IN LOVE WITH A GIRL WHO'S OUT OF REACH!
AZUSA WON'T NOTICE US UNLESS WE TAIL HER.
THIS IS THE ONLY WAY WE CAN TOUCH HER.
TWITCH

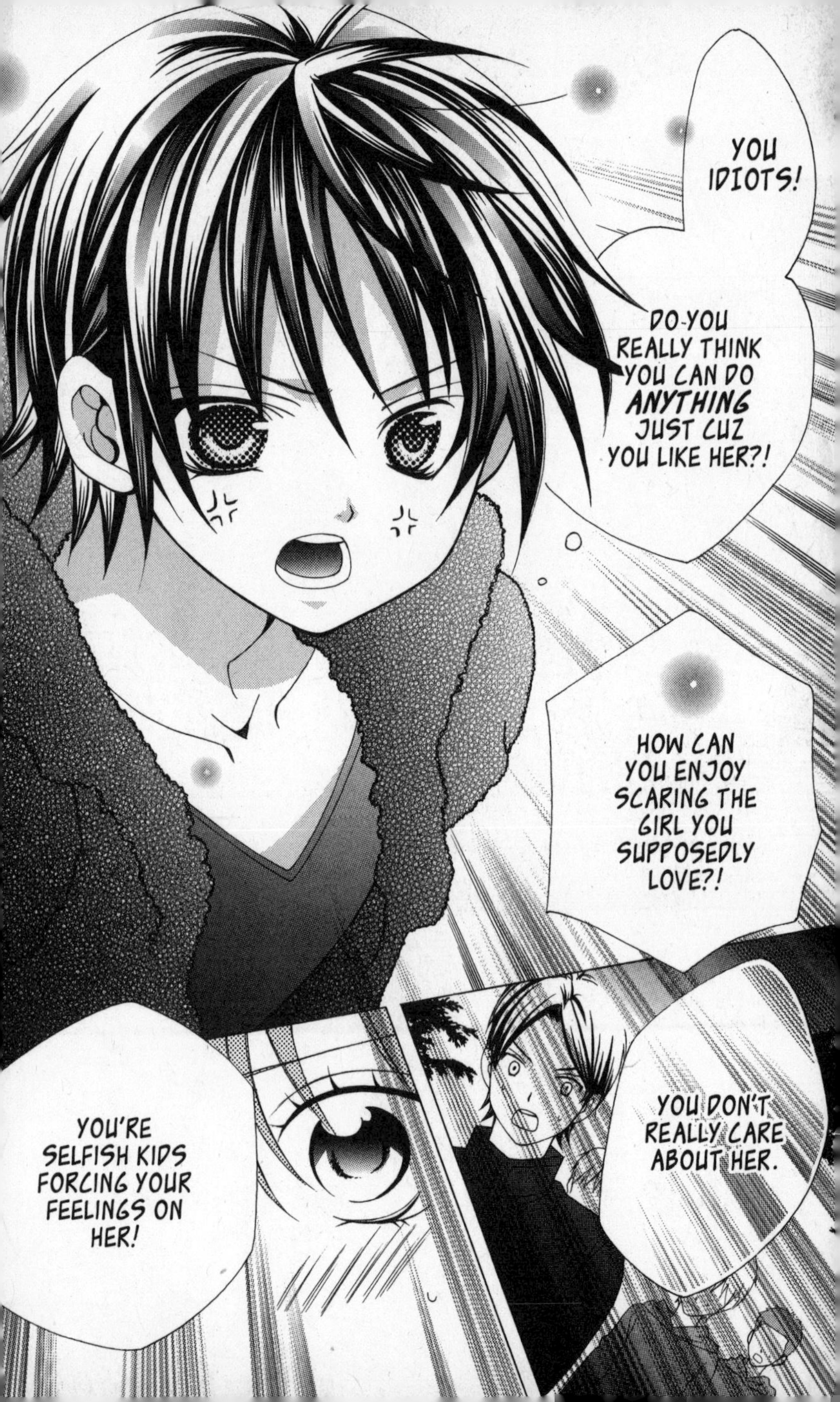
YOU IDIOTS!
DO YOU REALLY THINK YOU CAN DO *ANYTHING* JUST CUZ YOU LIKE HER?!
HOW CAN YOU ENJOY SCARING THE GIRL YOU SUPPOSEDLY LOVE?!
YOU DON'T REALLY CARE ABOUT HER.
YOU'RE SELFISH KIDS FORCING YOUR FEELINGS ON HER!

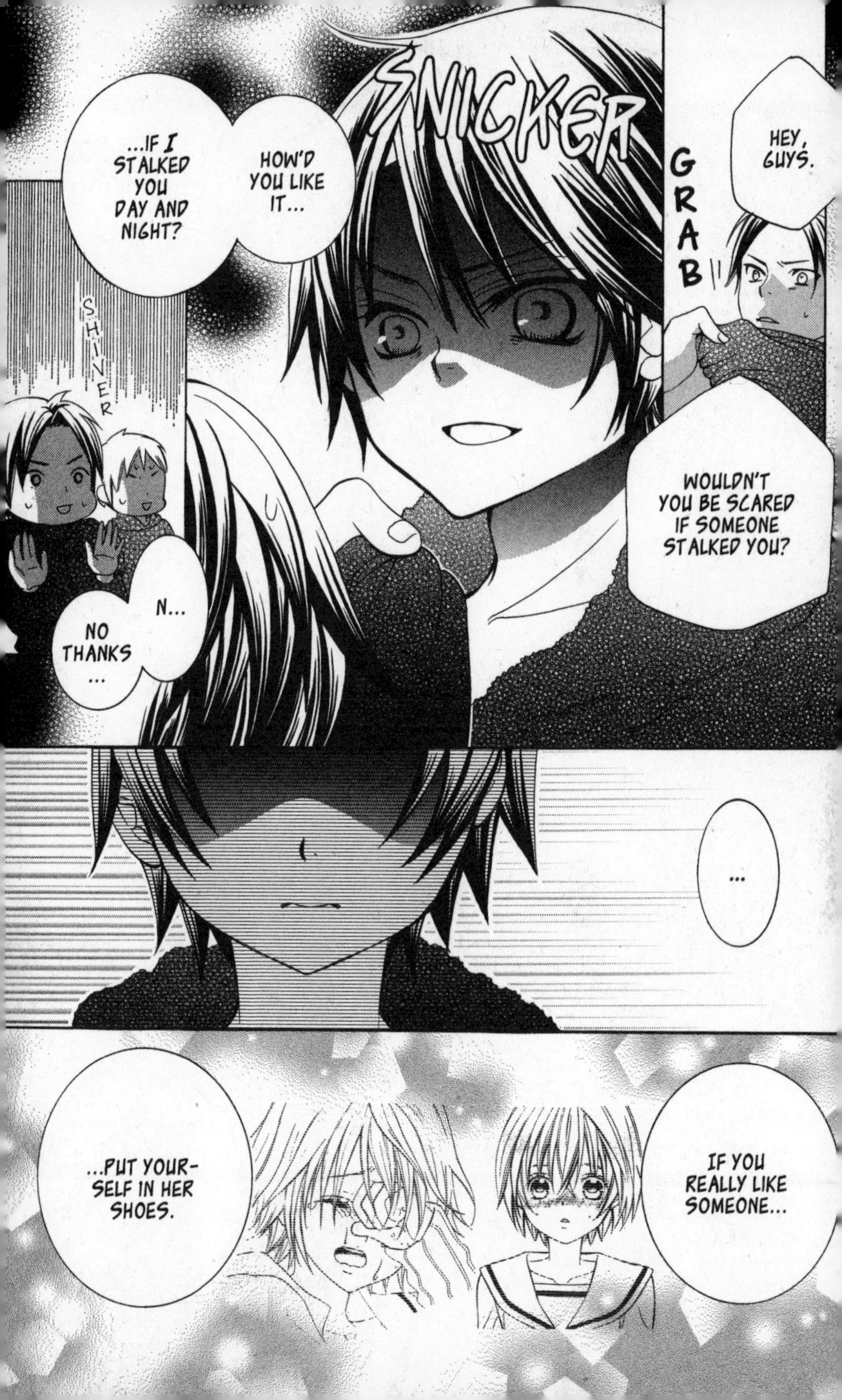
HEY, GUYS.
GRAB
WOULDN'T YOU BE SCARED IF SOMEONE STALKED YOU?
SNICKER
HOW'D YOU LIKE IT...
...IF I STALKED YOU DAY AND NIGHT?
SHIVER
N... NO THANKS...
...
IF YOU REALLY LIKE SOMEONE...
...PUT YOUR-SELF IN HER SHOES.

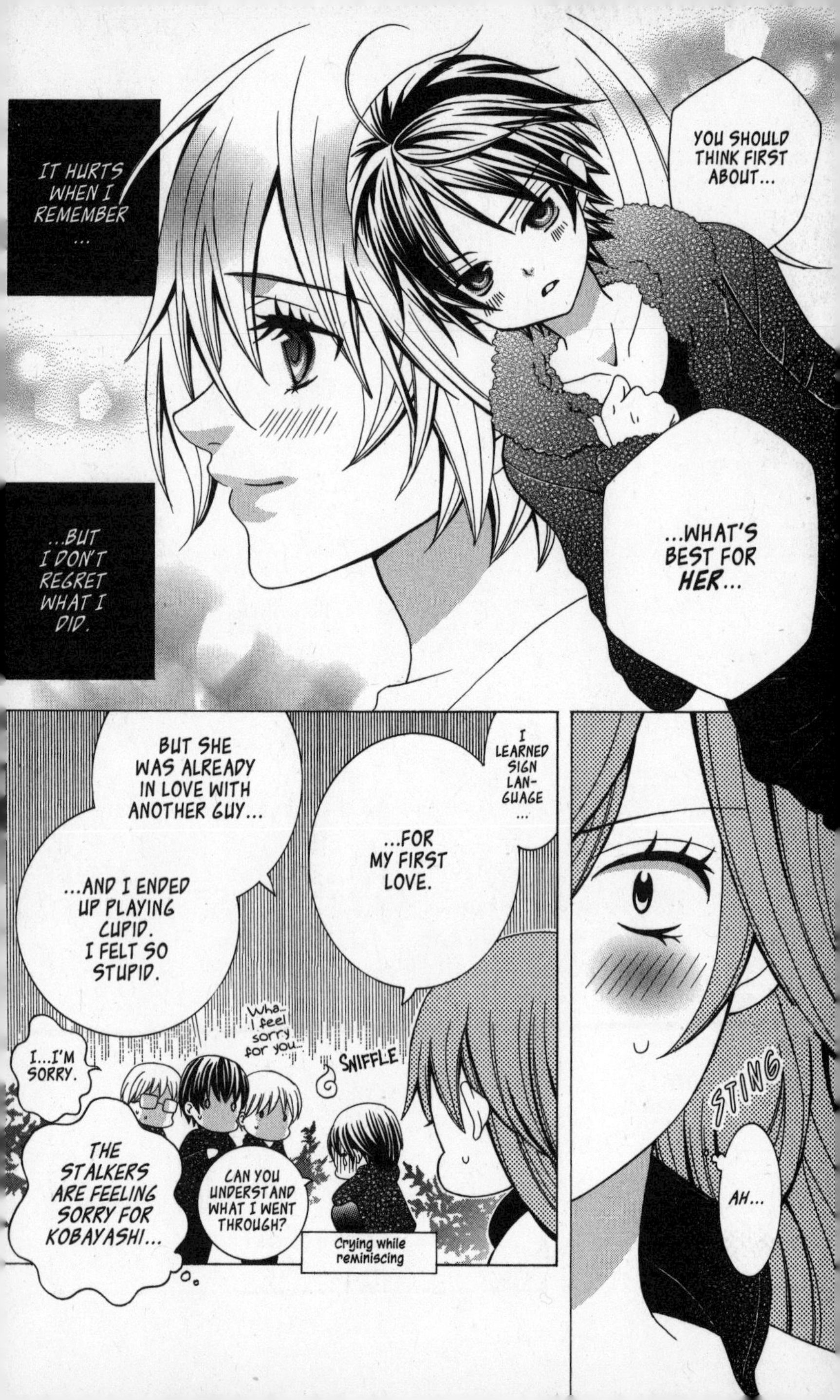
YOU SHOULD THINK FIRST ABOUT...
...WHAT'S BEST FOR HER...
IT HURTS WHEN I REMEMBER ...
...BUT I DON'T REGRET WHAT I DID.
STING
AH...
I LEARNED SIGN LAN-GUAGE ...
...FOR MY FIRST LOVE.
BUT SHE WAS ALREADY IN LOVE WITH ANOTHER GUY...
...AND I ENDED UP PLAYING CUPID. I FELT SO STUPID.
Wha... I feel sorry for you...
SNIFFLE
I...I'M SORRY.
CAN YOU UNDERSTAND WHAT I WENT THROUGH?
THE STALKERS ARE FEELING SORRY FOR KOBAYASHI...
Crying while reminiscing

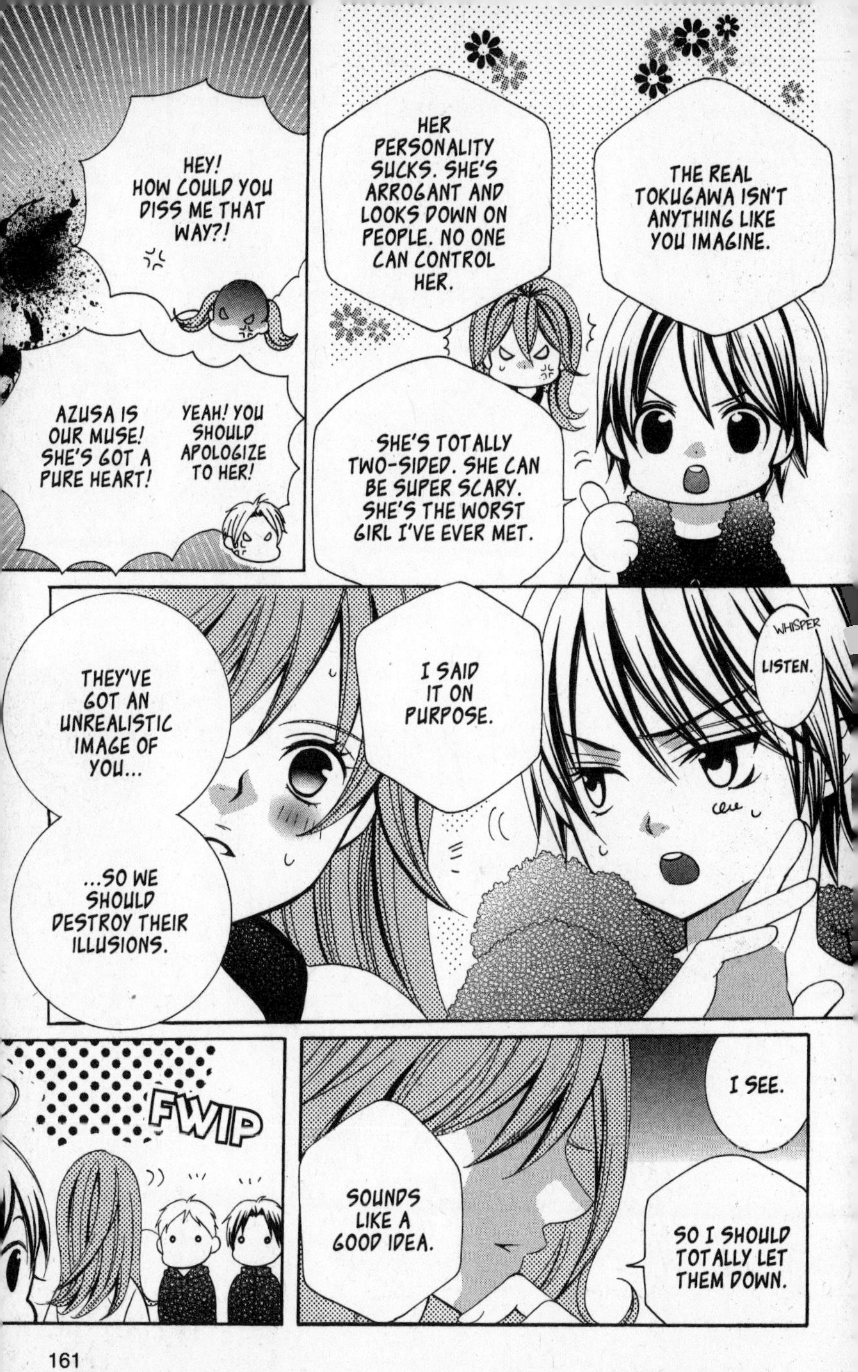
THE REAL TOKUGAWA ISN'T ANYTHING LIKE YOU IMAGINE.
HER PERSONALITY SUCKS. SHE'S ARROGANT AND LOOKS DOWN ON PEOPLE. NO ONE CAN CONTROL HER.
SHE'S TOTALLY TWO-SIDED. SHE CAN BE SUPER SCARY. SHE'S THE WORST GIRL I'VE EVER MET.
HEY! HOW COULD YOU DISS ME THAT WAY?!
YEAH! YOU SHOULD APOLOGIZE TO HER!
AZUSA IS OUR MUSE! SHE'S GOT A PURE HEART!
WHISPER
LISTEN.
I SAID IT ON PURPOSE.
THEY'VE GOT AN UNREALISTIC IMAGE OF YOU...
...SO WE SHOULD DESTROY THEIR ILLUSIONS.
I SEE.
SO I SHOULD TOTALLY LET THEM DOWN.
SOUNDS LIKE A GOOD IDEA.
FWIP

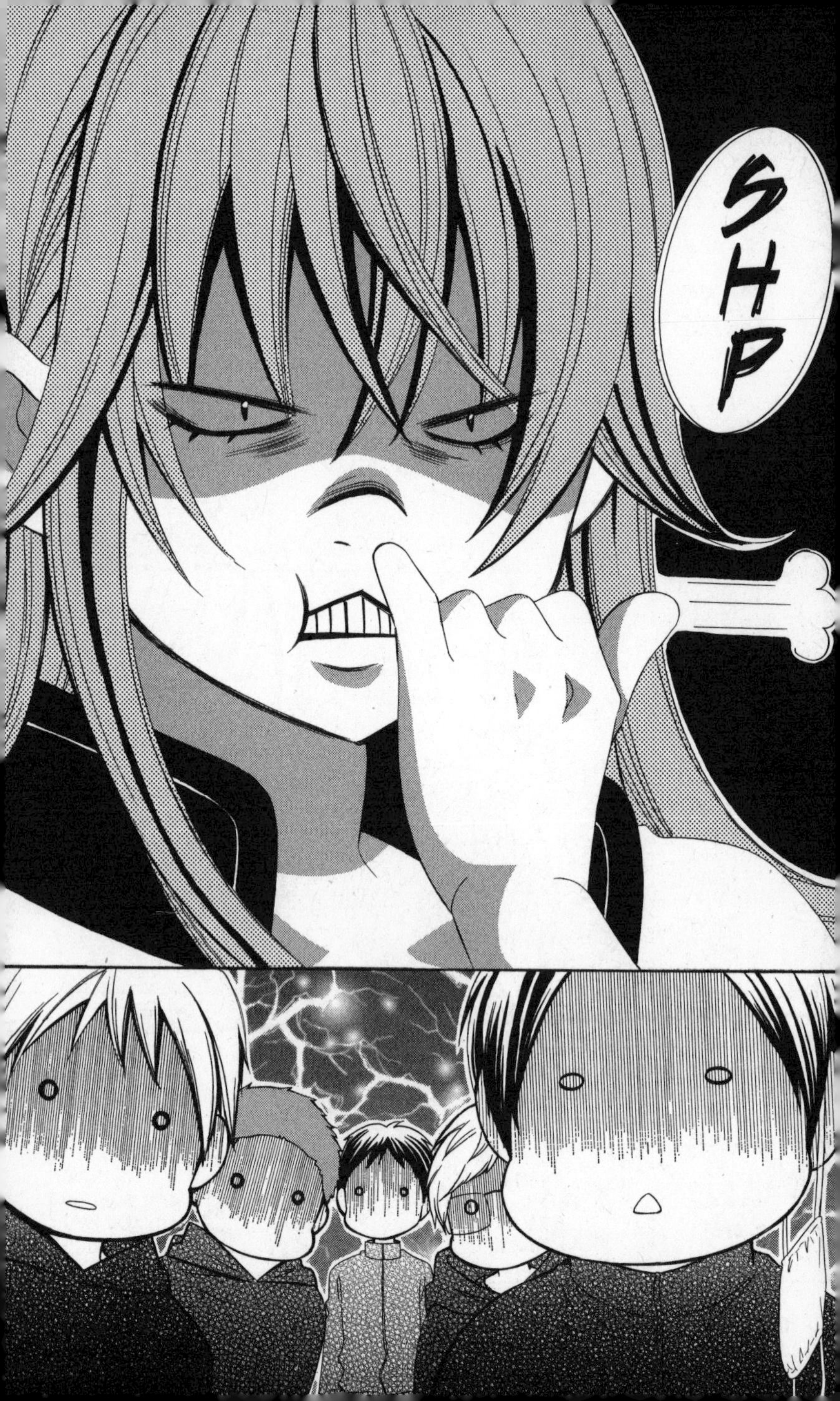
SHP

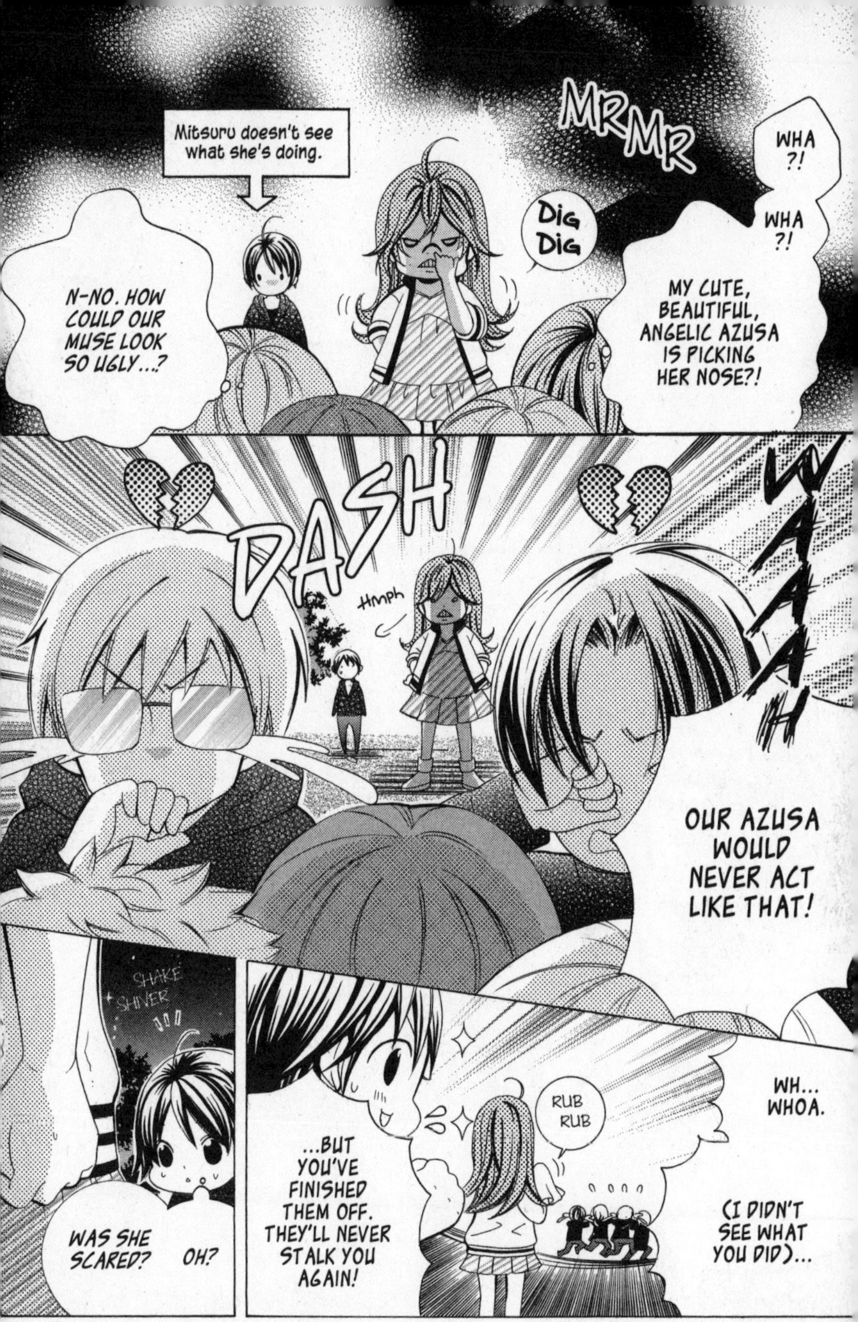

MRMR
WHA ?!
WHA ?!
MY CUTE, BEAUTIFUL, ANGELIC AZUSA IS PICKING HER NOSE?!
Dig Dig
Mitsuru doesn't see what she's doing.
N-NO. HOW COULD OUR MUSE LOOK SO UGLY...?
WAAAH
DASH
Hmph
OUR AZUSA WOULD NEVER ACT LIKE THAT!
WH... WHOA.
(I DIDN'T SEE WHAT YOU DID)...
RUB RUB
...BUT YOU'VE FINISHED THEM OFF. THEY'LL NEVER STALK YOU AGAIN!
SHAKE
SHIVER
OH?
WAS SHE SCARED?

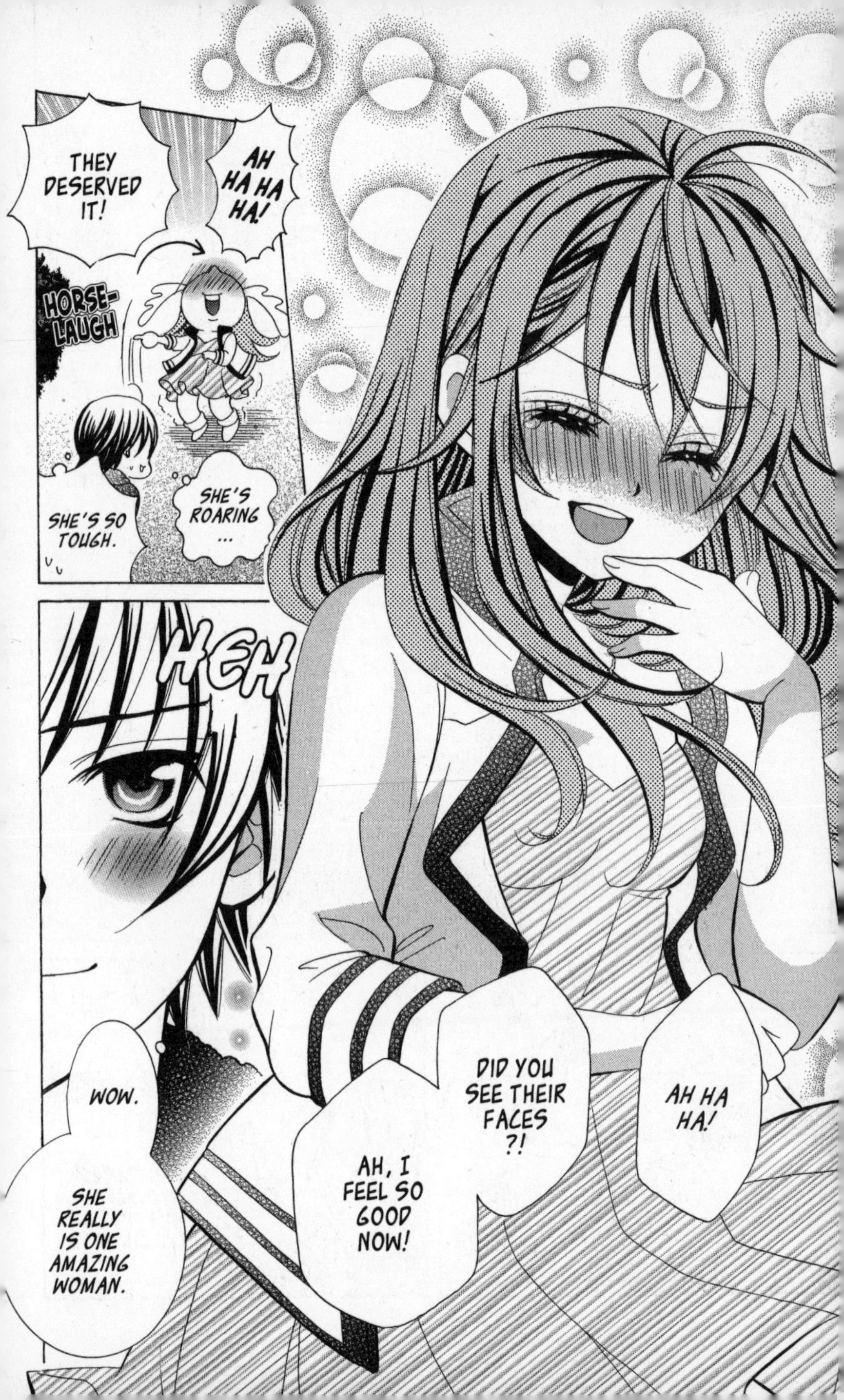
AH HA HA!
DID YOU SEE THEIR FACES?!
AH, I FEEL SO GOOD NOW!
AH HA HA HA!
THEY DESERVED IT!
HORSE-LAUGH
SHE'S ROARING...
SHE'S SO TOUGH.
HEH
WOW.
SHE REALLY IS ONE AMAZING WOMAN.

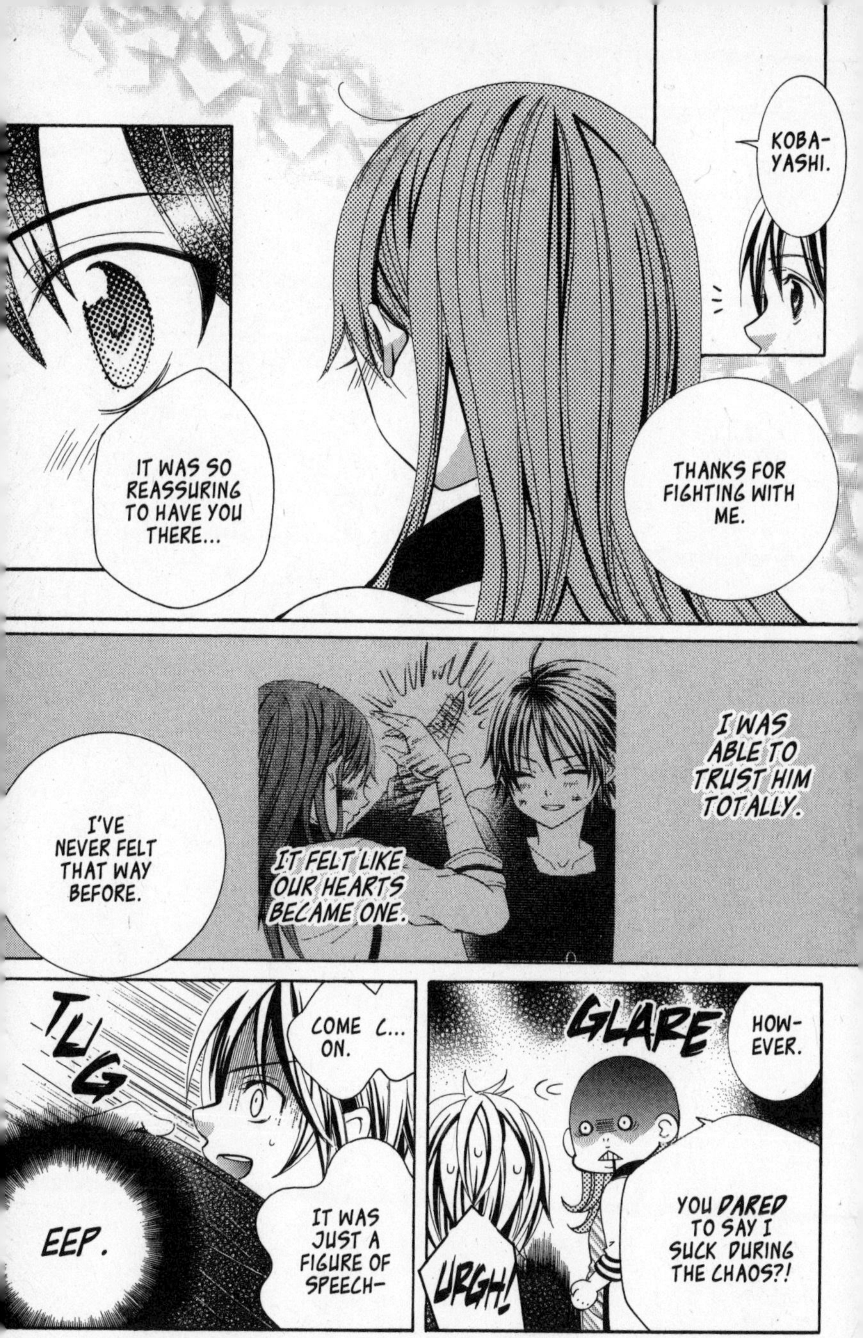
KOBA-YASHI.
THANKS FOR FIGHTING WITH ME.
IT WAS SO REASSURING TO HAVE YOU THERE...
I WAS ABLE TO TRUST HIM TOTALLY.
IT FELT LIKE OUR HEARTS BECAME ONE.
I'VE NEVER FELT THAT WAY BEFORE.
GLARE
HOW-EVER.
YOU DARED TO SAY I SUCK DURING THE CHAOS?!
URGH!
COME C... ON.
TUG
IT WAS JUST A FIGURE OF SPEECH-
EEP.

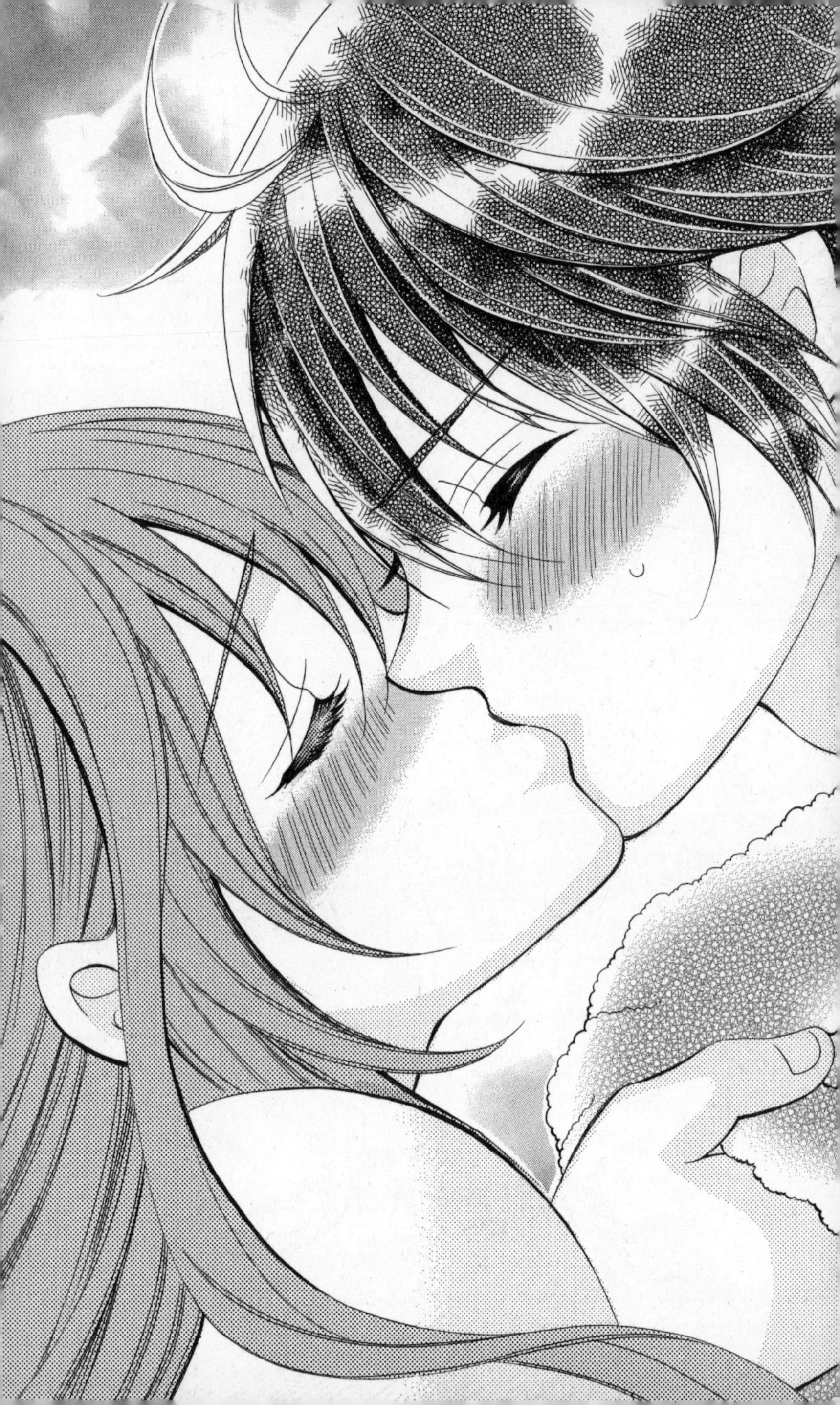

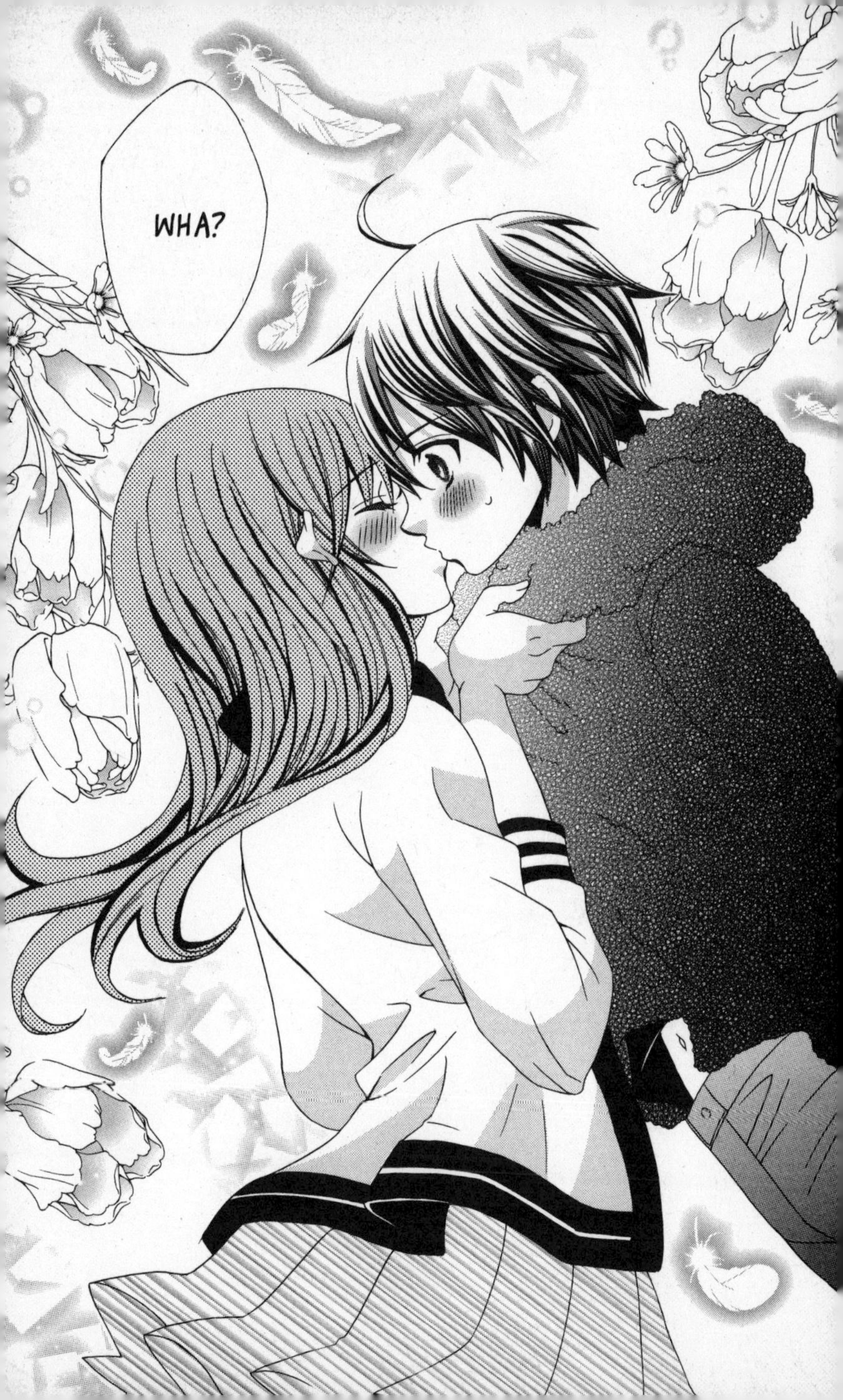
WHA?

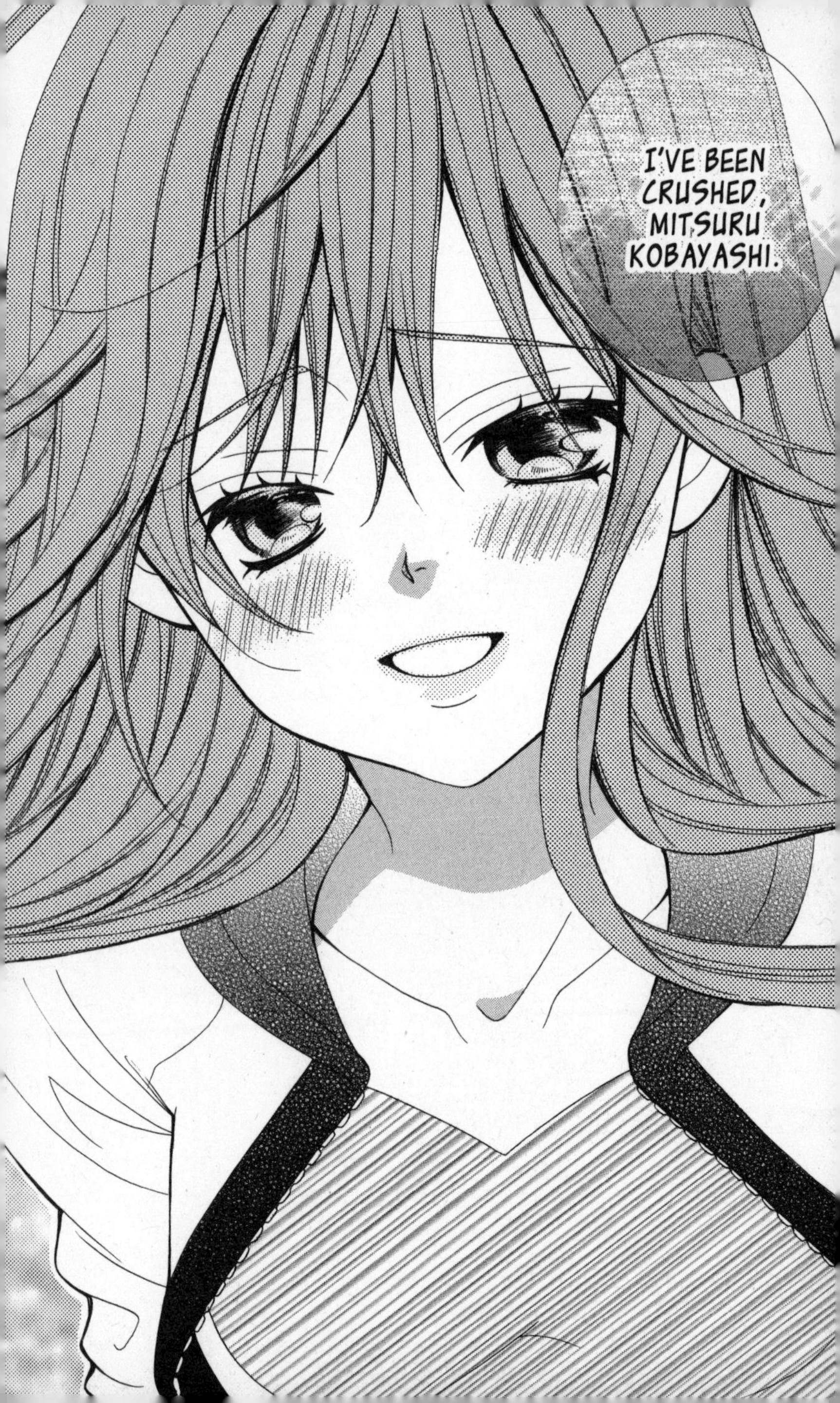
I'VE BEEN CRUSHED, MITSURU KOBAYASHI.

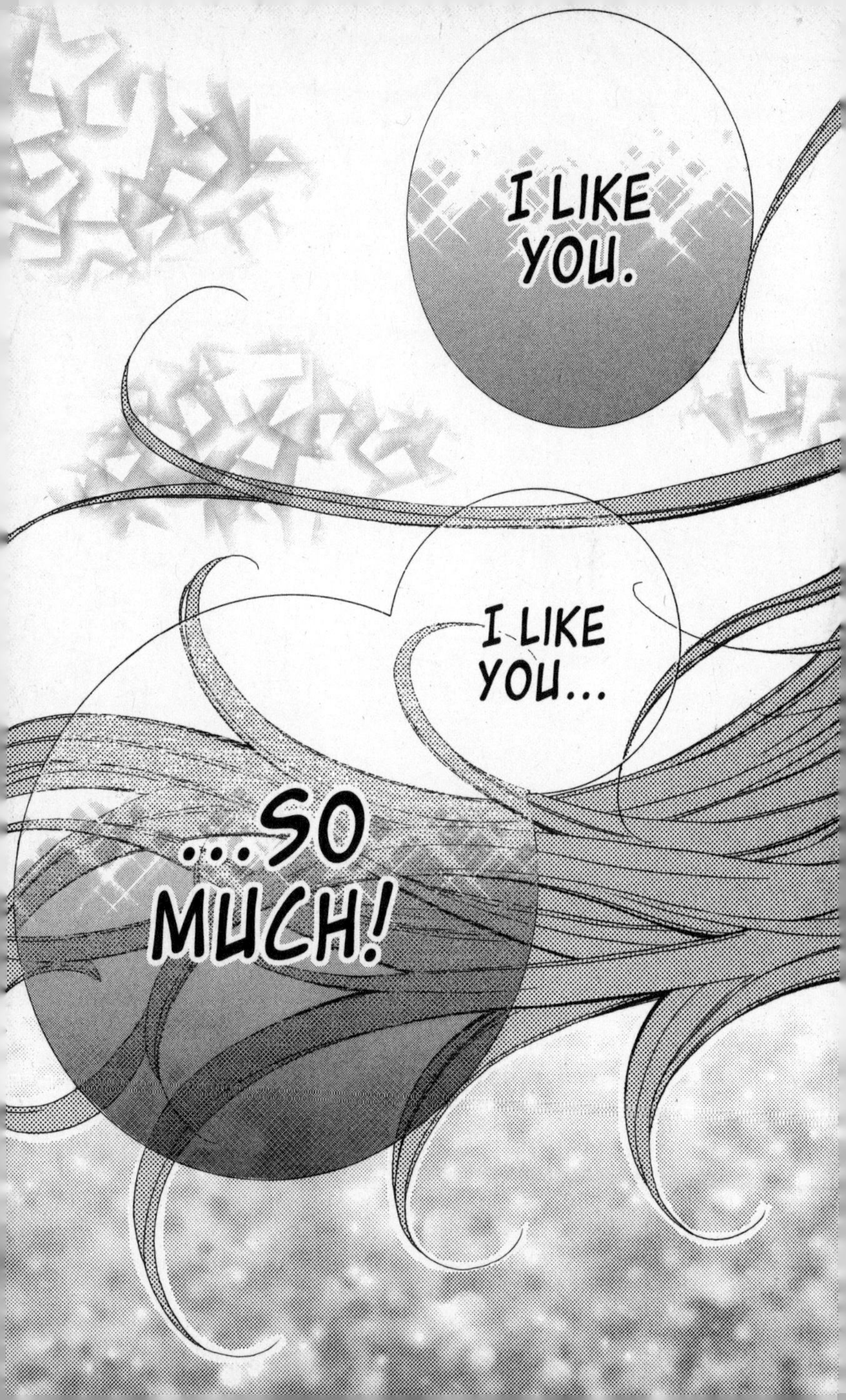
I LIKE YOU.
I LIKE YOU...
...SO MUCH!

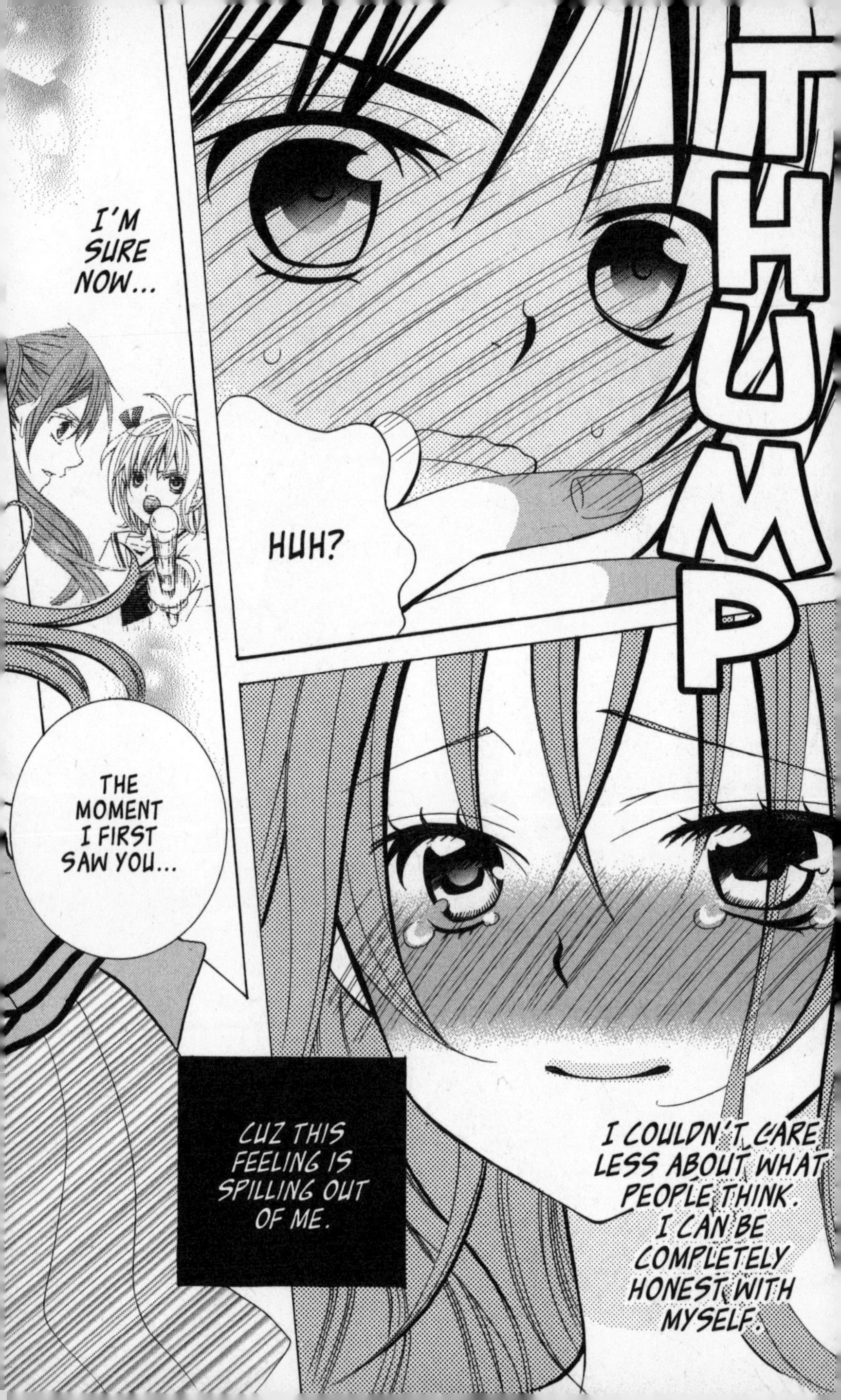
THUMP
HUH?
I COULDN'T CARE LESS ABOUT WHAT PEOPLE THINK. I CAN BE COMPLETELY HONEST WITH MYSELF.
CUZ THIS FEELING IS SPILLING OUT OF ME.
I'M SURE NOW...
THE MOMENT I FIRST SAW YOU...

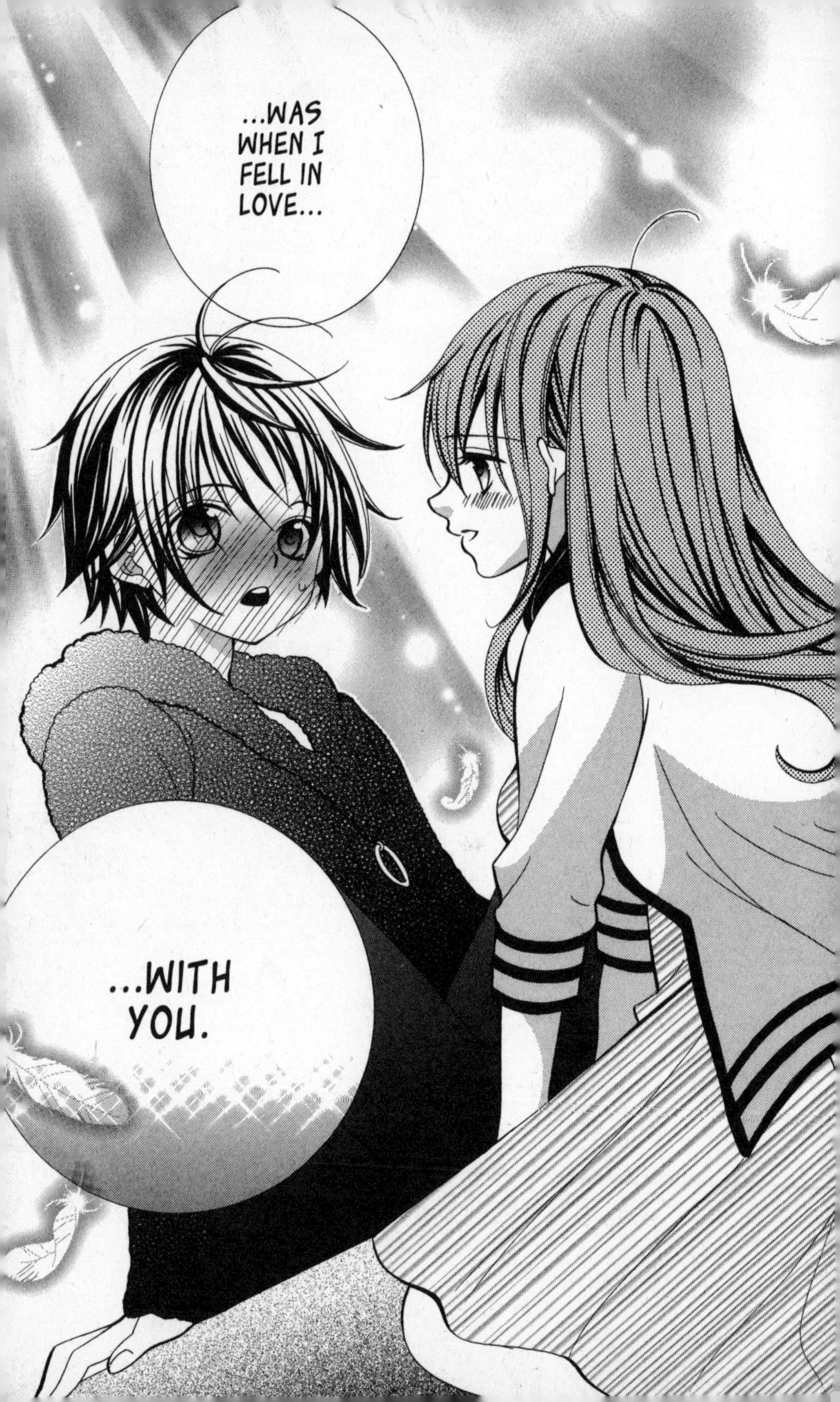
...WAS WHEN I FELL IN LOVE...
...WITH YOU.

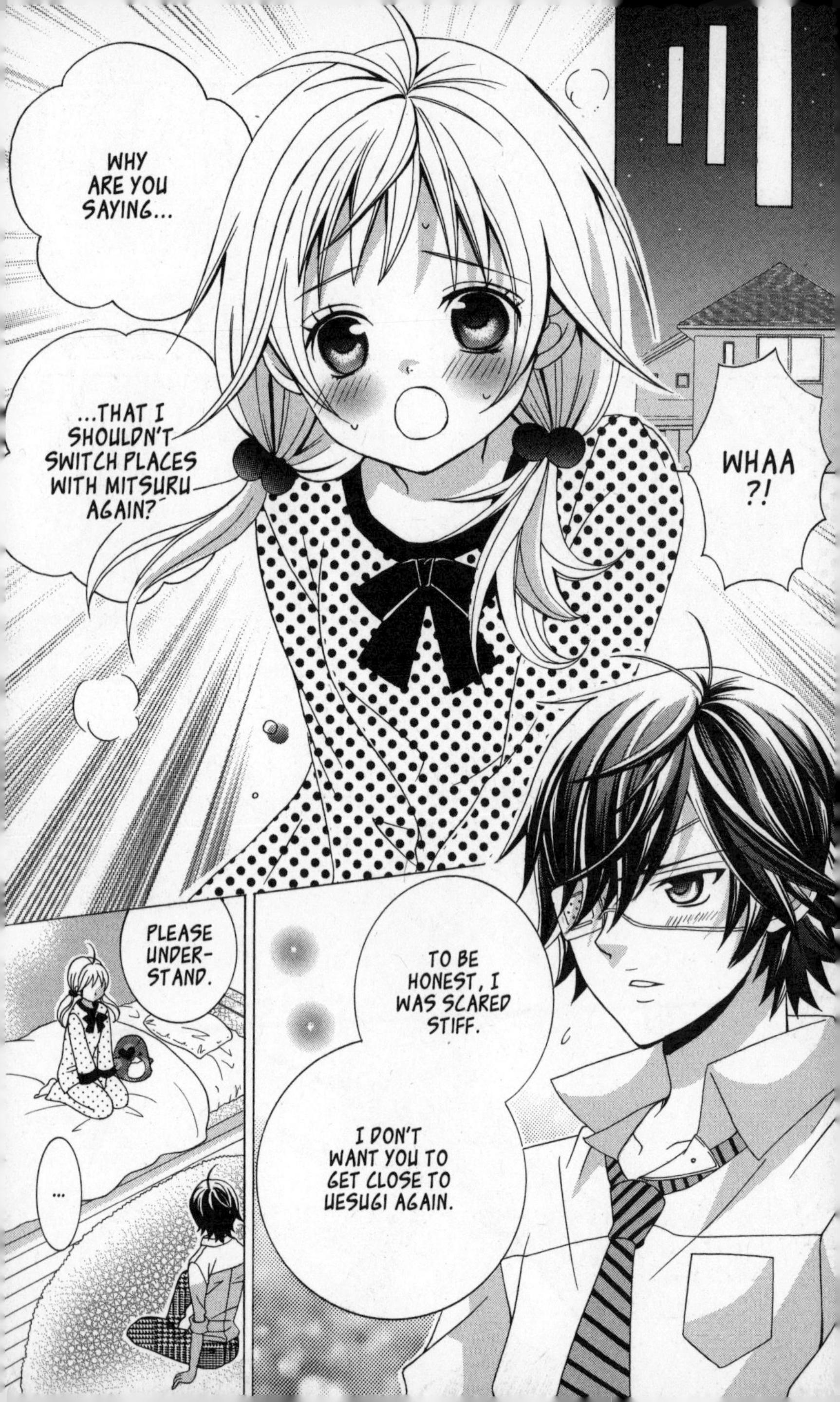
WHAA ?!
WHY ARE YOU SAYING...
...THAT I SHOULDN'T SWITCH PLACES WITH MITSURU AGAIN?
TO BE HONEST, I WAS SCARED STIFF.
I DON'T WANT YOU TO GET CLOSE TO UESUGI AGAIN.
PLEASE UNDER-STAND.
...

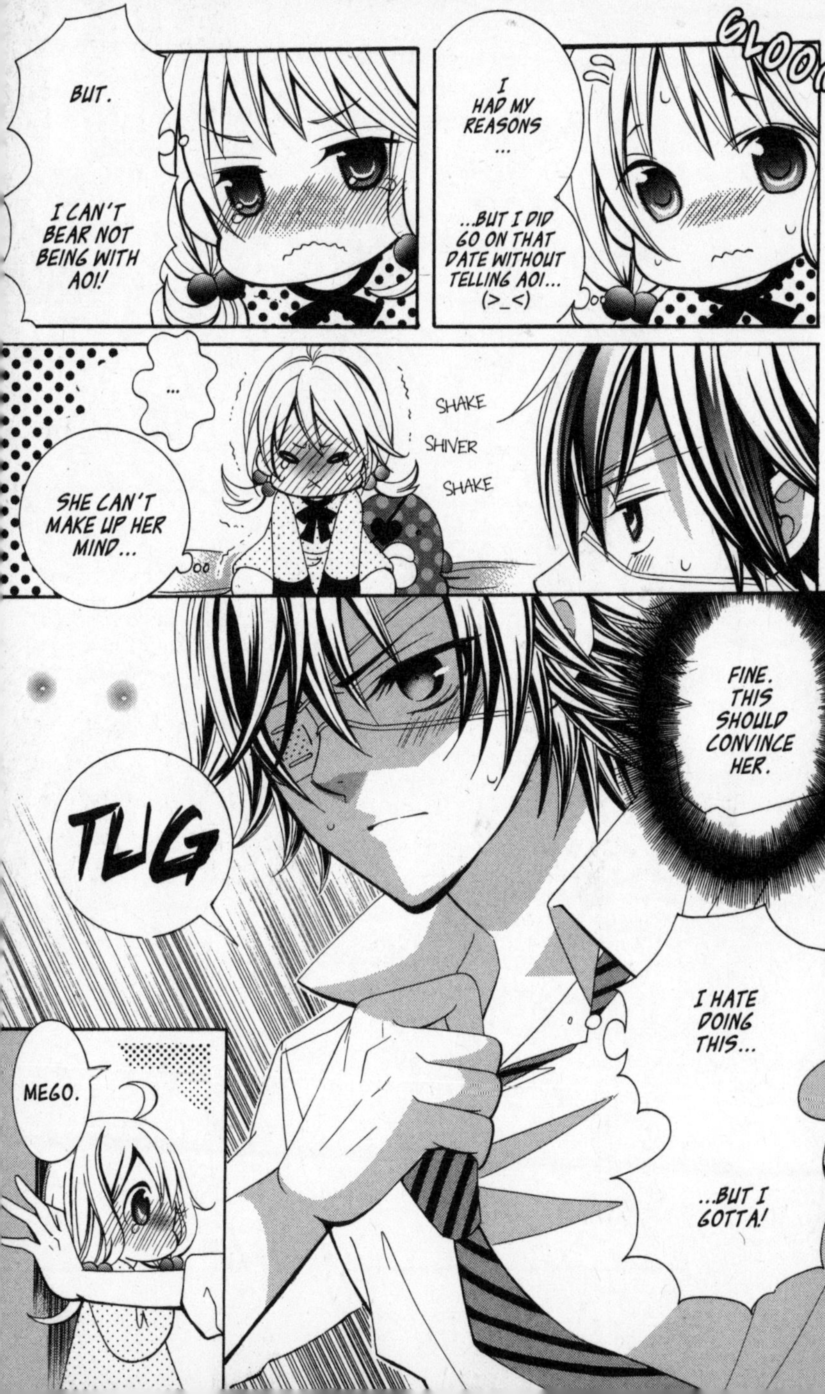
GLOOM
I HAD MY REASONS ...
...BUT I DID GO ON THAT DATE WITHOUT TELLING AOI... (>_<)
BUT.
I CAN'T BEAR NOT BEING WITH AOI!
SHAKE
SHIVER
SHAKE
...
SHE CAN'T MAKE UP HER MIND...
FINE. THIS SHOULD CONVINCE HER.
TUG
I HATE DOING THIS...
...BUT I GOTTA!
MEGO.

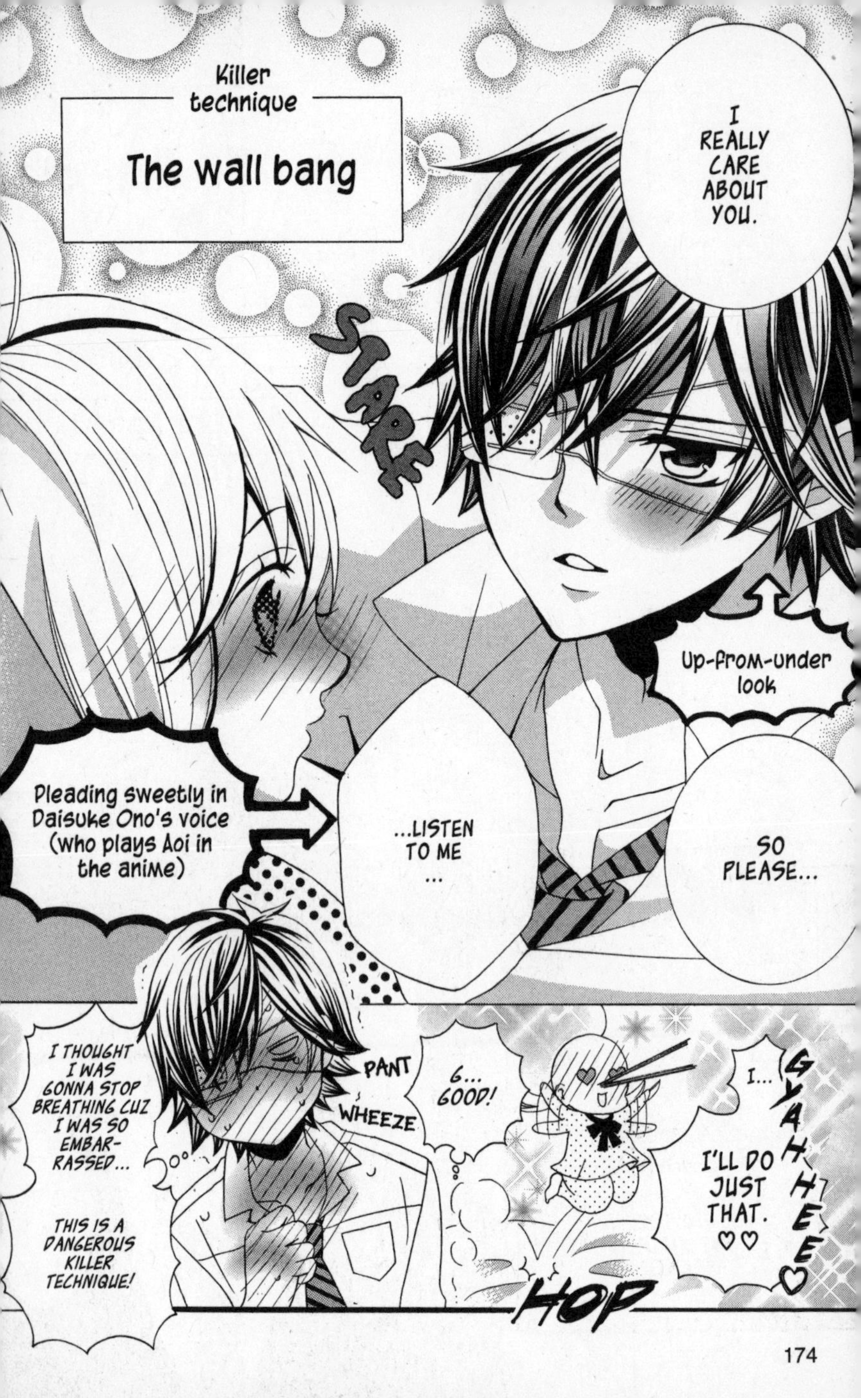

I REALLY CARE ABOUT YOU.
Killer technique
The wall bang
STARE
Up-from-under look
SO PLEASE...
...LISTEN TO ME ...
Pleading sweetly in Daisuke Ono's voice (who plays Aoi in the anime)
GYAHHEE♡
I...
I'LL DO JUST THAT. ♡♡
HOP
G... GOOD!
PANT
WHEEZE
I THOUGHT I WAS GONNA STOP BREATHING CUZ I WAS SO EMBAR-RASSED...
THIS IS A DANGEROUS KILLER TECHNIQUE!

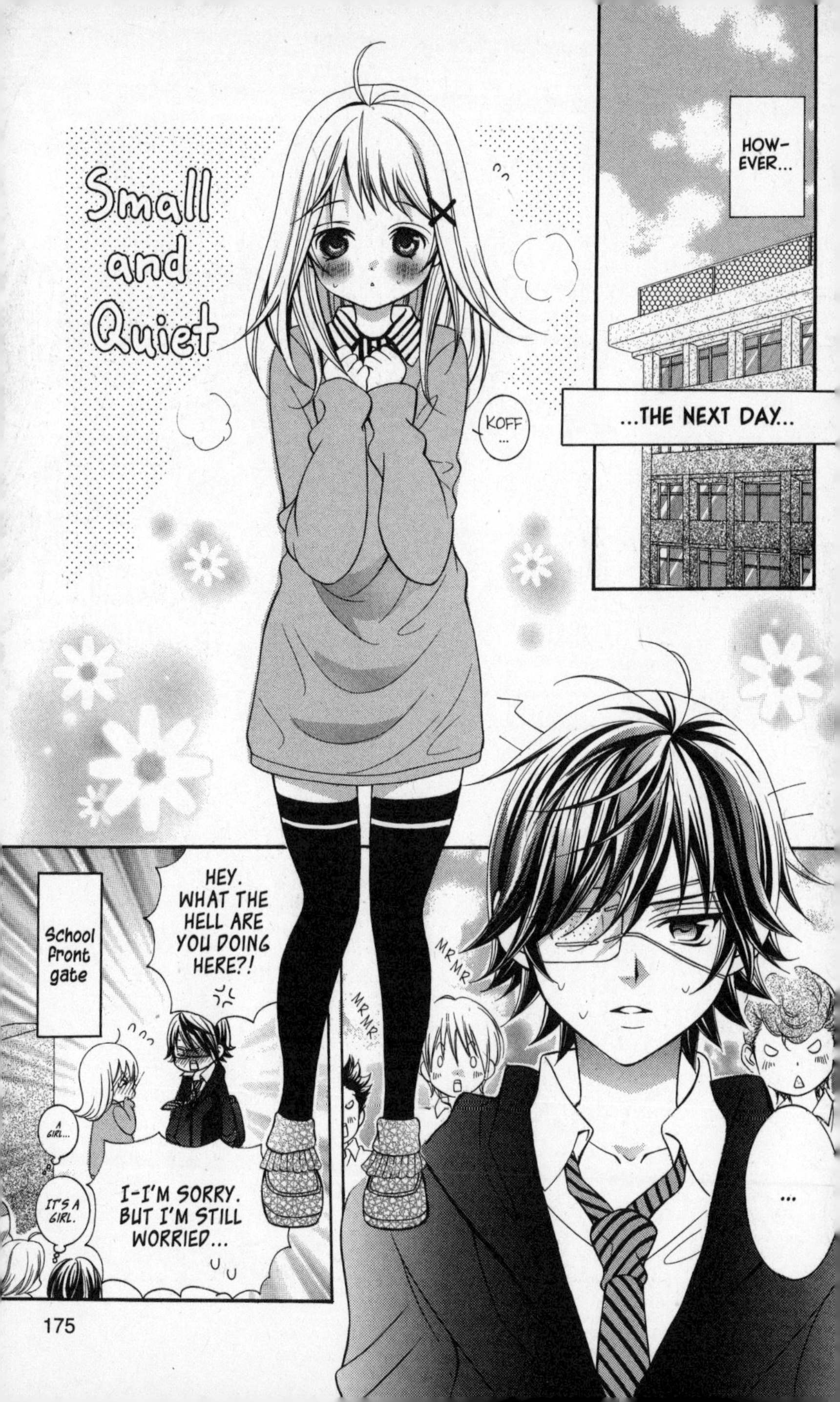
HOW-EVER...
...THE NEXT DAY...
Small and Quiet
KOFF...
MRMR
MRMR
...
School front gate
HEY. WHAT THE HELL ARE YOU DOING HERE?!
I-I'M SORRY. BUT I'M STILL WORRIED...
A GIRL...
IT'S A GIRL.

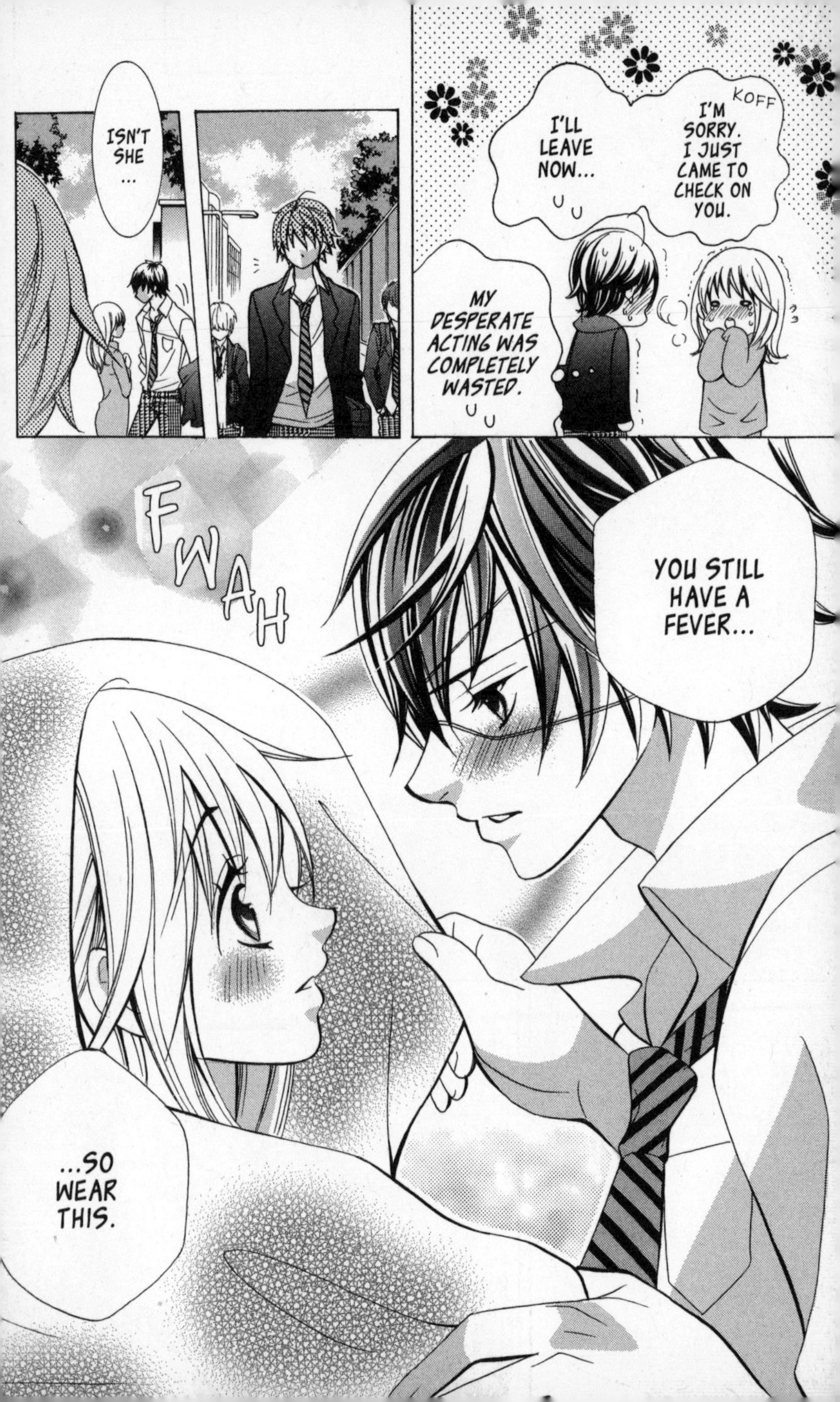
KOFF
I'M SORRY. I JUST CAME TO CHECK ON YOU.
I'LL LEAVE NOW...
MY DESPERATE ACTING WAS COMPLETELY WASTED.
ISN'T SHE ...
FWAH
YOU STILL HAVE A FEVER...
...SO WEAR THIS.

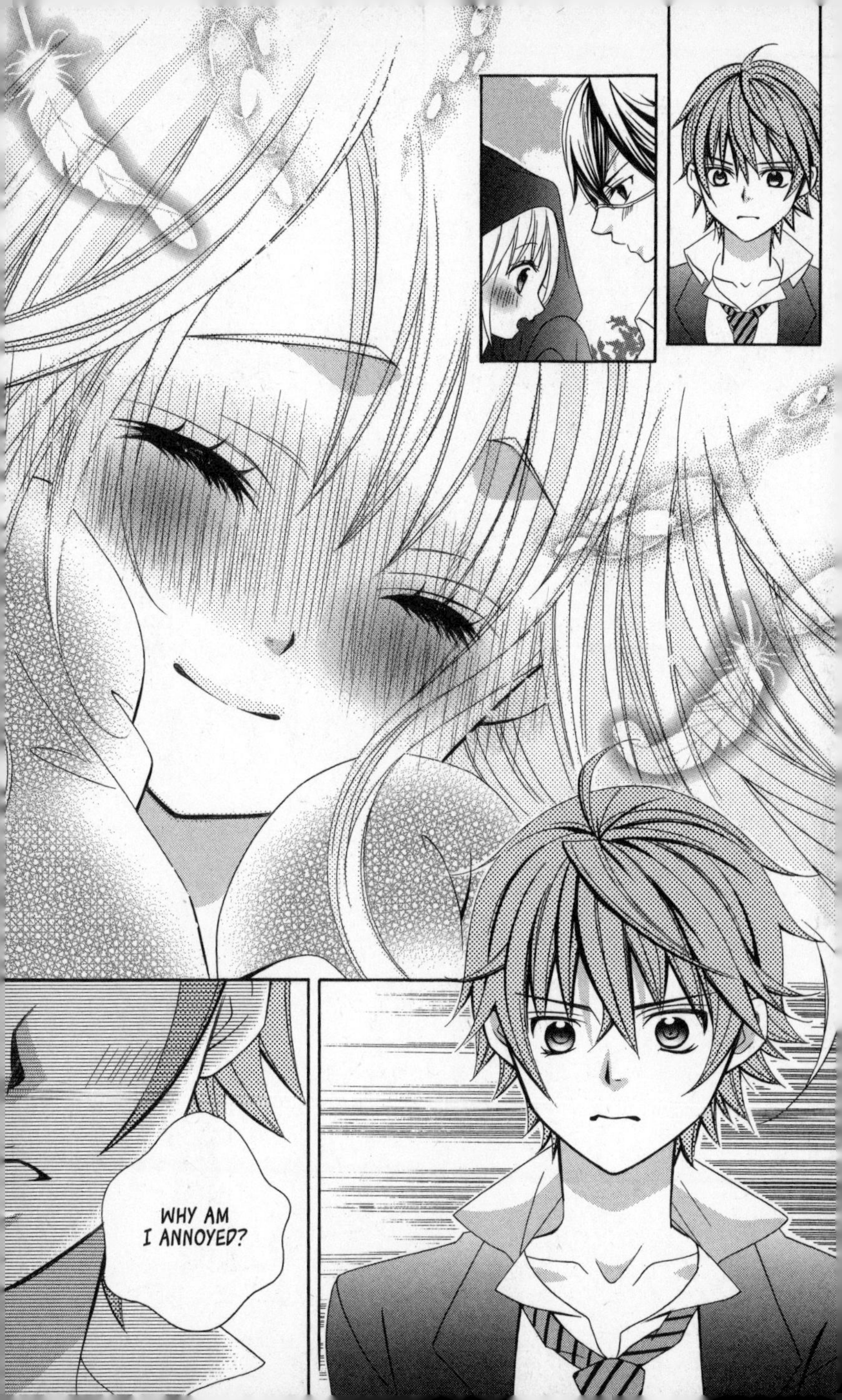
WHY AM
I ANNOYED?

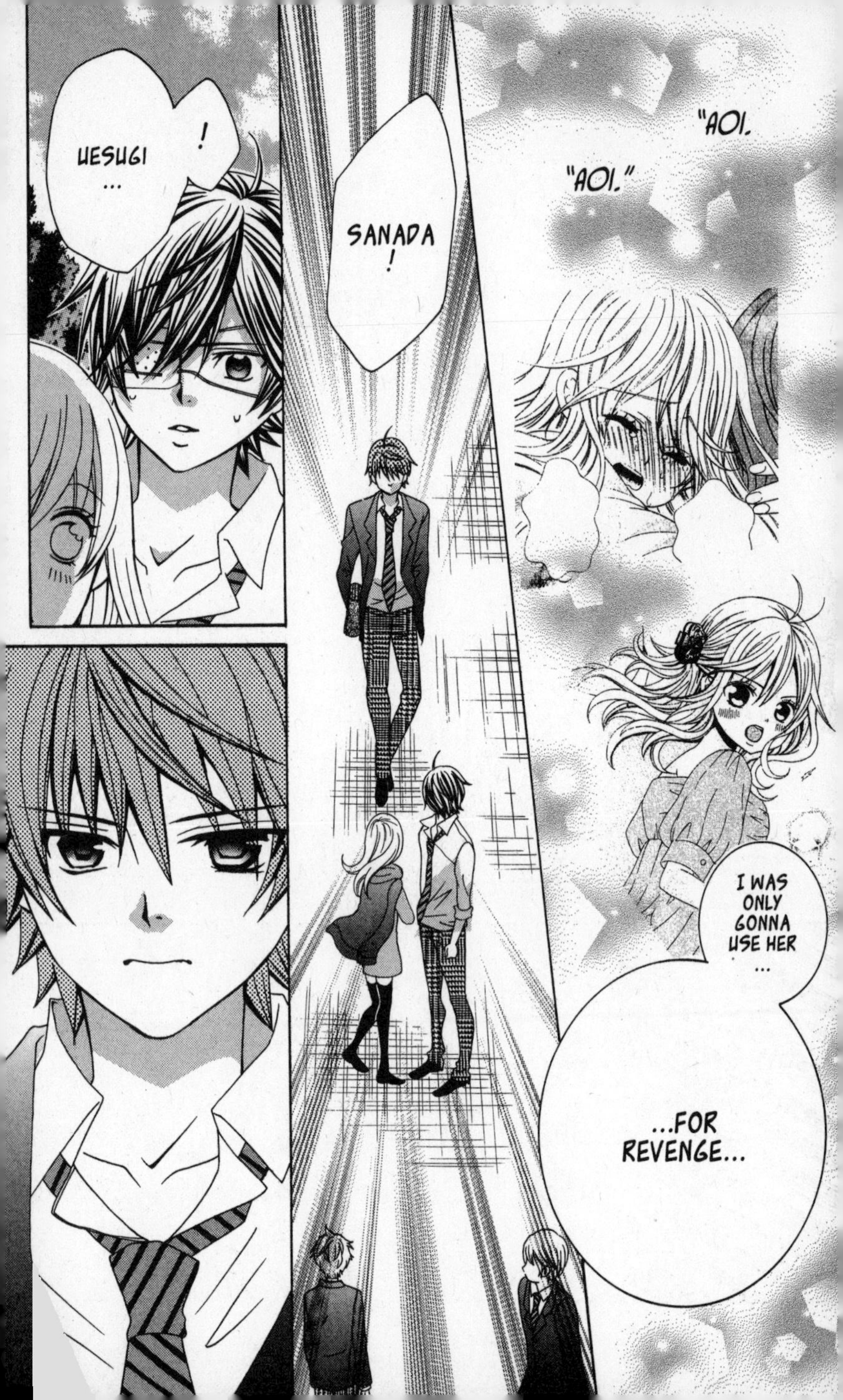
"AOI.
"AOI."
I WAS ONLY GONNA USE HER ...
...FOR REVENGE...
SANADA !
UESUGI ...
!

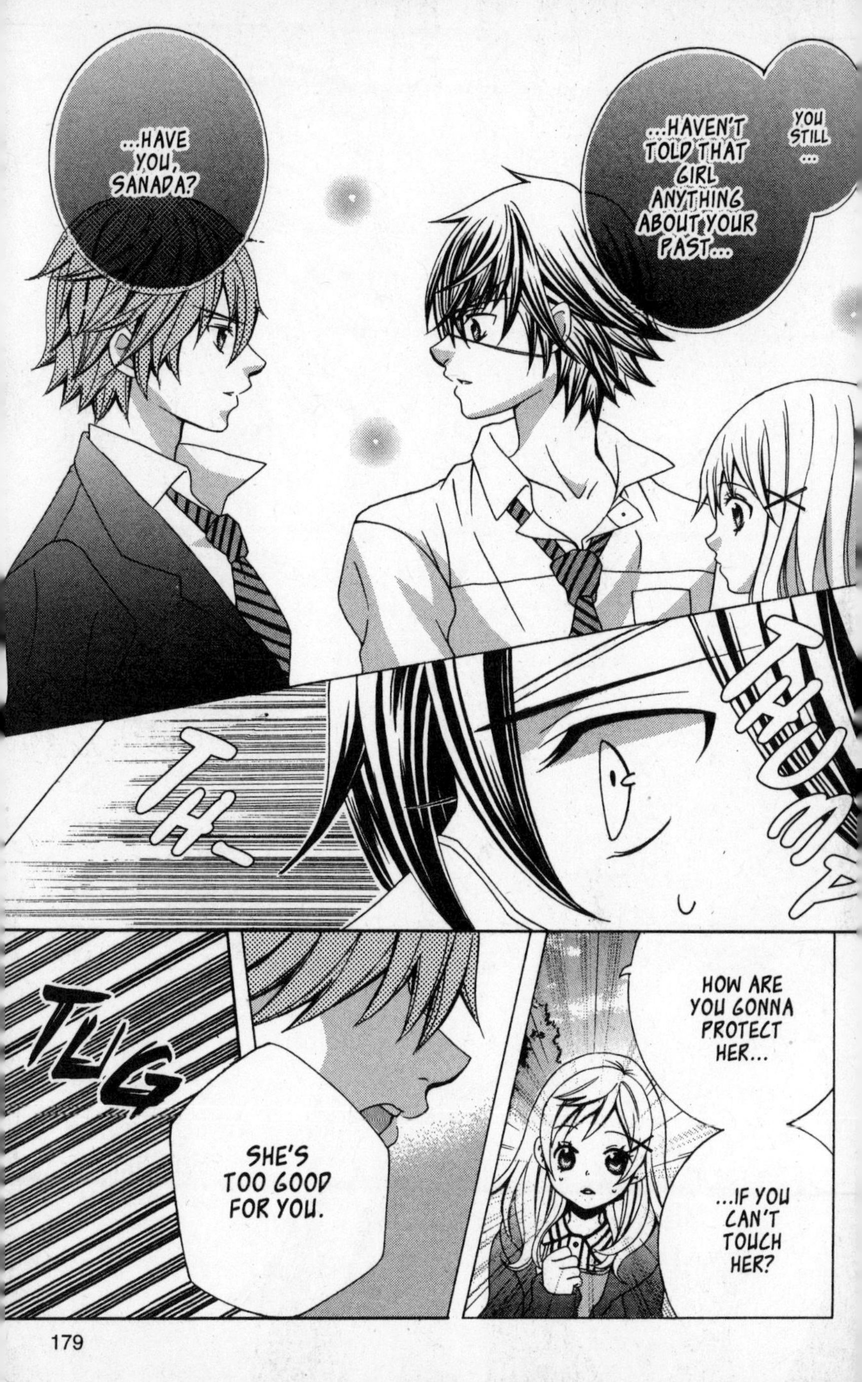
YOU STILL...
...HAVEN'T TOLD THAT GIRL ANYTHING ABOUT YOUR PAST...
...HAVE YOU, SANADA?
THUMP
TH-
HOW ARE YOU GONNA PROTECT HER...
...IF YOU CAN'T TOUCH HER?
TUG
SHE'S TOO GOOD FOR YOU.

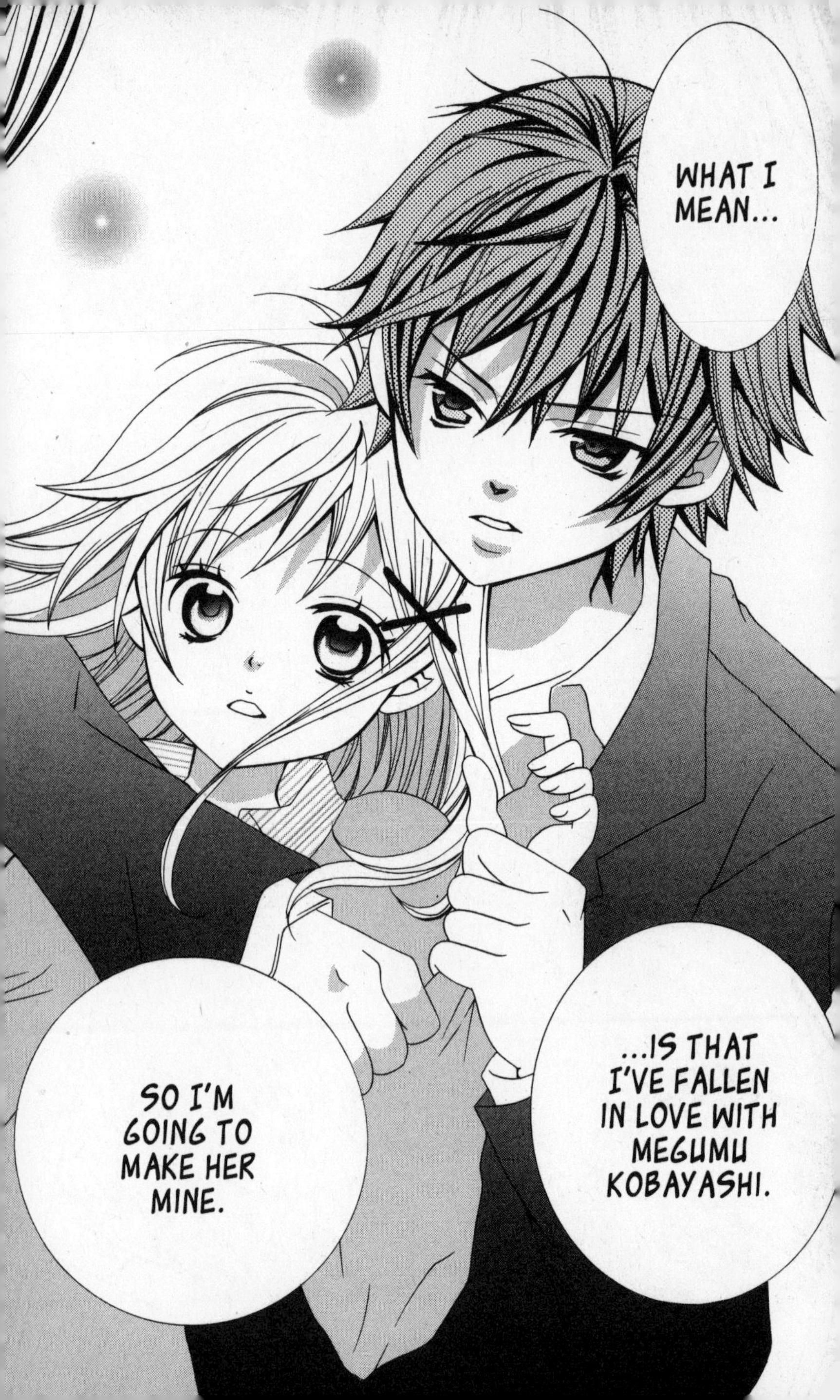
WHAT I MEAN...
...IS THAT I'VE FALLEN IN LOVE WITH MEGUMU KOBAYASHI.
SO I'M GOING TO MAKE HER MINE.

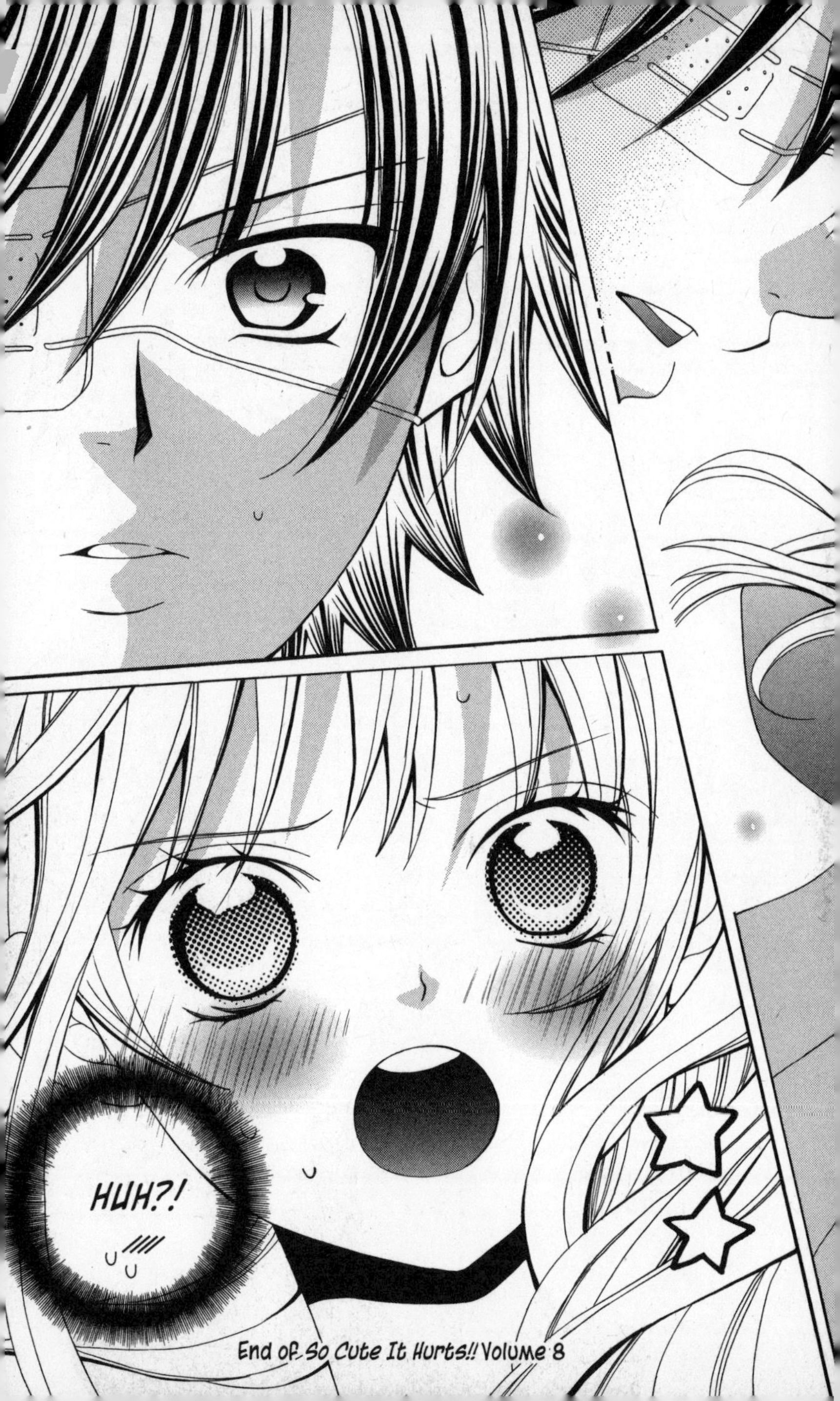
HUH?!
End of So Cute It Hurts!! Volume 8

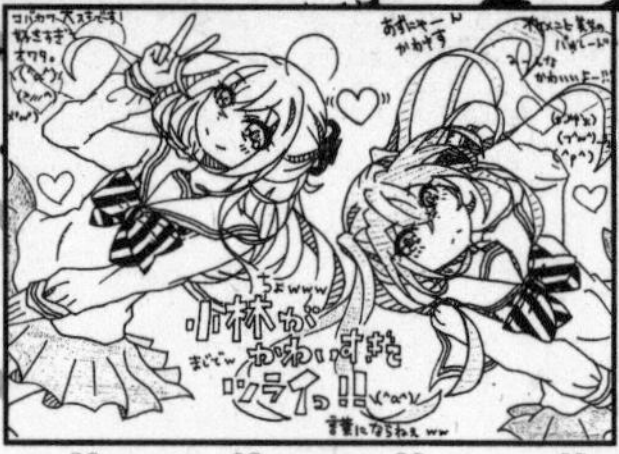
小林がかわいすぎてツライっ!!

Asuka (Gifu) ←

Ed.: Azunyan looks too cute!

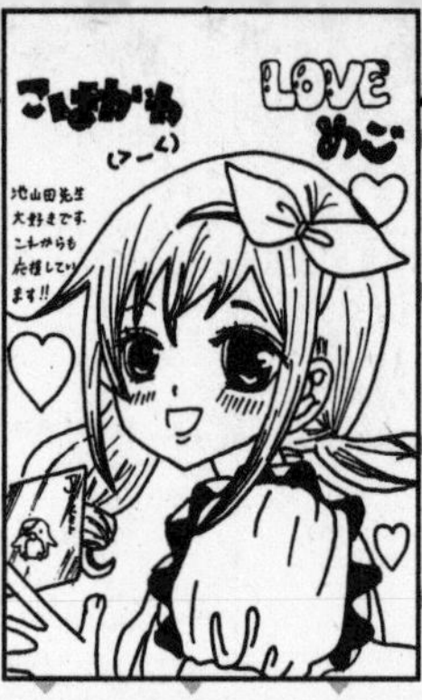
こばかわ
LOVE
めご

Mego Hime (Gunma) ←

Ed.: Mego looks cuter than usual!

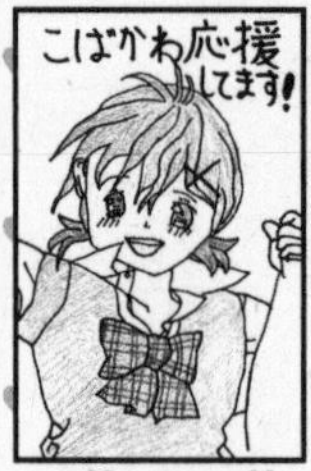
こばかわ応援してます!

Yuzuki Nakahata (Miyagi) ←

Ed.: Mego's full of energy!

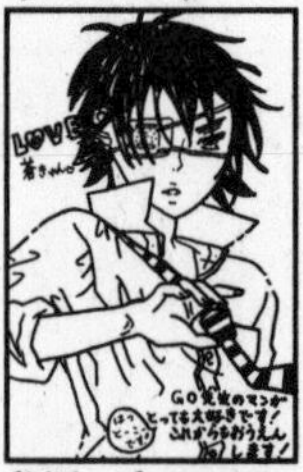

Chihiro Goroumaru (Iwate) ↑

Ed.: Aoi is always cool!

Rikako Noda (Aichi)

Ed.: Haven't seen Sayaka for a while. ♥ →

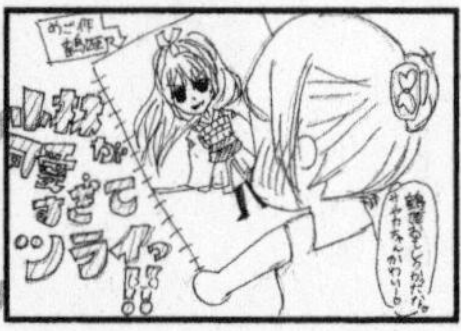
小林が可愛すぎてツライっ!!

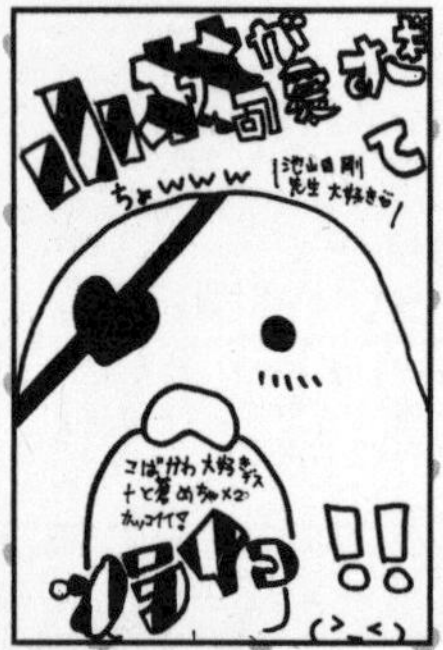
小林が可愛すぎて
ちょwww

Mio Aiba (Tochigi) ↑

Ed.: The eye-patch penguin is always popular!

Nichika Tanaka (Miyazaki) →

Ed.: Uesugi is becoming popular too?

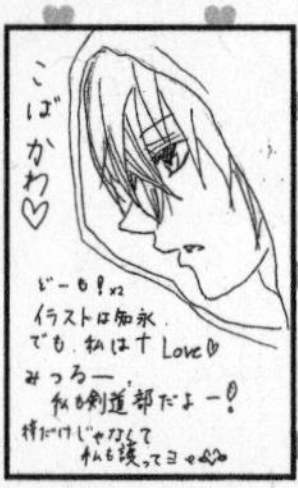
こばかわ♡

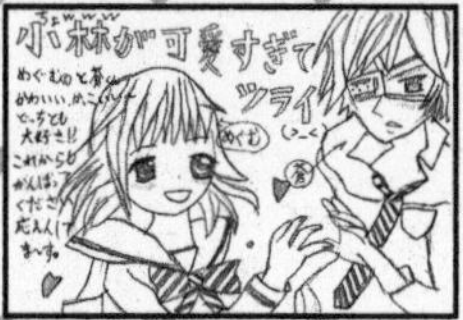
小林が可愛すぎてツライ

Yukky (Fukuoka) ↑

Ed.: They look innocent and cute. ♥

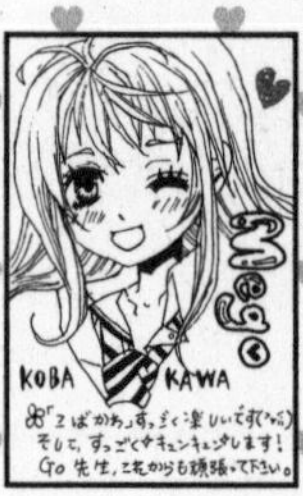
KOBA KAWA

Aena Kitau (Nagano) ←

Ed.: The mature-looking Mego looks dazzling!

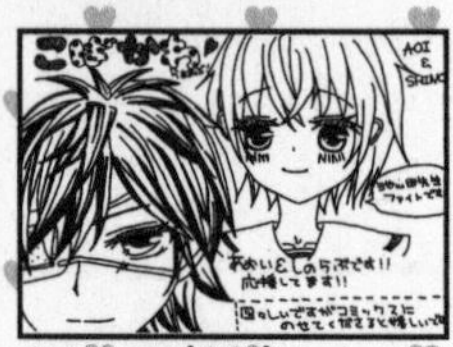

Shanaeru (Gifu) ↑

Ed.: I want to know about Aoi and Shino's past...

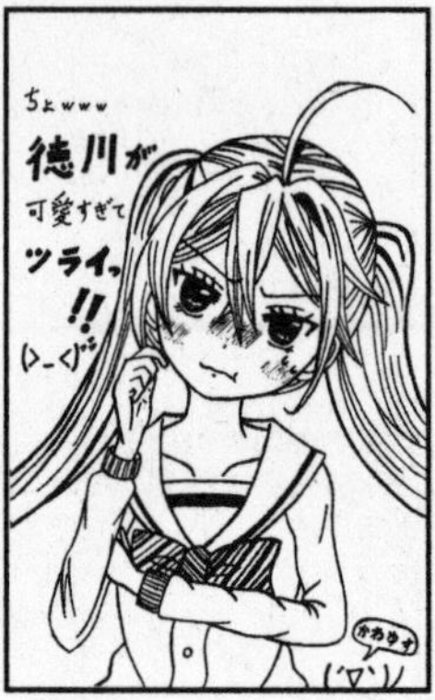
ちょwww
徳川が
可愛すぎて
ツライっ
!!
(>_<)

Kamo Asakura (Saitama) →

Ed.: Shall we start a spin-off?

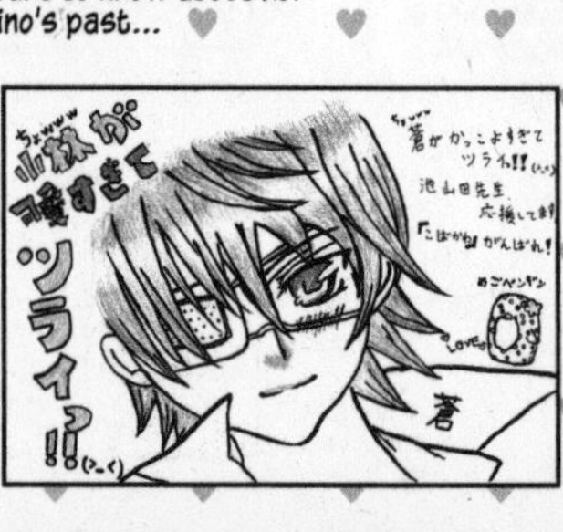
小林が可愛すぎてツライ?!!
蒼

Medaka (Yamanashi) ←

Ed.: Aoi is so cute it hurts!! (> <)

Arisa Yoshida (Shizuoka) ↑
Ed.: I've rediscovered how cool Mitsuru is!

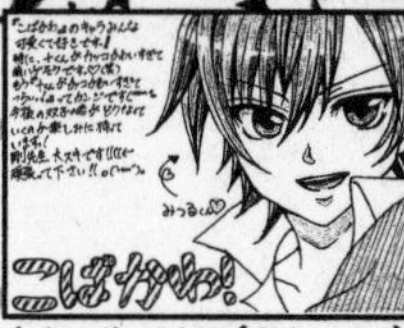

"GO (C) LOVE"
(Hyogo)
←
Ed.: Your drawing is good too!

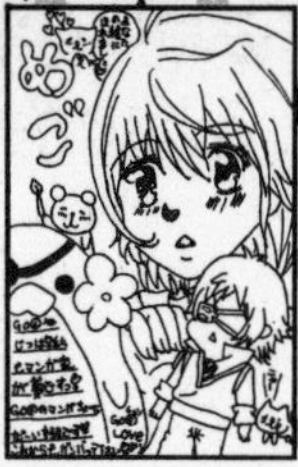

MIRAI ☆
(Kanagawa)
←
Ed.: I believe in you too!!

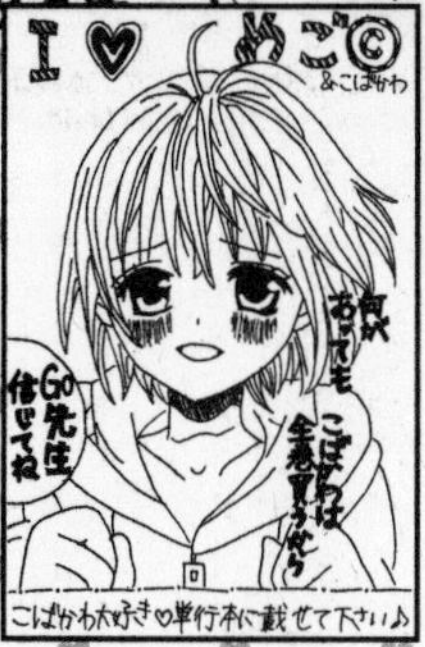
I ♡ めご©
&こばかわ
Go先生信じてね
何があってもこばかわは全巻買うから
こばかわ大好き♡単行本に載せて下さい♪

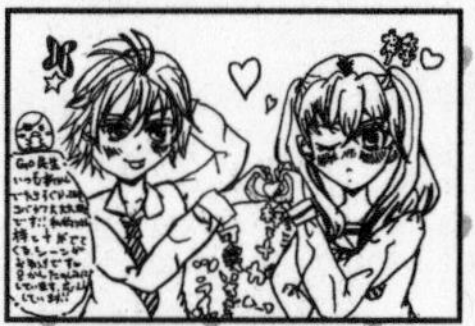

Risako Saeki ★ (Kyoto) ↑
Ed.: I'm also looking forward to these two!

I LOVE Aoi ♡
(Tokyo)
→
Ed.: This Masamune cosplay looks s-scary.
(> <)

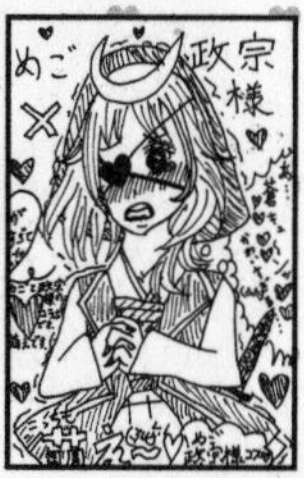
めご × 政宗様

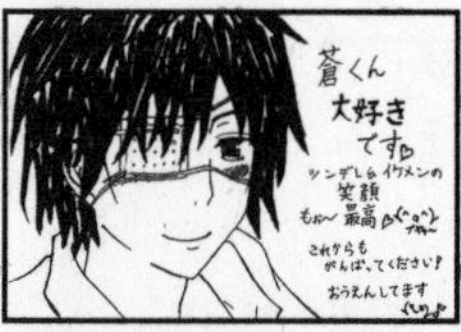
蒼くん大好きです♡
ツンデレ&イケメンの笑顔もぉ~最高
これからもがんばってください!
おうえんしてます

Shiori Mikasa (Tokushima) ↑
Ed.: Gently smiling Aoi is one cool dude!

Kazuki Yamauchi
(Kumamoto)
→
Ed.: I'm jealous that readers love Azusa.

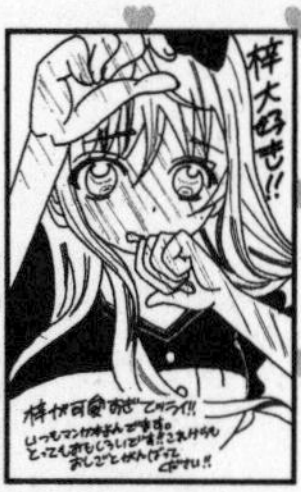
梓大好き!!

Kanayan
(Saitama)
←
Ed.: I'm so jealous that readers love Mego!!

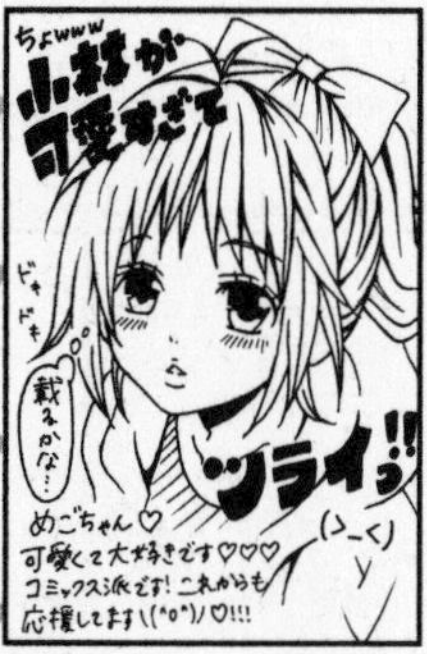
ちょwww 小梓が可愛すぎてツライっ!!
載るかな…
めごちゃん♡
可愛くて大好きです♡♡♡
コミックス派です! これからも
応援してます!

Saho
Watanabe
(Aichi)
→
Ed.: I find the naive Mego lovable!!

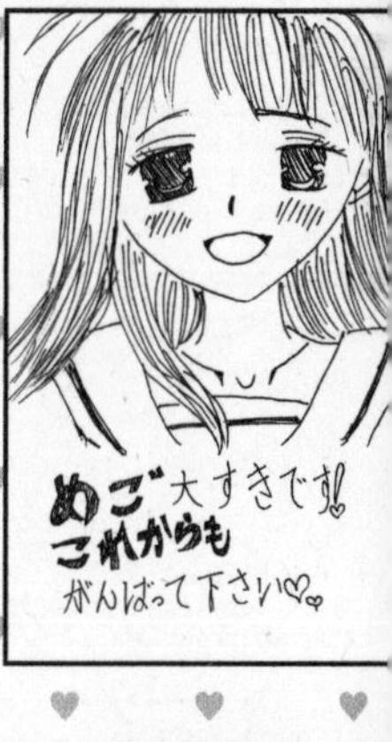
めご大すきです!
これからも
がんばって下さい!♡

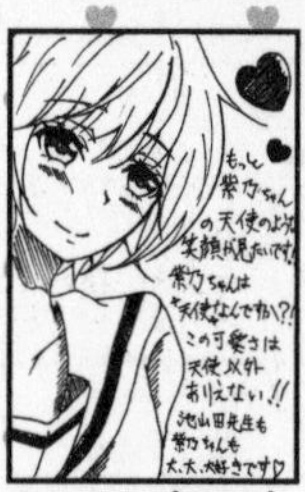
紫乃ちゃんは天使なんですか?!
この可愛さは天使以外ありえない!!
池山田先生も紫乃ちゃんも大、大、大好きです♡

Chiyuriru (Chiba) ↑
Ed.: I want to see more of Shino too.

ZZZ... (Chiba)
←
Ed.: Azusa the queen and Mitsuru the sadist...
(^o^)

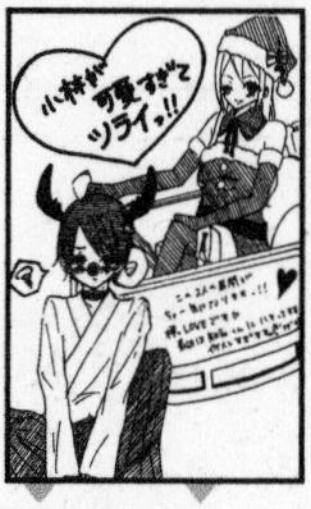
小梓が可愛すぎてツライッ!!

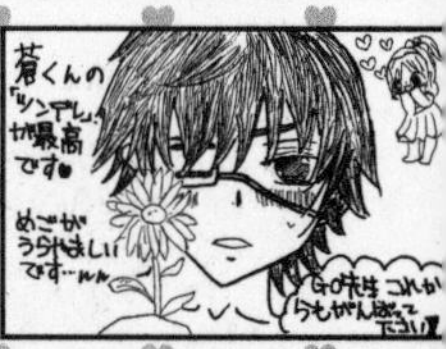
蒼くんの「ツンデレ」が最高です
めごがうらやましいです…

Irigoma Pudding
(Fukuoka)
→
Ed.: Readers always love Aoi!

Ayakamin ♥
(Nagasaki)
←
Ed.: Mego cries pretty!

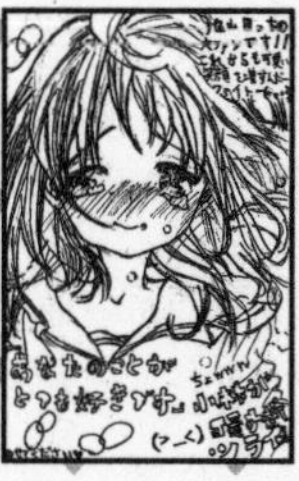

Myon
(Saitama)
←
Ed.: She's no longer alone!

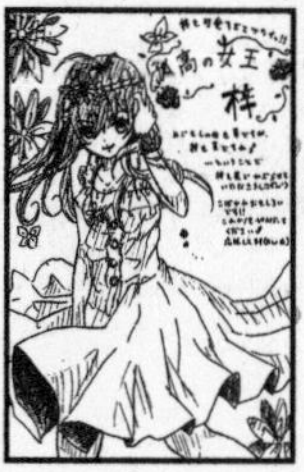
最高の女王 梓

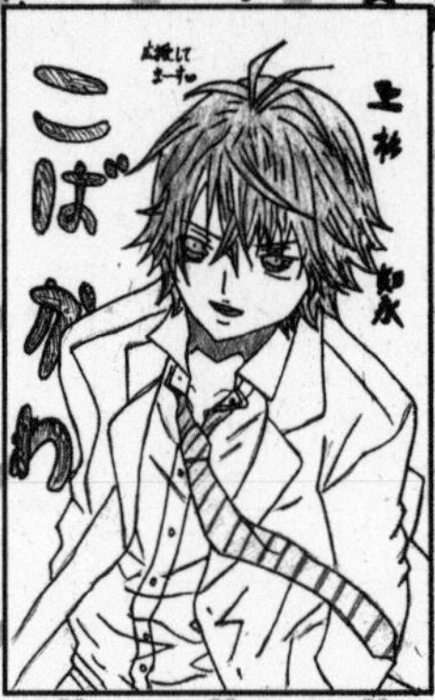

こばかわ

Chinatsu Kondo (Aichi) →
Ed.: Uesugi finally makes his appearance!!

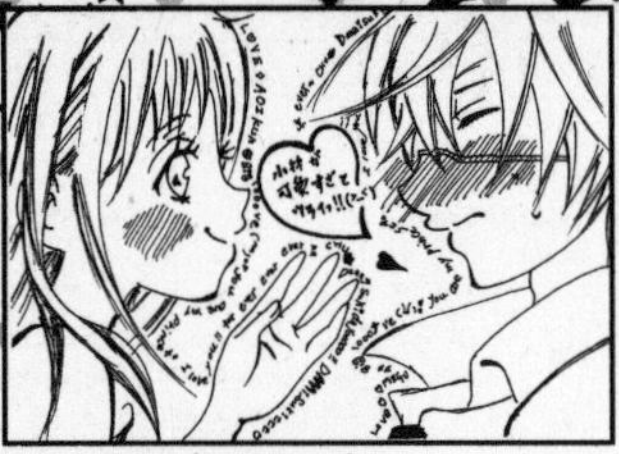

Noonnishi♡(Nagasaki) ↑
Ed.: Trembling Aoi looks cute!

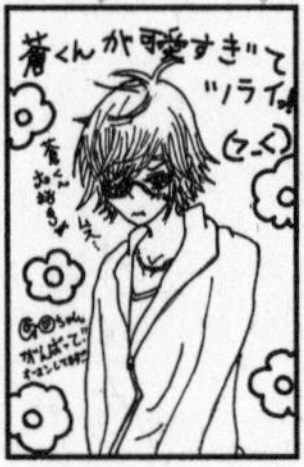

蒼くんが可愛すぎてツライ

Yuine Nakamura (Shizuoka) ←
Ed.: His mouth looks cute!

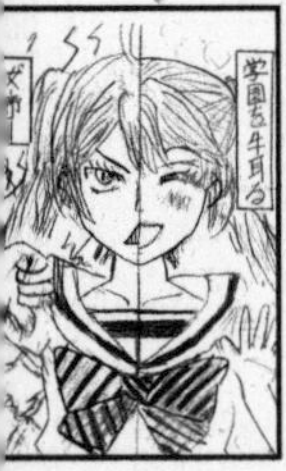

Midori Kojima (Fukushima) ←
Ed.: Ooh! That was quite a while ago!

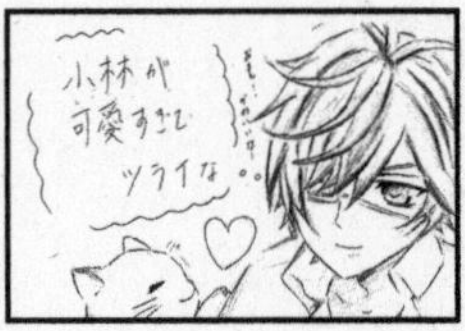

小林が可愛すぎてツライな…

Natsuyo Yasuhara (Saitama) →
Ed.: Mego the cat's cuteness is justice!!

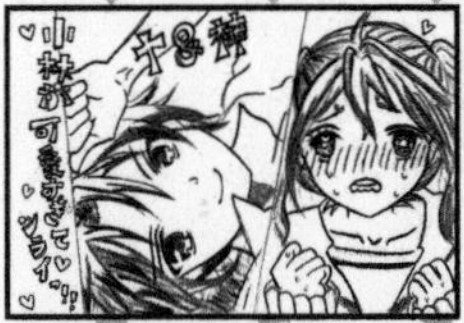

Hinaka Idemitsu (Fukuoka) ↑
Ed.: I really love sweet-looking Azusa!

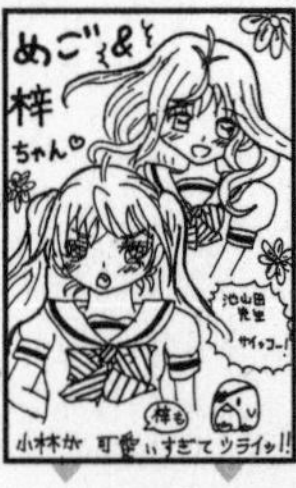

めご＆梓ちゃん
小林が可愛すぎてツライッ!!

Mango Cream (Kumamoto) ←
Ed.: These two look good together too!

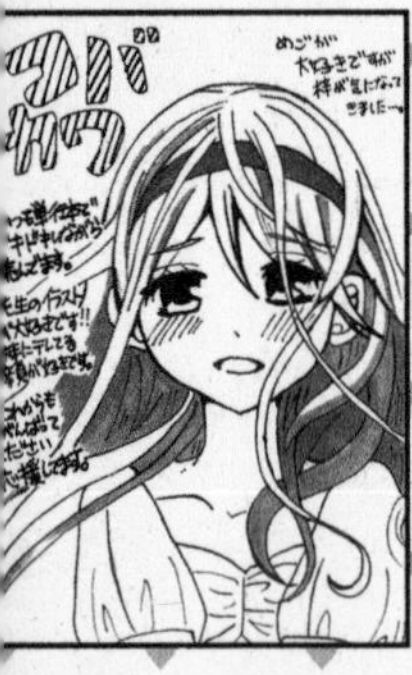

Ion (Osaka) ←
Ed.: I love the mature-looking Mego too!

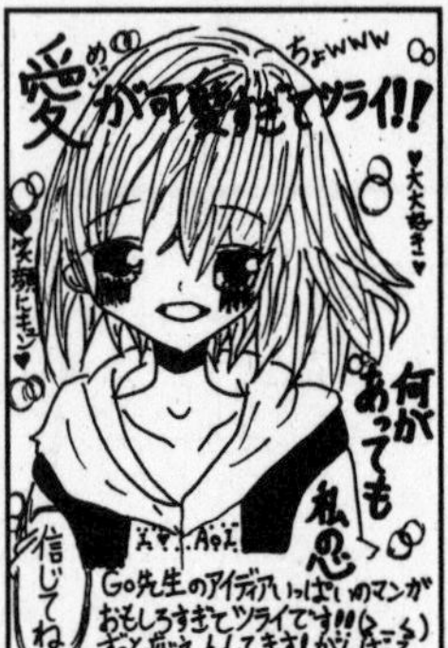

愛が可愛すぎてツライ!!
何があっても私の心
信じてね
Go先生のアイディアいっぱいのマンガがおもしろすぎてツライです!!

Chihotan♪ (Saitama) ←
Ed.: Yeah! I trust you no matter what. (> <)

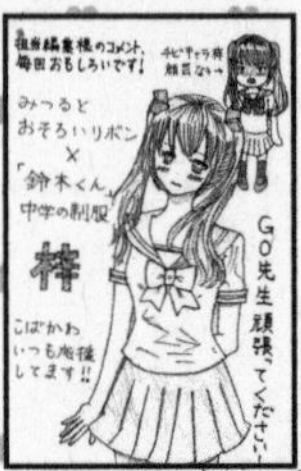

梓

↑ Komugiko (Tokyo)
Ed.: Having matching items makes you happy, right?!

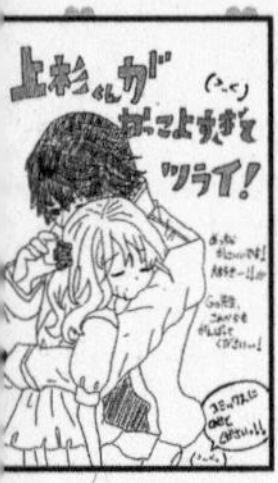

ツライ!

Yuuka Nakaoka (Gifu) ←
Ed.: Will Uesugi's popularity explode?!

Send your fan mail to:

Go Ikeyamada
c/o Shojo Beat
VIZ Media, LLC
P.O. Box 77010
San Francisco, CA 94107

lololololol

So Cute It Hurts!!

(>_<)

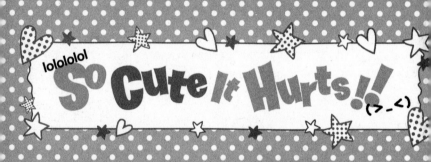

AUTHOR BIO

The fortieth anniversary of *Flower Comics* was in 2014! I always look forward to Miyuki Kitagawa Sensei's series in every *Sho-Comi* issue! I can't believe I now have a series running in the same magazine where Kitagawa Sensei had so many hits. I'll continue to do my absolute best, so do keep reading. (^O^)

Go Ikeyamada is a Gemini from Miyagi Prefecture whose hobbies include taking naps and watching movies. Her debut manga *Get Love!!* appeared in *Shojo Comic* in 2002, and her current work *So Cute It Hurts!!* (*Kobayashi ga Kawai Suguite Tsurai!!*) is being published by VIZ Media.

SO CUTE IT HURTS!!
Volume 8

Shojo Beat Edition

STORY AND ART BY
GO IKEYAMADA

English Translation & Adaptation/Tomo Kimura
Touch-Up Art & Lettering/Joanna Estep
Design/Izumi Evers
Editor/Pancha Diaz

KOBAYASHI GA KAWAISUGITE TSURAI!! Vol.8
by Go IKEYAMADA
© 2012 Go IKEYAMADA
All rights reserved.
Original Japanese edition published by SHOGAKUKAN.
English translation rights in the United States of America, Canada,
United Kingdom and Ireland arranged with SHOGAKUKAN.

Printed in the U.S.A.

Published by VIZ Media, LLC
P.O. Box 77010
San Francisco, CA 94107

10 9 8 7 6 5 4 3 2 1
First printing, August 2016

www.viz.com   www.shojobeat.com

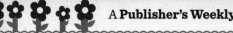 

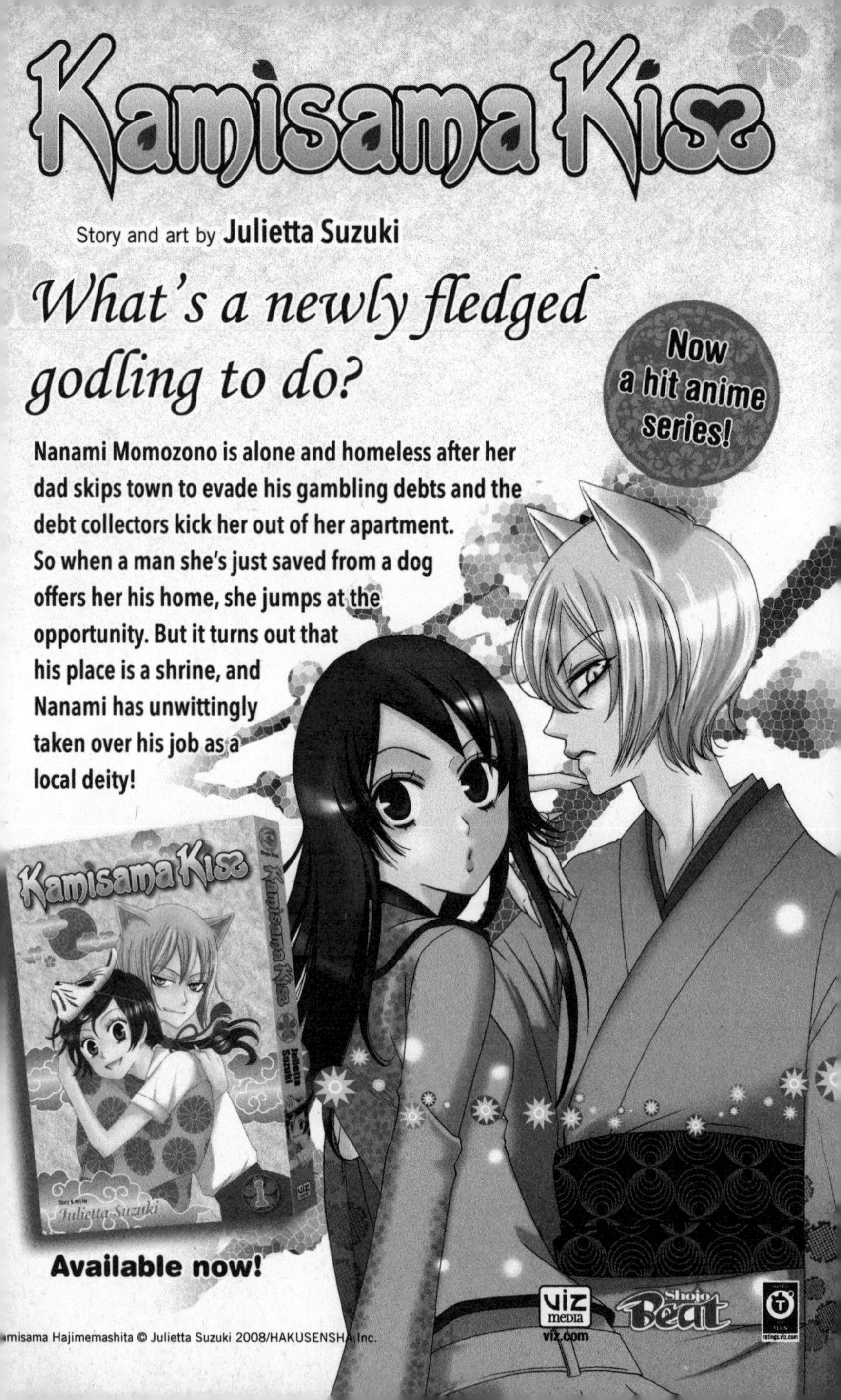

Kamisama Kiss
Story and art by Julietta Suzuki
What's a newly fledged godling to do?
Now a hit anime series!
Nanami Momozono is alone and homeless after her dad skips town to evade his gambling debts and the debt collectors kick her out of her apartment. So when a man she's just saved from a dog offers her his home, she jumps at the opportunity. But it turns out that his place is a shrine, and Nanami has unwittingly taken over his job as a local deity!
Kamisama Kiss
Kamisama Kiss
Julietta Suzuki
Story & Art by
Julietta Suzuki
Available now!
viz media
viz.com
Shojo Beat
misama Hajimemashita © Julietta Suzuki 2008/HAKUSENSHA, Inc.

This is the last page.

In keeping with the original Japanese comic format, this book reads from right to left—so action, sound effects and word balloons are completely reversed. This preserves the orientation of the original artwork—plus, it's fun! Check out the diagram shown here to get the hang of things, and then turn to the other side of the book to get started!

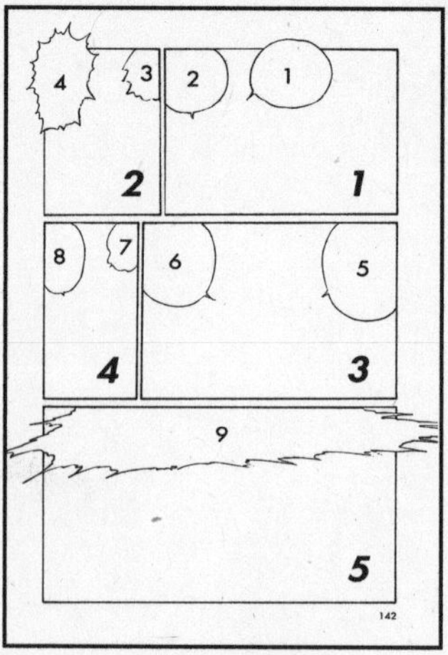
1
2
3
4
5

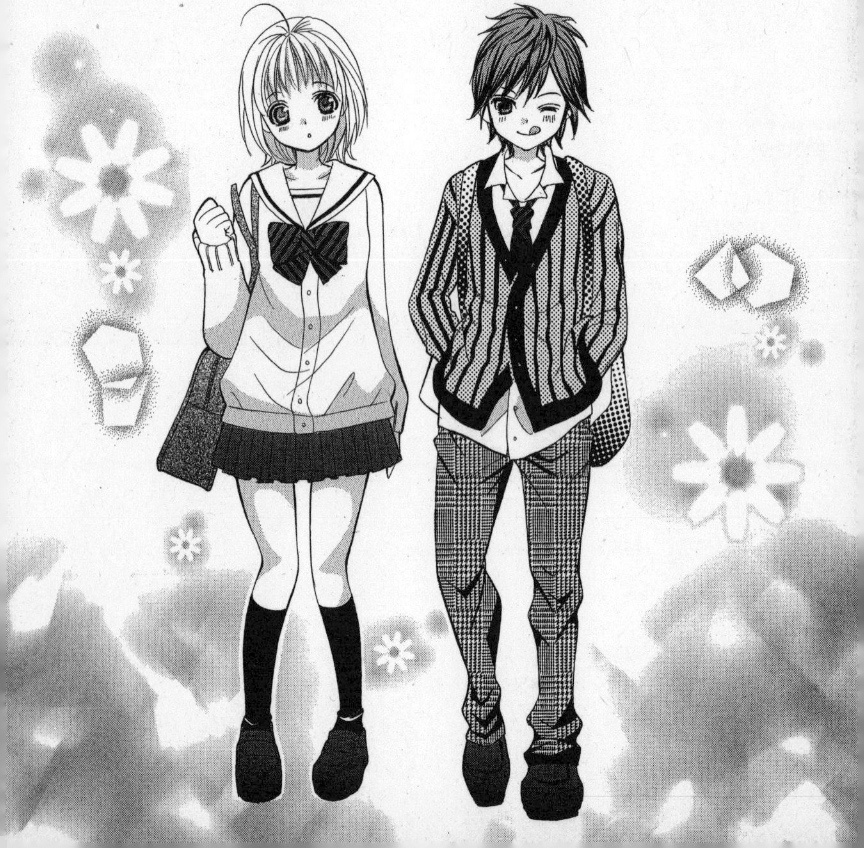